THE KEPHALAIA
OF THE TEACHER

NAG HAMMADI
AND
MANICHAEAN STUDIES

FORMERLY

NAG HAMMADI STUDIES

EDITED BY

J.M. ROBINSON & H.J. KLIMKEIT

Editorial Board

XXXVII

THE KEPHALAIA
OF THE TEACHER

THE EDITED COPTIC MANICHAEAN TEXTS
IN TRANSLATION WITH COMMENTARY

BY

IAIN GARDNER

E.J. BRILL
LEIDEN · NEW YORK · KÖLN
1995

The paper in this book meets the guidelines for permanence and durability of the Committee on Production Guidelines for Book Longevity of the Council on Library Resources.

Library of Congress Cataloging-in-Publication Data

Kephalaia. English.
    The Kephalaia of the Teacher : the edited Coptic Manichaean texts in translation with commentary / [edited] by Iain Gardner.
        p.   cm. — (Nag Hammadi and Manichaean studies, 0929-2470 ; 37)
    Includes bibliographical references (p.   ) and indexes.
    ISBN 9004102485 (cloth : alk. paper)
    1. Manichaeism—Early works to 1800.   2. Mani, 3rd cent.
    I. Gardner, Iain.   II. Title.   III. Series.
    BT1410.K4713   1995
    299'.932—dc20
                                                            95-922
                                                            CIP

Die Deutsche Bibliothek – CIP-Einheitsaufnahme

The **Kephalaia of the teacher** : the edited Coptic Manichaean texts in translation with commentary / by Iain Gardner. – Leiden ; New York ; Köln : Brill, 1995
    (Nag Hammadi and Manichaean studies ; 37)
    Einheitssacht.: Kephalaia <engl.>
    ISBN 90–04–10248–5
NE: Gardner, Iain [Hrsg.]; EST; GT

ISSN   0929-2470
ISBN   90 04 10248 5

To Carole

CONTENTS

PREFACE

This volume provides an English translation, together with commentary, of the presently edited Coptic text of the *Kephalaia;* as established primarily by A. Böhlig and H.-J. Polotsky in the 1930's and early 1940's. This is but part of a single codex of the Medinet Madi library of Manichaean writings, the entirety of which codex is considerably greater than will be found here. The editorial process still continues. Work on a second *Kephalaia* codex from the same find has hardly begun. There is also Iranian kephalaic material. Thus I am conscious of the limitations of what is presented here as an entry into the fantastic worlds of Mani and his followers in their search for the God of truth.

My own fascination with this text began in the latter 1970's as I prepared for a doctoral dissertation on the Christology of Manichaeism at the University of Manchester. At that time I attempted rough translations both as a means to understand the doctrine, and as an exercise in the language. At the beginning of this present decade S.N.C. Lieu was kind enough to remember our struggles as graduate students, and wrote to me wondering if I would be willing to revise some of these drafts for a collaborative volume containing Manichaean texts from the Roman Empire. I somewhat arbitrarily set myself to the task of a hundred plus pages from the *Kephalaia,* but rapidly discarded my youthful exercises. Towards the completion of this initial stage Dr. Lieu introduced me to D. Montserrat with the suggestion that we might work together on the complete edited text, and Dr. Montserrat began to prepare drafts of chapters on which I had not yet worked.

In 1992 Dr. Montserrat visited me in Australia, and we enjoyed the opportunity to develop ideas for the volume and to work together on first drafts of difficult sections. Since then other commitments have forced Dominic to withdraw from the collaboration, but I take this opportunity to thank him for his many fine suggestions, and to acknowledge the occasions that his phrasing may have influenced the final version. Similarly I thank Samuel Lieu, and acknowledge that phrasing from collaborative work appears in the introductory material.

However, sole responsibility for the published text is my own.

Now, in 1994, I have again worked through every line. As each reading has brought more light, so I become more aware of the impossibility of the translator's task. However, it is apparent that the density and complexity of this text have proved a barrier to the study of Manichaeism, particularly in the anglophone world. My hope here is to have rendered more accessible the greatest and most detailed of the available primary sources, and thus to encourage future work that will in time supersede my own.

I thank Edith Cowan University for the use of resources and the help of many colleagues, in particular Peter Bedford with whom I have often discussed problems of the translation process. My Faculty was kind enough to grant me time release from teaching during the early part of the work, for which I am indeed grateful.

Mount Lawley October 1994

INTRODUCTION

Manichaeology and the Religion of Mani

The self-declared apostle Mani (216 – 276 c.e.) was a native of Babylonia who founded a world religion in the early years of the Sassanian Empire. He believed himself to be the recipient of direct revelation from his divine Twin Spirit, which being is understood to be the Paraclete foretold by Jesus, and with whom Mani became 'one body and one Spirit (K.15.23 – 24)'. Thus, in his *Gospel* and *Epistles*, he introduces himself as the apostle of Jesus Christ (e.g. CMC. p.66). In Greek and Coptic his name is Manichaios; that is 'Mani the living', as derived from his native Syriac.

Modern scholarship has devoted much attention to the question of the nature and characteristics of Mani's teachings, and of the religion that he founded; and this history of manichaeology may be read as a commentary on that of the discipline itself. For the Christian theologians and leaders of the past Manichaeism had been a dualistic heresy that threatened and attempted to subvert the truths revealed in scripture, as held secure and preached by the church. Thus the origins of the discipline, for western culture, are to be found in the Greek and Latin sources of that world; particularly in the disputations, anathemas and parodies of the bishops such as Augustine (once himself a believer but turned champion of orthodoxy) and Archelaus (the fabled victor over a hapless Mani) and Epiphanius (the acerbic cataloguer of errors).

When western scholarship began to free itself from the heritage of heresiology a new approach to sources, especially by orientalists in the latter nineteenth century with access to Syriac and Arabic authors such as Theodore bar Konai and an-Nadim who quote from Mani himself, gradually started to write a more objective history.

The twentieth century has brought a succession of dramatic textual finds that have repeatedly shifted the focus of attention. The first actual Manichaean writings discovered were in Iranian and Turkic and Chinese literatures, and were plundered from Central Asia by the great European expeditions at the start of this century. In the heyday of the 'History of Religions' as a discipline Manichaeism was reinvented as a Persian religion.

However, even since the 1920's scholarly attention has been repeatedly forced to focus on gnostic and Judaeo-Christian origins and traditions in Mani's teaching. Such are evidenced particularly by the Medinet Madi library from the 1930's, of which the *Kephalaia* is part; and then since 1969 the Cologne *Mani Codex,* which text recounts the genesis of Mani's own life and the community that he founded. Also the flood of scholarship occasioned by the Nag Hammadi library, that is the inaccurately but popularly named gnostic Gospels, has provided a context for the growth of manichaeology as its heir apparent.

Now, near the close of the twentieth century, the student of Manichaeism is presented with a striking array of sources evidencing a religion that spread from Mesopotamia throughout the late classical and Islamic worlds of the Mediterranean and west Asia, and across the Silk Road to finally flare and die in south China. Throughout this century the discipline has been preeminently the domain of specialists, necessitating a high degree of philological and technical skill, particularly such as is preserved in the elite institutions of the European continent. However, developments and projects by the academic community now in process seem certain to render the subject both more accessible and of broader interest. These include the activities of the *International Association of Manichaean Studies,* with its conferences and publications; and the various renewed efforts both to complete the editing of sources and to make them more available.

The latest and still continuing development in the story of Manichaean textual discoveries is part of this process. This is the uncovering of a fourth century Manichaean community and its texts at the late Roman site of Kellis in Egypt, by an Australian archaeological excavation directed by C. Hope on behalf of the Dakhleh Oasis Project. For the first time the social context of a Manichaean church from the early period, indeed of any so-called gnostic group of antiquity, can properly be recovered. Thus the subject becomes part of the documentary record of the late classical world.

Every discipline is a product of its own cultural framework and its time. Manichaeology at the turn of the millenium takes its place in the story of the deconstruction of received histories. The finds at Kellis evidence that the Manichaeans there regarded themselves as the true and holy church. This story subverts that of the inevitable triumph of, for want of a better phrase, catholic Christianity. Instead, Christianities in context are found to be diverse, subjects of law and economics and inter-personal relations. Doctrine is imposed and undermined, theological orthodoxy is seen to be a social construct.

What then is the meaning of the religion of Mani? The *Mani Codex* is a nascent gospel for the apostle that compiles written testimonies by some of his closest disciples, together with quotations from his own writings; and contextualised by excerpts from Paul and other authoritative apocalypses of the past. While hagiographical elements are already apparent, such as the tutelage of Mani by his Twin (σύζυγος) from youth, it does provide clear evidence of his upbringing in a Judaeo-Christian baptist community. Mani conflicts with the elders over the food and ritual practices of the group (on the perhaps revisionist grounds of actualised Manichaean praxis), and appeals to the teaching of their leader (and founder?) Alchasaios. Thus the community seems related to the Elchasaites of Christian sources, although it is notoriously difficult to disentangle the various teachings of such sects from the available texts.

In any case, it is apparent that Mani broke with the community, and the evolution of his teaching overlaid diverse elements from gnostic and Syriac Christian traditions upon the restricted world of his youth. The influence of Bardaisanite and Marcionite teachings is apparent, although in his scriptures Mani also enters into dispute with such. The adult Mani embarked on his career as healer and apostle, travelling throughout the Persian Empire and to India and the boundaries of Roman power. He seems to have been favourably received by the Sassanian King Shapur I, to have travelled in his entourage, and to have been welcomed in the courts of the aristocracy. Zarathustra and Buddha were incorporated into the tradition of true apostles, together with Jesus, although recent scholarship has tended to downplay the extent of Iranian and Indian influence on the essential structure of Mani's teachings. However, after the deaths of Shapur and his successor Hormizd, Mani was imprisoned by Vahram I probably under the influence of the chief mobed Kirder and the Zoroastrian hierarchy; and there received his own martyrdom. This was then followed by a general persecution of his followers, especially in Mesopotamia.

Since its liberation from heresiology the study of Manichaeism has been driven by philological experts and historians of religion. This has tended towards a dominating interest in the texts in themselves, and in the various strands of Manichaean teaching. However, Mani's vision and the worlds of his followers must also be comprehended as integrated wholes. Mani believed himself to be the recipient of, and owner of, truth.

> This is how everything th[at] has ha[pp]ened and that will happen was unveiled to me by the Paraclete; [...] everything the eye shall see, and the ear hear, and the thought think, a[n]d the [...] I have understood by him everything. I have seen the totality through him! (K. 14.19–23 and see CMC pp. 66-7)

For Mani truth can both be accessed and comprehended. Error attacks and mingles with it in history, but revelation from the eternal world illuminates the good, and offers the sure hope of final victory. Revealed truth is the same as that good that has always been present in the universe, which holds it together, proving life and coherence within death and disorder. Thus, on their own terms, Mani's teachings can not be regarded as eclectic. If his revelations accord with those of earlier apostles it is because they derive from the same source. Where they differ the prior apostolic teaching has been corrupted. Thus Mani reiterates and reveals Zarathustra, Buddha and Christ. Other Buddhisms or Christianities can only be dull reflections of this truth.

In his lifetime Mani devoted himself to the building up of the true church. The superficiality of religious terminology ('church') is important to an understanding of Manichaeism, for as a persecuted minority the community was accused of dissimulation and subversion. Mani wrote his inspired scriptures so that the truth could never again become corrupted by error. He sent out missionaries to east and west, and claimed that no previous revelation had been universal and thus final, as was the one that had been given to him.

From the late third century Manichaeism challenged the Christian hierarchy of the Mediterranean world; but with the triumph of catholic Christianity in the Roman empire, and the common interest of church and state, these western communities gradually failed and died under persecution. In west Asia Manichaeism remained a vibrant force well into the Abbasid era, and

Arabic authors had access to the canonical scripures. However, the religion of light had its longest history in central and east Asia, perhaps surviving in south China until the early modern period. Despite the widely varied cultural forms in which it represented itself, Manichaeism retained an essential unity of vision and expression, and acted as an important conduit for the transmission of cultural ideas between east and west[1].

Manichaeism in Egypt

Manichaean missionaries would have first arrived in Egypt about 260 c.e. By the end of the third century the religion had attracted enough attention to be condemned by both the state, which feared its Persian origins and regarded it as harmful to the fabric of society; and the ecclesiastical authorities, who were particularly shocked by Mani's claim to be the apostle of Jesus Christ, come to restore and renew the true church. Nevertheless, although fiercely combatted and persecuted, Manichaeism attracted a radical and often sophisticated following. The pagan neoplatonist Alexander of Lycopolis, who informs us that the first missionary to reach Egypt was Papos[2], wrote against the doctrine surprised at its attraction for his philosophical colleagues. The religion also spread further west to Roman North Africa, where the writings of Augustine are an eloquent reminder of its appeal in the latter fourth century.

Upper Egypt seems to have become a particularly fruitful area for the Manichaean mission, and Christian writers made frequent attacks upon it. It is highly possible that missionaries reached the Thebaid not only via Alexandria and along the Nile valley, but also directly by sea from Mesopotamia to the coast (Berenice). The region features in the mercantile travels of Scythianus, the proto-Manichaean of Christian polemics. The largest corpus of extant Manichaean texts, the Medinet Madi library including the *Kephalaia,* can perhaps be traced to this area according to dialect. Although Manichaean success in the Roman Empire peaked about 400 c.e., it seems probable that communities survived in areas such as this into the Islamic period.

---

[1] For a detailed introduction to Manichaeism and its history see Lieu 1992.

[2] Alexander of Lycopolis, *c. Manich.* II, p.4, 17-19; and see PsBk2. 34.12.

The documentary texts from Kellis will provide much new detail about this process of Manichaean expansion in fourth century Egypt. It is apparent that the believers understood themselves to be the true and holy church. Presumably the mission to Kellis began as an outreach from an established centre such as Lycopolis. At Kellis there appears to have been significant success, for the documentary texts evidence Manichaeism integrated into the life of the community, and psalms have been found in two different parts of the site. Whether this success was an isolated instance, or more common across the Oasis is unknown. The Dakhleh Oasis is even today a relatively remote region, at the edge of habitation. The excavations at Kellis evidence that the pagan temple was still functioning at the beginning of the fourth century, and it seems reasonable to suppose that the process of Christianisation was less advanced here than in major centres. These features may have aided the Manichaean mission.

Certainly the discovery of bilingual glossaries of Manichaean phrases evidence the remarkable fact of translation from Syriac into Lycopolitan Coptic at Kellis. This, together with allusions to persecution in some of the letters sent to Kellis from the Nile valley, supports the hypothesis that the Oasis became a significant Manichaean centre and safe haven for the community. Unfortunately the archive as yet recovered breaks off at the end of the fourth century, and so the future of the community is unknown. Presumably the strengthening of ecclesiastical control, married to state power, means that Kellis would not long have remained immune from the attention of the authorities.

The finds from Kellis evidence a link between the use of Lycopolitan Coptic and Manichaeism. Dialect and text connect these finds to the Medinet Madi library, for the same psalm tradition is a feature of both finds. Minor textual variants indicate that the Kellis material predates that of Medinet Madi, and thus uncover some of the history of the latter codices. It becomes apparent that codices such as the *Psalm Book* and *Kephalaia* are constructed works in the process of evolution.

As regards the social context of Manichaeism: it was a highly literate and transportable religion that in its conscious universalism appealed to and indeed targeted educated elites. It spread along the trade routes and was regarded by the authorities as subversive. It also evidences a strong role for women who are remarkably visible in the documentary texts from Kellis, as in other Manichaean material such as the doxologies in the *Psalm Book*. The church was strongly structured, programmed for evangelical mission. It developed an elaborate network of what might today be termed safe houses and propaganda factories, for the writing of texts was part of the religious praxis. The letters from Kellis evidence a powerful concern for communication, full of news and greetings and introductions.

Success was founded on the two-fold structure of the community with the elect supported by the catechumens for the full-time service of God, and thus able constantly to travel and to build up the churches. Lay believers, that is catechumens or hearers, could engage in the every day life of family and business; while through their alms-giving they could ensure their eventual salvation. The actual divine work could then safely be left to the elect. Thus the religion, despite its powerful evangelical mission and other worldly focus, was well placed to become an integral part of the community. It is reasonable to presume that Manichaean communities were able to maintain themselves, in areas such as Upper Egypt, for a number of centuries; despite almost continual attack and sporadic enforced persecution.

The Medinet Madi Library

The sensational news of *Ein Mani-Fund in Ägypten, Originalschriften des Mani und seiner Schüler*, announced in 1933 by C. Schmidt, H. Ibscher and H.J. Polotsky, marks a decisive turning point in the modern rediscovery of the religion. The cache seems to have come from a wooden chest in the ruins of an old house in Medinet Madi, to the south west of the Fayoum in Middle Egypt. The codices were already broken up before they reached the Cairo market, where they were first seen by the Danish egyptologist H.O. Lange in November 1929. However, it was C. Schmidt in 1930, while on his way to Palestine to collect manuscripts for the Prussian Academy, who was shown a codex entitled *Kephalaia* and made the connection with Manichaeism. By sheer coincidence Schmidt was in the process of checking the proofs of the late K. Holl's edition of Epiphanius' *Panarion*, and he remembered that among the books that Mani was alleged to have received from Scythianus was one with the same title. Further examination revealed the characteristic clause: 'Once more the enlightener speaks to his disciples ...'

News of the discovery was immediately communicated to A. Harnack in Germany; but, before adequate funds could arrive in Egypt for their purchase, part of the find was acquired by the Irish-American philanthropist and collector A. Chester Beatty. His famous collection of classical and biblical manuscripts was housed first in London, but after the second world war transferred to Dublin, where they remain. The rest of the codices were then purchased by Schmidt with financial aid from the Stuttgart publishing company Kohlhammer, and shipped to Berlin.

The entire collection comprised seven codices, four in Berlin and three in London (now Dublin). In Berlin were: the *Kephalaia of the Teacher* (a small part of this went to Vienna); the *Epistles* of Mani; the *Acts,* a history of Mani and the early community; and the *Synaxeis of the Living Gospel,* (this codex also contains an at present unidentified text). In London: the *Psalm Book,* together with an index; a collection of *Homilies*; and the *Kephalaia of the Wisdom of my Lord Mani.*

The Coptic texts themselves date from about 400 c.e., and are translations of Syriac originals which reach back to Mani himself (the *Epistles*), or to the first generations (as with the *Homilies*). They are written in a form (*L4*) of that dialect known as sub-Achmimic or Lycopolitan; and thus seem not to have originated in the Fayoum, but were carried perhaps by missionaries or believers fleeing persecution.

The conservation of the extremely fragile codices from Medinet Madi, both of London and Berlin, was entrusted to the renowned H. Ibscher; and the task of printing the editions consigned to Kohlhammer Verlag. A special Coptic font was cut to resemble as closely as possible the hand of the original. For the first ten years publication proceeded apace: in 1934 H.J. Polotsky's edition and German translation of 96 pages of *Manichäische Homilien;* in 1938 the latter 234 pages of *A Manichaean Psalm-Book. Part II,* with an English translation by C.R.C. Allberry; and fascicles of the Berlin *Kephalaia* by A. Böhlig and H.J. Polotsky reaching page 244 in 1940. Unfortunately the rise of National Socialism in Germany, and the advent of the second world war, heralded a number of tragedies. These included the departure from Germany of a number of the leading scholars due to the threat of anti-semitism; the death of Allberry; and the loss and probable destruction of some of the codices housed in the soviet sector of Berlin. Specifically the historical work (*Acts*) and the *Epistles* seem to have been removed, and now only portions of these codices remain.

Such events led effectively to an end of work on the Medinet Madi texts for over forty years. Admittedly, A. Böhlig published a further fascicle of the *Kephalaia* (pages 244 – 291) in 1966, but the material for this was largely prepared in 1943. However, the current outlook is much more positive. With the financial support of the Carlsberg foundation S. Giversen has published a facsimile edition of all the Dublin texts in four volumes: *Kephalaia; Homilies and Varia; Psalm Book Part I; and II (Cahiers d'Orientalisme* XIV-XVII, Geneva 1986, 1988). Meanwhile, a separate team under the direction of J. Robinson is working on the remaining texts from Berlin, the *Kephalaia* and *Synaxeis* codices, together with such leaves as remain of the *Acts* and *Epistles*. Another team directed by M. Krause is currently in the process of reediting part II of the *Psalm Book,* before turning to Part I; and S. Giversen is coordinating the reedition of the *Homilies* codex. Also, I. Gardner is editing the new Coptic literary texts from Kellis, and coordinating work on the rest of the Manichaean material there together with other members of the Dakhleh Oasis Project.

The Kephalaia of the Teacher

Two codices of *Kephalaia* (that is 'of the head', thus chapters or summaries) were found at Medinet Madi. Their titles differ slightly, the wording of the Dublin one indicating more explicitly that it is the work of a disciple. However, this may not be of any great significance; and the two codices could well belong together. Until a full edition is made, their relationship will remain unclear. Certainly all the work is apocryphal in terms of Mani's canon of scripture. Still, the reference to the *Kephalaia* in such an early work as *The Sermon of the Great War* (H.18.6) indicates that it belongs in essence to the first generation after the death of the apostle (late third century)[3].

---

[3] 'I am weeping for the *Kephalaia*'. A reference in the *Acta Archelai* evidences that the work was known of in Christian circles by the 340's at the latest (for dating see Lieu 1994: 46-47, 135-140).

Indeed, in the introductory section to the text there appears to be a justification from Mani himself:

> The world has not permitted me to write down [...] all of it; and if you, my children and my disciples, write all my wisdom [...] the questions that you have asked me [...] and the explanations that I have made clear to you from time to time; the homilies, the lessons, that I have proclaimed with the teachers to the leaders, together with the elect and the catechumens [...] all that I have proclaimed from time to time. They are not written. You must remember them and write them; gather them in different places; because much is the wisdom that I have uttered to you. [...] according to your capacity, and even as you may find strength; remember! And write a little something from the great wisdom that you have heard from me (K. 6.16–27 9.5–7).

In a sense this is curious since it was intrinsic to the Manichaean scheme of things that the messages of previous apostles had been adulterated because they themselves had not written their own canon, unlike Mani, and their disciples had then corrupted their words. Nevertheless, kephalaic material has also been found in Manichaean writings in the east, in Parthian and Chinese, and clearly became an important genre for the propagation of the religion.

The Berlin codex opens with a grand survey of Manichaean cosmogonic doctrine; a listing of the canon; and a justification for the text itself, as above. Chapter One then relates the advent and task of previous apostles, culminating in Mani's own call, and the revelation from the Paraclete (his Twin Spirit or Counterpart). However, whilst the earliest chapters might be supposed to evidence some coherent structure to the work, there rapidly follows perhaps two hundred more linked in the most tenuous fashion if at all. The work illustrates a fascination, presumably Mani's own, with all aspects of the natural world, with astrology and the worlds of gods and demons. All such are ordered into elaborate taxonomies, underpinned by the detail of Mani's revealed doctrine, in order to establish a highly structured and holistic understanding of the cosmos and universal history.

The chapters vary greatly in length, appearing to incorporate blocks of oral and perhaps written tradition from a variety of sources. In general they follow a standard pattern wherein a disciple (occasionally an opponent) asks a question of the apostle, the 'enlightener' (various epithets are used). Usually contextual or historical detail is missing. The body of the chapter is then taken up with a summary of doctrine on that particular question which convinces all listeners; and may then end with a prayer of praise for Mani and thanks for his revelation. Similar catechetical methods can be found in early Christian and Buddhist texts. Certainly an introductory knowledge of the broad sweep of Manichaean teaching, as provided below, will help before attempting the *Kephalaia*.

The translation offered here is from the edited Coptic text concluding with kephalaion 122 (K. 295.8)[4]. The original extent of the Berlin codex is difficult to ascertain. The last reported page is 501/502, but a fragment with the pagination 514 has been identified. This may indicate an original total of 22 quires (528 pages). W.-P. Funk is currently editing the latter part of the codex and reports that from K. 296 there can now only be traced records or remains of 139 further pages, some of these in early transcriptions by Polotsky and Böhlig. It thus appears that 70 pages are no longer extant, counting to K. 504 (21 quires)[5].

The total number of chapters in the Berlin codex can be calculated as approximately 210/220. Since the lowest number for a kephalaion yet noted in the Dublin codex is 221 (pl. 17), it seems probable that this is in some sense a second volume, despite some apparent variations in the terminology and structure of the work[6]. The facsimile edition contains 354 plates; but the original extent and order of the codex has not been established.

The Kephalaia *as Text*

The *Kephalaia* is a dense and complex work, evidencing a great concern for detail and structure. Who were its authors and readers? Each kephalaion purports to be the verbatim record of a lesson by Mani, yet it is apparent that it is a constructed text in the process of evolution. The sequencing of chapters shows only a limited rationale, with links established by content (e.g. the

---

[4] The editors are H.J. Polotsky (K. 1 – 102); A. Böhlig (K. 103 – 291); W.-P. Funk (K. 292 – 295).

[5] See Robinson 1992:46-51; and W. -P. Funk, 'On completing the edition of the Berlin Kephalaia codex', paper read to the *IIIrd International Symposium of Manichaean Studies,* Royal Asiatic Society, London 1992.

[6] See Funk 1990.

actions of the Living Spirit in 42 – 44) or by terminology or some catchphrase regardless of theme (e.g. 'five' in 12 – 16). The incorporation of the number into the title, as with 'The Seventh (kephalaion)', evidences that the sequence is beginning to be fixed; but this is likely only to be true of the very earliest chapters.

Redaction history is also apparent in the body of the material itself. For example the description of the five worlds of darkness that occurs in both chapters 6 and 27, (and in the Mandaean *Right Ginza*), must rely on some prior source. However, since the redactors must have had ready access to Mani's scriptures, they would not have directly incorporated parts of the canon. Indeed, the lessons are presented as secondary to the scriptures, for on occasion they follow requests for the reiteration in condensed form or explanation of what Mani has written elsewhere (e.g K. 16.25 – 28). Therefore, kephalaic material can be understood to evolve as commentary to revelation.

Given the mass of the text the occasions of true historical reminiscence can be supposed to be limited. Sometimes the chapter begins with a narrative, such as Mani's visits to King Shapur (chapter 76) or his observation of the Tigris in flood (chapter 61). However, such examples are few, and in general the framing sequence for each lesson is minimal and to be regarded as a formal device. One of the wooden boards found at Kellis (T. Kell. Copt. 1) enumerates the 'five σχήματα (properties)' of the Father of Greatness as reflected in the Third Ambassador. It could be termed a kind of 'flip card' or easily memorised summary used for teaching purposes. In style it resembles much of the kephalaiac material, but here lacks the framing sequences where a disciple asks Mani some question.

It would be easy to construct such a sequence, for instance: 'At one of the times when the enlightener (Mani) was sitting in the midst of the congregation, one of the disciples stood up and asked him: Tell us, our master, what are the five properties of the Father about which you have spoken?'.

It can be supposed that a rapid multiplication of kephalaic material occured in this way, as providing apostolic authority for the constructed teachings of the community. Similarly, the repetition of blocks of material in different settings evidences an extended textual history, which belies the assertion that they are verbatim accounts of Mani's teaching.

A number of sequences appear to have attained a stylised form. This is particularly true of the abbreviated summaries of Mani's teaching, which have hints of creedal formulae; and of the concluding thanks given by the disciples. Thus:

> [Mani] says [... the] two essences that are present at the beginning [...] the [lig]ht and the darkness, that which is good and that which is evi[l, life and] death (286.27 – 30).

> I proclaimed there the word of [truth and li]fe. With [the voi]ce of the proclamation I se[parated the light from the dark]ness there, what is good from [what is evil ...] (186.27 – 30).

The body of the text is constructed in that some individual chapters appear composite, with blocks of material incorporated where seems appropriate, often with minimal connecting sequences. Thus chapter 26 links together five miscellaneous parables. In chapter 65 Mani lists seven benefits of the sun and seven wickednesses brought by the night. Then follow five further qualities of the sun; and then another set of three. It must be supposed that such blocks circulated independently; and also that some may derive from the teaching of the church after Mani. It seems probable that the source of some material may ultimately be from outside of the community, but for its utility it is brought in to the tradition. Chapter 70 contains two separate schema for relating the zodiacal signs to the parts of the body, schema that have long histories within western astrological tradition.

The delight in numerical sequencing is certainly a feature of Mani's own teaching, thus the five sons of the First Man and the five sons of the Living Spirit. Often the doctrine must be forced to accord to this, such as when pentads are fitted to duodecimal lists. Nevertheless, there are clear catechetical benefits in the approach, especially with a system as complex as this.

Thus, kephalaia develops as a form of discourse within the Manichaean community. In that its basis is the aural memory of the disciples, and this dates to the latter third century c.e., it is perhaps not strictly restricted text. However, it is not basic proselytising material, for the scriptural allusions and sequences presuppose an extensive grasp of the macrotext. Thus, it belongs to the inner circle of the elect and could become a means for argument and demonstration between believing communities; a Manichaean form that has social usages analogous to, for instance, hadith literature in Islam. The Iranian parallels evidence diverging traditions[7]; and the mass of material from the two Medinet Madi codices shows the utility of the form for the development of the tradition. It is thus best not regarded as an apocryphal book, but as an evolving and fluid discourse that retained its vitality in relation to the life and needs of the community.

Summary of the Doctrine

Manichaeism may be termed a gnostic religion; that is, both in a structural-systemic and in an historic sense. As a religious system it offered the promise of acosmic salvation through the revealed knowledge (gnosis) of transcendent realities, including the divine nature of the soul, and the details of the pathway to eternal life. Again, in its historic origins Manichaeism is to be considered together with the mass of related gnostic traditions that flourished during late antiquity. Thus Mani directly utilised prior revelations, and in this way gnostic concepts can be tracked from the esoteric forms of prior Judaisms and Christianities, through Manichaeism, and into later metamorphoses such as in Shi'ite Islam and the neo-Manichaean sects of the medieval period.

Nevertheless, the gnostic character of Manichaeism must be qualified, for Mani turned his revealed knowledge outwards to a universal evangelical purpose. While the elect learnt the secret workings of the divine nature, all were offered the call to faith, and the religion firmly grounded itself in time and the existential world. Therefore, the religion promulgated faith, knowledge and good works; and rose above the obscure and short-lived irrelevancies of most gnostic sects.

While it is possible and important for the historian to trace the diverse elements that Mani drew upon in his revelation, it is first vital to understand Manichaeism as a discrete and coherent entity, for this is how one can enter the world of the believer. The following account of the teachings of Mani will emphasise this inner structure and coherence. Nevertheless, any such summary inevitably tends towards artificial synthesis. Manichaean knowledge was carefully graded and tailored to the needs of its audience, as with any other avowedly evangelical ideology that

---

[7] See Sundermann 1992.

seeks the power to change people's life and thought. For the lay
faithful in the Roman Empire it was a kind of superior Christianity, and the metaphysical details that attract the attention of
scholars (and the higher echelons of the elect) had little profile.
In the personal letters of the believers at Kellis there appears to be
scarce knowledge of or interest in the many gods and demons, or
the intricacies of cosmology, such as dominate kephalaic
material. The evidence from Kellis shows how carefully the
hierarchy attempted to draw adherents further into the church
and the gnosis.

Whereas Christianity took centuries to formulate its doctrines,
and the controversies of the great councils seem far removed from
the teachings of Jesus, Mani took great pains to establish a total
religion based upon his own comprehensive scriptures and
preaching. He may be said to have combined the charisma of
Jesus, the missionary purpose of Paul, and the doctrinal strin-
gency of an Augustine. He understood himself to be the final and
universal apostle of God, called to restore the truth of all prior
messengers, including Jesus, the Buddha and Zarathustra. There
is thus less scope in the study of Manichaeism to trace the
evolution of doctrine, since all teaching was rigidly tied to the
very details of the divine word in Mani's scriptures. Nevertheless,
the eschatological urgency of earliest Manichaeism may be said
to have slowly turned towards an accommodation with the world.

The revelation was systematised, in substance at least by Mani
himself, into an elaborate and holistic account of the cosmos,
human history, and the natural world. Manichaean thought was
highly structured and maintained a remarkable uniformity from
Roman North Africa to medieval China, claiming to provide a
coherent and quasi-scientific explanation of everything from the
movement of the stars to the origins of fire and the genera of
creatures. The claim to knowledge would have been a source of
great appeal, but the provision of such detail in the scriptures also
demanded a rigidity that finally undermined the religion. For
these reasons it can be misleading to describe Manichaean doctrine as a myth; and it was certainly not intended as an allegory.

Mani's teaching was summarised by the catchphrase, that 'of
the two principles and the three times (or moments)'. The two
principles are those of light and darkness: whose realms in the
beginning are separate, the dark unknowing of the light; then

during the *middle* are in part mingled, the reality of this present universe; but at the *end* will be the triumph and eternal victory of life and light over death.

In Manichaeism what is true in the macrocosmos is also true for the microcosmos. The individual soul partakes of this whole history, so that our present enfleshment in a demonic body is only the *middle* time between two eternities. Note too that the dualism is not the hellenistic one of spirit and matter, but of two essences, even substances. The divine life is visible, has spatial and quantifiable elements; and evil matter is the active principle of lust, the elements and 'thought of death'.

Manichaean theology is not easily categorised. The Father evokes or emanates powers of himself for purposes in the cosmic drama, and these too may call forth further gods or angels (chapter 50). The language of 'calling out' the powers of light is crucial, to avoid any suggestion of generation, for sexuality is inextricably tied in Manichaean thought to evil matter and the lust that is its nature.

The Manichaeans, or at least the elect, delighted in establishing elaborate systemisations of these beings; but all the divine is ultimately one, so that the diversification represents levels of descent into or entrapment by darkness. Relationships between spiritual levels, for instance a lay believer or catechumen to an elect, will be an exact image of that relationship all the way back up the scale through the gods to the Father. The same is true of all the representatives of the essence of darkness; so that Manichaean teachings are characterised by elaborate series of parallels and shifts of scale.

In the 'first time' the Father of Greatness rules the realm of light, which indeed is an extension of himself, and has four divine attributes: purity, light, power and wisdom. He resides in five intellectuals or limbs: mind, thought, insight, counsel and consideration. These are otherwise substantially detailed as the five elements: living air, light, wind, water and fire. Surrounding the Father are the twelve aeons, distributed three each to the directions of heaven, and refracted also to the one hundred and forty-four aeons of the aeons.

To the south of this kingdom of life is the realm of the King of Darkness. His form combines the shapes of the animals representative of his five warring worlds and their own Kings, also the corresponding five elements of darkness, (chapter 6). This realm is a seething manifestation of the conflict and carnality that is its essence, Matter, the thought of death. In the course of its constant turmoil, by accident for darkness blindly grasps but can not know, the demonic powers glimpse the light and desire to possess its life. Since peace is the nature of the light the Father must call out from himself the great divinities, both as the only means to defend his kingdom, and to distance the inevitable conflict from the land of light. In the ensuing 'second time' the drama is driven by these gods in the arena of mixture, the universe, while the Father himself remains apart until he can again reveal himself and his inner treasury after the final victory.

First the Father evokes the Great Spirit who is the Mother of Life, and she in turn calls forth the First Man. This is the first emanation, that of the gods of *descent*. It also evidences a consciously trinitarian structure embedded in Mani's system, which in common with other Syriac forms of Christianity details the Spirit as feminine.

It is the Man who descends to battle. This first born son of God is armed with the five light elements, personified as his five sons; and it is this portion of the divine that is devoured by the powers of evil when the demonic forces defeat the warrior of heaven. This living soul comes to be compounded with the dark elements of matter throughout the universe, and is in need of redemption for the duration of the 'second time'.

So, while this first conflict appears outwardly to result in tragedy, as with the crucifixion the believer understands that it was a necessity for the binding of evil, and will lead to the ultimate victory of the life and light over death. Nevertheless, the inevitable consequence is the distress and suffering of the divine soul, (termed the Cross of Light particularly in the context of vegetation), and personified as the suffering Jesus awaiting redemption. The entire resultant history of the 'second time' involves the mechanics of once more separating the light from darkness; not simply as a return to the first eternity, but rather to fundamentally alter the status and relationship of the two principles by so fatally weakening the power of death that it can never again threaten the life.

In order to establish the arena in which liberation can take place, that is the universe, a new divine trinity is called forth: the

Beloved of the Lights, the Great Builder, and the Living Spirit (also termed the Father of Life). This is the second emanation, that of the gods of *creation*.

It is the task of the Living Spirit to rescue the First Man, which is a prototype of all future redemption; and then to fashion the universe from the powers of darkness in which the light elements, the five sons, are mixed. Thus the Living Spirit descends to issue a 'summons' (or call) to the Man who responds with his affirming 'answer'; and who is then lifted up out of the abyss. This is the archetype of the assent proclaimed by the community at prayer (chapter 122).

Summons and answer are themselves hypostasised into a pair of divinities. Together they are the 'counsel of life' that throughout the time of mixture personifies the awakening and motivating force of the soul and light elements that are sunk in darkness (K. 178.2 – 5). To prepare for that, the Living Spirit and the Mother of Life descend to the abyss. There they defeat the demonic powers and rulers, and out of their bodies fashion the universe. Thus the demiurge is a light god, though the dead matter of the creation is darkness, albeit shot through with the elements of life. The structure of the universe is divinely conceived, even if its matter is evil.

The Living Spirit constructs ten heavens and eight earths, flaying and crucifying some of the evil powers above, and forming the earths out of the bodies of others. To hold the whole elaborate structure in place he evokes his own five sons: the Adamant of Light, the Keeper of Splendour, the King of Glory, the King of Honour, and the Porter (or Atlas). By means of three wheels or garments, fire and water and wind, the three evil vessels of fire and water and darkness are swept down from the heavens; and then finally swept into pits that have been prepared for them. The light elements are freed to ascend to purity and rest (chapters 42 – 43).

The Keeper of Splendour oversees the eighth, ninth and tenth heavens; whilst the King of Honour watches over the lower heavens from the seventh. The King of Glory turns the wheels so that the light elements may ascend. The Adamant humbles sporadic demonic uprisings on earth. The Porter supports the entire structure from below. The sun and the moon are vessels of purified light, and stations on the path of ascent or descent for the redeemed soul and the gods. However, the planets and stars are evil rulers.

Once the machinery for the purification has been made ready by the second series of evoked gods, they all turn to the Father to plea for a new emanation to set the cosmos in motion, and thus to achieve the process of redemption through time (K. 273.15 – 274.11). The Father approves and calls forth his Third Ambassador (or Messenger), so termed because he introduces the third age of the world. He dwells in the ship of the sun; whilst the Virgin of Light, his feminine doublet, has her throne in the ship of the moon. Jesus the Splendour, another in the series of salvific deities, is closely related in Manichaean systematics to this androgynous sun-moon god. This is the third emanation, that of the gods of *salvation* or *ascent*.

The Ambassador and Virgin achieve a first redemption of trapped light, again turning the uncontrollable lust of the darkness, which is its nature, back upon it. They reveal their images, or more graphically appear naked, before the male and female rulers (archons) chained in the heavens. These powers spontaneously ejaculate or abort across the cosmos. Some light is drawn to the heights, while the remainder that is more deeply embedded in matter sinks downwards and must endure further degradation before it is redeemed. A part falls into the sea and rises as a monster that the Adamant subjugates. Other dross falls to the earth to become the seeds of plant life that the abortions eat. Such complicated details of prehistory were drawn from a variety of prior traditions, which seem to have fascinated Mani and his followers. Inevitably they drew the attention and ire of their opponents.

The abortions formed a rampaging demonic group from which the different genera of creatures originate, corresponding to the varieties of the five worlds of darkness from which they stem. Adam and Eve are fashioned by demons 'after the image of God' that they have glimpsed, that is the Ambassador who had appeared to the rulers in the heavens; and are procreated after various cannabalistic and sexual acts by the dominant demonic pair: Saclas and Nebroel.

Thus, lust is endemic in human nature. Mankind has been deliberately fashioned by demonic forces in an attempt to prevent the redemption of the light, for through the urge for sex humans

will multiply, and further entrap the divine soul in multitudes of
material bodies. This inverts the core of Hebrew tradition, that
God approves of the creation of man and woman, and ordains that
they should 'be fruitful and multiply'. Nevertheless, as with the
macrocosmos, the structural form of humans is in a sense
divinely conceived (in the 'image'), and acts as a mechanism for
the purification of soul.

Since the human soul is a principal repository of the trapped
divine, the abortions having concentrated therein such that they
had gained from the buds and fruits they had eaten, humans
become the focus of the salvific mission of the gods. In an archetypal episode Jesus the Splendour approaches Adam, lying as
dead after his creation and without consciousness, and awakens
him to the saving knowledge of his own condition. Here Manichaeism has inherited and developed the widespread gnostic
retelling and inversion of the 'fall' narrative, so that now the
serpent has become entirely transformed into the heavenly
redeemer.

The process of redemption enters human history. Again Mani
drew upon a variety of non-biblical traditions to develop a complex
narrative about the family of Adam. Note the veneration of the
virginal Seth, a characteristic feature of esoteric traditions; and the
fierce antipathy to female sexuality. In another episode from the
early generations it is related how the demons guarded by the
King of Honour rebelled, and two hundred of these watchers
escaped to earth to wreak havoc and unveil to mankind the
mysteries of heaven (K. 92.24 – 32). In these episodes prior Judaic
material has been reworked and integrated into the Manichaean
system.

The revelation by Jesus the Splendour to Adam is the exemplar
for all future human redemption. Gradually over the generations
more of the divine soul is liberated, so that 'they that are begotten
today, in these last generations, stand diminished and maimed
(K. 147.10 – 11)'. To achieve this liberation Jesus evokes the Light
Mind, and in turn summons forth the Apostle of Light who
becomes incarnate in the great religious leaders throughout
history and the world. So, the process of redemption is the work of
the Light Mind who transforms the human soul by enlightening
and freeing the five intellectuals of light from the shackles of
the body and the five members of sin. 'He shall set right the

members of the soul; form and purify them and construct a new man of them, a child of righteousness (K. 96.25 – 27)'. This 'new man', a concept ultimately to be derived from Paul, will now display the five virtues of love, faith, perfection, patience and wisdom.

Mani believed that he had been commissioned to make the final and universal proclamation of truth for the last generations. The cycle of true apostleship was important to him. It included patriarchal figures such as Seth, Noah and Enoch; also founders of true religions, in particular Buddha, Zarathushtra and Jesus; and more recent apostles such as the gnostic Nikotheos, and Paul upon whom Mani modelled his own style of mission. *Kephalaia* chapter 1 provides an extended simile wherein the advent of the apostles is compared to the months of seedtime and harvest. Each apostle is a farmer who plants a church, labouring over it till it matures and ripens. As it finally comes to fruition another will be seeded: 'There is not any time the tree is bare of fruit! (K. 11.26 – 27)'.

The various listings of the apostles evidence Mani's concept of universal revelation-history, and indicate sources that he regarded as authentic. Nevertheless, it is the figure of Jesus that dominates all the others who in comparison are little more than names. Preeminently Mani regarded himself as the apostle of Jesus Christ. United with his divine Twin he becomes the Paraclete foretold, as according to John 14:16 where Jesus promises the disciples that he will ask the Father who will send them another helper, the Spirit of truth, who will remain with them for ever.

As a whole Manichaean Christology draws upon a range of influences that are woven into a coherent thread running through the entire revelation. Regarding the historical Jesus the influence of prior docetic tradition is evident. Christian polemic against the Manichaean Jesus as a phantasm without human birth, and capable of only an illusory suffering, reiterates the arguments raised against the second century heretic Marcion. Similarly, the Manichaeans in their missionary endeavour in the Roman Empire drew upon the Marcionite critique of the Old Testament and the Jewish God, even though in contrast to Marcionism the Manichaean demiurge is good. Again, following Marcion, Mani believed that he had been called to restore the true teaching of Jesus. This had been corrupted and falsely interpreted by Judaisers, against whom Paul had preached, as evidenced by a particular reading of the Pauline epistles. Thus it lay upon Mani to establish a firm canon of scripture that could never again be adulterated.

Mani and the first generation of his church believed that they were living in the last days before the return of Jesus as judge. The powerful salvific and apocalyptic emphases of his teaching are evident in the rich details of the eschatology, both individual and cosmic. At death each soul will be judged, and if triumphant will be greeted by the Form of Light and angels with victory prizes. Devotional texts, such as Manichaean psalms, developed a powerful symbolic language to express this hope.

There are three paths for the soul at death. Gross sinners beyond any hope of redemption will be damned to hell to await the second death at the end of time, when all of matter and the darkness will finally be bound and sealed in its eternal grave. In contrast, the souls of those such as the catechumens, who are not inextricably compounded with lust, will be reborn in new bodies and have the hope of final purification.

The third way is that of the elect, and indeed of all the light freed from dead matter to life, such as that liberated from fruits and vegetables. This divine ascends up the Pillar of Glory, the great porter of souls, to the moon. This Pillar is itself divinised as a god of the third emanation. It is the Perfect Man (see Ephesians 4:12 – 13), the representation of the church as the body of Jesus in its ascent to the Father. The moon in its waxing and waning then provides visual and actual evidence of its role as a ship and stage in the transit of souls; thence to the sun. From the sun the redeemed light passes to the new aeon that has been built by the Great Builder for the time of mixture. Here the gods rest, and the souls must await the final burial of darkness, before the Father will again unveil to them his image, and can once more receive them into his treasury (chapter 39).

Individual and cosmic eschatology are interwoven in Mani's teaching, for each soul's own tragedy and victory are but a microcosm of the history of the universal soul and its liberation from matter. *The Sermon of the Great War* is an apocalyptic treatise (found in the Medinet Madi codex of *Homilies*) from the first generation after Mani's death, wherein the eschatological event is understood to have already begun. It utilises material from the gospel tradition; as Mani himself did in his earliest writing, the *Shabuhragan*. After the horrors of persecution and the final terrors Jesus will return to take the judgement seat that is prepared for him, to separate the sheep from the goats and to reign in glory.

Then will come the great fire that will achieve such final purification of the light still in the world as is possible. This soul will gather up and rise as the Last Statue, a divinity that in essence recapitulates the descent into the abyss of the First Man. The five sons of the Living Spirit will leave their tasks, and the dead husk of the universe will collapse in upon itself to sink to the depths. All the evil will be sealed in an eternal tomb; but the males and females separated so that they can never again renew themselves and threaten the light.

Time in the sense of the workings of the universe and the history of redemption has come to an end. The 'third moment' is a new eternality without fear.

> (The Father) can give the grace to his fighters, they whom he s[ent] to the contest with the darkness. They will roll back and gather [the cu]rtains, and he unveils to them his image. The [e]ntire l[ight] will be immersed in him. They will go in [to the] treasury. They will also come forth from him in glory (H. 41.13 – 17).

Now there will be two kings, the Father in the aeons of light, and the First Man reigning with the gods in the new age.

The Manichaean Ethic and its Practice in the Church

In the *Kephalaia* chapters 79 – 93 form a distinct section concerned with the religious praxis of the elect and catechumens. It seems probable that they were gathered together prior to their redaction into the work as it now appears. Indeed, chapter 76, concerning the missions of Mani, has some indications of being a new beginning; whilst 77 and 78 (linked by 'four') seem poorly placed. In any case, this sub-work provides much detail on the actuality of Manichaean concerns and community life.

Mani was himself brought up within the confines of a narrow religious sect; and his teachings, although able to drive a religion of world-wide significance, made radical demands upon his followers. Indeed, the question of submission to the demands of the world was the focus of the Manichaean accusation that the 'Christians' were only half believers who had betrayed the teachings of Jesus. The sudden influx and even visual appearance of these new ascetics from the late third century on may well be taken as one spark that lit the fire of Christian monasticism in the decades that followed.

It is certainly true that the teachings that underpinned this new ethic provoked fierce polemic from the leaders of the catholic community, and indeed also the imperial authorities. On the one hand the belief that the divine substance was scattered through all the material world led to devotional attitudes, for instance towards fruit and vegetables as vessels of the soul, that were received with horror. Christian polemic focussed on the complex food rituals intended to liberate the divine light from matter and pain, and accused the Manichaeans of worshipping the sun and the moon. On the other hand Mani's negative account of creation, and fierce antipathy to matter and sexuality as intrinsically demonic, was equally abhorrent.

For Mani the whole rationale for history, and any continuation of human existence, is the liberation of the light elements from the dark. The Manichaean attitude to marriage was entirely negative as the act of procreation prolongs the imprisonment of soul, which would now be further diversified into matter. Moreover, if a peasant works the land, or if a craftsman uses his tools or a soldier his weapons, then they harm and pain the living soul. The same applies to speech that calls for such activites; or incites immorality, anger or envy.

The principal symbol was that of the Cross of Light, the universal divine stretched and bound upon matter. Particularly the Cross was associated with plant life as manifested in sweetness, colour and translucence; in comparison to the heavy carnality and odour of flesh.

The Manichaeans strove to consume food and drink with as high a percentage of light as possible, such as melons and cucumbers; and indeed were much concerned with the classification and preparation of foods, which inevitably attracted the scorn of opponents. Specifically, meat and wine were regarded as dominated by the dark elements that would reinfect the believer striving for personal purification, and lead directly to sensuality and ignorance.

On the positive side, while the very act of eating caused pain to the light elements, the body as a microcosm of the universe also acted as a machine for the liberation of the divine; so that the righteous person could literally discard the gross elements below, and breathe forth angels to rise above. Chapters such as 85 and 93 express the determination to rise above quietism by showing that the purification of soul achieved by positive action in the world far outways the temporary pain caused.

Such an ethic could only really be applied by a small group of people. Yet, the goal that Mani felt to be his vocation was the foundation and propagation by mission of a world religion. The compromise was achieved, possibly under Indian influence, by instituting a two-tiered structure incorporating a doctrine of transmigration of souls.

The community was divided into an inner circle of the elect ('the virginal') who lived a life of extreme asceticism; around which a greater number of hearers or catechumens ('the continent') gathered, who were able to profit from the piety and righteousness of the spiritually more advanced. In actual fact the catechumens were allowed to marry and carry out normal daily activities; but they were obliged to see to the alimentary needs of the monks, and to dedicate a proportion of their work to the church. This duty brought merit to the hearers who could hope to advance to perfection in a future life (e.g. chapters 80 and 91). Mani was anxious to stress that both hearers and elect depend upon each other.

As the final apostle of God Mani led the community for as long as he lived, and after his 'crucifixion' was believed to have ascended to the moon to wait in attendance upon the faithful. During his life-time, concerned at the corruption of earlier churches, he endeavoured to establish the community for the rest of history through writings, missions, and a strong hierarchy. Until the tenth century the Twin-Cities (al-Mada'in) remained the seat of his successor: the *archegos* or *imam*. In standard lists ecclesiastical authority was mediated downwards via twelve teachers (*magister* or ⲥⲁϩ), seventy-two bishops (*episcopus*), three hundred and sixty elders (*presbyter*), and thence to the general body of the elect and hearers[8]. However, the *Kephalaia*, and

---

[8] See Lieu 1994:272.

indeed the new texts from Kellis, evidences a more fluid use of these terms[9].

In the Roman Empire the religion established an elaborate network of cells both to facilitate evangelism and to avoid detection. In later centuries the episcopal hierarchy seems to have been better preserved in the east, especially whilst it was the dominant religion in the Turfan area during the early medieval period.

In central Asia the Manichaeans finally had the freedom to worship openly, to observe their regular fasts, and to develop church practices. However, the most important festival remained the commemoration of Mani's martyrdom when a judgement seat (*bema*) was raised in the middle of the worshipping congregation. Upon this was placed a portrait of Mani to celebrate his continuing presence in the community of the elect; and to symbolise his position as proxy for Jesus until his return as judge.

---

[9] E.g. the use of *archegos* at 193.33. Note also deacons (ϣⲙϣⲉⲧⲉ) at 42.4

COMMENTS ON THE TRANSLATION

The translation provided here is as complete as the surviving edited Coptic allows. Some passages are very fragmentary, where the overall meaning relies more on the impression given by key terms than actual content. With experience an entire episode such as the Third Ambassador displaying his image, and the establishment of life on earth consequent upon the ejaculation and abortion by the heavenly rulers, can be hung by the reader on a slight recurrence of terminology: '[... Amb]assador [... fell to] earth'. Thus the translation attempts to render the lacunose text as accurately as possible. The placing of brackets reproduces the reconstructions of the edited text, with the aim to aid the reader with limited Coptic. Perhaps this is over zealous.

Similarly, the heavily didactic and repetitious style of the original is reflected in the English. The translator's problem is to reproduce intention and not to be misled by the structures of language as system. Inevitably this becomes a matter of interpretation: when is it that the text is repetitive for didactic purposes and when is it the nature of Coptic? This translation errs towards inclusion and faithful representation, hopefully not at the expense of sense. It seems that the style is dense and loaded; terms are ossified and even social and political frameworks appear archaic in the original.

Whilst the English translation endeavours to reproduce the style of the original, the format has been altered in order to try and render it more readable. In particular the text has been broken up into shorter units of paragraphs and lists. Some of these are warranted in accordance with indentations used by the scribe, but the practice has been applied with more consistency. Also, each chapter has been provided with a brief introductory commentary to provide context for the reader, and to aid review of the work as a whole. The Coptic word ⲥⲉϫⲉ ('word' or 'saying') has, where applicable, been rendered as 'lesson'; for this seems best to indicate the quality of Mani's discourses that are the basic material for the constructed *Kephalaia*.

In general there is an attempt to reproduce significant terms and phrases consistently. However, some latitude is necessary to balance consistency with readability. Policies that have been followed are always to use an English term rather than, say, the Greek (thus 'lump' for bolos); to be sparing in the usage of capitals; and also to attempt to provide an equivalent even where the exact meaning of the original is unclear (thus 'sect of the basket' in chapter 121). Often translations can make the original appear overly arcane by the constant highlighting of the technical. This is a problem with a system as complex as Mani's, with a universe populated by numerous gods and demons. In general capitals are used only for the 'great' gods such as the Living Spirit, while subsidiary figures ('five sons of') and epithets are not capitalised. It is difficult to make this policy entirely coherent, but the index will evidence the intention.

The index itself is an aid to the reader. The listing of epithets and alternative titles (the 'Father of Life' is the Living Spirit) helps to clarify the text, whilst hopefully not being overly interpretative. The many epithets and fluid functions of the spiritual entities in Mani's universe make it difficult to achieve closure in this process, and total consistency can not be claimed.

ABBREVIATIONS

CMC.   Cologne *Mani-Codex.*
H.   *Manichäische-Homilien,* ed. H.-J. Polotsky (Manichäische Hand-
         schriften der Sammlung A. Chester Beatty 1, Stuttgart 1934) =
         Homilies and Varia, facsimile ed. S. Giversen (The Manichaean
         Coptic papyri in the Chester Beatty library II, Geneva 1986).
K.   *Kephalaia,* ed. H.-J. Polotsky and A. Böhlig (Man. Hss. der
         Staatlichen Museen Berlin 1, Stuttgart 1940); ed. A. Böhlig
         (ibid. 1.2, 1966).
K (Dub). (Dublin) *Kephalaia,* facs. ed. S. Giversen (ibid. I, Geneva 1986).
PsBk1.   *Psalm-Book,* I, facs. ed. S. Giversen (ibid. III, Geneva 1988).
PsBk2.   *A Manichaean Psalm-Book,* II, ed. C.R.C. Allberry (Man. Mss.
         Chester Beatty 2, Stuttgart 1938) = facs. ed. S. Giversen (ibid. IV,
         Geneva 1988).

SELECT BIBLIOGRAPHY

Alfaric, P., *Les écritures manichéennes*, I/II, Paris 1918, 1919.

Arnold-Döben, V., *Die Bildersprache des Manichäismus*, Köln 1976.

Bagnall, R.S., *Egypt in late antiquity*, Princeton 1993.

Beltz, W., 'Katalog der koptischen Handschriften der Papyrus-Sammlung der Staatlichen Museen zu Berlin (Teil 1)', *Archiv für Papyrusforschung und verwandte Gebiete* 26, 1978: 57 – 119.

Böhlig, A., *Die griechisch-lateinischen Lehnwörter in der koptischen-manichäischen Texten*, Studien zur Erforschung des Christlichen Ägyptens, I, München, 1953.

——, *Mysterion und Wahrheit*, Gesammelte Beiträge zur spätantiken Religionsgeschichte, Leiden 1968.

——, 'Ja und Amen in manichäischer Deutung', *Zeitschrift für Papyrologie und Epigraphik*, 1985: 59 – 70.

Boyce, M., *The Manichaean hymn-cycles in Parthian*, Oxford 1954.

——, *A catalogue of the Iranian manuscripts in Manichaean script in the German Turfan collection*, Berlin 1960.

Brown, P., 'The diffusion of Manichaeism in the Roman Empire', in *Religion and society in the age of St. Augustine*, London 1972: 94 – 118.

Burkitt, F.C., *The religion of the Manichees*, Cambridge 1925.

Cameron, R., Dewey, A.J., *The Cologne Mani Codex: 'Concerning the origin of his body'*, Missoula 1979.

Crum, W.E., *A Coptic dictionary*, Oxford 1939.

Decret, F., *Aspects du manichéisme dans l'Afrique romaine*, Paris 1970.

Dodge, B., *The Fihrist of al-Nadim*, 1/2, New York 1970.

Funk, W.-P., 'How closely related are the Subakhmimic dialects?', *Zeitschrift für Ägyptische Sprache und Altertumskunde*, 112, 1985: 124 – 139.

——, 'Zur Faksimileausgabe der koptischen Manichaica in der Chester-Beatty- Sammlung, I', *Orientalia*, 59, 1990: 524 – 541.

Henrichs, A., Koenen, L., 'Ein griechischer Mani-Codex', *ZPE*, 1970: 97 – 212.

Kasser, R., *Compléments au dictionnaire Coptic de Crum*, Le Caire 1964.

Klimkeit. H.-J., 'Gestalt, Ungestalt, Gestaltwandel. Zum Gestaltprinzip in Manichäismus', in *Manichaean Studies*, ed. P. Bryder, Lund 1988: 45–68.

Koenen, L., 'How dualistic is Mani's dualism?', in *Codex Manichaicus Coloniensis*, Atti 2, ed. L. Cirillo, Cosenza 1990: 1 – 34.

Lattke, M., *Hymnus. Materialien zu einer Geschichte der antiken Hymnologie*, Novum Testamentum et Orbis Antiquus, 19, Göttingen 1991.

Lieu, S.N.C., *Manichaeism in the later Roman Empire and Medieval China*, 2nd ed., Tübingen 1992.

——, *Manichaeism in Mesopotamia and the Roman East*, Leiden 1994.

McBride, D., 'Egyptian Manichaeism', *The Journal of the Society for the Study of Egyptian Antiquities*, XVIII, 1988: 80 – 98.

Murray, R., *Symbols of church and kingdom*, Cambridge 1975.

Nagel, P., Die apokryphen Apostelakten des 2. and 3. Jahrhunderts in der manichäischen Literatur, in *Gnosis und Neues Testament*, ed. K. -W. Tröger, Berlin 1973: 149-182.

——, 'Bemerkungen zum manichäischen Zeit- und Geschichtsverständnis, *Studia Coptica*, Berlin 1974: 201 – 214.

Puech, H.-C., Le prince des ténèbres en son royaume, *Satan*, Paris 1948: 136-174.

——, *Le Manichéisme. Son fondateur – sa doctrine*, Paris 1949.

——, 'The concept of redemption in Manichaeism', in *The mystic vision*, ed. J. Campbell, New York, 1968: 247 – 314.

Reeves, J.C., *Jewish lore in Manichaean cosmology*, Monographs of the Hebrew Union College, 14, Cincinnati 1992.

Robinson, J.M., 'The fate of the Manichaean Codices of Medinet Madi 1929 – 1989', in *Studia Manichaica,* ed. G. Wießner and H.-J. Klimkeit, Wiesbaden 1992: 19 – 62.

Rose, E., *Die manichäische Christologie*, Studies in oriental religions, 5, Wiesbaden 1979.

Rudolph, K., *Die Mandäer*, I/II, Forschungen zur Religion und Literatur des Alten und Neuen Testaments, NF, Heft, 56, 57, Göttingen 1960 – 1.

——, *Theogonie, Kosmogonie und Anthropogonie in den mandäischen Schriften.* Eine Literarische und Traditionsgeschichtliche Untersuchung, Göttingen 1965.

Schaeder, H.H., 'Urform und Fortbildungen des manichäischen Systems', *Vorträge der Bibliothek Warburg, 1924 – 1925*, Leipzig, 1927: 65 – 157.

Schmidt, C., Ibscher, H., and Polotsky, H. J., 'Ein Mani-Fund in Ägypten, Originalschriften des Mani und seiner Schüler', *SPAW*, 1, 1933: 4 – 90.

Smagina, E.B., 'Some words with unknown meaning in Coptic Manichaean texts', *Enchoria*, 17, 1990: 115 – 122.

——, 'Die Reihe der manichäischen Apostel in den koptischen Texten', in *Studia Manichaica*, op. cit. 1992: 356 – 366.

Stroker, W.D., *Extracanonical Sayings of Jesus*, SBL resources for biblical study, 18, Atlanta 1989.

Sundermann, W., Namen von Göttern, Dämonen und Menschen in Iranischen Versionen des Manichäischen Mythos, *Altorientalische Forschungen*, VI, 1979.

——, 'Der Lebendige Geist als Verführer der Dämonen', in *Manichaica Selecta*, Manichaean Studies I, ed. A. Van Tongerloo and S. Giversen, Louvain 1991: 339 – 342.

——, 'Iranische Kephalaiatexte?', in *Studia Manichaica*, op. cit. 1992: 305–318.

Van Lindt, P., 'Remarks on the use of σχῆμα in the Coptic Manichaica', *Manichaean Studies*, op. cit. pp. 95 – 103.

——, *The names of Manichaean mythological figures. A comparative study on terminology in the Coptic sources*, Studies in oriental religions, 26, Wiesbaden 1992.

Van Tongerloo, A., 'An odour of sanctity', in *Apocryphon Severini*, ed. P. Bilde, H.K. Nielsen and J.P. Sørensen, Aarhus 1993: 245 – 256.

Vööbus, A., *A history of asceticism in the Syrian orient*, I/II, Louvain 1958, 1960.

Vycichl, W., *Dictionnaire étymologique de la langue Copte*, Leuven 1983.

Winbush, V. L., ed. *Ascetic behaviour in Greco-Roman antiquity*, Minneapolis 1990.

Woschitz, K. M., Hutter, M., Prenner, K., *Das manichäische Urdrama des Lichtes*, Wien 1989.

Wurst, G., 'Zur Bedeutung der `Drei – Zeiten´ – Formel in der koptisch – manichäischen Texten von Medinet Madi', in *Peregina Curiositas*, ed. A. Kessler, T. Ricklin and G. Wurst, NTOA, 27, Göttingen 1994: 167 – 179.

An extensive bibliography of primary and secondary sources may be found in Lieu 1992. Recent studies are listed in the *Manichaean Studies Newsletter* (ed. A. van Tongerloo and published by the International Association of Manichaean Studies); together with details of conference papers, publication and research projects et al.

THE KEPHALAIA OF THE TEACHER

CONSPECTUS SIGLORUM

[...]   Lacuna of any length, together with vestiges of letters or words with undetermined meaning.

{ }   Unknown word or phrase.

< >   Words or phrases added to the primary text.

[[ ]]   Dittography.

++   Corrupt text.

( )   Explanatory material added by the translator.

/   Line break; (each multiple of five and the pages are numbered).

LIST OF KEPHALAIA

••• (Introduction) •••

(1,1 – 9,10)

The introductory section cannot properly be termed a kephalaion. Rather, it is a framing sequence; and a justification for the entire work.

The text (when readable) begins with a grand survey of the crucial moments in the cosmogonic drama: the eternal separation of the two principles at the beginning; the attack by the darkness, and consequent emanation and descent of the First Man in defence of the light; the construction of the universe by the Living Spirit; the role of the Third Ambassador as supreme redeemer; the destruction of the cosmos in the great fire, and final binding of the darkness; the reintegration of the divine, and victory of the Father (– 5.20).

Mani then asserts his revelation of total wisdom in his canonical scriptures. However, he also stresses his oral teaching; and urges his followers to write down what he has taught them. This appears to provide justification for the *Kephalaia,* as a sub-canonical text (– 7.6).

Mani acknowledges the true proclamation by earlier apostles, detailing Jesus, Zarathustra and Buddha. However, they did not write their own scriptures; and so their teachings were adulterated, and their churches will decay and pass away (– 8.28).

In consequence, Mani again admonishes his disciples to remember and write down his teachings (– 9.10).

(1) [...] [17] light [...] [33] which he has unveiled [... (2) ...] [21] h i s disciples [... (3) ...] entire [...] of wisdom [... / ...] word in the beginning [... / ...] concerning the separation [... / ...] the heights [... [5] ...] to the hei[ghts ...] and they spread out [... / ... unt]il they should make war [... [17] ...] kingdom [... / ... l]ight [... / ...] in the heights [... [20] ... f]rom all the aeons [... / ...] the light, the one that no [... / ...] in it. /

[...] the darkness, the wo[rld / ...] their roo[t ... [25] ...] which poured for[th ... / ...] the one that the earth has [... / ... / ...] darkness [... / ...] it is far from the light [... [30] ...]

Thi[s] is the first [... / ...] concerning the eternality; he [... / ...] to you, for each one of them exis[ts ... / ...] they are divided from one another by their [... / ...] in an eternality since the [... [35] ...] which I have written for you (pl.); this is, that [...] (4) the darkness has made war against the light, desiring that it would rei[gn / over an] essence not its own. It spread a quarrel / [...] it disturbed

[... / ...] came up, it [... in ⁵ this great] need. The power came forth from [... / ... which] is [the Fir]st Man. He [... / ...] the armour of ligh[t ...] / all [the enmity]. He cruc[if]ied it in [... / ...] the armour [... ¹⁰ ... / ...]

[... ¹⁵ ...] he brought the sun [... / ...] the lig[ht] aeons [... / ... the] L[i]ving [Spirit] spread [out the] universe / [...] the earth [... / ...] the light and the da[rkness in] the beginning [... ²⁰ ...] and the garments. He gave [them ... / ...] He set in order the [... / ...] and the wheel of the cou[rse ... / ...] in the heights, that they would [... / ...] of the darkness. He stood [firm ... ²⁵ ... f]ixed. He constructed the found[ation / ... al]l of it was set up. Unde[rneath ... / ... a]ll of them; and also above he [... / ... thre]e earths, they being conjoined. He enclosed the earth i[n / ... f]our mountains and three vesse[ls ³⁰ ...] in its seas and its mountain[s ... / set in] order upon it. This uni[v]erse stood f[irm / ...] a bond for the evil powers [... / ... li]ght that they joined with the darkness [... /

The]n the Third Ambassador! [He purified the ³⁵ li]ght by his image. He became [redeemer of] / all [thin]gs.

(5) [...] they are in all the [... / ... / ... u]niverse, and the fire blazes in it, and it is devo/[ured ...] all [...] of the light al[s]o, and he bec[omes] ⁵ purifier, and goes up to his essence. Conversely, the darkness [wh]ich is in / [...] out, and it is gathered in to a bond [... ¹² ...] unveil [... / ...] and they go in to him and become [... / ... pe]rfume [... s]¹⁵et up [... an]/d they reign for ever, and a single God comes to be [... ov/er] the totality, being above [the to]tality. You (sg.) find no opponent / from this time on again[st the Father], the King of the Light and the [... / ...] which they occur in, from the [beginning ... ²⁰ ...] they are mixed and joined with one another. /

[... unv]eil in these three lessons*¹ / [...] in them. I have written [them in / my bo]oks of ligh[t: i]n *The Great Gospel* and *Treasu[ry] / of the Life;* in *The Treatise;* in *The One of the Mysteries;* [in] ²⁵ *The Writing,* which I wrote on account of the Parthians; and also all my *Ep[ist/le]s;* in *The Psalms* and *The Prayers.* For the[se three] / lessons are the measure of all wisdom. Everything that has

---

*¹ ⲥⲉⲝⲉ Perhaps the 'three times'.

occ[ured], / and [th]at will oc[cu]r, is written in them! Have strength to discrim[inate / ...] and know it through them. [Every] wri[ter, [30] if he re]vea[ll]s these three great lessons: that on[e is / the writer of truth]. Also, every [te]acher, if he gives instruction and proclaims these th[r/ee lessons, is] the teacher of truth. I also, for my part, behold [I] have / [revealed] these three great lessons. I have given them to yo[u / ...]

The first gr[eat lesson (6) [...] which in the [... / ...] / that walks in it because of the twel[v]e [... / ...] in it, which in the cities and the dwelling places found in the [5] [...] because of the doors that are opened in them [... / ...] upon the earth, which in the four corners [... / ... / ... / ... [10] ... / ...] and my pains. For also [... / ...] and my afflictions [... / ...] to them [... / ...] suffices for the person [... [15] ...] wise person.

[Yet], now [I will] entrust to you (pl.) [... / ...] The world has not permitted me to write down [... / ...] to me all of it; and if you, my childr[en and my discip]/les, write all my wisdom [... / ...] the questions that you have asked me [...] [20] and the explanations that I have made clea[r to you from t/im]e to time; the homilies, the lessons, that I have proclaimed with the teache[rs / to] the leaders, together with the elect and the catechume[ns; / and] the ones that I have uttered to free men and free women; [... / ...] all of them, that I have proclaimed from time to time! Th[ey] are [not] writt[en. [25] Y]ou must remember them and write th[em; ga]ther them i[n / differ]ent places; because much is the wisdom that I ha[ve ut]tered [to y/ou].

I did pay heed to each one. I spoke [in (wisdom) about them], / with person after person. Each [one ...] / I have given to him a conviction. The elec[t ... [30] ...] I have given them psychi[c] wisdom [...] (7) psychi[c ...] The suckling babe[s], according to their ability, [... / ...] it, even a[s] is fitting for them; so that they would lis[ten /] like th[is]. Also, even the sects and the he[resies ... / o]ut. I have open[ed] the eyes of each one of them [... its [5] wi]sdom and its [scr]ipture, for the truth is this that I have unvei[led. / I have] revealed it [i]n the world. Also the apostles have [... / ...] and the earliest fathers past unveiled it in th[eir scriptures / ...] Concerning this I [...] in haste, in that [... / ...

eve]ry explanation and every wisdom, as I proclaimed in e[ach
pl[10]ace], in each c[it]y, in each land [... / ...] and they [...] as he
may form it in [... / ...] and [...] truth since [... / ...] which they
have [... / ...] the church [... [15] ... / ... / ...] according to [...] book. /

[...] you [... my] beloved ones: At the time that [Jesus t/r]od [...]
the land of the west [... [20] ... proc]laimed his hope [... / ...] his
disciples [... / ...] which Jesus uttered [... / ... a]fter him they wrote
[... / ...] his parables [... [25] ...] and the signs and wonders [... / ...]
they wrote a book concerning his [... /

The apostle of] light, the splendrous enlightener, [... / ... he came
to] Persia, up to Hystaspes the king [... / ... he chose d]isciples,
righteous men of trut[h ... [30] ... he proclaimed hi]s hope in Persia;
but [... / ...] Zarathustra (did not) write books. Rather, hi[s /
disciples who came a]fter him, they remembered; they wrote [...
/ ...] that they read today [... / ...]

Again, for his part, when Buddha came, [... (8) ...] about him,
fo[r] he too proclaimed [his / hope and] great wisdom. He
cho[se] his chur[c/hes, and] perfected his churches. He
unve[iled] to them / [his hop]e. Yet, there is only this: that he
d[id not] write his wi[5][sdom in bo]oks. His disciples, who came
afte[r] him, are the ones who re/[membered] somewhat the
wisdom that they had heard from Buddha. They / [wrote it in
sc]riptures.

And this, in that the fathers of righteou/[sness] did not [wri]te
their wisdom in books [... / ...] know that their righteousn[ess]
and their chu[r[10]ch will pass aw]ay from the world; because they
did not writ[e / ...] Since [...] write it in book[s / ...] will lead
as[tr]ay [...] fall / [...] and they [...] lead astra[y / ...] adulter[at]e,
and they [... [15] ...] mix [... / ... / ...] all of it, of the knowledg[e / ...]
will unveil [... / ...] in the world, in a [...] Since the fa[thers of [20]
righteo]usness know this, that also [... / ...] in the [... / ... / ...]
from [... / ... [25] ... / ...] lead astray and [... / ...] as they illuminate
[... / ...] write [th]em for you (pl.) in books. /

[... [30] ...] it was not unveiled, nor was it [... / ...] every [...], together
with the commandments and [... / ...] unveiled for you in my
script[ures ... / ...] to you, that the wisdom and the in[terpretation

... / ... from] time to time, which I did not write [... ³⁵ ...] and you write after me, so that [...] **(9)** it leads you not astray! For you yourselves k[now] / the great wisdom [I have uttered in] / city after city, in each land separately. What [I have written] / in books no human mouth will suffice to write. ⁵ Nevertheless, according to your capacity, and even as yo[u] may fi[nd] / strength; remember! And write a little something from [the] great [wi]/sdom that you have heard from me.

When [y]/ou write a[nd] are amazed by them [... en]/lighten greatly; and they shall give benefit and make free [...] ¹⁰ of the truth.

••• 1 •••

(9,11 – 16,31)

/ *Concerning the Ad[vent]* / *of the Apostle.*

The succession of apostles and churches is compared to the continuous cycle of
seedtime and harvest. A new apostle releases the spiritual forms of his
church, (the heavenly twin motif); and then is sent to earth to sow the seed
of his election, at the very moment that the previous church finally ripens to
harvest and ascends. Thus, there is no moment when the world is bereft of
the means of salvation (see 11.26 – 27).

This recognition of the authenticity of each cycle of revelation is one of
the most striking aspects of Mani's teaching. While Mani is likely to have
developed it from the concept of the true prophet, found in his Elchasaite
heritage and in other Jewish-Christian sects, and it also owes something to
Marcion's idea of the renewal of Jesus' true revelation by Paul and himself;
nevertheless, the universal application seems to be the product of Mani's
particular religious genius. It also, by an historical connection which is not
yet clear, may well have influenced the notion of cycles of prophecy that
appears in emergent Islam.

The chain of apostles is traced from Sethel, (as in other gnostic teachings), through Enos and Enoch to Sem. Two figures from Indian tradition
are then included, the Buddha and Aurentes (from 'arhant'?); and finally
Zarathustra and Jesus. Other Manichaean texts provide similar lists, and the
concept was open-ended enough to allow the inclusion of other apostles such
as Hermes Trismegistus or Lao-Tzu to accord with the missionary expansion
of the religion (see Puech 1949: 144 – 146 and now particularly K (Dub).
299). Nevertheless, while universality is obviously the intention, it is noticeable that only Jesus receives any significant detail or historical context. It is
difficult to find evidence that Mani had any real knowledge of the lives and
teachings of figures such as the Buddha.

Docetic emphases that can be traced back to Marcion are embedded in the
Manichaean accounts of Jesus. This kephalaion is particularly interesting for
an understanding of Mani's religious heritage because he follows the chain
of apostles from Jesus to Paul, and then to one (or two?) righteous man in
the Christian church (13.30 – 35). The identity of this figure has been much
debated, but the obvious candidates are Elchasai, Marcion, and perhaps
Bardaisan.

After the ascent of the church of Jesus Mani's apostolate begins. Thus, the
authenticity of later Christianity is rejected. As he foretold, according to the
gospel of John, Jesus sends after him the Paraclete. This is Mani's own
Twin-Spirit who reveals to him the totality of truth, the knowledge that
Mani will then preach and write in his canonical scriptures. The summary
of the essentials of revelation given here (14.27 – 15.24) is one of the best
known from Manichaean texts; and has an almost creedal ring to it. Mani
finishes with a brief summary of his missionary journeys, and a repetition

of his claim to direct revelation. His own apostolate is superior to those
before him because it has spread throughout the world; and thus it will last
till the final judgement and the return of Jesus (16.3 – 17).

In the framing sequence at the end the disciples are enlightened and
thank Mani; and assert that he is the Paraclete. Thus he has become one
with his heavenly Twin, 'a single Spirit (see 15.23 – 24)'.

15 The first chapt[e]r is this: His disciples [questioned / h]im
concerning his ap[os]tolate and his coming to the wor[ld; / fo]r
[h]ow did it happen [... his] / journeying in each city, in each
la[nd]; / in what [manner] was he sent [... 20 ...] first, before he
had yet chosen h[is church]. /

The apostle [sa]ys to them: I [... / ...] but I will recount to you [... /
... / ...] Understand, O my beloved ones: [A]ll the apost[les] 25
who are on occasion sent to the world re[semble] / farmers;
while their churches, which they choose, [are] / like Pa[rm]uthi
and Paophi. For, the way Parmuthi [occ/u]rs not in all the
months of the year; nor [does Paophi / ...] in all of them. Rather,
the season [... 30 ...] for it alone, as they know [... / ...] its vegetables
[... / ...] the time they are cropped; also the vegetables and the [... /
...] season; and they tend and ripen the pickings, and they / [...]
to Paophi. Of course, now that farmer (10) [...] Parmuthi; in that, if
he will come and sow some corn seed th/[ere ...] cereal. And he
shall be involved from the beginning / [...] a corn seed and toil
for it. Yet, when the summer / [comes] each year, and his corn
comes to the season of its harvest; 5 [then] the farmer comes forth
and harvests it. Even the ga[rdener] from the begin/[ning ...]
shall toil for his fruits; and he tends them and he / [...] and they
ripen; and he comes forth and picks them from the tree. /

[This is the way of the] apostles who are come to the [wo]rld.
They are l/[ike] a [...] of the greatness [...] the season that [... 10 ...]
flesh. Rather, they are sent before [... / ...] before they had yet [...]
in the wo/[rld ...] from the greatness. They [...] to the [whole]
created order; / [and they] choose a selection of the [..., as t]hey
make [... / ...] the elect and the catechumens [... 15 ...] their forms,
and they make them [free ... / ...] in the flesh [... / ...] the world /
[...] to above / [...] as he may make his [...] the winter, and he
harvests it 20 [...] also tend to the fruit in the summer and the / [...
P]aophi, and he takes them away.

Also the way [... / ...] many years before [... / ... the w]orld, as he
journeys below to the [... / ... makes the f]orm of his church free,
and [... 25 ...] of the flesh, whose form[s] he had made free / [...]

Like the farmer, for when he will [... / ...] that moment he shall
begin [... t]end / [...] it reaches Parmuthi also, he may harvest it
[... / ...] toil for the fruits of Paophi [... 30 ...]

Again, this too is [how] the apostl[es ... / ...] from the beginning
of the moulding of humanity [... / ... a]s I have t[ol]d you, that
when they [... / ...] before every thing he shall [... / ...] free above,
first.

Yet, when (11) it [will be] born in the flesh, he shall come down
to it and at once [...] it in the [...] / which comes out from the [...]
is [r]aised up / to the greatness. [He] shall continue in the world
at this time [...] / him, corresponding to the season when the
world will come to his [...] 5 when the season will mature he is
raised up from the world [...] / and he leaves his church
{behind}*2 and goes forth. Still, he [... / ...] and he helps and aids
his church. / Whoever comes out from their body after him, he
shall be[come] / for them a s[uppo]rt and a leader; and he goes
on before them [...], 10 excepting the othe[rs] who are set firmly in
the fles[h]. He is the one who [will / be]come for them a h[e]lper
and a guardian; he shall not take [... / ...] in se[cr]et, until his
church [... / ch]ange it [...] when [h]is church [... / ... 15 ...] he
was raised up after it, and went [in / to the l]and of glory. And he
rejoices and rests at the last [... / ...]

Like the far[me]r who shall be glad of heart in [...] / he was
bringing in (the harvest). Or like the merchant who [shal]l come
up from [a coun]/try with the doubling of his great cargo; and the
riches [of his tr]20ading.

When the apostle will be [rais]/ed up from the world, he and his
church [... / ...] for [every] apostle / [...] in the [...] Since [... / ...]
tree, that still [is l]aden with its first fruits 25 [...], and they are
picked; they shall propagate other ones th[ere], / and they mature
to the season to bring them forth. There is not any time [the tree]

---

*2   ⲙ̄ⲛ̄ⲍⲱⲥ

/ is bare of fruit! Rather, instead, those about to ripen as they pick them / shall propagate other ones there. When they bear these [... / t]hem on the tree; they come up and are brought forth upon it[s bran]³⁰ches. They shall pick from it those that mature and ripen. [The far]/mer do[es not] rest at any time from the labour and the pain. / At what hour [may he] cease? When he can finish harvesting the corn in P[armu]/thi! [...] them in the winter, the fruits of the summer shall [...] / grow [up and] be picked in the month of Paophi.

³⁵ The apostles are like [t]his [also]. N[o]w, (12) when the apostle will be raised up to the heights, he / and his church, and they depart from the world; at t[h]at instant / another apostle shall be sent to it, to another ch/u[rch ...] it [...] Yet, first, ⁵ he shall make the forms of his church free in the heights, / as I have told you. When [...]; / again, he too shall come down and appear [... / ...] and he releases his church and saves it from the flesh [of / sin ...]

The advent of the apostle has occured at the occasion ¹⁰ [... a]s I have told you: From Sethel / [the first] born son of Adam up to Enosh, together with / [Enoch]; fr[om] Enoch u[p] to Sem [the] son of [Noah; / ... / ...] church after it [... ¹⁵ ... Bu]ddha to the east, and Aurentes, and the other [... / ...] who were sent to the orient; from the adve[nt] / of Buddha and Aurentes up to the advent of Z[a/ra]thustra to Persia, the occasion that he came to Hystaspes / [the k]ing; from the advent of Zarathustra up to the advent of Jesus ²⁰ [the Christ], the son of greatness. /

[The advent] of Jesus the Christ our master: He came [... / ...] in a spiritual one, in a body [... / ...] as I have told you about him. I [...] him; / for he came without body! Also his apostles have preached ²⁵ in respect of him that he received a servant's form, an appearance as of / men*³. He came below. He manifested in the world in / the [s]ect of the Jews. He chose his twelve / [and] his seventy-two. He did the will of his Father, who had / sent him to the world. Afterwards, the evil one awoke ³⁰ envy in the sect of the Jews. Satan went / in to Judas the Iscariot, one am[ong the twe]lve / of Jesus. He accused him before the sec[t of the J]ew/s, with his kiss. He gave [him] over [to the han]/ds of the Jews, and

---

*3   Phil. 2:7

the cohort of the soldie[rs. The Jew](13)s themselves took hold of the son of Go[d. They gave judgement on] / him by lawlessness, in an assembly. They condemned him by i[ni]/quity, while he had not sinned. They lifted him up upon the wood of the cro/ss. They crucified him with some robbers on the cr[o]s[s. 5 Th]ey brought him down from the cross. They placed him in the grave; [and] / after three days he arose from among the dead. He / came towards his disciples, and was visible to them. He laid upon them a / power. He breathed into them his Holy Spirit. [He sen]/t them out through the whole world, that they would preach [the grea]10tness. Yet, he [hi]mself, he rose up to [the heights.

... / ...] Jesus, [h]is twelve [... / ...] land [... / ...] master [... / ... 15 ... / ...] them. They were not faint-hearted, nor [... / ...] they were all active [... they were raised] / up and rested in the greatness.

[... while] / the apostles stood in the world, [Pau]20l the apostle [reinforced them]. He also came forth. He preached [... / ...] He gave power to the apostles. He made [them] stro[ng ... / ... the] church of the saviour [... / ... / ...] he preached a [... 25 ...] he too went up and rested in [...] /

After Paul the apostle little by little, day [after] / day, all mankind began to stumble. They le[ft righteousness / b]ehind them; and the path which is narrow and sticky. They preferred [...] / go on the road which is broad.

30 [A]t this same time also, in the last church, a righteous [m]an / of truth app[ea]red, belonging to the kingdom. He reinforced [... / ...] they cared for*4 the church of our master according to [their / capacity; bu]t they too were raised up to the lan[d of / light. A]fter those ones again, little by little, the ch35[urch] perished. The world remained behind without (14) [c]hu[r]ch. Like a tree

---

*4 Or 'carved': p̄ⲧⲁⲕ lit. 'make knife'. See also 218.6 Kasser 1964:50 suggests 'prendre soin de'; but in this context it may indeed mean to separate the righteous Christians from the falsifiers. The switch to plural has been taken by most commentators to mean that the first righteous man (e.g. Marcion) agreed with (ⲧⲙⲉⲧⲉ, here translated as 'reinforced') a second (e.g. Bardaisan) who together p̄ⲧⲁⲕ the church. However, as E. Smagina (1992:365) points out, the lacuna could easily be filled by such a term as 'his disciples'.

will be plucked, and the fr/uits on it taken away. And it remains
behind without fruit. /

[Wh]e[n] the church of the saviour was raised to the heights, my
apo/stolate began, which you asked me about! From that time on [5]
was sent the Paraclete, the Spirit of truth; the one who has /
co[me] to you in this last generation. Just like the saviour sa/id:
When I go, I will send to you the Paraclete. / [Whe]n the
Paraclete comes, he can upbraid the world concerni[ng / sin,
and] he can speak with you on behalf of right[eou]sness, and [10]
[about] judgement, concerning the sinners who believe / [me
not; ...*5 he] can speak with you [... / ... / ... / ... [15] ...] he can
s[p]eak with you and preach [... / ...] that [...], the one who will
honour me and [... / ...] and he gives to you. /

[...] preach on behalf of the Paraclete of truth, that he / [...] he
came to manifest the one whom he had known [... [20] ...] the
appointed time of all these years, as they [... / ... from] Jesus until
now [... / ... / ...] until he [... / ...] and he makes them free. Yet,
when the church as[25]sumed the flesh, the season arrived to
redeem the souls; like / [the mont]h of Parmuthi that cereal shall
ripen i[n], / to be harvested.

At that same season he [...] / my image, I assuming it in the
years of Arta[b]anus / the [ki]ng of Parthia. Then, in the years of
Ard[ashir], the ki[30]n[g] of Persia, I was tended and grew tall and
attained the ful[lne]ss of the sea/[so]n. In that same year, when
Ard[ashi]r the ki/[ng was c]rowned, the living Paraclete came
down t[o me. He sp]o(15)ke with me. He unveiled to me the
hidden mystery, / the one that is hidden from the worlds and the
generations, the myster[y] of the dep[ths] / and the heights. He
unveiled to me the mystery of the light / and the darkness; the
mystery of the calamity of conflict, and the w[ar], [5] and the great
[...] the battle that the darkness spread about. Aft[erwards], / he
unveiled to me also: How the light [...] / the darkness, through
their mingling this universe was set up [...] / H[e o]pened my
eyes also to the way that the ships were constructed; [to enable the
/ go]ds of light to be in them, to purify the li[ght from] [10] creation.
Conversely, the dregs and the eff[lue]nt [... to the] / abyss. The

---

*5   Jn. 16:7–9 +ff.

mystery of the fashioning of Adam, the fir[st ma]/n. He also informed me about the mystery of the tree of knowledge, [wh]/ich Adam ate from; his eyes saw. [Also], the myste/ry of the apostles who were sent to the wor[ld, to enable them] 15 to choose the churches. The mystery of the elect, [with their] / commandments*6. / [The] mystery of the catechumens their helpers, with [their] / commandments. The mystery of the sinners with their deeds; / and the punishing that lies hidden for them.

This is how everything th[at] has ha[pp]20ened and that will happen was unveiled to me by the Paraclete; [...] / everything the eye shall see, and the ear hear, and the th/ought think, a[n]d the [...] I have understood by him e/verything. I have seen the totality through him! I have become a single body, / with a single Spirit!

In the last years of Ardash[ir] 25 the king I came out to preach. I crossed to the country of the Indians. [I] / preached to them the hope of life. I chose in that place / a good election.

Yet, also, in the year [that Ar/da]shir the king died Shapur his son became king. He [...] / I crossed from the country of the Indians to the land of the Persians. Also, from 30 the land of Persia I came [to] the land of Babylon, Mesen[e] / and Susiana. I a[pp]eared before Shapur the king. He rece/i[v]ed me with great ho[nou]r. He gave me permission to journey in [... / ... pr]eaching the word of life. I even spent some year[s / ...] him in the retinue; many years in (16) Pers[i]a, in the country of the Parthians, up to Adiabene, and / the bor[de]rs of the provinces of the kingdom of the Romans. /

[I have chosen] you (pl.), the good election, the [h]oly chur/c[h] that I was sent to from the Father. I have 5 [sown] the seed of life. I have [...] them [... / ... fr]om east to west. As you yourselves are seeing, / [my] hope has gone toward the sunrise of the world, and / [every] inhabited part; to the clime of the north, and the [... / ...] Not one among the apostles did ever do these things [... 10 ...]; because all the apostles who were sent / [... / ...] they preached [... / ...] the world [... / ...] (my hope) will remain in the world until

---

*6 [[the mystery of the sinners with their de[eds]]]

[(Jesus) ... [15] ...] his throne in it, and he will make [...] in / [...] church, which is the righ[t] side, / [...] which belongs to the left. /

[...] about which you questioned me. S/[ince the] Spirit is of the Paraclete, the one who was sent to me from [20] [the greatness; what has] happened and what will happen [has been] / unveiled to me. For you I have written about it, in full, in my / books already. Today you have again questioned me. Behold, now I have repeated / the lesson to you in brief!

Then, w[he]n his / disciples heard all these things from him, they rejoiced greatly. [25] Their mind was enlightened. They say to him in their joy: We th/ank you, our master! For while you have written about your advent in the / [scri]ptures, how it came to be, and we have received it and believed in it; / still, you have repeated it to us in this place, in a condensed form. And / we, for our parts, have received it in full. We have also believed that you are the [30] Paraclete, this one from the Father, the unveiler of all these hi/dden things!

••• 2 •••

(16,32 – 23,13)

/ *The Second, concerning* / *the Parable of the Tree.*

The use of Jesus' parable about the two trees as a proof-text for dualism was already a key feature of Marcion's exegesis (e.g. Tertullian *adv. Marc.* 1.2.1; 4.17), from which it must be traced to Mani, and is thence found throughout Manichaean texts (e.g. PsBk2. 56.21 136.20-21. Augustine *c.Adim.* XXVI).

In this kephalaion Mani begins by discussing sectarian interpretations of the parable. Unfortunately this section is very fragmentary, but it seems to be concerned with the mixture between the two principles that occurs during time and in the cosmos, so that no person or thing of composite nature can be singularly good or evil (17.16 – 19.28).

Mani then presents his own definitive revelation. The limbs of the good tree are the five intellectual qualities through which the soul ascends to the Father and the aeons of glory (20.21 – 31). This equation of the internal mental process of salvation with the eschatological journey through the heavens indicates a living spirituality in Mani's teaching that is often missed by commentators. The fruit of the good tree is Jesus the Splendour, that is Jesus as the universal redeemer and incarnation of divine Intellect, and thus the 'father of all the apostles'. Consequently, its taste is the community of the church.

As an exact negative of this the evil tree is also made up of five intellectual qualities. However, in this case the mental process is directed towards sin and darkness; and the corresponding eschatological journey takes this soul to the ultimate death where it is compounded with the final 'lump' beyond all hope of redemption (21.27 – 22.20). The text does not preserve the fruit of the evil tree; but its taste is the sects that always oppose the true churches.

The chapter ends with an important semi-creedal assertion of belief in absolute dualism (22.35 – 23.13).

³⁵ The first parable that they asked him about! They besought [him to ex]/plain it for them.

This is the [occ]asion that [... (17) ...]; for his discip[les, who sat] / before him, questioned him. They say to him: We beseech y[o]u, our / master, that you may re[coun]t and explain t[o] us about these / two [tr]ees [that Jesus pre]ached to his disciples. As it is written in ⁵ [the] Gosp[el, he says]: The good tree shall give / [good fr]ui[t]; also [the] bad [tr]ee shall give b[ad] fruit / [... There is no] good [tree] that shall give bad fruit; / [nor a bad tree that] shall give [g]ood fruit. [One / kn]ows [each tree by] its fruits*⁷.

¹⁰ Now, [we] entreat you, that you may [...] / two trees, [an]d explain them [... / ...] as they grow u[pon the] earth; because it is written [...] / scriptures [...] them [... / ...] saying [... ¹⁵ ...] mystery by mystery. /

While there are some among the sects who explain about these [tw]o tr[ees], / as they reckon them, that a good tree [... remai]/ns behind, on this composite earth; another [...] / to them, comparing them with [...] ²⁰ in a single explanation. /

Then speaks our master Manichaios, the apostle [of gre]/atness, to his disciples. Great is [...] ²⁶ by his own mouth [...] bad / [...] The sec[ts ... / ... / ...] ³⁰ Yet, [th]is that they [expla]in about the two trees, as they reckon the[m, / ...] the trees [...] in an explanation [... / ...] because [... / ...] tree, as it grows on this composite ea[rth, / ...] date palm, because [... ³⁵ ...], for not absolutely every part of the date palm is used! (18) [...] their child, as it strikes [... / ...] while first one [...] in them / [...] at the end there is one [...] it

---

*⁷ Lk. 6:43–44

occurs / in its fibres and its branches [...] [5] There is a bad dust in them [...] / date palm [...] before the tree that [...] bad; / because they give the decision [... / ... / ...] the one that they name [... [10] ...] the type [... / ...] name it: tree [... / ...] is sweet [... [17] ...] writing [... / ... / ...] they shall establi[sh ... [20] ...] man [... / ...] it is sweet [... / ...] seed of the [...] and it is us[ed] / for their nourishment [... [31] ...] will explain [... / ...] may not join to the [... / ...] mankin[d], as they are named [... / ...]

[35] [... / ... / ...] for as they [... apo(**19**)s]tle. They counted him in the number of [the twelve]. Yet, [at] / the end, it is written about him that Sata[n entered him]*[8]. / He gave the saviour into the hands of the Jews; they [...] / upon the wood.

Now, Judas Iscar[iot], first [they] [5] called him a good man; [(but) ... / ...] and traitor and murderer [... It is written about] / Paul, that first he was acting persecutor [... chur]/ch of God*[9], he persecuting [... / ... [10] ...] / a great rev[elat]ion. He [...] / the church [of m]y master. He [... / ...] bad first [... / ...] explain [... [15] ...] their explanation [... / ...] good man, upright [... / ...] completely bad; because [...] / they were fashioned through the mingling of the [...] / they all standing firm in [...] [20] they gave likeness to them, they established them in the [...] / which is mingled in all things.

Behold, [... the ex]/planation of the sects [... / ...] listen and I will revea[l] to you concerning the [... th/at the] saviour preached in the [parable] about the good tree and [25] the bad tree [...] / they know not, for what are [...] and their inner p[ar]ts / [...] know, they being like [...] in their explanation [... / ...] what are th[ese t]wo tre[es]?

[...] / how I will reveal to you [...] the expound[er ...] [30] the trees [...] the Father [... / ...] all of them, as he [...] in the [... / ...] world [... / ...] this g[o]od tree, the [... / ...] the light of this good tree [... [35] ...] the [P]illar [... (**20**) ...] the intellectuals that are cloaked upon its body [... / ...] this good tree. They are the light elements / that are mingled, being compounded in the totality. The fruits / of the

---

*[8] Lk. 22:3
*[9] I Cor. 15:9

good tree are glorious Jesus the Splendour, the father [5] [of] all [the apo]st[l]es. Yet, the taste of the fruits of the [good] tree / [is the] holy [c]hurch, in her teachers and her / [...] the c[atech]umens. Behold, this is the [good] tree / [... / ... [10] ...] bad [f]ruit / [... r]evea[l] to you [... / ...] it has five limbs. / [They are considera- tion, counsel, insight, tho/ught, mind. I]ts consideration is the ho[ly] church. [Its counsel] [15] is [the Pil]lar of Glory, the Perfe[ct] Man. [Its insight / is the Fir]st Man who dwells in the ship of [living] wat[ers]. / Its thought is the Third Ambassador / [who dwells in] the ship of living fire, that shines in / [... A]lso, the min[d] is the Father who dwells in great[20][ness, who is perfe]ct in [the] aeons of light. /

[...] this one, for the souls that ascend and attain / [h]oly [...]; together even with the alms that the cate/[chumen]s give, as they are purified in the [holy] church; / [...] everything. It is conside- ration that shall [... [25] ...] they shall be raised up [...] is counsel; / [they sh]all be raised up to insight, which is the First Man / [who d]wells in the ship of the night; fr[om] insight they shall ris[e / u]p to thought, which is the Ambass[ad]or who dwells in / [the sh]ip of the day. And he too, great glor[ious] thought, [30] [shall bring] them in to mind; which is the Father, the Go/[d] of truth, the great Mind of all the [ae]ons of glory. /

[Th]is is the good tree that shall give [good] fru[it, ... / ...] is [the] entire life and light for ever [... / ...] occurs [...] ever, it is bles[sed ... [35] ...] goo[d ...] bad [... (21) ...] happen in [... / ...] from [... / ...] also [... / ...] the way that it i[5][s ... [12] ...] the good tree [... / ...] of the fire [... / ...] they are the rul[ing-power ... [15] ...] heaven and the wheel [... / ...] they are the five fleshes that walk [... / ...] fruit [... / ... te]aching as of error, the mystery that [... wh]/ich Satan appointed in the world.

However, the [taste of these] [20] bad fruits is these evil people, the sects [... wh]/ich are bound in law after law, they and their teachers [... / the l]aw of death; they taking taste for it, they being thirsty fo[r it / ...] the soul[s] of death.

This is the tree that [shall / give g]ood [fruit]; the one that our master called [25] [the good tree that shall] give good fruit. He [...] / in the scriptures [...] all [the] sects know it. /

[... I will] reveal to you and you [... / ... The] bad [tree] has five limbs. / Th[ey are consid]eration, counsel, insight, thought, [mind]. 30 [It]s c[onsideration is] the law of de[at]h from which the sect[s] / take instruction. I[t]s counsel is [t]ransmigration [...] / in typ[e after type]. Also, its insight is the furnaces of [fire / ... ge]henna; which is full of [s]moke. Thought [... / ... ve]ssel. Its mind is the [... 35 ...] the lump, the last b[o]nd, the [... / ...], they that Satan ca[st away. (22) ... 11 ...] the great [... / ...] and they fall [... / ...] the darkness [... / ...] all [...] and they take away [... 15 ... are swall]owed i[n] to the lump, and they are bound [... / ...] the fruit of darkness, the one that they [... / ...] for ever and ev[er / ...] his face [... / ...] will arrive at that place; and they have no 20 repentance therein. /

[...] this is the e[x]planation of the bad tree, as I have e[xpla/ined ...] to you, which you [...] to it [... / ...] good fruit [... / ...] its fruit bad [... 25 ... i]n it, in its existent days [... / ...] in it.

Concerning this [... / ...] and my be[loved on]es [... / ...] them in truth, it being changed from [... / ... 30 ...] which lies in its go[o]d earth [... / ... life] and light; as death and darkness do not ex[ist ... / ...] Also, [the] bad tree is Matter [... / ... i]t, I understand it alone among the [... / ... wh]ich occurs in its bad earth [... 35 ... darkness] and death.

Blessed is [every one (23) ...] these [t]wo trees, and separates them on[e] from [an]other. / He understands that they did not arise out of one another, nor did [th]ey come / from one another. They did not come from one! The person / who can separate them out may go up to the aeon of light. 5 [... as I have] revealed it to you. And he sees / [...] bad fruit di[d n]ot arise from / it [...]; but whoever will not separate out [... / ...] from [o]ne another, he falls to the land [of / darkness ...] until he arrives at the [... 10 ... / ...]

Ble[s]sed is whoever can believe! He [... / ...] darkness; which grows out of the [... / ... for e]ver and ever.

••• **3** •••

(23,14 – 25,6)

[15] *The Interpretation of Happiness, / Wisdom and Power; what they signify. /*

Mani contrasts true happiness, wisdom and power to their perceived meaning in the world. In a schema that will be repeated throughout the *Kephalaia,* these principles are successively identified with the various levels of divinity (here five) as it descends into time and the universe.

Thus the archetypes are the great Gods in the eternal kingdom, untouched by the conflict with darkness; reflected then in the first evoked gods who have entered into time for the purpose of redemption, and who inhabit the two ships (the sun and moon), which can be regarded as the gateways to eternity for the purified light; then the divine elements and subsidiary gods who have descended into the mixed universe; and finally the human members of the church.

[Once aga]in the enlightener speaks to his disciples, whil[e / he si]ts in the assembly of the church: [What] are these thr/[ee things] that in the world are called 'happine[ss', [20] 'wisdom]', and 'power'? People boa[s]t of th[em / ...] the happiness of the world [... / ...] in the world it has a [... / ...] of the world shall pass by. /

[People boa]st of them. They praise [... [25] ...] Now, [the] thing is revealed in a [... / ...] as I have told you. /

[I will t]each you of another happiness [... / and another wi]sdom [...] and together another power [...] / So, now, listen that I may reveal to you [30] [how] it is [with] these three: [ha/ppiness], wisdom and power. /

[The happin]ess of the glorious one is the Father, the God of / [truth, who] is established in the great land of [light]. (24) His glorious wis[d]om is his Great Spirit that [... / ...] below, which flows through all his aeons, / and t[h]ey float therein. His great power is all the / gods, the rich ones and the angels who were [5] summoned from him as they [...] t/hey that are called aeons [... / ... /

... / which is called] the sun [... [10] the ship of] living fire, [... the Third / Amba]ssador, the second greatne[ss ... The] / glorious [happiness] is the [Living] Spirit, [... / ..., the wisdom] is the Mother of Lif[e ... / ... and great power] is [all] the gods, [the [15] rich o]nes and the angels who are within the ship. /

Again, [h]appiness, wisdom and power exist in the s[hip of liv/ing waters ...] the happiness [... / ...] the Mind of the Father. / Also, wisdom [is the Vir/gi]n of [Li]ght. And the power that is [i]n the ship is [all] the go[ds], [20] the [ri]ch ones and the angels who are established i[n it].

Again, these three exist in the elements: happiness, wis/d[o]m and power. The happiness is [the Pillar of Glory], / the Perfect Man. Wisdom is the [five sons of the] / Living Spirit; and great powe[r is ... the fi][25]ve sons of the First Man [... who are encl]/osed and compounded in the totality, that [...] / while he supports the totality. /

Now, moreover, happiness, wis[dom and power ex/ist] in the holy church. Great, glorious, [happines][30]s is the Apostle of Light [who has been s]/ent from the Father. Wisdom [is the leaders / and] the teachers who travel in the [holy] church, [proclaiming] / wisdom and truth. Great [power is ... (25) ...] all [the] elect, the virgins and the c[ontinent; / together with the] catechumens who are in the [holy] church. /

[...] five happinesses, the five wisdoms, [a]nd five powers [... / ...] in the five chur[ches]. Blessed, [5] [therefore], is every one who will know them, for he may [... / ...] the kingdom forever.

••• 4 •••

(25,7 – 27,31)

/ *Concerning the Four great Days* / *th[at have] come forth from one another;* [10] *together with the Four Nights.* /

The concept of the four days and four nights is temporal in the sense that, as each unravels from the last, it represents a descent / ascent from the polarity (the Father / the land of darkness) into the human sphere, where the choice between the two is met (the true church / the sects as representations of the new and the old man).

The schematic elaboration of days and hours is somewhat artificial. Certainly, as a systematisation, it is secondary to other doctrinal taxonomies. The purpose seems to be to enable Mani to link together a number of details around the theme of 'twelve'; and thus to strengthen the coherence of the revelation as a whole.

The twelve aeons or rich gods of the land of light are met elsewhere (see PsBk2. 1.13). Also, the twelve virgins of the Ambassador are known as a variant or elaboration upon the Virgin of Light, his feminine identity. Since Jesus is really the Ambassador's doublet, and the Virgin is sophia, this explains the twelve wisdoms of the fourth day. The summons and the obedience are the vocalisation of the salvific process, the archetype of which is the rescue of the First Man by the Living Spirit. The pairing of these divinities with the respective sets of Five Sons is used variously to elaborate doctrinal details (compare 43.2 – 4).

The necessary sets of twelve hours for the nights appear mostly artificial, since Manichaean doctrine regarding the land of darkness and the worlds of flesh is dominated by pentads. Nevertheless, the link between the sects and the zodiacal signs is found elsewhere (see 48.34 – 5); and the idea that false religions are determined by the planets and the stars is a mainstay of gnostic systems and Mandaeism. The emphasis upon the First Man as a snare is a recurrent feature of Mani's knowledge, and indicates the Christological basis for this doctrinal complex.

Once again the enlightener speaks: Four great days have come / [forth from one another; they] were evoked [out] of one another! The first / [great day] is the Father, the God of truth, the fir[st ... / ... m]idst the aeons of his greatness, in his [l]iving [ki^{15}ngdom]. The twelve hours of this great day / [are the] twelve great rich Gods of great[ness. / These], who are the first evocations that he evoked (to mirror) / [h]is greatness, he spread out to the four climes, three b/y three before his face.

^{20} The second day is the Third Ambassador, the one w/ho dwells in the light ship. His twelve ho[urs] are / [the] twelv[e v]irgins that he evoked in his greatness. /

[The third day is the Pillar of Glory, the great po/rter that is greater than] all [the po]rters; the one that supports all [...], ^{25} those above and those below. Its twelve hours are / the five sons [of the F]irst Man; the five sons of the Living Sp[ir]it, / who support all the weights of the uni/[v]erse; together with the summons and the obedience, which are counted to their ten / brethren. These are the twelve light hours of the th^{30}ird da[y].

The fourth day is Jesus / the Splendour who [dwells in] his

church. His twelve / [h]ours are the twelve wisdoms, which are his / [light] h[o]u[rs].

These are the four great days that have come / [forth from one another, wh]ich were evoked out of one another. They [35] [... Blessed is] every [o]ne who will know them, and / [...] the light!

(26) [...]: For just as four day[s ex]/ist, s[o] too four nights exist. / The first nigh[t] is the land of darkness. It has t[w]e/[l]v[e] black [shadows] therein, which are its [5] dark h[o]ur[s]. The twelve shadows of the f[irst ni]/ght a[re] the five elements of the land of darkness, [which] / poured [fo]rth from its five sense organs; and [...] / which [...] in its [fi]ve elements and its five [...] / the five [sp]irits that dwell in its elements [...] [10] These a[re] the twelve shadows and spirits of the fi[rst] ni[ght]. /

The second night is Matter, the sculptress [... / ...] who has sc[ulpted ... / a]nd the entire [ru]ling-power that is in the worl[ds of darkness]. / She has fashioned it in five sense organs, five [male] [15] and five female, two per world; together with the fire and [the lu]/st [that] dwell in men and women, inflaming [them] / inward to one another. These are the twelve spirits of this [sec]/ond night. Indeed she, this Matter, the thought of death, / ga[ve] the King of the realms of Darkness and his powers strength for the w[20]ar and the fight, against the aeons of greatness. Yet, / he was caught! They laid a snare for him through the Fi[rst M]an. [He] was ta[ken] / t[o ...] through the powers [... He] was brought [u]/p from the land of death and s[et ... ab]/ove and below in the [whole] universe; in the five par[t[25]s] in the heavens above, as well as the five [parts] / in the earths below; together with the heat [and the] cold that / are the father and the mother, their fire and their l[u]st. /

This is the second night that is begotten [fr]om the first ni/ght. They laid a snare for her through the First M[a]n. She was brought u[p] [30] by the hand of the Living Spirit, and set in this composite univers[e ...] / he[r], above and below. The [upper side is the sense] / organs of males; the lower side [...] / fe[mal]es.

The thir[d night is the five] / worlds of flesh [... five (27) mal]e, and five female; that were begotten from the powers / [abo]ve.

They have fallen upon the earth, being displayed in wh/[at is d]ry and what is moist; together with the fire and the lust / [that d]we[ll] in them, which drives them inward to one another. 5 [Mat]te[r] herself, the thought of death, is the / [mother] of them all; as among them she is named 'the night'. / [The worlds] of male and female fleshes, together with the fire and the l/[ust], shall [...] twelve hours of [... / ...] night. Again, [it] too, the third night that is in 10 [the] worlds of fl[e]sh, was begotten from the sec[o]nd / [ni]ght; which the Living [Spir]it crucified in the uni/[verse ..., ab]ove and below in heaven [... /...]

The fourth night is the law of [si/n, which] is the dark spirit who speaks in the twelv[e 15 spirits], the twelve sects. They are the nakedne/[sses], the twelve zodiacal signs of Matter. They / [are] her thrones; she who is made public, as she sculpts and is dis/[p]layed in the old man. And, also, the hours of this four[t/h] night that is the old man, who reigns in the sects, are the [tw]20elve e[vi]l spirits; the [...] of the old man, which / [are ... / ... / ... / ... di]fferentiate the day and night [... 25 ... of] death. This is the fourth ni/[ght ...] that have come forth of one another. One has [... / ...] just like the days of lig[ht / ...] they manifested one another. So als[o / ...] they did arise out of one another.

30 [Bl]essed is he [who wi]ll know them, and separate them, and / [... for] ever! (28)

••• 5 •••

(28,1 - 30,11)

/ Concerning Four Hunters of / Light and Four of Darkness. /

The parallel reverse imagery evident in this kephalaion is typical of Manichaean doctrine. In this instance the powers of light and darkness are compared to hunters trawling various seas from ships and with nets. The teaching is structured in terms of the cosmic history, presupposing a prior knowledge of the entire cycle from the descent of the First Man to the ascent of the Last Statue and the everlasting death of sinners. Thus, the redeeming work of the Third Ambassador, achieved by the revelation of his image in the heavens, is prior to that of Jesus, whose net is the wisdom cast from the church.

Once again the apostle speaks to his discipl[es]: [5] There are four hunters who were sent from [the li]/ght to fulfill the will of the greatness. /

The first hunter is the First Man who was sen[t] / from the greatness. He threw himself down to the five storehouses / [of] d[ar]kn[ess, h]e caught and siezed the enmity [... [10] ...] his net also [... / ...] out over all the children of darkness [... / ...] His ship is his four sons who are swathed / over his body. The sea is the la[nd of darkness ... / ...] his net is [...] [15] and his powers.

The second [hunter is the Th]/ird Ambassador. This one, for by his [lig]ht image, / which he revealed to the depths be[low], / he hunted after the entire light that is in al[l] things; [as it is establ/i]shed in them. His net is his light image, [20] [...] the whole universe and took it prisoner, / to this likeness [... His] / ship is his light ship. [The sea] is the universe [...] / which were hunted after by his n[et ... / ... [25] ...] his [glorious] image. /

The third hunter is Je[sus the Splendour, who came from the] great/[ness], who hunts after the light and lif[e; and he ...] it / to the heights. His net is his wisdom, [the] lig[ht wisdom] / with which he hunts the souls, catching them in the n[et]. [30] His ship is his holy church [... The sea is / the] error of the universe, the law o[f sin ...] / the souls that are drowning in it [...] He catch[es] / them in his net. They are the souls [... / th]em by his light wisdom.

[The fourth] [35] hunter is the great counsel that [...] / that lives in the circuit [...] (29) entire universe in it today. Yet, at the end, in the dissoluti/[on] of the universe, this very counsel of life / [will] gather itself in and sculpt its soul in the / Last [St]atue. Its net is its Living Spirit*[10], becau[5][se] with its Spirit it can hunt after the light and the life that is in / all [t]hings; and build it upon its body. Its ship, in which it / [is est]ablished, is this light cloud whereby it itself trav/[els] in the five elements [... / the] great fire that will burn all the buildings of [... [10] ...] in its net is the light and the [life. It can] / rescue and free it from all bonds and fetters. /

---

*[10]   See 54.22

Blessed is ev[ery] o[n]e who will be perfect in his deeds, so that / at his end [he may escap]e the great fire that is prepared for the uni/verse at [the end of] its time!

[15] O[nc]e again he [s]peaks: As I have revealed to you the four / living hunters of light who belong to the greatness, / [I will] also [t]each you about four other evil hunters who ca/me from the darkness.

The first hunter is the King / of they who belong to the darkness, who hunted after the living soul with his net [20] at the beginning of the worlds. His net is his fi/re and his lust that he has put upon the living soul, / with which he has entangled it [...], through all his powers. /

[The] sec[ond] h[unter i]s the evil counsel that lives in / [...] [25] that hunts after [the] light [...] and [...] / up from [...] the earths to heaven. It binds them with / its powers, which b[ring] them to the heavenly worlds above. / [I]ts net is [...] whereby they are drawn up / [fr]om the abyss [to the heig]hts.

The third hunter [30] is lust [...] walks in every power of the flesh that wa/[lks ...] in the [...] the living souls [... / ... t]hem in its bodies, which [... / ... / ...]

The fourth [35] [hunter is the spirit] of darkness, the law of sin and (**30**) death, that rules in every sect. It hunts after the so[ul]/s of people and entangles them with this erroneo[us] teaching. / Then it drives them to eternal punishment. It[s] / net, whereby it hunts souls to death, is its [5] erroneous teaching full of guile and villainy / and wicked turns. It imprisons foolish people wi[th] / its teaching, subduing them under its net and co[mpelling them to] eternal punishment.

Blessed is e[very] one [w]/ho will recognise these evil hunters through know[ledge, and it will s][10]ave and free them from their bond and fetter [for ever] and ever!

••• **6** •••

(30,12 – 34,12)

*/ Concerning the Five Storehouses that have po[ured f]orth / from the
Land of Darkness since the [Beginning];* [15] *the Five Rulers, the Five
Spiri[ts], / the Five Bodies, the Five Tastes. /*

Elaborate and highly schematic descriptions of the kingdom of darkness,
and its powers, are a feature of Manichaean (and anti-Manichaean)
writings that must derive from canonical sources. The overall conception,
with its delight in pentads, and a certain attention to what can be termed
the psychosymbolism of evil, has a stamp that is unmistakably Mani's.
Specific features such as the 'five trees' appear in other gnostic writings, and
may serve to indicate Manichaean influence, rather than vice-versa.

Kephalaion 6 (and compare also 27) evidences some textual development;
and probably some corruption in the tradition. The redactor appears unsure
about the relationship of the supreme King of Darkness (30.33 – 33.1) to his
five warring rulers in the various sub-kingdoms; but tends toward
identifying him with the King of Smoke (33.2 – 4). He is thus to be
distinguished from the ruler or King of the sub-world of Darkness (33.33 –
34.5). Manichaean writings are also unclear about the relationship of the
supreme King to personified Matter, who here appears to be prior to him as
his fashioner (31.8 – 16). These points have been discussed by H. -Ch. Puech
(1948); who also shows that the parallel passage in the Mandaean *Right
Ginza* XII, 6 (278 – 282) is secondary to the *Kephalaia.*

O nce again the enlightener speaks to his disciples: Five
s[to]/rehouses have arisen since the beginning in the land of
darkne[ss! The] fiv[e] / elements poured out of them. Also, from
the five e[le][20]ments were fashioned the five trees! Again, from
the five tre[es] / were fashioned the five genera of creatures in
each wor/ld, male and female. And the five worlds thems[el]ves
[ha]/ve five kings therein, and five spiri[ts, five] bodies, five
[tastes]; / in each world, they n[ot] resembling [one another]!

[25] The King of the world of Smoke [...] / who came up from the
depth of [darkness; this is he who is] / the head of all wickedness,
and [all] mal[ignity]. The beginning of / the spread of the war
occured [thr]ough him; all the battl[es], / fights, quarrelling,
dan[ger]s, destructions, f[i][30]ghts, wrestling-contests! That is the
o[ne who fir]st [made] arise [dan]/ger and war, with his worl[ds
and his] powers. Af[te]/rwards, also, he waged war with the
light. H[e pitched] a battle wi[th] / the exalted kingdom.

Now, regar[ding the King] of Darkness, / there are five shapes on him! His head [is lion-faced; his] ³⁵ hands and feet are demo[n- and devil]-faced; [his] / shoulders are eagle-faced; while h[is] belly [is dragon-faced]; (31) his tail is fish-faced. These five shapes, the marks of his / [fi]v[e] worlds, exist on the King of the realms of Darkness! /

Now, [th]ere are five other properties*[11] in him. The first is his / [dark]ness. The second is his putridity. The third is ⁵ h[i]s ugliness. The fourth is his bitterness, his own soul. / The fifth is his burning, which burns like an / iron {}*[12] as if poured out from fire. /

[There are] also th[r]ee oth[ers] in him! The first, that hi[s body / is ha]rd and very tough, even as she has formed him [...] cru[10][el-hear]ted; namely Matter, who is the though[t] of death, / [the o]ne w[ho] sculpted him from the nature of the land of dark/ness. T[his] is the manner [of] the body of the ruler of Sm[oke]. He is h/[ar]der than every [ir]on, copper and steel and / [lea]d; as there is no cleaver at all, nor any iron implement, can ¹⁵ [...] him and cut him. For Matter, his fashioner, has formed him / [...] strong and hard.

The second, that he wounds / [an]d kills by the word of his magic arts. His recitation and / hearing, all his foolish instruc- tion, make magic / and invocations for him. When it pleases him, he can make an invocation ²⁰ [o]ver himself, and by his magic arts be hidden from his compan/[ions]. Again, when it [plea]ses him, he can be manifested over his powers / [and] appear to [them]; so that these enchantments nowadays, which peo/[ple] utilise (?) [...] this world, are the mysteries / [of] the King of Da[rkness]. Concerning this, I command you (pl.) ²⁵ all the [ti]me: K[ee]p away from the magic arts and enchantments / [of] darkness! For any person who will be taught them, / and who [d]oes and accompl[ishes them]; at the last, in the place wh[ere] will be bound the King / [of] the realms of Darkness with his powers, there they will bind t/[ha]t one also, [the s]oul of whoever has lived freely among them and ³⁰ [wal]ked in the

---

*[11] Read ⲥⲭⲎⲙⲁ (W.- P. Funk).
*[12] ⲡⲉⲓϣ

[magic ar]ts of error. Whether it is a man or a / [woman, this is] the sentence given, cut / [... f]rom God's judgement, that whoever will / [...] with their King.

(**32**) The third, that the King of the realms of Darkness knows the [co]/nverse and language of his five worlds. He understands / every thing he hears from their mouths, as they address one / another; each one of them in his language. [Every] design [5] they will consider against him, every snare they d/ebate with one another to bring upon him, he knows them! / He can also understand the gesturing they signal / between one another. Yet, his powers and his rulers, / who are s[ub]ject to him, can not understand his wordy converse. While all these things [10] are unveiled to him; still, their heart is not manifested to him. He k[n]/ows not their mind nor their thought; he can not ponder their / beginning and their end. Rather, he only knows and ap/prehends what is before his eyes. /

Also, another different thing is found in the King of [the] realms of Darkness! [15] For when it pleases him to move, he spreads all his limbs / out and walks. When it comes to mind, he with[draws] / his limbs and takes them in, and is rolled (?) to / his companions; and he falls to the ground like a grape and a / great iron ball! He terrifies by his cry, [20] he is frightful. He frightens his powers with his [s]ound; bec[a]/use when he speaks, being like thunder / in the clouds, he resembles the [...] of the rocks [...] / When he cries out and [...] and calls [...] / over his powers, they shall tremble and to[tter a]nd fall under f[oot]; [25] even as some birds would be [...] the bird [... / ...] and they fall down to the earth. Still, [thi]s thing only: / he knows not what is far from him, he sees not w[ho is at] / a distance, nor does he hear him. Rat[her], whoever is befo[re] / his face he sees, hea[ri]ng him and [30] knowing him.

These sign[s a]nd these evil mar/ks are found in the chief of the d[e]mons and / fiends, the King of all the mountains of Darkne[ss ... the one] to [whom] / the land of darkness has given birth, be[gotten in its cru]/elty, in its wickedness and its wrath [...] (**33**) more than all his fellow rulers, who are in all his worlds. /

Gold is the body of the King of the realms of Darkness. / The

body of all the powers who belong to the world of Sm/oke is gold.
And also, the taste of its fruits is s⁵alty. The spirit of the King, of
the realms of Darkness, is this one who reigns / today in the
principalities and authorities of the earth and the entire un/iverse.
I mean these who reign over the entire creation, / humiliating
mankind with tyranny, according to their heart's desire. /

In contrast, the King of the worlds of Fire is lion-faced, the
fore¹⁰most of all the beasts. Copper is his bo[dy]. Again, [the
bo]/dy of all the rulers who belong to Fire is copper. / Their taste
is the sour taste that is in every form. / Also, the spirit of the King,
of they that belong to the world of Fire, is this one / who reigns
i[n the] greater ones and the leaders; who are under ¹⁵ the
command of the principalities and authorities and the kings of
the wo/rld. Also a spirit of his is found in these sects / that
worship [fi]re, as their sacrifices are offered to fire. /

Again, the King of the wor[l]d[s] of Wind is eagle-face. His /
body is iron. Also, the body of all they who belong to ²⁰ the Wind
is iron. Their taste is the sharp taste th/at is in every form. His
spirit is the one of idolat/ry to the spirits of error who are in every
temple, the sit[es] of ido/[l]s, the sites of statue- and image-
worship, the shrines o/[f the] error of the world.

²⁵ For his part, [the K]ing of the w[o]rld of Water is fish-face. His
/ body is silv[er]. All the other rulers who belong to Water, /
silver is their body. Also, the taste of their fruit is / [the] sweetness
of water, the sweet taste that is in every (form). / Again, the spirit
of the King, of the rulers of Water, is this one who r³⁰eigns today
in the sects of error; these that / [d]ip the baptism of the waters,
(setting) their hope / [and] their tru[st] in the baptism of the
waters. /

Again, [the Kin]g of the [wor]ld of Darkness is a dragon. His /
[body is lead] and tin. All the other rulers ³⁵ [who belong to the
world of] Darkness, their body is lead and (34) tin. And also, the
taste of their fruits is bitt/erness. Again, the spirit who reigns in
them is the spirit / who speaks till today in the soothsayers,
giving oracl[es]; / in the givers of portents, every typ[e]; in they
who are poss⁵essed; and the other spirits that give oracles, every
type. /

Concerning this I tell you, my [bret]hren and my li/mbs, the perfect faithful, the holy elect: / Hold your heart close to you, and you stay away from the / five enslavements of the five dark spirits. Put [10] behind you the service of their five bodies. Li/ve not in them, that you may break loose their chain / and their chastening for ever!

••• 7 •••

(34,13 – 36,26)

/ The Seventh, concerning [15] the Five Fathers. /

This is one of the best known of the kephalaia, due to its full and ordered account of the evocation of various Manichaean divinities. However, it is important to note that the schema of the 'five fathers' is not an archetypal classification prior to all the other theological taxonomies evident through-out the texts; but, rather, only a partial and conditioned representation of the overall system. Thus, temporally, the Third Ambassador is the principal divinity of the third evocation (redemption). In the first evocation (descent) the Father summons the Mother of Life, who then calls forth the First Man and his five sons. In the second (creation) it is the Beloved of the Lights, and then the Living Spirit and his five sons. Kephalaion 7 is concerned with the sequence from the Father through the Ambassador; and its purpose is, therefore, the emanation of the divinities from the aspect of redemption.

Once again the enlightener, our father [the] apostle of / truth, is sitting in the midst of his disciples and pr/eaching to them of the greatnesses of God. Again, he speaks t/o them like this, in his revelation: Five fathers [20] exist, they were summoned forth one of one. [Also], one did come / out of another!

The first Father is the Father of Grea/tness, the blessed one of glory, the [on]e who has no measure to his gr[ea]/tness; who also is the first o[n]ly begotten, the f[i]/rst eternal; who exists with fiv[e fa]thers for ever; [25] the one who exists before every thing that has existed, and th/at will exist.

Now he, the glorious Father, summon[ed] from him / three emanations. The [fi]rst is the Gre[at] / Spirit, the first Mother, who came out of the Father. She app/eared first.

The seco[nd i]s the Belo[ved of] [30] the Lights, the great glori[ous] Beloved, [the one w]ho is honour[ed; w]/ho came out of the Father. [He ma]nifested ou[t of h]im. /

The third father*[13] is the Thir[d Ambassador], / the eldest of [al]l the counsell[ors; who came out of] (35) the first Father. He appeared.

This is the first Father, / the first power, the one from whom the three great powers came out, / This is the first Father, the first eternal, the root / of all the lights; from whom the three emanations came out. [5] They have humiliated the darkness. They have brought its heart's desire to naught. They have / given themselves the victory. They have also given the victory to their aeons. /

The second father, who came out of the first Father, is the Th/ird Ambassador, the model of the King of lights. / And again, he too summoned and sent out of him thr[10]ee powers.

One is the Pillar of Glory, the Perfect Man; / the one who bears up under all things; the great Pillar / of blessing; the great porter, who is greater than all the po/rters.

The second is glorious Jesus the Splendour; / [the] one through whom shall be given life eternal.

The th[15]ird is the Virgin of Light, the glorious wisd[o]m; the on/e who takes away the heart of the [rul]ers and the powers by her image, as she fulfi/lls the pleas[u]re of the greatness. /

The third father, who came out of the second father; h/e is glorious Jesus the Splendour. And, again, he too summoned [20] three evocations after the pattern of the second father. /

The first power whom he summoned is the Light Min[d], / the father of all the apostles, the eldest of [a]ll the [ch]urches; / the one whom Jesus has appointed corresponding to our pattern in the holy chur/ch.

The second power whom Jesus summo[25][n]ed is the gre[at

---

*[13] Textual error: the Ambassador is the second father, but the third emanation of the first Father.

Jud]ge, who gives judgement on all the souls / [of] mankind, [his] dwelling being established in the atmosphere under [... / ...] wheel [...] stars.

The third power is / [the Y]outh, the gre[at ...] light in his two pers/ons, in [...], I am speaking about that which has been established [30] [i]n the summons [and] the obedience. [He] too [stood] with his fa[ther / the] king [...] the savio[ur ...] seen, as he tells / [...] I, what I have seen with my Father, / [I tell to] you. For yourselves, what you have seen / [with your fath]er, do that*14.

(**36**) The fourth father is the Light Mind, the one who chooses all the / churches. And, again, he too summoned three / powers after the pattern of Jesus.

The first power is the Apostle / of Light; the one who shall on occasion come and assume the chur[5]ch of the flesh, of humanity; and he becomes inner leader of ri/ghteousness.

The second is the counterpart, who shall come to the apo/stle and appear to him, becoming companion to him, / sticking close to him everywhere; and providing help to him all the time, from / all afflictions and dangers.

The third [10] is the Light Form; the one whom the elect and the ca/techumens shall receive, should they renounce the world. /

And also the fifth father is this Light Form; the one who / shall appear to everyone who will g[o] out from his bo/dy, corresponding to the pattern of the image to the apostle; and the thr[ee] [15] great glorious angels who are come with her.

One (angel) ho[ld]/s the prize in his hand. The second bears the light garment. / The third is the one who possesses the diadem / and the wreath and the crown of light. These are the thr/ee angels of light, the ones who shall come with this Light Form; [20] and they appear with her to the elect and the / catechumens.

These are the five fathers who have come out / of one another. They have appeared and man[ifes]ted through one ano/ther!

----

*14 Jn. 8:38

Blessed is he who will know and understand th[em]! / For he may find life eternal; and receive these light garments [25] that shall be given to the righteous, [the faithful], the givers of peace, / and the doers of good things.

••• 8 •••

(36,27 – 37,27)

/ Concerning the Fourteen Vehicles / that Jesus has boarded. /

The fourteen vehicles correspond to the stations through which Jesus passes as he descends deeper into matter for the purpose of salvation; and to the divine elements that he assumes and thus sanctifies in this descent. The listing of the ten 'carriages in the zone' reverses an order most familiar in accounts of the ascent of the light elements, the qualities of the living soul, as they pass through the redemptive process of summons and obedience, and finally ascend perfected from the Pillar to the moon and thence to the sun (see 71).

[30] Once again, the light-man speaks to the congregati[on that] is sitting in front of / him: When Jesus the son of greatness [came] to these world[s], / at the time that he unveiled the greatness, [he boarded ten] / vehicles! He journeyed in the universe [by them]. /

The first vehicle is the ligh[t] ship, [since] [35] he received instructions from the Ambassador [there].

(**37**) The second carriage is the ship of the First Man, sin/ce his dwelling is established there. /

The third is the Pillar of Glory, the Perfect Man, sin/ce he shone forth there. He came below, he appeared in the wo[5]rld.

The fourth is the summons that he clothed / upon his body. The fifth is the obedience that he swathed / upon the summons.

The sixth is the living air, and since / he assumed it too, he received anointment there. / The seventh is the living wind that blows. The eighth [10] is the light that illuminates. The ninth is the living w/ater. The tenth is the living fire that is above them all. /

He was journeying in these ten carriages among all the orders and / all the [...], those above and those below. /

After he had assumed these ten, he came and manifested in the [15] flesh. He chose the holy church in four vehic/les. One is all the holy brothers. The second is the / pure sisters. The third is all the catechumens, / the sons of the faith. The fourth is the catechu/- mens, the daughters of the light and truth.

These ten carria[20]ges that he boarded in the zone, and the other four that are in the flesh, / they complete and make fourteen carriages! He has done in them / the pleasure of his Father. He has made alive, has redeemed, and given the victory to / [th]ese who are his. Conversely, [h]e has killed, bound, and destroyed / they who are strangers to him. He has given glory to the Father who sent him, [25] and the entire kingdom of life. Blessed is he who will k/now these mysteries; for he will count to the portion of Jesus, / the son of greatness.

••• 9 •••

(37,28 – 42,23)

/ The Explanation of the Peace, what it is; [30] the Ri[gh]t Hand; the Kiss; the Salutation. /

The ritual actions that occur in human society, and which Mani has instituted in his church, are presented as reenactments of divine archetypes. Mani's lesson is carefully structured, and provides many important details and insights into Manichaean doctrine and church practice.

38.13 – 39.9 The descent of the First Man from the land of light was a favourite theme. Full of the pathos of loss and estrangement, it is in a very real sense the story of each soul. Thus, this text makes much of the familial love and care within the divine household.

39.10 – 40.19 Once the sacrifice of the First Man has been achieved, he is saved by the Living Spirit and returns to the kingdom. This establishes and sanctifies the process of redemption; and, while it occurs at the beginning of the history, it also anticipates the triumphant return at the end of time of the collectivity of the divine, with the First Man at their head, to enter the new aeon.

40.24 – 41.10 Now that the primordial archetypes have been established, Mani immediately relates them to the individual's experience and the practice of the church.

41.11 – 25 Mani then utilises the symbols to focus on the glorious hope offered to the victorious soul, when it meets the Light Form and receives its prizes.

41.26 – 42.23 The lesson ends with the injunction to its hearers to honour and practice this divine teaching.

[O]nce again the disciples questioned the apostle, saying / [to him]: This peace and this greeting that occur in the world, / [from w]hom [did they come fo]rth? Or likewise, the right hand that occurs in / [the world, it being h]onoured by mankind, of whom is it? Or the my³⁵[stery of the ki]ss that they embrace one another with, / [...]? Or who is the one that reveals this (38) salutation with which they make obeisance to one another? Or this laying on of h/ands, which an immensely great one bequeaths upon his inferior, / giving him an honour and making him great; of / whom is this laying on of hands?

Then he says to his disciples: ⁵ You have questioned me about these five lessons. Now, they are display/ed in the world as miniatures, being made little; / and yet indeed they are great and honoured. I am the one who can reveal to y/ou their mystery! So, these five signs / are the mystery of the First Man. He came forth wit¹⁰h them from the aeon of light. Also, when he finished / his contest, he went up with these good signs. / They received him into the aeons of light. /

The first peace is the one that the gods and the [an]gels in the land / of light gave to the First Man; when he comes ¹⁵ out against the enemy. The gods and the angels / were walking with him; escorting him, giving to him their peace and / power, and their blessing and fortification. This is the first / peace that the gods and the angels gave to the First / Man; as he comes forth from the aeon of light.

²⁰ The first right hand is the one that the Mother of Life gave to the First Ma/n; when he comes out to the contest. /

The first kiss is this one with which the Moth[er] of Life embrac/ed the First Man; as he separates from her, coming / down to the contest. Even all the gods and the [an]²⁵gels who are in the aeons of light were making to em[br]ace him! [...] / all of them also, and the church tutelaries (?), and the kinsf[olk w]/ho

belong to the household of his people. They were making to
embrace him as [he] / separates from them, accompanying him
out, em[bracing] / him with the kiss of affection and love.

30 The first salutation is the salutation with which the F[ir]st
Ma[n] / made obeisance; when he comes ou[t to the depths] /
below. He was bending his kn[ees, making obeisance] / to the
God of truth, and all the aeons [of light] (39) who belong to the
household of his people; entreating them for a power to / escort
him*15, as he comes forth. /

The first laying on of hands is the one that the Mother of Life
bequeathed upon / the head of the First Man. She armed him and
made him 5 mighty. She laid hands on him, and sent him to the
battle. He des/cended. He completed his struggle with the great
powers and the en/mity.

By the[se] five signs and these five myst[e]ri/es the First Man
came forth from the aeons of light / against the enemy. He
humbled him. He was victorious against him by [th]em.

10 Also, when he ascended from the w[a]r, he came i[n] / to the
kingdom of the household of his people by these five mysteri/es!

The peace with which h[e ascen]ded is the peace that the /
summons gave to him, [w]hen it was sent forth from the [Fa]ther
of L/ife. It gave him the peace in the world of darkness. 15 Also,
that peace with which he descended is th/[e sam]e as the one
with which he ascended from the struggle! Therefore, appropriate
to the my/[s]tery of that peace, which the summons gave / the
First Man, did this peace here and now come about. / It was
named and heard among the powers of the Father.

Again, this 20 second right hand is the one that the Living Spirit
gave the First / Man, when he [brou]ght him upward out from
the struggle. Appropriate to / [the] mystery [of t]hat right hand
this right hand has come about; / the one that occurs in the [midst
of] mankind, as they give it to their companions, / [it b]eing
honoured and [...]

---

*15 Perhaps the angel Nahashbat referred to in the account of Theodore
bar Konai *Lib Schol.* XI.

Also, this second ki[25][s]s is the one with which the [Father o]f Life and the Mother of the living / embraced the F[irst] Man, when he ascended / from the struggle. Again, this kiss occurs among / mankind, as they make to embrace their companions with it; whether then [they] / go away from home and be far from their friends, or else [30] [if] they approach one another, according to the mystery of (the First Man). /

[The] second [s]alutation with which the First Man made obeisance / [... this] time to the God of truth and / [...] the blessed aeons and al[l] the aeons / [... the] whole [land] of light, whe[n] (40) the Father of Life and the Mother of the living brought / the Man upward from the abyss of the struggle. Appropriate to the myste/ry of the second salutation this salutation has come about; this one / that occurs today in the midst of mankind, as they make obeisance to one [5] another, doing an honour to their companions.

The second / laying on of hands is this: When the Living Spirit brought the First / Man upward from the war, he saved him from / all the surging waves. He brought him upward, he gave him ease in the great / aeons of light, which belong to the household of his people. [10] He set [him] firmly before the Father, the Lord of the totality. / Now, when he went up before the great Father of the / lights, a voice came forth to him from the heights, saying: / Make my son, my first-born, to sit at my right hand side, until I / set all his enemies for a footstool under his feet.*[16] [15] He received this great laying on of hands that he may become leader / of his brethren in the new aeon. Again, appropriate to the myster/y of the second laying on of hands, this laying on of hands has come / about; the one that occurs in the midst of mankind as they lay hands on one / another, the great giving authority to the lesser.

These five myste[20]ries and these five signs came about first in the divi/ne. They were proclaimed in this world by an [a]postle. Ma[nk]/ind has been taught them; and they have instituted them in their mids[t ... but] these myster[ies] wer[e] / not at the beginning amongst the / powers of darkness.

The Light Mind al[so], who co[mes] [25] to the world, shall come

---

*[16]   Mk. 12:36

with these several mark[s]. With these five / lessons he shall choose his church.

First, before / everything else, he chooses his church with peace. / And he gives the peace first to mankind; so that the person receives / the peace, and becomes a child of peace. Afterwards he is elected [30] to the faith. Now, when he may receive the peace, he shall receive [the rig]/ht hand and count to the right hand. Then, whe[n he receives] the right hand, / the Light Mind s[h]all draw him to him, and cause [him] to app[roach the ch]/urch.

With the right hand he receives the k[iss of lo]/ve and becomes a child of the c[hurch ...] (41) With the kiss he shall receive salutation, and make obeisance to the God / of truth. Also, he makes obeisance to the holy church [...] / the hope of the faith, good works.

When they / will receive the peace and the right hand, the kiss and the salutation, [5] the last of these things shall be bequeathed upon them from the right hand of charity. They / too [receive] the laying on of hands, which will be bequeathed upon them. A/nd they are conformed and built up in the truth, and made strong in it for eve/r. They shall come in to the Light Mind with these good signs; / and become fulfilled people. They make obeisance and [10] [give] glory to the God of truth. /

[On]ce again: At the time of their coming forth, the Light Form / shall come forth before them; and she redeems them from the darkness to the li/ght [...] This Light Form calms the per/son, with the kiss and her quiet, from fear of the [15] demons w[ho de]-stroy his body. By her asp[ec]t and her im/age [the] heart of the elect one, who is come forth from his bo/[d]y, shal[l] be calm for [him]. Afterwards, the angel who h[o]lds the victo/ry prize ex-tends to him the right hand. And it draws him out of / the abyss of his body, and accepts him in with the [k]iss [20] and love. That soul shall make obeisan[ce] to its red/eemer, who is this Light Form. And also, at the inst[ant / when ...] he shall be perfected and increased according to [... / ...] in the household of the living ones, with the go/[ds] and the angel[s] and all the apostles and the chosen. [25] [An]d he receives the crown [...] glory in the life for ever. /

[Concern]ing this I tell you, my brethren and my limbs: / [L]et you (sg.) find these fi[ve signs] in your hands, honoured before / [ea]ch one of [yo]u. They are: the peace; the right hand; the k/[i]ss; the sa[luta]tion; and the laying on of hands. I have brought this [30] [to] you from the household of the living, out from the Father who / [se]nt me.

[Hap]pen you know, that a great myster/[y ...] him, by these five signs that I have brought / [...] you may part from the world, beca/[use ...] you have understóod about the first (42) peace and the first right hand and the first kiss / [and] the first salutation and the first laying on of hands.

Therefore, le/t them find this laying on of hands being esteemed in your presence; as you give / honour, and make obeisance to the teachers and the deacons and the presby[5]ters, they whom I have laid hands on. I have bequeathed upon them the great / laying on of hands; because they are set in a great myste/[r]y, the laying on of hands of the divine, which is bequeathed upon the h/ead of the teacher. Now, whoever will reject and dis[da]in i/t, and it is made nothing by him: he commits sin subject to God, with gre[at] [10] sin; and also against me too. /

Still, you, my beloved ones, hasten in to these five / [...] you, and you [... / ...] fulfill at these occasions [... / ...] wishes he may answer you [... [15] ...] as he told y[ou ... / ... / ...] that are in the storehouses of [... / ...] your (pl.) heart [...] them, for he [... / ...] which is set right by you [...] each [one [20] ...] listen to him. He knows [ev]ery deed that you d/o, all of them, [...] with your companions [... / ...] this [... / ...] he turns to you [...] and he [...] / from you the afflictions of [...]

••• 10 •••

(42,24 – 43,21)

[25] *Concerning the Interpretation of the Fourteen [great A]eons, / about which Sethel has spoken in [his P]rayer. /*

Mani regarded Seth as the first in the line of true apostles (12.9 – 11); and the various references to him in Manichaean texts show some dependence

upon prior gnostic traditions. The *Cologne Mani-Codex* quotes from an unknown apocalypse of Seth (pp. 50 – 52). The question about the prayer of Seth
in this kephalaion may well indicate such a tradition.

However, Mani provides his own interpretation consistent with his
revealed teaching. The fourteen great aeons of light are: the five elements
or sons of the First Man; the call and the hearing; the five sons of the
Living Spirit; the two respective fathers. The fragmentary final section (43.10
– 21) seems to indicate that these fourteen underpin the visible universe; and
that the Ambassador, as the principal god of redemption, has become their
leader and king after the image of the first eternal Father.

Once again the disciples question the apostle. They sa[y] to him:
We be[seech] / you, our master, that you may enlighten us
a[bou]t this lesson that is wr[itten / in] the prayer of Sethel, the
first-born son of [Ad]am. As he says: [30] 'You are glorious, you
fourteen great [ae]ons of [lig]/ht'. Tell us, our master, what are
the [f]ourteen grea[t / a]eons of light?

Then the enlighte[ner speaks / to the]m: I am the one who will
interpret for you [the fourteen] / great aeons of light abou[t]
which he has spoken!

[35] Happen you know this, that the [... (43) ...] below abide in
fourteen [great aeons /...] the five elements, the sons of the First /
Man, together with the call and the hearing. They anoint them, /
living in them. These shall make seven, five plus two. [5] [... the]
f[ive s]ons of the Living Spirit who / [support] all [the wei]ght of
the universe; together with the [Li]vi[ng] Spirit / [and the Fir]st
Man, their fathers. These are the fourt/een p[raises that he has]
proclaimed, the praise that is made of fourteen / pra[yers], by
which the universe is established.

[10] [There are fourt]een aeons of light [...] / of Seth[el ...] about
them in his prayer, for they are expl[ai]ned / [... the la]nd that is
not revealed. This land [... /... is estab]lished. They bore up under
the enemy [... / ... equa]ls them. The hidden plenitude that [... [15]
...] the Ambassador who came from the Father, the [... / ...] He
came and stood firm in the midst of these [...] / he is called the
good father of [all] the ae[ons and gods] / who are holy and
conjoined. He has become leader and a / great king after the
likeness of the first Father, the lord of all these cou[nse[20]ls]. This
universe is held together by their will / [...] to the end of all
things. /

••• 11 •••

(43,22 – 44,18)

/ [Concerning the Interpretation of] all [the] Fathers of / [Light], who are distinguished from one another.

Summary of the characteristics of principal divinities; perhaps for catechetical instruction.

25 [Onc]e again [the enlig]htener speaks: Happen you know, / [m]y beloved ones, that [the beginn]ing of every good grace is the / [gr]eat Father of the [ligh]ts; since [a]ll [graces] are given by his hand. /

The beginning of each blessing and every prayer / is the Mother of [L]ife, the first Holy Spirit.

30 Also, [the] beginning [of] every good [co]unsel is the T[h/i]rd Am[bassad]or, the king of the glorious realm that lies in this / [wo]rld, [...] of the King of the lights.

The beginning of / [... and] each [hono]ur (?) is the Beloved of the Lights, who is honour/[ed.

The beginning of a]ll [the trappers] and hunters is the First 35 [Man.

... of] all fighters is (44) [the] Living [Spirit], the Father of Life, who has distribu[ted about] / his five sons from place to place.

The beginning of all the archit[e]/cts and builders is the Great Builder, who is glo/rious.

Also, the first of all the porters of the gr[e]5a[tness is the Pillar of Glory ... / ...]

The beginning of [all] the deliverers [is Jesus the Splendour]; / or the one who delivers, as he frees whoever belongs [...] / from his words.

The beginning of every wisdom of / truth is the Virgin of Light, [...]

[10] [The beginning of] all [the great]est honoured ones [...] / is the Light Mind; who is the awakene[r of they] / who sleep, the gatherer in of the ones who are sc[att]ered. /

Blessed is he who shall lodge this treasure within hi[m, and] fasten [the knowledge] / of these fathers in his heart! For they a[re] the [root (?) of] [15] all the lights, and such as belong to all life; as [...] / of all souls beside them.

Blessed is he who wi[ll kn]/ow them, and continue in their belief, that he may inh/erit with them eternal life for ever.

••• **12** •••

(44,19 – 45,15)

[20] *Concerning the Interpretation of the Five Words that are / proclaimed {} *17 / in the Univer[se]. /*

These five words appear to be the divine names used by other sects. Mani explains their significance by equating them with the appropriate Manichaean divinities. Mani was himself brought up in an Elchasaite community; and the *Kephalaia* makes a number of references to contemporary groups such as Baptists, Nazoreans, and Purified Ones (Catharioi). However, the exact identity of and relationship between these diverse Jewish-Christian sects remains unclear. The First and the Second Life are characteristic Mandaean terms.

Once again the disciples [questioned the apostle. They say to] / him: Recount to us, our master, of these five words that are procl[aim][25]ed in the sect of the Baptis[ts ... they] / occur in other sects. [Also, thei]r name is proclaimed by they [w]/ho are called 'Purified Ones', as they say this '[First] / Life' and the 'Second Life' [... / ...] make a heart together with the mind [...] and the l[aw [30] ... /

... / ...] / call it by this name is the Father, the l[ife ...] / this unnameable, whom no one [... [35] ...] his name.

The second [word is the Thi(45)r]d Ambassador [...] / of life, whom they also call the father of [... / ... / ...] [5] the first Father.

---

*17   ⲙ̅ⲛ̅ⲧⲡⲁⲣⲁⲛⲉϩⲟⲩⲧ

The law [...] / living [...] law of the good and the evil ones. / For it, it was given victory by the aeons of lig[ht against the en]/mity. It humbled the rebels [... / ... their] 10 essence and their universe. It overcame*18 th[em ... t]/hem in th[is b]order until the end time.

[... / ...] the powers [...] the universe is established [... / ... al]l of them are a single living body / [... 15 ...] against one another.

••• 13 •••

(45,16 – 46,12)

/ Concer[ning] the Five Saviours, the Resurrectors / of they who are Dead; together with the Five Resurrections. /

Chapter 12 has begun a series of kephalaia connected only by their pentadic structure.

[O]nce again [the] enlightener speaks: [...

24 ... i]25t therein [...] /

[The] sec[ond resurrector is ... / ...] /

And [the] third resurrector is the father, the first [... / ... b]ecause by his word shall a[ll] lives 30 [...] gather in and go to him, and they receive / [...] and re[s]t. /

[The fourth res]urrector is the Light Mind, becau/[se ... (46) ... / ...]

The fifth resurrector to the good [... / ...] is the Father, the first [es]tablis[he]d on[e / ...] all the powers, and [he] stands fir[m 5 ...] he shall unveil the [...] over them / [...] and he draws them to him [... / ...] his will [...] and he / [...] them, and he stands them u/[p ...] there, and they remain until 10 [...]

Bl[es]sed is every one who / [...] day of / [...] complete [...] for ever. /

---

*18 Reading ⲥⲱⲧ‹ⲡ›

••• **14** •••

(46,13 – 47,21)

/ The Interpretation [of] the S[i]lence, the Fast, [the Peace], 15 the Day,
[and] the Rest; [what] they are. /

Mani provides cosmological archetypes for the ritual practices of the church.

[Onc]e again the discipl[es] questioned the enli[gh]tener. They
say to h[im: Re/coun]t to us of the five [le]sso[ns] that [a]re
proclaimed in the [wo/r]ld, [one] being cal[le]d [...] 'the peace',
another called '[the] / silence', [...] another 'the day', ano[ther 20
... We implore you, our] father, that you may p[/roclaim ...

28 ...] the gatherer in [... / ...] then he shall cau[se] the body [...] 30
all the lusts of the world [... / ...] of the body in righteousness [... /
...] is the Pill[a]r of Gl[or]y [... / ...] because [... (47) ... / ...] up to
the [... / ...]

The one they call [...] it is the / [Fi]rst [M]an who dwel[ls i]n the
ship of living waters 5 [... li]ght [...] he is c[alled / ... / ... / ...] that
they have [... / ...] glorious [...

10 ...] the enlighten[er ... / ... cal]l it 'day' [... / ... uni]verse as they
shall [... / ... / ...] in the great aeon [... 15 ...] are spread in the
universe, it is [... / ...] established in the [... / ...] and the so[uls ... /
...] /

Blessed is he [who ...] gives joy by [...] for ever. 20 The great [...]
remains for ever and e[ver] / and ever.

••• **15** •••

(47,22 – 49,9)

/ [Concerning the ... / ...] Five [Parts ...] 25 Worlds of [...] /

The disciples ask Mani why the realm of darkness became active and death
streamed forth against the light. Mani explains that the driving force is
fire and lust, charged by the doubling of the evil pentad (five elements,

worlds, categories of creation or flesh) into male and female. Thus there are twelve parts (5 x 2 + fire and lust) ; corresponding to the zodiacal signs and the spirits of the evil sects.

[Once again, the enlighten]er is sitting in the midst of his discipl[es, / explaining to them about] the great and secret matters of Go[d / ... the] two ess[e]nces. His disciples say / [to him ...]: Did death ari[se] and stand firm [30] [...] up? Or else did it turn itself from [... / ...] its armo[ur ...] in its [... / ...] but it finished [...] the tw[o / ... /

... [35] ... (48) ...] it moved it and [... / ...] they that are in the [... of] the earth of dark[ness /...] first part. /

Yet, after a long time, as there was not [... [5] ...] / it gushed and streamed u[p ... the five eleme]/nts of death that gushed [... / ...] which are [smoke, fire, / wind, wa]ter and dar[kness ... [10] ...] the second time [... / ... / ...] they were sculpted [...] / those in which death was established [... /

The] fourth part is the ev[il] fruits [... [15] ...] in the five trees that are in the five [worlds of] / the land of darkness. /

The fifth time it spread itself out to its creatures that exist [in the five] / worlds; the ones that were formed and generated from the fi[ve] / fruits of death. They are the five worlds of fl[20]esh, the five creations of darkness in which death has been established. It / spread itself out to ten parts, five male parts and five fem/[ale ... / ...] /

Now, like the land of darkness, in that its spirit and i[ts ...] [25] they nourished the five elements [...]; / this is also [how] the ten parts that are in [male and / fe]male, the fire and lust of the flesh[es ...] / them, as they yoke them with one another [... they were est]/ab[li]shed against the First Man. This is [... [30] ...] of the darkness, / it was condemned for ever.

Alongside the mystery of these twe/lve parts that came about in the darkness [...] / against the First Man. The twel[ve ...] / the twelve spirits of error that [came] [35] about from the twelve signs of the zodiac [... (49) ...] They are estab[lished agai]nst the second living man, w/ho dwells in the [h]oly chur[ch]. They pursue him the way t/hat they pursued [... at] the beginning of the First Man in the land / of darkness.

As the First Man humiliated the darkness [5] [... / ... the li]ght th[at] dwells in the church / [...] the twelve sects. /

[...] his holy father for ever and / [ever].

••• 16 •••

(49,10 – 55,15)

/ *[Concerning the Five] Greatnesses who / [went forth] against the Darkness. /*

49.15 – 31 Four of the 'greatnesses' are the Father himself and the standard three series of emanations (corresponding to descent, creation, and ascent). Interestingly, Jesus the Splendour (and his powers) is given a separate place as the fifth greatness, which may be a later development of Manichaean doctrine that attempts to regulate the increasingly dominant role of this god.

49.31 – 50.6 The text remarks on the characteristic pentads of the doctrine; and then notes, in an undoubtedly forced calculation, that together with the summons and the obedience twelve major gods (not counting the series of five sons) can be counted.

50.7 – 55.15 The major part of the chapter is in effect a separate and unrelated kephalaion concerned with the advent of five divinities. The role of each is given a useful summary, and Mani develops similes to aid his hearers' understanding.

[Once again the enlightene]r [speaks] to his disciples: / [... the] darkness, it was defeated by five greatnesses.

[15] [The first gre]atness is the Father of Greatness who [exi/sts] in c]alm and hiddeness; as he is established in his [light] / earth, in his own essence.

Four greatnesses were mani/[feste]d and came forth of him. They were appointed to ten parts, and estab/lished in total twelve.

The second gr[20]eatness poured out and was manifested. It was revealed from the first / greatness. It is the Mother of Life, the Great Spirit. Together with / the First Man [and his] five sons; [these are the second / great]ness.

The third [greatness is the Bel/oved of the L]ights, the Great Builder, the Living Spirit, and the five [s]o^{25}[ns] of the Living Spirit. These are the third greatness. /

[The fou]rth greatness is the Third Ambassador, and / [the P]illar of Glory, and all the light powers who were revealed / [from him. These are the] fourth greatness. /

[The fi]fth greatne[ss] who came from the Father is Jesus the Splendour, and ^{30} all [h]is powers whom he summoned, his emanations who were [... / They] poured out and were manifested from him.

This is, so that they were [spre]ad out and / [...] five[s]: these five sons of the First Ma/[n ...] the entire building; another five are the five / [sons of the Living Spirit] who are spread out to five places, supporting ^{35} [...]

[...] total in tw(50)elve parts that [... There are] another two [ad]/ded to them who are the summons and [the obedien]ce. They are the father and the mother whom Jesus the Sp[lendour] by his advent has [appointed] / as successors to his place [...] the great earth ^{5} and the [... / ...] in them. /

[The advent ...] / of the First Man who came [... / ... ^{10} ...] belonging to [...] / ex[isting i]n a kingdom [...] / esteem [befo]re they who belong to his [household ... / ... / ...] his enemies [...] ^{15} and suffering by their wickedness; and they take from him [...] / and a richness; and they imprison [him in] / captivity and take from him their companies (?). Yet, h[e ...] / by his humility; and he takes heart and restrains his en[emy / ...] in silence.

Just as with this man, this noble ^{20} son whose enemies surround him; this also / is how the advent of the First Man happened, / [... rul]ers, the enemies of [the l]ight. /

In contrast, the advent of the Living Spirit and the [comman]dment that he received, / whereby [he] came upon all the rulers; it differs from that of the ^{25} First Man. His adv[ent ...] the advent of the F[irst] / M[an].

The advent of the Living Spirit is lik[e] / this, when he was sent from the greatness that he might br[ing] / up the First Man. He resembles a [ju]/dge the king would send to overturn the violence to [30] that man, the noble son against whom his enem[ies] / sinned. And he, this [judge, ...] / hard and cruel [... / ...] and he gives the means [... by his right] (51)eousness and his st[rengt]h; and he also judges all who / are condemned according to their rebellious heart, and re/pays each according to his deserts. They who are worthy of / blows he strikes with hard leather whips. Again, these [5] who are worthy of cutting off their limbs, or indeed their / [...] and he repays them accordingly. / [...] and he binds and fetters them, and hangs by / [...] and thus he does to them with a / [righteous] judgement. And he kills them to flay their skin [10] [...] so that they will be killed by a death / [...] until they die. Again, [they for] whom it is fitting / [...] to banish from their dwellings he may / [remove according to] a righteous judgement; just as they had faulted / [and sinned against] the noble son. Also, the associates in the mystery [15] [and the assis]tants of this judge, these who belong to / [him in] great strength; in an instant and / [h]aste they shall do the will of their master. /

Now, just as this genuine judge, who was sent f/rom the king to overturn the violence to this man, the [20] noble s[o]n; this is also the case with the Living Spirit. / He also was sent from the King of the lights / [to] over[turn] the vengeance [a]nd violence to the First Man, / against whom the King of the realms of Darkness had sinned. He faulted / [and] sinned against him, and also his rebellious powers. [Therefo]re, when (the Living Spirit) came, [25] he bore up the First Man.

Also, a[l]l the rulers, / the powers of sin who had faulted and sinned against the sons / [of] the First Man, he has judged them according to a right[e]ous judgement. / He has bound them in heaven and earth. He put each one / to the place fitting for him, he weighed each of them [30] [acco]rding to his c[ru]elty and oppression. [While] some [of] the[m] he enclosed in / [the prison, ot]hers he hung head down. Som/[e ...] are crucified, others are (52) sat down all the time. Some among them are fixed be/neath their associates, restricted by a strong chain; / others he made the holders of authority over their companions / beneath, so that they may do their pleas[5]ure amongst these below them. /

Happen you know this [...] that w[h]e[n] / the Father of Life established the judgements [...] / He was revealed to all the powers o[f darkness. He] / judged them as a [true] giver of judgement [... 10 ... / This] is the first judgement that the [Living] Spirit [gave] / the rulers [in respect of the] First Man. [Indeed, he] gave victory to the [First Man] / corresponding to his victory; [but] he condemned the [King of the realms of Darkness] / corresponding to that [by] which he had erred.

[... 15 ...] this chain, of this sort, became [...] / the earth till the en[d] time when the [universe] will be dissolved; / and it perishes in the great fire and is separated. While [the li]/ght goes to its country, the darkness remains in / [the chain] and fetter for ever.

20 The advent also of the Third Ambassador, when he came / [to inspect] they who are imprisoned in the zone. He is / like a great king who comes and inspects cra[f/tsmen ...] and [...] and [... / ...] Also, they who are good, of the craftsmen and archi[te]25cts and artisans whom he has there in ea[ch] / place; he shall see that [th]ey have worked well, / and have fallen to his works in their fashion. He shall rejoice with / [great joy ...] He shall thank the artisans / who have constructed his works [and completed] his orders.

30 Now, just as this great king w[ho c]omes and insp[e]/cts his works and fortific[ation]s; so a[lso] / is the advent of the Third Amb[assa]dor. [F]o/r, when he too came, he saw [his works] / established and prepared and [...] (53) series of the rulers prepared and established there; / above and below, outside and w/ithin, in the great pattern that his brothers had made. / They had come before him to the contest, they who had fixed and cre5ated the universe before he came. He saw the gods and the / a[ng]els est[abl]ished and controlling the fortifi/[cations ...] guarding the [ent]ire ruling-power [... / ...] which his first powe[rs] had done. / [They are the F]irst Man and the [Living Spirit]; 10 a[nd the] Great [Spirit, the M]other of Life.

Therefore, when h[e s]aw / them, that they had [created] everything [with] great wisdom; / [...] as they looked he plundered (?) [... / ...] in h[is adve]nt, by which he came, he was

un[veil]ed / to [them]. He says to the Living Spirit: 'The
judgement that [you] have [... [15] ...] good, what you utt[ered ...] /
you [gave to] them correspondingly; so that they were moved
and raised up to that of w/h[ich t]hey were not worthy'. /

[The] advent also of Jesus the Splendour, the time when he came
to [a]ll [...] / being just like a man if he is [se[20]n]t to pull out a [... /
b]urn a difficult f[ig]-garden with fire. Therefore, [aga]in, /
when he has [fi]rst cu[t] the bad trees with his a/[x]e and has
pulled out [... / ...] and their body with his fire; so that they should
not return to sprout [25] [from] this time, no[r] bear fruit bad to eat /
[...] Afterwards, [he] also planted [good] plants; [the / t]ree of
lif[e] that will make good fruit. /

Again, this is [like] this simile of the advent of Jesus the
Splendour. / [It] happened l[ike this]; because he too set out [30] [...
h]is power and his wisdom, in his / [...]-ness [... a] king and a
saviour / [...] in his glorious wisdom (54) he destroyed them. He
bound and crushed them like / the fire that shall burn and
destroy trees. This is also how / he performed his will in the
zone, / among the many powers; until he reached the form [5] of
the flesh of Adam and Eve, the first humans. [He perfected] / his
will in Eve, he [... He a]lso [gave / h]ope to Adam, and the g[ood]
news [...] / glorious [...] He went up to [the heights ... / ... of li]ght.

T[hen the summons and the obed][10]ience, the great counsel that
came [to] the el[emen]ts, / which are set in conjunction. It
[mixed w]ith them, i[t was es]tabl/ished [i]n silence. It bears u[p
...] un[til the end t]i/me when it can arise and stand f[ir]m in the
g[reat] fi/re. It will gather to it its own soul, and sc[ul]p[15]t it in the
Last Sta[t]ue. You will a[ls]o find it / sweeps out and casts from it
the polluti[on] / that is foreign to it. However, the life and the
li[gh]t / that are in all things it gathers in to it, and builds / upon
its body. The time when this Last Statue [20] will be perfect in all its
limbs, then it can become free / and ascend from that great
struggle thr[ough] / the Living Spirit its father, the one who
comes and brings a [... l]/imb. He brings it up from within this
gathering(?), the melting do[wn] / and destruction of all things.

Now, th[is co][25]unsel, tha[t] summons <and> obedience, resembles / thus cooled butter. If a pers[o]n will take an[d s/e]t it in

hot milk, it melts [dow]n and soak[s] / in with this hot milk. It m[elts] in another [time / i]n silence and quiet to the mids[t ...] 30 yet also, of the power and the taste of this m[ilk ...] / is drawn to (the butter), and (the milk) sets and becomes [cold ...] / in [...] and the [... this mi](55)lk it shall clarify and discard. However, the oil and the grea/se and the 'beauty' of the [m]ilk it shall gather in to it. /

Again, this too is what the advent of / that thought is like; the counsel of life, which 5 is the summons and [o]bedience that came to the el[e]ments. / This is the one that at the end c[an a]rise and stand firm, and will gather / [i]n to it all [the] lives, a[nd] the light that has / [remai]ned behind [in] everything. It can bui[ld] them upon / [it]s body, it will [gath]er them in to it [... 10 ...] in its im[ag]e for ever and ever [... / ...] from this time.

B[l]essed is / every one w[ho will be]lieve in these five advents and [b]e confir[med / in the] knowledge. [He will come to] the heights and be saved [... / ...] and not be counted [... 15 ...]

••• **17** •••

(55,16 – 57,32)

/ The Chapter of the / Thr[ee] Seasons. /

Manichaeism designated itself as the religion 'of the two principles and the three times (or seasons)'. The two principles are light and darkness; and the three times are the beginning, the middle and the end.

In Manichaean tradition there are two primary ways of delineating the three times. Often the whole of history, the time of mixture, is encapsulated in the middle period between the twin eternities before and after its events. Alternatively, as in this kephalaion, the history itself is separated into three: descent, creation, redemption.

It is notable that the primeval events when the First Man is in the land of darkness, before the construction of the universe, cover the longest span. In contrast, the entirety of human history, from the fashioning of Adam and Eve 'after the image of God (the Ambassador)' to the final redemption, occurs in the third period. Thus, it is all eschatological.

O[n]ce again the apostle speaks to his disciples: Fr[om] 20 the time when the light came forth and was crucified in the darkness; / [t]o the season when the Statue will ascend an[d] / the entire light, w[hic]h was conjoined with the darkness, will be puri[fied] and c[lean/sed]. He [s]ays: [Fr]om that time on, [from tha]t time / to the season of the end totals three seasons.

25 [Thre]e season[s from] the time when the First Man / [went] down to the abyss, and waged the war and the struggle / [against] the King of the realms of [Dark]ness and his other powers. He was victorious, / [whi]le h[is sons remain behi]nd with them in the worlds [... / ...] in the [...] until he shall catch all of them 30 [... he bou]nd them all up, so that not one o[f / them escaped] his hand. He won a great victory [... / ... The First] Man spent human lifetimes and / [generations in the land] of darkness, until he prevailed / [...] (56) he fulfilled the will of the greatness that was [commanded] / of him.

Then they sent the Living Spirit, the Father [o]f / Life. He brought the First Man up from the struggle, he / [brought him up to the] land of light. This is the first 5 peri[o]d, from the descen[t] of the First Man / to his ascent. /

The second seas[o]n is from the time [when the F]irst [Ma/]n ascen[d]ed. The Living Spirit came, an[d the] Mother of [Life. / They set in order the th]ings o[f] the univer[se, they] set u[p 10 ... the Father of] / Life [an]d the Mother of the living set in order [... / ...] the u[n]iverse, up to the moment when they go out / [...] it was reckoned to the second season. /

[...] the universe [... 15 ...] the Third Ambassador spread [... / ...] that is in the [...] living; he [... / he separated] beauty from all the powers and scooped [it up] / to the heights, he swept the waste to the abyss, and he [... / ...] Now, from the moment when the Ambassador revealed 20 his image he purified the light. Sin spur[ted] / up towards him. He hid his image. Sin came / [...] from [the dark]ness. It sculpted the trees and the abortion[s fe/l]l down. Afterwards they sculpted Adam a[nd Eve] / in the flesh. Until the moment when Jesus wa[s se]nt and he [... 25 ...] as he performed there h[is w]ill. He gave the [hop]/e to Adam, and ascended to the heig[hts]. /

Now, from the time when the Ambassador [displayed] his

ima[ge] / until the season when [the Sta]tue will [as]/cend at the end, shall be reckoned to the t[hird sea]son.

[30] T[hen] the disciples asked the apost[le ... / ...] / with each other in the ligh[t] earth [... / ...

The apost]/le says to them [... (**57**) ... / ...] lasts long in the time t[hat the] First [Man spent in the wo]/rld of darkness. It is a very great count [of t]ime [more] / than the (other) two seasons!

His discipl[e]s say to h[im: The] [5] first season, wh[ic]h the First Man spent in the [world of] dark/ness, is how mu[ch] longer than the time that this univer[se has been? While it is / es]tablished?

[He replies to them]: If you should say th[at ... / ...] it is small, if y[ou] sho[uld ... / ...] to him [...] and [y]ou consult [... [10] ...] you will tel[l] him: Twe[nty times]! / [It is grea]ter again in this other one that you will c[onsult]. / Th[ir]ty times! Less also is this other o[ne ... / ...] people will receive the {}*19 of the trees [... / ...] the years and the generations [... [15] ...] earth to the heights. This is [...

This / is] the third period, from the time w[hen the Ambas-sa/d]or revealed his image until the [S]tatue will asc/end from the lump. It again, th[at] time, is / greater than the intermediate; but it does not come equal to the ti[20] [me of the Firs]t Man. For this intermediate season, / in [which] the Father of Life and the Mother of Life [constructed the un/ivers]e with its orders, is shorter than that of the First / [Ma]n.

Gr[ea]t [i]s the period of the First Ma/[n]! It lasts longer than the season in which the Ambassador disp[25][l]ayed his image, until the dissolution of / [the] world and [the S]tatue ascends. [From the time / to]o when the Ambassador displayed his image, until / [the dis]solution of the universe [... / ... [30] ...] when the Father of Life and the / [Mother of Life s]haped the universe.

These are the / [... thre]e periods of time that o[ccur]. (**58**)

---

*19 ôòλε

••• **18** •••

(58,1 – 60,12)

/ *[Concerning the Five] War[s that the] Sons / of [Li]ght waged wi[th the*
   Sons] of Darkness. /

Five major cosmological events in the history are, in sequence, presented as
wars in which principal divinities have vanquished the powers of darkness.
     58.7 – 19 The descent of the First Man who sacrifices his five sons, the
living soul. While this is sometimes presented as a primal tragedy, like the
crucifixion it is the bait that ensures the defeat of death.
     58.20 – 59.2 The creative activity of the Living Spirit who imprisons the
rulers in the universe.
     59.3 – 18 The displaying of the divine image by the Third Ambassador
who seduces the demons chained in the heavens, thereby drawing out of
them their light. Mani develops a short parable to explain this crucial
moment.
     59.19 – 28 The descent of Jesus the Splendour who subdues a rebellion by
evil (see 93.29 – 94.11) and imparts knowledge to Adam.
     59.29 – 60.8? Perhaps the eschatological work of the counsel of life that
sculpts the Last Statue upon itself, achieving the final victory and redemption
(see 81.1 – 6)?

[Then] the enlightener [s]peak[s]: The sons of light waged five [5]
[war]s against the sons of darkness. The sons of light /
[humiliated the s]ons of darkness in them all. /

[The first w]ar is that of the First living [M]an, which [he /
waged against the] King of the realms of Darkness, an[d] all the
rule[r]s that had come / [forth from] the five worlds of [...] He
hunte[d [10] them with] his net, which is [the] living soul. He [... /
...] in the snare and [...] the face of the [... / ... h]is virgin, the
living fire [... / they did not find] how to escape h[is n]et [... / ...
h]e caught them like fish [... [15] ...] the five counsels of the five
elem[ents ... / ...] He cut and dug out the root of [the fi]ve [tr/ees,
...] r[o]ot of the evil tree, like an ax[e. / As] the saviour has said:
Behold, the axe is put to the roo[t / of] the evil tree, so that from
this time it can not bear evil fruit*[20].

[20] The second war is that of the Liv[ing] Spirit [... / ... h]e has

---

*[20]   Mt. 3:10

constructed the things and the worlds of l[ight; / he spre]ad out
the rulers and chained them in the middle [of ... / ...] the stars in
[...] the earths [... / ...] them in the three vessels. For the rulers 25
rebelled and were set [a]gainst the Living Spirit. They wished to
[... / ...] since they knew and realised that he might bind [and] /
fetter them with a strong chain. Yet he, the L[ivin]g Spirit, /
(appeared to them) with many aspects, with numerous [...], with
m[a]/ny hands and great cruelties. [He was revea]led to them, 30
he imprisoned them with mu[ch] skill. Not one [of] / them was
able to save (himself), and he {}*21 [... / ...] Now, since he [... / ...]
he trapped them [... (59) ... / ...] /

[The third war] is that of the Third A[mbas]sa/[dor who has
display]ed his image [... 5 ...] what is below [... sc]ooped / [...] all
[l]ight and the property [... / ...] the ones that are consumed [... /
... the] entire [r]uling-power [... / ...] pride of the li[ght ... 10 ...]
extending it [... / ... a] person comes, who is powerful [... / ...] he
takes his riches [... / ...] silver [... / ... his] pride and wantonness.

15 This i[s what] the ruling-[power] is like [...] / all riches [...] as
they travel [... / ...] light / [... he] cleansed and purifi[ed] i[t]. /

[The] four[th] war is this that Jesus the gl[orious] one waged
against 20 all [the re]bels who had rebelled above and be[lo]w. /
[W]hen the light was purified from them by the imag[e of the]
Th[i/rd] Am[b]assad[or], their chains loosened [... / ...] the
glorious one in the fourth war; he came and brought [... / ... a]
rebellion of the entire ruling-power. He girded [himself ... 25 ...
a]ll of it another time. [H]e constructed the whole structure and
he made [... / ...] a great contest; [h]e humiliated therein. / [...] he
fulfilled the will of the greatness, [he / gave the] hope to Ad[am
...] to his light ship. /

[The fifth war is this] that the [co]unsel of li30[fe ... wh]ich is the
summons and the obedience [... / ...] great [... / ...] and it placed
[...] upon the [... / ...] and the [... (60) ... / ...] of death, which [... /
...] with it. And it was victorious over [...] / for [eve]r, and it gave
the kingdo[m ... 5 ...] great wa[rs ... / ...] with the sons of darkne[ss

---

*21 ϭⲁⲩⲙⲉ Smagina 1990:116 suggests 'get out' (from ϭⲱⲩⲙ); Vycichl
1983:206 'se libérer'.

... / ...] the good are victorious over the [wicked ... / ...] for ever
and eve[r ... /

Blessed is] every [el]ect one who will [... [10] ... li]ves therein and is
victorious over it [... / ...] after the likeness of these five [... / ...]
receives the victory without [...]

••• 19 •••

(60,13 – 63,18)

/ Concerning the Five Re[le]as[es; [15] *what] they [are]. /*

These five 'releases', or moments and processes in the redemption of the
light, correspond to the five wars in the previous chapter.

[Once again] our father [s]peaks: [There are] five [releases / by]
which the light is saved f[rom] / all [the rulers and] powers of
darkness! /

[The first loo]sening and saving is that of [the] First Ma[20]n, since
when the First M[a]n was freed fro[m / the prison of] the rulers
by the Living Spirit, who had come [... / ...] / of the First Man,
much light and [much] power was / saved from the entire
ruling-power. They ascend[ed] [25] with the First Man to the aeons
[of] greatn[ess]. This [is the first] / release. /

The second saving is that of the Liv[ing] Spirit, since whe[n] /
the Father of Life and [the] Mother of [Li]fe constructed [the ... /
...] and [w]orlds [... wo][30]rlds, the earths and their [rulers;
im]measurable light / was saved f[r]om them [... the First] /
Man, who w[a]s devoured [...] lig[ht ... **(61)** ... / ... th]ree wars [...
/ ...] to the time when he [... / ...] above [... [5] ...] them upon the [...
/ ...] universe. /

[The third red]emption is that of the Thi[rd / Ambassador ... he]
displayed [his / image ...] he [... [10] ... the r]uling-power; he [... / ...
/ ... / ...] from them [... / ...] So this is [how] the [... [15] ... his]
image that [... in the Th/ir]d Ambassador. /

[Th]e fourth s[av]ing is that of Jesus [the Splendour, since whe/n

he was] re[ve]aled in the zone he displayed [his im]/age in front
of the firmaments and purified [the light] [20] that is above. He
established the first righteous o[ne*22 ... / ...] all the churches. He
took the likeness*23 [... / ...] he made himself like the angels in
[...] un/til he travelled and descended to the form of flesh. He set
in order / [t]he earths and all the fastenings. He also loosen[ed [25]
...] light without measure in the entire structure. He gave / [the
s]ummons and the obedience to the elements, he formed /
[J]esus the Youth. He as[ce]n[d]ed and rested himself in the /
light [land].

The fifth release / a[nd s]aving is that of the great counsel,
w[30][hich is the s]umm[ons an]d the obedience, since it also / [...
the] soul from the [land] of greatness (62) [... [5] ... the] Living Spirit
[... [9] ...] as he gave [... [10] ... the r]elease [... /...]

The first [... / ... he] ascended and he [... / ...] as he [... / ...]
wisdom [... [15] ... / ...]

The fourth [... / ...] its wisdom / [...]

And also, the fifth [... / ...] in to it, and it sets it in order [...] its [20]
light image in this Last Statue.

These five grea[t] / powe[rs ...] were revealed. They came to a
profit [... / ...] they were established upon [... / ...] First Man [...]
when he came to/ward [...] from the struggle. He set in order and
constru[25]cted [...] universe [... / ...] the First M[an / ...] his advent.

In / t[his way ...] they st[an]d with [... (63) ...] because of the light
[th]at had rushed from [... / ...] the Amba[s]sa[d]or.

The counse[l of] / life, which is the [s]ummons and the
obedience, will make [... / ...] seal the commandment and the [...
[5] of] all [the] apostles. In this last season they [... / the] life of the
S[t]at[ue and] he judges the sou[ls / ... he] can send [... /

...] powers, they [...] from the [... / ...] it is alive [...] of the will [of
the ...] [10] Father, the establ[ished one ...] / powerful; they g[o ...]

---

*22   Read ⲁⲣⲭⲓⲁⲓⲕ[ⲁⲓⲟⲥ] after P. Kell. Copt. 2 line 139 and PsBk2. 88.15
139.43
*23   Phil. 2:7

enemy, they [...] / all of them [...] conquer this land that they have [... / ...] in it for ever [... / ... t]hey came fr[om h]im in the beginning, as t[hey will r]eturn ¹⁵ again to the light. They [as]cend to him at the la[st]. /

Blessed is every person [who can] understand these mysteries! [... / ...] up [...] from the first to [...] / it [...]

••• 20 •••

(63,19 – 64,12)

²⁰ *The Chapter of / the Name of the Fathers. /*

The name 'father', as the Father of Greatness, supremely designates the ultimate God and source of all divinity. However, it can also properly be used of the derived gods in their own realms of greatness. Compare chapters 7 and 25.

[On]ce again the enlightener speaks to his disciples: The [Father / of] Greatness, as he is named; due to what reason is he given the name 'the Father / [of] Greatness'?

His disci²⁵[p]les say to him: We beseech you, our master, that you may enlighte/n us about this [g]reatness; for who is it that is named / 'the Father o[f G]reatness'?

Then he speaks / [to] his disciples: Now, the Father, who is the first esta/[b]lished thing, [shall be cal]led 'the Father of Great-ness'. ³⁰ His greatn[ess is the gr]eat earth where he lives, he being established / [i]n it [...] the essence of the light that swathes / all the [r]ich go[d]s and the angels and the dwellings / [...] is set over it. /

[Furthermore, they shall c]all the Third Ambassador ³⁵ ['father'. His greatness i]s the light ship of living fire (**64**) [wherein he lives], he being established in it. /

[Once again, J]esus the Splendour shall himself also be called 'father'. / His [greatn]ess is the ship of living waters where he lives, / [he being established in it].

[5] [They shall] also [call] the Pillar of Glor[y] 'father'. It[s] gre[atness / ...] the five gods of hol[y ...] which [li/ve and are establ]ished in them. They [... / ...]

Again, [the] Li[ght] Mind shall be / [called] 'father'. His gre[atness] is the [holy] church; [10] becaus[e] he lives [and is established i]n it. It also / [...] in it [...] alone. They / [... li]ght.

••• 21 •••

(64,13 – 65,13)

/ [C]oncerning the Father of Gr[eat]ness: [15] [ho]w he is established and / determined. /

The kingdom of light is a manifestation of the Father himself, which he pervades by his qualities or limbs. The kingdom is variously described in the texts, which have difficulty reconciling the sets of five and twelve that structure Mani's system.

Once [again] the apostle [speaks] to h[is d]isciples: Hear / [this lesson t]hat I will recount to you. Very great is / [land of] light*[24] in the presence of they who will hear and kno[20]w it, due to the first Father of Greatness. How he ex/[ists and is] established in his five light limbs, which are / [... the store]houses that have neither limit nor measure to the[m / ...] mind, thought, insight, counsel and [consid/eration ...] his twelve light limbs that [25] are his twelve wisdoms. Now, there are five great light lim[bs] / in each one [...] five grea[t] / springs of praise gush for[th ...] five great / [...] lig[ht ...] /

The first is his light that enlig[htens ...] it gushed [30] forth from him and pour[ed ...] a[ll] aeons. /

The second is the perfume of the [...] / and pervades all the aeons of greatness. /

The third is his living voice of [... / ...] all his aeons [...]

[35] The fourth is his [...]-ness [... (65) ... gus]hes forth from him [... o]ut [...] /

---

*24 Suggested reading: ⲡⲕⲁϩ ⲙ̅ⲡⲟⲩⲁ̈ⲓⲛⲉ

The fif[th] is his great glorio[us ...] that [..., w]/hich [has been
ma]nifested all the tim[e], whi[ch contin]ues [...] / all of them. It
was sculpted in them [...] ⁵ se[a]led in the[m ...] sea[led ...] / as
they send [...] in [... / ...] they too receive nourishment [...]
immediately [... his] / living voi[ce ...] joy [...] / set up anew. It
shall gush forth from it [...] ¹⁰ they shall [...] and become rich in
the [...] / too is beautiful [...] portray[al ...] / adornment [...] and
they live [... / ...] for ev[e]r. /

••• 22 •••

(65,14 – 66,27)

¹⁵ *[... / ...] the Land of Light. /*

The theme of the previous kephalaion is here continued with a description
of the land of light.

[...] in the great land of greatness / [... a]s I will reveal to you [... ²²
...] above. /

[... f]ace is [... / ... ²⁵ ...] living / [... / fr]om [... / ...] upon him. /

[...] light and ³⁰ [... / ...] face / [... (66) ...] out; he has [... f]ace of
the [...] / in the [...] now fi[ve ...] of prais[e ... / ...] in the [...]
living [am]bros[i]a [...] / five [...] compound [...] they become an
image ⁵ [...] the li[v]ing air [...] also living. [As] / those five shall
[...] from all the contests of the greatness / [...] and a beautiful [...]
to the limbs of their body / [... w]hich exists [...] the land of light;
their / [... l]ife. Just as all the gods and the rich ones and the ¹⁰
[angels w]ho were summoned came from the Father, so also / all
[the moun]tains [...] springs and trees / [...] gush forth [...] great
is / a [...] every thing that you [... / ...] neither water nor [...]

¹⁵ These ar[e ...] which [... / ...] /

The [...]-th [...] great light, the living air [... / ... in which the
aeons of grea]tness dwell, being established therein. [... / ...
ang]el[s] that [... ²² ...] and the [... / ...] the gi[fts] of the great
Father [... / ... ²⁵ ...] in the [...] /

Blessed is whoever will k[now ... / ...]

••• 23 •••

(66,28 – 70,7)

/ [...] ³⁰ *which [...]* /

Mani begins by telling his disciples that no one can explain the ultimate
origin of the two eternal kingdoms, for no prior power has been revealed
(66.31 – 67.20). However, the apostle can preach about the time from when
the darkness first stirred against the light, to attack it. Thus begins the
history of war and conflict (67.20 – 30).

The essence of darkness stirred into the thought of death, and spread and
generated the hideous warring powers through its five elemental worlds.
These are the five trees that bear evil fruit (67.31 – 68.28). The chief ruler
then took charge of his powers; and, noticing the light, conspired to attack
(68.29 – 32 and ff.).

The Father of Greatness knows that death can not be allowed to intrude
into the eternal land of light; and thus must emanate the gods to take the
conflict to the darkness and into the arena of mixture. The plan that will
ensure ultimate victory is entrusted to the living soul (the five sons of the
First Man), for it will destroy evil from within, using that uncontollable
lust that is at the heart of death. Therefore, the First Man puts on his sons as
garments, or as armour in preparation for the war (68.33 – 70.7).

O[nc]e again it happened [... / ... / ... / ...] essence in [... ³⁵ a]s I
have told y[ou ... / ...] is the land of [... (67) ... / ...] and [...] / their
last.

What the essence of [...] / no person could re[cou]nt or unveil [or
say how it] ⁵ exists [... f]or ever [...] / all [...] and [...] unve[i]l /
[...] etern[ity ...] great [...] / again and the [...] tend [...] / the
beginning of eter[nity] and the end [...] ¹⁰ set th[at one] down. /

Now, my [...] the land of d[eath ... / ... nat]ure of the essence [... /
...] which exists [... for e]/ver and ever [...] ¹⁵ in [...] / with one
another.

As for the eternity of [... / ...] which exists from ever, no person is
able to / [understand] how they exist. For no other power / [is
manifes]ted to them, in that it might speak or recount about their
[origin*²⁵], ²⁰ how [they e]xist. However, from the time w/[hen

---

*²⁵   Perhaps read ⲁⲣⲭⲏ

it] stirred itself and rose up against the light [... / ...] it might come
and rule over the land of the living. /

[The Fi]rst Man came forth against it and prevented it, [he k/ept]
it apart from the house of the living. He prevented i[25] [t]. From that
time, when the light was mixed with / [the] darkness, and life
[wi]th death, there was a measure of approval and an ability / [for
the] first-born [and the a]postle[s] to teach about it. They spe/[a]k
and unveil how the reproach and the fight did hap/[pen], [how]
the light [was] entwined with the darkness, which they [30] [...] life
in death. /

[... after it] stirred itself in its essence, its th/[ought ...] in its own
land. It [... / ...] the entire land of darkness in its [... / ...] of light
in the abyss. For (68) [...] essence in [i]t [... / ...] because a [...]
they reckoned [... / ...] on its side [...] this first nature / [...] it,
bec[ause i]ts body is made strong [5] [... more] than the Adamant
[...] every [...] as it exists / [in the univer]se.

[...] of death [... / ...] envy, which [...] the land of [darkness / ...
consi]deration in [...] wickedness / [...] for as it [...] the wounds
[...] against this land [10] [...]

Then he will run [... f]rom the land / [...] darkness. It drew [...]
his members / [...] is deep [... / ... / ...] in them.

[15] [...] every [...] It spread itself o[ut. It] generated itself / [of the
five dark elements]; which [are] sm/oke, fire, wind, water and
darkness. [... / ...] sprouted trees. It came up [... / ...] it formed its
own self in the [... [20] ...] it generated its own self with its birth [in]
/ numerous [emana]tions, not resembling each other; [in] / the
storehouses of its abyss, many [dark] creatures / [...] destroyers
and dragons an[d] evil [beas/ts]. It was established and {}*[26] and
grew strong [... [25] ...] in the ugly forms of those in the darkness
[...] / dark, and by the [...] impetuosity, by their wickedness
an[d] / hatred they slaughter [...] / each other as they war with
one another. /

Then the counsel of their ruler humbled [it]s world an[d] [30] its

---

powers. It sensed the essence of the [light ... / ...] It conspired to wage a war [...] / with the exalted kingdom and the [...] /

However, he, the Father of Great[ness ... **(69)** ...] / it also knew [... w]/ar, to disturb the [land of] light [...] / in the wisdom of his [...]-ness [...] [5] he transformed himself against it [... / ...] against it. /

Indeed, at t[hat t]ime [... / ... / ... [10] ...] / go agains[t ...] God [...] /

[... fr]om its [... p]/oured it out [... i]n the elemen[ts]: in the smoke, / the fi<re>, the win[d], the water and the darkness. It came up from the [great] [15] d[epth], it being set in the trees [... / ...] against it.

Also, at the time when it generated itself / [...] it formed the fruits, it still being set in t/hem. They summoned the five garments, the sons of the Fir[st] / Man.

And at the time when it generated its own self [20] [f]rom the fruits through its offspring, they fell upon the earth and [...] / strength from the elements and were nourished by them. [... / ...] wickedness, together with cruelty [...] / in the ruler, the leader of all the demons. He hum[bled] / his worlds and his powers; he gathered them all in [to [25] hi]m. He made himself ready for the battle; he set himself [to / the] war with that light earth, and the great / King who dwells in it.

At that very moment / the First Man approached his garments, the gods / [who sh]ine forth. He spoke with them, that he might entrust to them a [... [30] ...] he [reve]aled to them and taught them about everything that [... / ...] them. He assumed them. He arranged them [... / ... He] draped them over one another upon his li[mbs ... **(70)** ... / ... d]anger, it [... / ...] the heights of the earth [... / ...] with all its powers [5] [... beg]inning, it being immeasurable / [... / ...]

••• 24 •••

(70,8 – 76,14)

10 *[... / ...] /*

This chapter is concerned with the measurement of time and eternity; and consequently with the question of why apostles can speak of certain episodes in the history, but not of those others that are eternal. In this it is linked to the opening question of the previous kephalaion. Chapter 24 appears also to be composite, with series of textual material loosely strung together on these related themes.

70.12 – 72.27 The duration and process of emanating the Great Spirit, the First Man, and his five sons; from the Father. It is notable that the Mother of Life is in part distinguished here from the Great Spirit (71.25) who comes into existence prior as the female archetype of the divine.

72.28 – 73.3 The other gods were also emanated at the same time.

73.4 – 74.9 Apostles can speak of the middle time, the history of descent and ascent; because it is temporal in contrast to the twin eternities of the beginning and the end.

74.9 – 75.10 The parallel process of evil emanation from Matter.

75.11 – 76.3 A list of six related points; but the exact context is unclear.

76.4 – 14 Reiteration of the theme about time and eternity.

[...] a great ju[d/ge ...] now also a ti[me ...] that they sculpt/[ed ... he was revea]led in the Father, the first est[ab]lished thing.

W[he[15]n ...] the two summonses that he called [... / ...] the Mother of Life [... / ...] a long duration in the first Father [... / ...]

For someone, if he might set a measure and rule / [...] the earth {particles}[*27] and the {pebbles}[*28] of the mountains and [20] [... of the] s[e]a and the body of the firmaments. Should they be po[ured / ...] the body of the four mountains and the three ve[s]/sels that [s]urround the universe; if they shall al[l] be poured out / [...] these fine {granules}[*29]. /

Happen you know that the grains of the earth {particles} are measurable, [and those of] [25] the [entire] uni[verse]. It is possible to count the {particles} of the earth eac[h] / ye[a]r [...] the sand

---

[*27] ⲕⲁⲏⲁ Cf Vycichl 1983:76 – 77.
[*28] ⲁⲗⲟⲁⲉ
[*29] ⲙⲉⲥⲁⲏⲥ

grains of the entire universe; / but the duration of the time that the Great Spirit spent in the Father, [the] / first established thing, one will not be able to make a count of it!

He first / sculpted her like this. He established her in his inner storehous[es] 30 in quiet and silen[c]e. When [they had] / need of her she was called and came forth of the Father [of Greatness]. / She looked at all her aeons of lig[ht]!

Once again, from the time when she was called to [...] (71) go to [...] she gave [...] / upon his [bod]y [...] al[l] the aeons [...]; / she also [...] all of them. This [is also the case] / with the First Man.

This is how the Man 5 spent a long time being anointed in the Mother, set fast in her / inner storehouses [...] the extent of time that I have rec[ounted] / to you; from when the First Man went d[own to] / the contest, till the time when the [Statue (?) co]mes i[n ...] / this time [... 10 ...] he appeared [... / ...]

Ag[ain], from when he was / [c]alled and came forth, till the time when he [himse]lf call[ed / the five] shining [gods] who are his sons; they / themsel[ves also spent a long] time existing in their father! 15 I[t is the ti]me that occured from the coming down of the Fi/[rst Man] till the going up of the Last Statue. The f/[ive god]s spent this much duration being anointed in the First Man. / Yet, [at the] t[i]me when they were awaited, they were called and came [f]orth. /

Listen also to this, how I would teach you it. At the 20 time when the Mother of Life was called from the Father of Greatness, / when she expelled herself and came down by her [o]wn [wish], / from the heights of the Father to the earth, [she would spend / thousands of] years and many ten thousands until she reached the earth. / [Fo]r there is no measure nor rule to the heights of the Father. Rather, [just as] 25 he had called her in his Great Spirit, so he set her upon / [the] land of greatness thr[ou]gh one of these three that are counted to the twe/[lv]e hidden ones withi[n] the light veil, the ones / [esta]blished after the [...] region of the south. /

[The] matter of the Mother [of L]ife is like this. When 30 [the Fath]er called her he established her in the place he pleased, /

[to] establish her there as the instruction of the people that / [...] many [...]; and she examined everywhere that / [...] a blink of an eye, or like a (72) [...] bir[d ... / ...] This also is lik[e / ... the] Mother of Life in [...] whenever / [...] cast her out [... u]pon her to the place [... 5 ...] him. He perfected her in his Great Spirit and set her in / [the place he pl]eased, according to [his wi]ll. /

[Th]is [also is how] they called the [five g]ods from the [Fi/rst Man. They were se]t befo[re him], as he wished that [... / ... 10 ... / ... / ... / ...]-ness [...] / down, that they would rule in them [...] 15 one another. He ordered and distributed them [... / ...] the son. He stripped himself of them [...] and he [... / ...] he girt and bound himself to [...] / in a [...] of silence upon the border of the earth [... A]/gain, he too, the First Man, spent a long period and [time] 20 until he gave power to his sons; until he assu[m]/ed them. After he came to wear them he stood fast in the hei/ghts between the borders. Again, he spent a duration and ti/[me] like this, corre-sponding to such amount and measure as the rain/drops and dew and falls of mist that come down in 25 the universe. This is how he spent this duration also, [stand]/ing between the borders, until the hour when he cast himself [d]/own to the contest! /

Whenever the Father of Greatn[e]ss [calle]d the Great Spir[it] / and the First Man and the gods [of] the glorious one, who are provide[d to] 30 enable them to reveal him; at that ve[ry ti]me [he] / sculpted the Great Builder in the [land of] light, [and] / the Living Spirit with the might[y] and active gods who came [from] / him. Also, at that time, he sculpted the [Amb]/assador, with Jesus the Splendour and the Vi[r]gi[n] of Lig[ht] 35 and the Pillar of Glory, and the gods who [came from them. (73) All these the Father of Greatness sculpted at] / a single time. They came for[th of] one another, one after on/e; the time when [...] and the work./

[...] to recount it to you [...] 5 from the time when the da[rkness] raised itself up to / [...] essence of the light / [...] these three emanations / [...] from the [w]ill of the Father against the enemy [... / ...] he has [... 10 ...] darkness [... / ...] according to the will [... / ... / ... / ...] the universe [... 15 ...] in it [...] separate out [... / ...] rest him in which way, and he rejoices [... / ... i]n his kingdom; until [the time when / the face] of the Father will be unveiled over

[all] the gods / of glory, and all the rich ones of [... the em]^{20}anations who came forth against the enemy. /

[From] that time when he sculpted these three [... / ...] till the time when the Father would unveil his face, / [and they g]o in to his hidden storehouses, and he calls them / [...] establishes each one of them to [his place. There is no measure ^{25} nor ru]le to this period until that time.

It is po[ss]ible / [for] all [the teachers] and saviours and apostles of / greatness, that they can speak and reveal about what has / [ha]ppened and what will happen; but before [... / ...] they are sculpted in heaven there is no possibility for any apost^{30}[le] a[nd teacher] to proclaim about this beginning, because / [...] for ever. Nor also is it possible for [al]l the apo/[stles] and teachers to be able to speak and revea[l / ...] the time when all the fathers (**74**) [of lig]ht [go in to the hid]den (places) of the Father, and [dw]/ell [...] power in them to i[t]s / [...] of God [...]; because it exists for e/ver. It is continuous till the a[e]ons. It has no time ^{5} to the end; but their establishme[nt ...] et/ernal is their life [... gener]ation by generation. /

[If] a person [s]hall ask [...] an/d about th[a]t etern[a]l end [...] in the devastation / [...]

However, [... ^{10} ...] to enable him to recoun[t ... / ...] who asks him [... / ...] of the disciples [... / ...] because [... / ...] and he gives [... ^{15} ...] about this Matter, this though[t of death ... / ...] which I have told you; for [this] is the way that [... / ...] came up to its storehouses. It has [... / ...] in its five elements. Again, it also [... / ...] the period and the time that it spent, until it rev[eal]^{20}ed itself to its elements, before it came to the trees. It spent / a great period and a long time established [... / ...] before it came up to the trees. It was [...] / in the trees. It spent a long time and duration [...] / existing in them, before it sculpted the fru[its ... ^{25} ...] and sculpted the fruits. Again, it spent a long [time] / in the fruits. Not little is the period and the tim[e that it / spent] existing in the fruits, before it sculpted [... / ...] after a long time [...] the d[emon]s / of its five worlds in various forms [can not (?)] be measured ^{30} [...] in p[erfec]tion of the fruits in the de[mons] / and fiends. They fell upon their earth and [...] / were nourished. Not little is the period that they [spent in the wo]/rlds, until they were nourished [a]mong[st ... (75) ...] to make [... / ...] t[h]at [l]and which shin/[es], and the great [King] who dwells there.

[Y]/ou know that [...] that in [... 5 ...] at the time when he / [... i]ts essence. It assumed / [... Mat]ter [...] to the war [... / ...] the Perfect Man. / [From the time] when the [wa]r occured [... 10 ...] /

[The first is ... h]e came to be in some [... / ...] when they ensnared a [...] /

[The second is ...] that h[e] built [... / ... the] universe was established. The zone [... 15 ...] down until the time when it will be / [dissolved].

The third is the [... / ...] the things and the universe will [... / from the] time when they were established there, till the time [when] / their end will be complete and their existence ceases [...]

20 [The f]ourth is the dissolution when they will dissolve the universe / [th]ere, and all things are destroyed. Obliteration / [reaches] them in that great fire, [which wi]ll burn them for fourteen / [hundred] and sixty-eight years. /

[The fift]h is the way that the Last Statue will be sculpted 25 [from] the remnant of all th[in]gs. The light separates / [ou]t to its place, and goes up and rules in its kingdom. / However, [the da]rkness [...] and they take it in to the tomb [... / ... and t]hey are bound with it in an et[ernal] chain. / Now, from [the tim]e when this first war 30 occured, till the [ti]me of this chain [...] these five things [... / ...] li[g]ht. /

[The six]th: From the time when it stirred and raised itself / [up in its] land, till the time of its chaining, it is possible / [for the apostles and the] chosen and the teachers to speak and recount (76) about it. However, before [...] / from it out of the powers [... / ...] and measure it; because it is eternal. /

[From the time] when it will be taken in to the chaining and bound 5 [in] the lump [...] / to give to it. No pe[rson] is able [...] /

the apostle and the teacher is enabled to [...] / chaining is eternal [in the] lum[p ... / ...] {}*30. From the time when [... 10 ...] with one anothe[r, till] the t[ime ... / one] another; and eac[h one ... / ...] fetter [... / ...] and they proclaim about the [...] / time and period.

••• **25** •••

(76,15 – 76,25)

/ *[Concerning the Advent of Five Fathers / from the Five Limbs of the Father]. /*

Once again the apostle speaks concerning [the advent of five fathers / fro]m the Father, one after another. [He] speaks t[hu]s: 20 [The Ambas]sador [came] from his mind; the Beloved of the Lights / [from his thought]; the Mother of Life from his insight; [Jesus] / the Beloved from his counsel; the Virgin of Lig[ht f]/rom his consideration.

So in this way were summone[d these five] / fathers. These five advents came from the five limbs [of the Father]. 25 One came from another and was manifested in its season.

••• **26** •••

(76,26 – 77,21)

/ *Concerning the First Man and the Ambassa/dor and the Ship; what they resemble. /*

Mani frequently used parables and similes in his teaching. However, the miscellaneous set of five in this kephalaion have little coherence beyond the concept of redemption. Their collection here evidences that the original contexts have been lost during a period of textual transmission.

76.29 – 34 The First Man rescues his treasure, his sons (the living soul), from the powers of darkness.

76.34 – 77.3 The significance of the two sons (usually five) and the two powers is unclear.

77.4 – 7 The Great Spirit has its throne in the sun (see 82.30 – 31); and its role is to beautify and to set matters in order (see 79.29 – 30 102.27).

---

*30 ⳁⲙⲏⲧⲉ

77.8 – 10 The Living Spirit redeems the First Man.

77.11 – 16 The Third Ambassador is the principal god of redemption. The living soul is continually reborn in the material forms in which it is imprisoned.

O nce again he speaks: The First [Man] is like a grea[t] [30] distinguished man wh[ose treasu]re has been taken away from him. H[e came] / to pursue his treasure. This [is] how the [First] / Man too came after his sons [f]rom the heights, [so that he] / might redeem[*31] them and retrieve his treasure, which had been scattered among[st] / his enemies.

Once again, [he is like a man] [35] whose two sons were taken away from him by [... He] / came out toward them to redeem them. [Again, this is how **(77)** the F]irst Man [...] shines in the heights because of h[is] / two sons, who were separa[t]ed from him. They are his / living soul that exist in two powers, which makes four. /

[Once] again, the ship [of the day] is like a great spear [... 5 ... The Grea]t Spirit too, which is in it, / is like a wise [crafts]man who might beautify and / set aright [all] the armou[r] for war. /

Once again, the Living Spirit is like a combatant / who might go towards a king's [so]n who has been taken prisone[r of war], [10] and he redeems him [from the] hands of his enemies. /

[The Amba]ssador to[o] is like a great man / [...] because of the treasure / [...] hand of his priso[ners / ...] these light powers [... [15] ... the] sons and their soul, so that they would [... / ... (the soul) might] be brought forth in the land [wherein it] was imprisoned. /

Again he turned, and he says to his discip/[les]: You yourselves must be purifiers and re[dee]/mers of your soul, which is established in every place, so that y[ou [20] may be counted] to the [c]ompany of the fathers of light [... / ...] of the kingdom in the new aeon, in the place of joy.

---

*31 Reading: ⲥⲁⲧⲟⲩ for ⲥⲁⲧϥⲟⲩ: 'purify them'.

••• **27** •••

(77,22 – 79,12)

/ *Concerning the Five Forms that exist* / *in the Rulers of Darkness.*

Compare chapter 6.

²⁵ [Once agai]n, the apos[tle] is sitting among the congregation. He says [to] / his disciples: Cons[id]er the ruler, the leader of all the powers / [of dark]ness. Now, f[ive forms] exist in his body, corresponding to / (the archetype)*³² [of the five] creations that exist in the five / [wo]rlds of darkness.

Indeed, his head is lion-faced, wh³⁰[ich] came about from [the] world of fire. His wings and his / [shoulders] are eagle-faced, after the likeness of the children of the wind. / [His hands] and [h]is feet are daemons, after the likeness / [of the children] of the [w]orld of smoke. His belly is [dragon]-faced, / [after the likeness of the] world of darkness. His tail [is the] **(78)** form of the fish , which belongs to [the world of the ch]ildren of water. These [five] / shapes are in him, and [they came] from the five [creations] / of the five worlds of darkness.

[S]hould he wish, h[e shall walk / on] his two feet [...] world of [sm⁵oke]. Also, when he wants, he shall [... f]our [...] / on his hands and feet [...] like [the] children of f[ire]. / Sh[ou]ld he wish, he shall rise up on h[is] wings, like the children of / the [wind]. Also, should he wish, he shall [plun]ge down to the waters / [like the] children of water. Again, shoul[d he w]ish, he shall crawl on ¹⁰ his [bell]y like the children of dark[ness. These] five shapes are / i[n hi]m.

Also, there are three other (qualities) in h[im.

The first]t: / [...] his powers [...] /

The second: Shall a [...] / his magic arts. When he [wishes, he shall make an invocation over ¹⁵ himself], and hide from his

---

*³² Lit. '[the appearance] of the seal'.

powers*[33]. [When he wants], / he shall show himself to them and strike a [death]-blow [by his] / magic arts. Any word he might utter at that moment, he shall [wreak magic] / by it.

The third: His body is strong, a[l]l [...] / nails and claws of his powers are not able to penetra[te it]. [20] No iron nor copper body will equal hi[m ...] / they will not be able to destroy him, because he was formed and fash[ion]ed / from the hard hearted counsel of Matter, the mother of d[emons and] / fiends.

Again, there are three others in him.

Wh[en he wants], / his fire shall {blaze}*[34], and his entire body be made like the [... of] [25] fire.

Also, when he wishes, he shall send out / frost, and his entire body freezes like a [... of] / snow.

The third: Whenever his powe[rs are sto]/od before him, he shall look at them and understand; for [whatever ex]/ists in their heart he shall understand, what is in th[eir heart] [30] and their face so long as they are stood before him. W[hen] / they retreat before him and distance themselves from him, [he shall not und]/erstand what is in their heart. There is no life [in him] / whatsoever, but his 'life' is the bile of [anger] that is app[arent] / on his face and in his fear. Shall a [... (**79**) ...] destruction that is establ[ished be]fore him.

Behold, do not [lay up/on] yourselves, my beloved ones, the shapes of this ruler, the ro/ot of [all] piercing evils and the camp / of every ugliness. Hold yourselves secure [5] from his midst and [h]is wicked teachings that dwell in your / body; so that they may not agree with you and ruin your sweet/ness, nor transform your truths to a lie. /

Rather, do you become zealous and perfect / in the presence of the Mind of truth that has been manifested to you, [so] [10] that you may [...] and they draw you [... u]/p to the he[ights. And you inhe]rit [li]fe for [ever / and] ever.

---

*[33]   Cf 31.30 which has the same phrase. The powers are subsidiary demons.
*[34]   ⲙⲉⲕⲣⲉ

••• 28 •••

(79,13 – 81,20)

/ *[Concerning the T]welve* ¹⁵ *Judges [of] the Father.* /

While the Father of Greatness is the transcendent and eternal Judge, twelve of the emanated gods act as judges as they take their roles during the course of the history. Mani instructs his followers similarly to walk in the path of righteousness.

[O nce again] he s[peaks] to his disciples: Twelve jud[ges / ex]ist; the great mighty givers of judgement! They were sen[t and / came] from the [ex]alted greatness to this place. They were assigned to different wo[rk]s / according to the command that the Judge, who belongs to the great[ness], ²⁰ [en]trusted to all these judges. Now he, [the gr]ea[t / Ju]dge, he who transcends all the judges, who exists and [/ is e]stablished in the aeons of greatness; [he] is the Father of [Greatness]. /

[The fir]st judge is the First Ma[n, he w]ho humiliated [the ruler / of Darkness in the] beginning. He judged him ac[cording to a ju]dgement of righteousn²⁵[ess]; for he had exalted himself [against a kingdom] that [was not] his own. /

[The se]cond judge is the Living Spirit, he who came and bore / up the Man. [He t]oo [made] a judgement on a[ll] the powers [of] / darkness; which had woun[ded] the garments of the First Man. /

[The th]ird judge [is the] Mother of Life, the Great Spirit, [she who ³⁰ beauti]fied and set up [the] heavenly part of [the un]iverse, [according to / her] pleasure; which [...] her. She j[udged] the rulers / [abov]e; she f[ettered] and set them firmly in the place / [that is fitting for them.

The fo]urth [judge] is the Great Bu/[ilder, he who built the] new aeon of joy. He ³⁵ [judged, according to a judgement of righte]ousness, the [storeho]uses of the [enemy]; (80) that death may not well up from this time on. He has constructed a prison for the / enemy. Also, upo[n] the crown [of the] building he has constructed a / throne for the First Man and all the fathers of light; / they who engaged the struggle with the evil one and were victorious over him.

5 The [fif]th [j]udge is the great King of Honour, he who dwells / and is established in the seventh firmament. He is the jud/ge of all the firmaments who gives a true judgement, according to / [a] judgement of righteousness, upon all the powers and all the [king]doms / [of the] firmaments.

The sixth judge is 10 [the Th]ird Ambassador, he who came and displayed / [his image]. He purified the light [...] which his own / [...] also of the enemy, he has [... /

The seventh judge is ... /...] the worlds [... as he gives the victory 15 to] they who are steadfast; but he condemns the on[es who are convicted ... / ...] he shall become for them the steps of the way (?) [...]; / but the convicted he sweeps and ca[sts out / to the] depths.

The eighth judge is Jesus the [Spl/endour], the father of all the apostles; because after 20 [the Am]bassador had displayed his image and the l[i]gh[t] was taken / [...] a mass of rulers rose up from abov[e] / and below. Then they sent Jesus the Splendour. He came [... / ...] he descended and made a judgement in the / [firmaments. He separated] the steadfast [from] 25 the convicted.

The ninth judge i[s the Vir]/gin of Light, [she who took the heart] of the powers by [her] / image, gathering her own ones in to her. She mak[es] / a judgement on the ruler of the moist, and the ru[ler] / of the dry.

The tenth judge is [the Jud]30ge who dwells in the atmosphere, judging all mankind. He [ma]/kes a separation between they who are good and they who are evil, setting [apart] / the righteous from the sinners. /

The eleventh judge is the Light Mind, he w[ho shall] / come and appear in the world. And he [choos]es the holy c[hur]35ch, and he unveils [...] / and separates light from [darkness, and sets the truth apart from] (81) lawlessness.

The twelfth judge is the great / counsel, which is the summons and the obedience, which is appointed in / the elements. It is the one that makes a separation between / the good and the evil ones. At the end also it can gather itself together [5] and sculpt its own self in the Last St/atue. And it separates [light] from [darkness]. /

These are the twelve great and mighty judges who / were sent. They came from the great Judge, he who transcends / all the judges. He is the Father that is hidden and [immeasurable], [10] the one who exists; who is established in the aeons of gre[atn]ess [upon] / the great throne of honour, which is the King of Ho[nour / ...] in his kingdom. /

[I am telling] you [about this], my beloved ones, so that you / [yourselves may w]alk in true heart on this path o[f [15] righteous-n]ess that I have revealed to you. Judge, / according to a true judgement, as judges of righteousness! / May a brother speak with his brother in truth; so that / when you depart (the body) you can receive the victory from these / twelve great judges, and go to rest [20] in this place of rest for ever.

••• 29 •••

(81,21 – 83,16)

/ *Concerning the Eighteen great / Thrones of all the Fathers.* /

There are nine thrones established for the great gods in the eternal realm. Another nine are appointed in this universe, the arena of conflict, and thus of loss and redemption. The last of these thrones is that upon which the apostle of a particular time sits; and Mani illustrates to his audience that he is now occupying it.

[On]ce again he speaks to his disciples: Eighteen [25] [great thrones for all the fathers] exist and are appointed, which are es/[ta]blished in eighteen places! While there are nine among them / [appointed in] the outer aeons, they ex[is]t / [i]n all the worlds of the damage. /

[The fir]st throne is the throne of the Father, the God of [30] [trut]h, the King of the aeons of greatness, the one who exists; who is esta/[blished ...] he alone, in his own essen[c]e, / [... he ap]art. This is the first throne / [...] the one that surpasses all the thrones.

(82) The second throne is that of the [gl]orious Mother of Life. / She is the origin of all the emanations that have come / to this world.

The third throne is / constructed for the father, the First Man. He is the one who [5] humiliated the entire first enmity, which existed in the / worlds of darkness.

The fourth throne is / that of the Beloved of the Lights, the great honoured Beloved o/f the aeons of greatness.

The fifth throne / is that of the glorious Great Builder; the great architect [10] who built the new aeon for a newn[ess], for [a ...] / for [the] fathers of light; also for a place of binding [and] a pri/son for the enemy and his powers.

[The sixth thro]n[e] / is that of the Living Spirit, the [glorious] mighty one, he who bore / up the First Man out from the [land of darkness]; [15] who also set in order and constructed the world[s ...] / both for a cleansing of the light, [and] for a binding [of the] / powers of the enmity.

The seventh th[rone is] / that of the Third Ambassador, the king of the zone, also the / master of all advices.

[20] The eighth throne is that of Jesus the Splendour, who [is] / the releaser and redeemer [of] all souls. /

The ninth throne is the throne of the great M[ind, he to whom] / all the churches shall gather; and all the [life] / that will be purified from the world returns to him.

[25] These are the nine thrones of ho[no]u[r] appointed in the outer aeo[ns], <which are established> / for the fathers of the glorious realm; [in the kingdom of the King of] / Honour, for ever and ever, amen. /

In contrast, these are the other nine thrones that are appointed in this world o[f] / the zone.

Three thrones in the ship of [the d][30]ay: one is that of the Ambassador, the second i[s that of] / the Great Spirit, the third is that of the Living Spirit. /

Once again, there are another three in the ship that [belongs to the night]: / the first is the throne of Jesus the Splendour, [the second is that of] / the First Man, the third is tha[t of the Virgin of] (83) Light. These six thrones are established in the two ships. /

Also, the seventh throne is established in the sev/enth firmament. The great King of Honour si/ts upon it.

The eighth throne is establis⁵hed in the atmosphere. The Judge of truth sits upon it, / he who judges all mankind. Three paths shall / be distinguished be[f]ore him: one to death, one to life, on[e] to / the mingling.

The ninth throne appointed and established is / for the [a]postle in the holy church. The apo¹⁰stle who has come to you at this time sits up[on it]; / thus, [as jud]ge of righteousn[ess]. They shall proclaim [true] judgem[ent] / every t[ime]!

Th[ese] are the [nin]e great [th]ro/[nes ...] that are established in this world of / [...] of the glorious realm, the one that the [... ¹⁵ ...] honour them [... / ...] and the [...]

••• 30 •••

(83,17 – 84,4)

/ *Concerning the Three Garments.* /

As the creator the Living Spirit establishes wind, fire and water across the entire universe. These are three garments that he carries with him; and which have to be divested and stretched over the zone from the bottom edges to the topmost point.

[On]c[e again] he speaks to his disciples: Happen you know this, ²⁰ my beloved ones, that when the Living Spirit / came he brought the three garments; that of wind, that of fire, and / that of water. He assumed them from [...] he has / [...] in them in th[ose] three garments / [...] he established [them] for all the things of [this ²⁵ univers]e, both above and below. He arranged them in the [... / he was displ]ayed. After[wards ...] his works / [...] the [... h]e stripped them off before / [the ri]ghteous ones.

Now, when he was about to loose[n them, / ... he] divested himself of them from their {clasp}*35 and he {}*36 and 30 [... i]n them, and thus these three g[arme]nts are arranged / [...] from below the edges of the zone as they clothe i[/t al]l [...] up [...] above [... / ... u]p [...] above them (84) strips them of the zone from that place at its topmost point; / and it is placed below them and ra[ised u]p to the hei/ghts above, from which it had been sent o[u]t at / their beginning.

••• **31** •••

(84,5 – 85,18)

/ *Concerning the Summons, / in which Limb / of the Soul it descended to the First Man. /*

This chapter discusses the relationship between the First Man, who was saved from the abyss by the Living Spirit; and his limbs or sons, the living soul that is scattered throughout the material universe. The summons is the call to salvation, and together with the answer or obedience it forms the counsel of life. This is the active will for redemption that drives the soul (see 178.1 – 5).

Mani shows that the First Man is the head upon which the soul depends for its life. Although hidden in this time and space, his presence is still with us in his image and love which is the virginal soul. The Man gathers in the soul, and builds it up, so that as his trunk it eschatologically ascends back to the land of light. This trunk is the Pillar of Glory which reunites with the First Man at its head. At the end of time it is the Last Statue.

Once again one of the teachers questioned the enlightener. He says to h[im]: 10 In which limb of [the liv]i[ng] sou[l] did [the] summons descend / [to] the Man, who exists in the [a]eon? F[o]r it is written in / the [s]criptures about the Man that he spread himself through the [...] / aeon as to a wooden house.

The [enli]ghtener speaks: / Indeed, the First Man dispersed himself and he [...] 15 limb o[f] the living soul as I have written f[or you ...] / of the living soul; he has [...] he did not know [... / ...] but the blessed, glorious Man c[a]me [in] / secret; in his

---

*35   ⲧⲟⲩⳓⲱⲡⲉ

*36   ⲥⲁⲣⲙⲉ Smagina 1990:116 suggests 'pulled off', (from ⲥⲱⲣⲙ); Vycichl 1983:206 'se libérer'.

image; in his shape; in h[i]s lo/ve; in his holy virgin, she who is
the v[ir]g^{20}in of light, the soul of the father. /

After the fashion of this fleshly body: as the root of / all the
lim[bs] hang upon the head, so that should one of / the person's
limbs be cut off, while the head exists he has hope for [...] / but if
his head should be cut off, the entir[e] body [w]ill d[ie] ^{25} and he
is lost.

This is also the case for the Firs[t] Ma[n]. / He is the head, while
his sons attach to it the l[i]mbs [of] / his soul. Or, conversely, like
the l[i]ving air, on [w]/hich all flesh entirely lives as it breathes
an[d ...] / therein. His head is placed on the body of the Pill[ar of
Gl]^{30}ory in the heights of the universe.

[This i]s also the case [for] / the father, the blessed Man; as he is
like the he[ad that is upon the] / body and the air that upon the
Pillar is set i[n ...] / being made strong by his l[ight] virgin, [she]
who is / his soul that he clothes [...] (85) t[h]ose [...]: the mind,
thought, insight, counsel and / c[on]sideration that he produced
and sent forth from / hi[m to] do his will. He sprang and
travelled behind them. / [...] of his living soul, which is entwined
among the rebel^{5}s; as they are like the limbs of its body, and / [...]
universe.

And when they were sent, / at [that ti]m[e] he was found with
the Virgin of [Lig/ht an]d [he] stood up, asking and entreating
for a p[o]wer*^{37}. / [... he] gave him peace and a ki[ss ^{10} ...] he
[gave] him goo[d] tidings / [... M]an. The Man him[s]elf gave
[his / ... h]is limbs and gathered his soul i[n / ...] he built it in its
place like this to[w]er*^{38} / [...] shaped it and beautified it skillfully
[... ^{15} ... f]or[m ...] the voices that he se[n]t / [... he] might sink in
and [q]uench [... / ...] so[u]l that was crushed by the enemy.
They were gathered in. They came, / [s]et firm onc[e] more, in
the image of their father.

---

*^{37} See 38.30 – 39.2
*^{38} See PsBk2. 198.5 – 6

••• **32** •••

(85,19 – 86,17)

20 *Concerning the Seven Works / of the Living Spirit. /*

The Living Spirit is the principal god of the second emanation (creation), whose tasks connect the first (descent) and the third (redemption). Therefore, he saves the First Man, defeats the demons who have devoured the living soul, and constructs the universe with the use of their bodies in which there is now both light and darkness. The universe is then held in place by the five sons of the Living Spirit and a multitude of other divine powers.

It is the Living Spirit who first called out the summons to redemption that, joined with the obedience of the First Man, becomes the active will to salvation. Thus it is mixed with the five sons of the Man, the soul.

[Once] again the enlightener speaks: The Living Spirit has done seven / [wo]rks with his strength.

[The fi/rst]: He brought the First Man up from the contest, the way 25 a pearl is [brought] up from the sea. /

[The s]econd: He spread about the one who had rebelled, he crucified / [h]im in every body.

The third: He / [tr]ampled, piled up, and pierced the essences of death. /

[The f]ourth: He constructed the ships of light.

The fi30[ft]h: He evoked his five sons, and distributed them about. They / [took] possession of the zone, they bore up under all the uni/[vers]e's weight. Also, he evoked three living words. He set / [them] upon the th[re]e vessels, another one upon the giant. / [Again, he evoked the] summons, that it might be mixed with the five shining 35 men.

(86) The sixth: When he had constructed the zone he aro[se] and s[e]/nt forth a multitude of powers and many [angel]s; / so that they would bound the circuit of the z[o]ne on every si[de], / un[t]il he finished [co]nstructing the works. And at the end [of] all the [wor]5ks he to[ok s]ome of them in to his storehouses, / and he appointed others at the watch-posts. /

The [sev]enth: A[t the] time when the Ambass[ador dis]-
pl/[aye]d his glorious imag[e], the L[iving] Spirit [established] /
many [go]ds and angels. They [...] ¹⁰ Th[ey to]ok hold of it, that
the entire building [...] not [... / ...] one another against [the]
light, which he had [...] /

Also another gr[ea]t and glorious work he will enact at the e[nd]
is [the] Last [Statue], / which he will bring up to the aeons of
[light]; / and he [...] in, and [he ta]kes hold, and he smites [...], ¹⁵
and [he] builds, and he [...], and he [... t]hem.

[Bless/ed is he] who kn[ows] him i[n the] new [aeon], and
[dwells in] that [ae]/on of glory and joy!

••• 33 •••

(86,₁₈ – 86,₃₀)

*/ Concerning the Five Things that he ²⁰ constructed with the hard Bodies /
of the Rulers. /*

This brief chapter follows the previous, for it discusses intricate details of the
work of the Living Spirit in the construction of the universe, utilising parts
of the demons that he has destoyed.

Once again the enlightener speaks: The Living Spirit constru[cted five] / great things from veins and skull[s in the] hard
[bodies]. /

The first is the disc that is placed upon [the sh]²⁵oulder of the
Porter.

The se[con]d are the arches of [the] / pillar that is before him.

[The th]ird is the [mou]/ld of the fo[r]m for the gehennas.

The fourth are the [seven (?)] / pillars that he has erected in the
great sea, in [the] / seven parts of the universe.

The fifth are the four ³⁰ walls that surround the vessels.

••• 34 •••

(86,31 – 87,13)

/ Concerning the Ten Things that the Am[bassa]/d[or] began by his Ad[vent]. /

While the Living Spirit had constructed the universe as a vast and complex machine for purification of the light, it is the advent of the Third Ambassador that begins the cycle of redemption. Now time begins, and the sun and moon revolve through the heavens; the different cosmic cogs start to move; and the various events occur that will lead to life on earth, and thus ultimately to the salvation of the soul.

Once again the enlightener speaks: The Am[bassador performed ten] [35] works by his advent.

[The first: (87) The] Great Builder came forth to build the new aeon. /

[The second]: The ships moved through the heights in the heavens. /

[The th]ird: The wheels begin to s[e]nd the lif[e / to] earth and the upper worlds.

The fourth: [...]

[5] [The fifth i]s the d[o]ors of the ships, that they were opened up / [...

The] sixth is the doors too [... / ... that they were opene]d to receive the waste.

The seven[th i]s / [the sin], which he had separated from the rulers by cause [of the Th/ird Amb]assa[do]r; it fell upon the earth.

[10] [The eig]hth: [Ni]ght and day were separated [... / ...]

The ninth: The abortio[ns fe]ll / [to the g]round.

[The] tenth: Transmigrations [came ab]out / [i]n [the] zone.

••• 35 •••

(87,14 – 87,29)

15 *Concerning the Four Works / of the Ambassador. /*

The displaying of the image of the Ambassador to the rulers of darkness is a crucial moment in the history of salvation, and achieves a first purification of the light that is bound up in the rulers. This leads to the establishment of the heavenly bodies; to the beginnings of life on earth; and ultimately to the completion of the salvific process in the ascent of souls to the sun and the return to the kingdom.

[On]ce again the enlightener speaks: At the time when the Amba[s]sa/[d]or displaye[d] his image, four great wor[ks] were re/[v]ealed that are very excellent and outstanding.

20 [The f]irst is his image that he displayed in [a] / glorious [image].

The second is all the doors of the f[irm]a/[ments] that were opened at that time. They ope[n / ...] and shut behind him. /

[The t]hird is the light [a]nd the releasing that was purified by 25 his image. That lig[ht] is more than the li/[g]ht that he shall [...] /

[The f]ourth: He has [made appar]ent, by the perfection of people, his / light [s]hip. He has [...] the living soul that sho/[ne forth in] perfection and fullness over the worlds of enmity.

••• 36 •••

(87,30 – 88,33)

/ *Concerning the Wheel that exists / i[n fron]t of the King of Honour. /*

The King of Honour is enthroned in the seventh firmament from where he is able to control and judge all the evil powers fettered in the heavens. The wheel is here presented as a divination device by which he can know the plans and tricks of these demons as they seek to escape; but also the location of the five shining men, that is the soul mixed throughout the material universe.

[Agai]n the [apostl]e speaks about the wheel that exists in front /
[of the King of Honour who dwells in] the seventh firma[35][ment
...] the root of the rulers above and (88) below in a great and cruel
fetter; as the entire will / of the great King of Honour is placed in
[it]. / Also, their entire enmity, which is in the firmaments, is
[...] / and ensnared in it. It exists in a blaze of splendour [with] [5]
ornamentation and great beauty. Now, there are twelve / seals in
it. The seal between i[s] every [fi]/r[ma]ment and the rulers
who are there [... / ...] are in it; for should one of them wish to
escape, he will be bound / [...] if he should wish to cause a trick in
his bond [... [10] ... will be] apparent and known in [that] wheel /
[...] the spheres and stars and [the] l[ea]der of all the powers /
exist there, and can be known by it; / i[n f]ront of the King of
Honour. /

The twelf[t]h seal that is in it is its five [15] shining men that are
conjoined and enmeshed through the entire zone; becau/se every
place where they are cramped, and every place where they have
s/p[ac]e, is displayed by that wheel. / For the root of all the
firmaments above and be[l]/ow, and that of their rulers, is
ensnared and fixed in it. The observation [20] [...] is set right at all
times opposite the great King o/[f Honour ...] so that fear, wh/ich
[...] will assume all the powers of mixture [... / ...] their root
affixed there, so that they can not make an esc[a]pe / from the
fetter of their bond. That wheel rese[m][25]bles, in this respect, a
chain in front of the chief gu/ard, for when [...] in th[ose / ...] in
the [... cha]in[*39].

This is / also the case for all the rulers who are in the firmaments, and every power / of the zone: If they should wish to
escape, they shall be [30] recognised and revealed by that wheel. /
[As] the wheel is like a great mirror, for [the di]/scrimination of
all things [... is] / in it. (89)

---

*39   Reading [ϩⲁⲗⲧ]ⲥⲓⲥ

••• **37** •••

(89,1 – 89,17)

/ *Concerning the Three Zones.* /

The three 'zones' are those of the five powers of darkness, both male and female; the five sons of the First Man; and the five sons of the Living Spirit. The universe is so constructed that the first must depend upon the second, and the second upon the third. Thus the material powers are placed in the most vulnerable position, being 'hung' from soul; and the sons of the Living Spirit are in the strongest, holding the universe in place. Of these the King of Honour in the seventh firmament has a key role.

[O]nce agai]n the enlightener speaks about the Living Spirit: W/hen he built and constructed the worlds, he suspended the zones [5] on their zones, and within another zone also. The first zo/[n]e is the five powers of darkness, males and females. / This is why he hung one zone on a zone! He hung the five / powers of darkness on the five shining men, the sons of the M/[a]n; because all the enmity is entwined and bound in them. [10] Also, within the zone are the five sons of the / [Living] S[pirit; b]ecause the entire edifice is suspended from them, it being [... / ... he]ard (?) him too, the oth[ers ... / ...] after them. And this is the one who came to [... / ... the fi]rmaments above [... [15] ...] which is in one zone, is the great [King of Honour] / who e[xists ...] within the [... / ...] of the universe.

••• **38** •••

(89,18 – 102,12)

/ *Concerning the Light Mind and* [20] *the Apostles and the Saints.* /

This long and complex chapter demonstrates the correlation between the macrocosmos and the microcosmos of the human body. The prodigious gods and demonic beings who inhabit Mani's worlds are here integrated with the more accessible workings of religious psychology. These insights into the life of the community aid an understanding of the appeal and success of Manichaeism.

89.21 – 90.14 A disciple asks Mani a series of questions about the Light Mind, the god who enters into the believer and transforms the old man

into the new man. How can this happen, and why does the old man continue to rebel? He also asks Mani about his apostolate.

90.15 – 92.8 Mani begins his discussion with the macrocosmos. The
universe is constructed in the form of a human. Its life and soul are the five
sons of the First Man. The five sons of the Living Spirit are the intellectual
qualities, who act as sleepless guardians, each firmly established in its place.
The summons and the obedience, that is the active will to salvation personified in Jesus the Youth, become the sixth sons of each. The Pillar of Glory,
the Perfect Man, is the Mind in the universe.

92.9 – 94.16 The five sons of the Living Spirit each have their appointed
watch-districts. Yet, demonic rebellions have occured in each during the
course of cosmic history; and have had to be dealt with by various gods.

94.17 – 95.1 Similarly the Light Mind dwells in the human body, and
needs to deal with the treachery of sin manifested by the old man who still
lies bound within. Mani assures his listeners that despite the recurrence of
evil the powers of light know the final victory; and thus always act for the
good.

95.2 – 10 Mani briefly answers the disciple's question as to how the mighty
Light Mind can live in this small fleshly body.

95.10 – 97.24 Sin constructed the human body from evil matter. Yet, its soul
is divine, being taken from the five sons of the First Man. The five intellectual qualities were bound in the body and overlaid by corresponding evil
qualities. This led the soul into error and forgetfulness of its true origin.
When the Light Mind comes it frees the divine qualities, binds the evil
ones, and imprisons sin. Thus the believer is transformed into a new man.

97.24 – 99.17 Nevertheless, sin can rebel and cloud the intellectual qualities, leading the believer once again into error. Mani explains the process
by which such a person may gradually come to turn against the true faith,
despite the love and support of church leaders and friends.

99.18 – 100.17 Mani emphasises to his disciple that he has now explained
the workings of the Light Mind in the body, whose role corresponds to that
of the watch-keepers in the macrocosmos. By purifying the spiritual intellect
the elect can ascend in their hearts to God the Father, and know everything.

100.19 – 102.3 Mani now turns to the disciple's final question about his
apostolate; and explains how he, although a solitary man against the world,
has been victorious over all the kings and earthly powers. Thus he has
achieved more than all previous apostles, excepting only Jesus.

102.4 – 12 The disciples thank Mani and promise to be strong in their
faith.

[O]nce again, at one of the times, a disciple questioned the
[apostle] / saying to him: You have told us that the / Light Mi[nd]
is this one who shall come and assume the saints. [You sai/d] it to
us like this: He too is one among the gods [... 25 ...] many gods are
with him. You have also told / us: [W]hen he enters withi[n the
body / of] the flesh and binds the ol[d ma]n with his five counsels, he / [set]s his five [couns]els upon him in the five limbs /
[of his] body.

[So], no[w], where is he? In that the old man is chained in the bo³⁰dy! For I see how rebellions arise there despite / his bondage, from ti[me] to time.

Also, secondly, I a/[s]k you: If then he is a great God, unchanging and im/measurable, how could he come and appear in the smallness of the bo/[dy]?

The third thing I want you to recount to ³⁵ [me ...] a holy one is the Mind, and he is pure; / [...] the defilement of this body?

(90) Fourthly: If truly the Light Mind exists in [the s]/aints, why is his likeness not displayed to us, the way th/at he is?

The fifth thing I want, for / you to tell me and explain about your apostola[te]. ⁵ Look, it is not clear to me! For they oppress / and persecute you in the world. /

I entreat you: Can you persuade me about these things that I have asked you? /

T[hen] he speaks to that disciple: My en[tire] revelati[on], / which I have unveiled, I have declared to my chu[r]¹⁰c[h]. In your presence! This one alone among [... / ...] him.

This disciple says [to the apost]/l[e]: All that you have unveiled you have [...] / in our presence. Yet, I wanted to kno[w ... the] / L[igh]t Mind, the way that he is.

¹⁵ Then the apostle says to him: If I shall repeat [... / ...] to you about these things that you are so set upon, and they become true [f]/o[r] you after you are so set upon them, will you understand what you [... / ...]? On your account I will give vision to they who see! I will / make the living fountain overflow for the thirsty, that they may drink and [l]iv[e].

²⁰ Then speaks the apostle to him: All the error, when the / en[e]my of the lights constructed it, he constructed after the likeness of / a man. The head of the universe is the beginning of the garments. / [H]is neck is the nape of the garm[ents]. His stomach [is / the] five unfolded ones (?), which a[re ...] of the garm[e]nts. ²⁵ His ribs are all the firmament[s]. His navel [is the] / sphere of the stars and the signs of the zodiac. And, also, [the

par]ts [that] / come from his navel to his hip are [... / ...] that come from the sphere t[o the corne]rs of the four / worlds. His loins are the th[ree eart]hs that are below [... u]^{30}pon the head of the Porter. His [...] from the [...] / to the earth upon which the Porter [is stood] firm. / His shins and his feet a[re ... / ...] and the entire zone that belongs [...] (91) His heart is mankind. His liver is the four-footed / animals. His lung is the race of birds that [fly in] / the air. His spleen is the race of fish that swim in the wat/ers. His kidneys are the world of reptiles that creep [up]^{5}on the earth. His outer skin is the wall that [... which] / surrounds the piercing and the great fire. His [...] / the vessels of the great fire. His [...] / of darkness. His gall is the [... His] / great intestine is the breadth of the great [... ^{10} ...] of the worlds. His veins [...] all [the spri]/ngs and wells. His e[yes (?) ... / ...] His feet are his [... / ...] /

This is how each of the worlds h[ave been ha]rmonised (?)^{*40}. ^{15} F[iv]e g[od]s are fastened in him. [...] / they are his soul and his life [... / m]an is a sinner [... / ...] the Living Spirit and the Ambassador [... / the] five sleepless guardians.

He has [...] ^{20} the Keeper of Splendour, the mind that is [... in the wo/r]ld of the mind that is above. He has [... who]le [...] / of the powers of hea[ven that] are in [... / of] the great King of Honour, [who is the thought that exists / i]n the seventh firmament. He has humbled [... ^{25} ...] also of the Adamant of Lig[h]t, who is the insight [... / f]rom {}^{*41} he has given [...] because of lust [... He has] / also appointed the King of Glory, who is the coun[sel ...] / patience over the three images; that of wind, that of / fire, and that of water. He has handed over to him the [... ^{30} ...] do evilness. / [...] the Porter, who is the consideration [... / the wi]sdom in the [...] which is below. He has made him [... / ...] the foundation [below ...]

(92) Furthermore: The Ambassador refined from them five / intellectuals of life. Also, the summons / and the obedience were situated there. Now, they made six sons of the Living Spirit, / together with the six sons of the First Man!

---

^{*40} Reading ⲉⲧⲁ[ⲩⲧ]ⲙⲏⲧⲉ as ⲧ]ⲙⲉⲧⲉ
^{*41} ϩⲛ ⲧⲙⲏⲧⲉ Also 93.6

⁵ Further: The Ambassador placed in them the great Mind; / who is the Pillar of Glory, the Perfect Man. /

Furthermore: Jesus the Youth was set there; who is the / image of the living word, of the utterance and the obedience. /

He has made strong these camps, those above and those below ¹⁰ [...] each one of them will be secure in the circuit of his [watch-]district, / so that neither uprising nor treachery are made in his watch-district. /

And look, see! The Keeper of Splendour is set firm in the / great mind, in the camp above the pris/on of the bound ones, for he brings to nothing [a]ll the gloo[m] of de[ath]. ¹⁵ An[d a] treachery came about, and an uprising! The sin abor[te]d, [it / tangled i]n with the soul. It became mixed with this light that it / expelled toward the image of the Ambassador. It went [... / ... in the] third firmament that is above the watch-t[ower / ...] the Keeper of Splendour. From that place also it tang²⁰led in with the light. It was detached and came down / to that which is dry and that which is moist. It [fashio]ned the trees [up/on] the dry (land); but in the sea it immediat[ely] took form and / made a great uprising in the sea. /

Again, look, see! The great King of Honour, who is ²⁵ the thought, he is in the thi[r]d firmament*42. He is made [...] / with wrath. And an uprising [came about]! A treachery and a[n] / anger happened in his camp. The watchers / of heaven, who came down to the earth in his watch-district, / they did all the deeds of treachery. They have revealed crafts ³⁰ in the world and have unveiled to people the mysteries [of] / heaven. An uprising came about, and a destruction, on the earth [... / ...] to it.

The Adamant [...] / the fulfillment. He is set firm upo[n ...] **(93)** and a treachery came about in his camp; the occasion / when the abortions fell to the earth. They formed Adam / and Eve. They begat them so as to reign through them in the world. / They fashioned every object of lust upon ⁵ the earth. The entire world was filled by their lust. / Also, {} they persecute the churches.

---

*42 Probably an error for the seventh firmament.

They kill the / apostles and the righteous in the watch-district of the Adam[ant] / of Light, time after time, and from generation to generation. /

Once again: In the watch of the great King of Glory, wh[o] [10] is the great counsel, he who exercises authority over the thre[e] / wheels. A [dis]turbance came about, and an affliction, for [they were ...] / pained and oppressed in the three earths. After the Ambassa/dor displayed his image, the paths closed to their / [... th]eir ascent was impeded by them [...] [15] the w[ind], the water, and the fire ascend on them. /

[O]nce again: In the watch of the Porter, he who humiliates [... / upr]ising of the abysses below [... / ...] bent, the fastenings underneath were loosened [...] / in the foundation below.

[20] [On] account of the earthquake that happened in the watch of the Keeper of Splen/[dour], the Pillar of Glory came forth; as it [... / ...] helper of the Keeper of Splendour. It bore up under all [burden]s. /

Conversely, because of the treachery and the uprising that / happened in the watch of the great King of Honour, which is the wat[25]chers who came down to earth from the heavens; / four angels were called upon about them. They bound the watche/[r]s with an eternal chain, in the prison of the blackened ones (?). / [Th]ey obliterated their children from upon the earth. /

[Th]en, again, the abortions descended in the watch of the Adamant [30] [and] begat Adam and Eve; because of that great treachery wh/[ich] happened, and the mystery of wickedness, he sent Jesus / [...] the prayer of the five sons. He assumed them / [...] the abortions. He fastened them beneath the / [... the] mind of Adam.

(94) Also, because of the earthquake that happened in these three / earths, and in that the paths were hindered and the springs of / wind and water and fire were impeded, Jesus cast himself down. He / assumed Eve; and he straightened the tracks of the [win]d, the water, and [5] the fire. He opened the springs for them, and he set [in ord]er the path / of their ascent.

Once [again]: Since the / earth beneath the Porter was loose[ned from] the fastenings that / [...] because of this too Jesus went down, assuming / [Ev]e until he reached tha[t] place. [H]e set in [or]der and stre¹⁰ngth[ened] the fastenings beneath. He returned, [he came] up to his / [...] rest.

Then speaks the a[po]stl[e] to him: / Look at all these watches of the zon[e], the ones in which these / great gods are master, w[atch]ing over them [...] / Uprisings have happened, and treachery, in them. The [... ¹⁵ ...] in them from time to time; with a great hum[iliati]on, / until they humbled the powers of the enmity. /

So also is this body! A mighty power lives / here, even if it is small in its stature. Nevertheless, s/in dwells within, and the old man who is lodged in it. Certainly he is cruel, ²⁰ with great cunning; until the Lig/ht Mind finds how to humble this body, and drive it [according to] / his pleasure.

Just so, in the w[atch-]districts / of his great outer brothers, they who are masters in the zone. / In them, in the great body: the earthquake and treachery happened ²⁵ from time to time. So, also, is the watch-district of the / Mind, which is the body of the flesh. Sin raises [up], / from time to time, its agitations in the body. /

Now you (pl.), understand thus, that the powers of light / are good. The beginning and the end are unveiled to them. ³⁰ All that they do is being done with correct judgement. / Indeed, because of this they may permit the enmity / to initiate error, and do its pleasure [for] / a moment. Then they seize [... **(95)** ...] they have acted first with a righteous judgement. /

And [with resp]ect to this other (question) that you have put forward: How may the Light / Mind come, this great and honoured mighty one, and assume this little / body of the flesh? Again, look, see! These gods, in that ⁵ [... are] great and mighty ones. And each one of them is enclosed and hard pr/[essed] i[n this pl]ace wherein he is set; like trees / [hol]ding to their taproot. So also this is how each / [o]ne of them has 'held to his taproot' in the world, according to / [the] k[ind] of place in which he is set, bearing up till ¹⁰ [...]

Now, also, happen you know / [...] the world is set firm, being ordered [... / the five sons of the] Living Spirit in all its members / [...] sin took this body out from [the] la/[nd (?) ... co]nstructed it in its members. It took its [bod]y ^{15} [from the five b]odies of darkness. (Sin) constructed the body. Yet, its / [sou]l i[t] took from the five shining gods. / [(Sin) bou]nd (the soul) in the five members of the body. It bound the mind / in bone; the thought in sinew; the insight in vein; the cou/nsel in flesh; the considera-tion in ski[n].

(Sin) set f^{20}[ast] its five powers: its mind upon the mind of the soul; / [its] thought upon the thought of the soul; its insight upon the insight / [of] the [s]oul; its counsel upon the counsel of the soul; its consider/[atio]n upon the consideration of the soul. It placed its five / [an]gels and authorities upon the five members ^{25} [of the] soul, which it had brought in and bound in the flesh. They / [...], pronouncing to the soul and continually leading it on to / every evil thi[n]g, to all the sins of lust, to the / [wor]ship of idols, to erroneous opinions, to humili/[ation]; in the humiliation of slavery! As it is set fast, wors^{30}[hipping] the things that [...] will not remain; making obeisance / [...] idols of wood and gold and silver. / [...] worshipping beasts (96) that are unclean and polluted! They are ugly in their appearances and their / forms.

(The soul) assumed error and forgetfulness. It for/got its essence and its race and its kindred; kn[o]/wing not the door of the place to pray to him, nor call up ^{5} to him. It became hostile to its father [... / ...] itself, being wicked [... / ...] its own light [...

The] Light / [Mind] comes and finds the soul [... / ...] it assuming it in the [... ^{10} ...] its wisdom [... / ...] he shall become for it [... / ...] the bonds [...] / members in the body. He shall loosen the m[ind of the soul and relea/se] it from the bone. He shall release the th[ought of the soul] ^{15} from the sinew; and s[o] bind the thought [of the sin in] the sinew. He shall release the insight of the soul from the vei[n]; / and so bind the insight of the sin in the vein. [He sh]all / loosen the counsel of the soul, and release it from the flesh; / and so bind the counsel of the sin in the flesh. He shall ^{20} release the consideration of the soul from the skin; and bin[d] / the consideration of the sin in the skin. /

This is how he shall release the members of the soul, / and make them free from the five members of sin. / Conversely, these five members of sin, which were loose; 25 he shall bind them. He shall set right the members of the soul; form / and purify them, and construct a new man of them, a child [o]/f righteousness. [And] when [he] fashions and const[r]/ucts and purifies the new man; then he shall bring forth five / great living members out from the five great memb[ers]. 30 And he places them in the members of the new man. He shall place his m[ind], / which is love, in the mind of the new man. Also, the th[oug]/ht, which is faith, he shall pl[ace in] the thought [of the] / new [man]; whom he shall purify. His insight, which [is perfection, he shall place] (**97**) in the insight of the new man. His counsel, which [is] / patience, he shall place in his counsel. Also, [w]is/dom, which is his consideration, in the consideration of the new m/an. He shall make the image of the word pure from the word of 5 sin; and he adds to it his word, so that his / [... be]comes nourisher and strengthener [... / ...]

Now, when he shall perf[ect / ... the tw]elve members. This [is how / ...] and his wisdom. His [... 10 ...] becomes righteous, as he perf[ects ... / ...] While formerly he was running [... / ...] but instead of this, now he runs [... / ...] his road and his path and his [...] / also [he mounts up] to the heights, to the great aeons [... 15 ...] thus the old man is bound in the [... / ...] and his lust, his [...] his / foolishness in these five members of the bo[dy ...] / the dark spirit is imprisoned with them in a bond and in / severe misery.

Also, the new man reigns 20 [b]y his love, by hi[s] faith, by his perfection, [b]y his / [p]atience, and by his wisdom. Yet, his king [... / the] Light [Min]d, he w[ho is] king over the totality. He re[igns] o[ver it / according to] his pleasure. While the members [...], / thus sin is imprisoned. Still, the Light Mind 25 [is] king, and an affliction may arise in the body from t/[im]e to time.

There are occasions when sin shall mount / [u]p with its foolishness; and it disturbs the consideration, and it clouds / the wisdom and the understanding of the person. It causes truth to be s/[pl]it into doubt in him, and he utters some foo[li]sh words 30 and some [... W]hen the manner of his foo/[lishn]ess will come to the [...] in the church, the teachers and / [the ...] and the [...] and the

presbyters shall gather / [...] helper. And they put straight his
wisdo/[m ...] His consideration has been set right (**98**) [about]
this. His wisdom has been set in its right place and ordered [... /
...] well.

Now, if he shall not accept the rebuke / and the edification of his
brethren and his helpers; then shall / sin mount up again,
another time, from the consideration to [5] the counsel. It takes his
patience f[rom him], and bestows upon him / faint-heartedness
and hurt. And the [si]n is displ/[ayed] in the midst of his
brethren. His [...] for / every [thing] that he shall do [...] / advice
of his brethren, and he becomes [...] [10] the [fo]olishness. A battle
and a war shall arise / (between) the Light Mind and the sin in
the counsel [... / they sh]all group together and become [... / ...
the]re, and they cause him to cease from the [... / ...] and they put
him straight in his place another ti[me ...] his [15] compa[nio]ns in
his struggle.

If again the [...] / to that place, then again sin shall rise [... / ...]
and clothe him with lust and vanity and / pride. He separates
from his teacher and his brethren. / [He sh]all always [w]ant to
go in and to come out alone. [20] He shall want to eat and to drink
alone, a solitary man. [He sh]all / always want to walk alone.
Indeed, this is the [si]/gn that the familiarity of his brethren does
not act on him.

Should he again not [...] / his heart from lust; again sin shall
mount / up, the thought of death, to his thought. He shall [...] [25] a
vanity; and causes his f[ai]th and his truth to le[a]/ve him.
When the sign of his foolishness will be [dis]/played, and his
reputation spreads in the church, the [wis]/e ones of the church
shall gather to him; so [that] they may set right his [heart], / and
encourage it with God's edification. If now he took [the adv][30]ice
of his brethren, and listened to [...] / and set himself apart from
his wrath and [...] (**99**) It is possible he could live and be victorious
over the sin, and all its wars. /

Yet, if he shall not make this watch secure, (sin) shall rise up /
and assume his mind; and disturb his mind, which formerly
was calm. / It shall disrupt his love, away from his teacher and
his [5] instructor. It shall take from his heart love of the churc/h,

and fill it full of hatred. And all his brethren become hateful /
before him. H[i]s brethren and his loved ones and his friends /
who love him; they shall be like enemies before him. / Now, that
person is disturbed like this, and he lets his 10 love and his will
turn from him. That person shall / [himse]lf become a vessel of
loss, and he separates fr[om] / the church, and his end comes
down to the world. / The Mind, who was in him, sh[a]ll disperse
from him and go / to the apos[t]le who sent him. He shall be
filled by evil spirits; 15 and they deal with [him], dragging [hi]m
hither and thither. And he himself becomes like / wordl[y]
me[n]. [He] will change and become as if a b/[i]rd, were its
feathers plucked out. He becomes an earthly man. /

[T]hen, have I taught you, and opened your (sg.) [eyes], as to
how / confusion shall arise in the zo[ne]; in the camps of 20 these
great mig[hty] gods? Again, this is how / disturbance shall come
about, from ti[me] to time, in the [...] of the / [Li]ght [M]ind. So
al[so] these watch-keepers, for they are set [... / f]i[rm in] the
zone, (but) they are not visible. Again, this too is the way / of the
Light Mind, [for he is] not visible in the body.

25 Also, [corr]esponding to th[ese] outer [watch-keepers]; in that
while they are great, / [y]et have they contorted themselves.
They have [...], they have become small, to the measure of the
task / [th]at is apportioned to each o[n]e [of t]hem. Again, this too
is like / [the] Mind, himse[lf] a great one, and exalted; but he is
bent over / and [has] become small, to this little worthless [bo]dy.

30 [Even so] the gods [in the] outer [z]one: they are transcendent /
and purified, they are set [f]a[st in] the mingling of the totality,
(but) are not defiled. / [This too is like the] Light [Mind]. While
he is placed in hi[s / ...]

(100) Again, behold the mightiness and the activity of the Light /
Mind: how vast he is over all the watch-districts of / the body! He
stays fast at his camp. He shuts off / all deliberations of the body
from the beguilements of sin. 5 He limits them and distributes
them out. He sets them down / at his pleasure.

Also, he does another work, surpassing and ex/ceeding (these).
He bestows a great spirit upon the ele/ct one. Indeed, now may

you find him, as he stands on the earth, / [r]ising up in his heart and ascending to the Father, the 10 G[o]d of truth. He who exists and is established above / all the things of loss. [Onc]e again, he may push dow/n [i]n his insight and his consideration, and descend to / the land of darkness, from where the darkness has poured forth. / His heart shall run and touch everything, as it [...]

15 Then he says to [th]at discip[le: I have taught you] / the deeds of the [Light] Mind! Whoever has / an open and percept[ive] eye, [he can] appear to him. Whoever / has not that eye, he can not appear to him. /

And, also, as to my work that [is] not [manife]st nor revealed to you, 20 the deeds that I have done; I will teach you about t/hem, and open your eyes [to] this wonder [...] / and of my leadership. /

Observe from this! That I, a single Manichaios, I have come to the wo/rld alone. And the races [and] kindreds of the body, 25 and the gold and silver and [br]ass [...] copper, and the / many gifts and breast[plates and] armour of [the] / multitude, and [m]uch humani[ty], submit to me. / Many types of gods and idols from / smelting furnaces! You (pl.) have beheld the k[ingdom] of the world. For, despite great effort, [ev]30en with many benefits and [gif]ts, with a / breastplate and a violent war; they have not subdued [the ci]/ties nor conquered the countries. [Yet, I, I have conquered] / without breastplate and without [armour] (101) distant [cities] by the word of God, and distant countries. / And they bless my name, and it is glorified in all countries. /

[Und]erstand also another thing that I will teach you. The k/in[g]s have striven with me, and the nobles and [offi]5cials and their powers, so that they might bring to nothing this truth. T/hey did not have the strength for this against me. Now, if I am alone, / why did they not have power against me? Namely, all these who have [striv]/en with me.

The third thing: [No on]/e in the world has given freedom to his children [a]nd 10 his brothers and his kin, and made them fr[ee] f/rom the variance of all things, the way I have. [I who have made] / all my children free from every toil and every [... / ...]

The fourth thing: I have [cover]ed them / with the breastplate [of

wis]dom; so that you will not find a single one among man[15]-
[kind ...] and he is victorious over them. For as no single per/son
is able to be victorious over me in the entire world; so it [i]s also
like this for my children. No person will be able to be victorious
over them! /

[The fi]fth thing: I have chosen with my power this entire great
elect/ion. I have given my children my emblems of authority [...
[20] a]nd the great springs of wisdom, so that [...] / apostle [...] of the
church [... / ...] I have made it mine. I have made my church
strong, and appointed in it / all [goo]d things that are beneficial to
it in every matter. / [I have pl]anted the good, I have sown the
truth in every land, f[25]ar and near. Apostles and ambassa/[d]ors I
have sent to all countries. Therefore, the former apo/[st]les who
came before them did not do as I have do[ne / in] this hard
generation; apart from Jesus only, the son of / greatness, who is
the father of all the apostles. [30] [S]o, all of the apostles have not
done as [I, / I have] done! Look again, and see now: How great is
my / [power] and my activity? For not one among the former
apo/[stles, ... i]n the flesh has reached my like in the / [...]
through me. For this great (**102**) door has been opened, opened by
me, to the gods and the angels and / mankind, and all the spirits
and the living souls, who are prep/ared for life and eternal rest. /

Then, after his disciples had heard all these sayings, which he [5]
proclaimed, his disciples answered. They say to him: Gre[at] /
and mighty are all these things that you have uttered to us; which
/ [you] have [do]ne by your power, and the power of the one who
sent you. Who / could fully recompense you for the grace that
you have d/one [u]s, except this one who sent you? Still, the
on[l]y gift [10] available to us, to repay you, is this: that we will
make ourselves strong in / y[our] faith; and persevere in your
commandments; and / also be per[s]uaded of your word, which
you have proclaimed to us.

••• 39 •••

(102,13 – 104,20)

/ Concerning the Three Da[15]*ys and the Two Deaths. /*

Patterns of temporal and sequential classification were of great importance
to Mani, who used them to structure his system, to teach, and to evangelise.
Compare chapters 4 and 17. The particular focus and interest in this
kephalaion is the eschatological detail. Life in this time and world is but a
precursor to the reign of the saints in the new age and the new earth.
There the First Man, the victorious son, will be king (H. 41.11-20). However,
this too comes to an end; when the hidden Father at lasts reveals his image,
and receives the souls and gods back into the heart of the eternal kingdom,
from where they have been barred since the beginning of the conflict. In
contrast to this glorious hope, sinners are warned of a second death,
eternally separated from life and the divine.

Once again the apostle speaks to his disciples: Hap/pen you
know, my beloved ones, that there exist three great / mighty days
in all; and also two great / and bitter deaths.

When his disciples hea[20]rd they say to him: Tell us our father,
what are th[ese] / three great days? Or again, what are these two
de[aths] / that are bitter?

He speaks to them. / The first day is our father, the Man. From
the ti[me] / when the First Man went down to the abyss of
darkness [25] and drowned in it; and the Living Spirit was sent, who
w[ent] / and bore him up. After the Man had ascended, the
Father o/f Life and the Great Spirit set things in order, and the
wo/rlds above and below.

Furthermore, the glorious [Am]/bassador came and dwelt in the
ship of the day. [30] He displayed his glorious image, and he
purified [the li]/ght out of all things. He walked in the heights of
the [hea]/vens. Till the time when the world will be dissolved, /
all things destroyed, the great [fire] released, / and the Last Statue
ascends. [35] These three deeds were be[gun] on this first [day,
when they sent] / the First Man with his five [sons].

In contrast, [the first death] (**103**) is the darkness that mixed with the five sons / of the First Man.

The second day / is the time when the fathers of light, who were victorious in the struggle, / will sit on their thrones in the new aeon and dw⁵ell on the new earth. And they reign in the new [aeon] / till the Father unveils his image / above them.

The {length of the sojourn}*⁴³ in the [ne]w aeon / equals the measure of the first day spent [in affli]/ction. They will reign like this and rejoice in [the n]ew [aeon].

¹⁰ The great third day [is the time] / when the Father will unveil over them his [image ... / ...] and he raises them up [...] / and he receives them in to his hidden treasur[y ...] / and he gives [...] his soul. He can pour out upon th[em ...] ¹⁵ his ambrosia and his sweet perfume, which ta[kes away] / all affliction that they have seen with their eyes. [...] / fullness and a joy eternal! When his / [g]race would sate them, he gives to them his [...] a/[nd t]hey are made anew in them. Also, he can summon them once more [in] peace ²⁰ and silence, and perfect their stature in sa[m]e measure / as his first aeons. And he sets each power / [i]n its aeon, in its dwelling-place. They will dwell in the [n]ew aeon / in their aeons! Now, when they dwell in / their aeons, they will become rich beyond measure, ²⁵ for ever, beyond time.

From then on they will not count / that season amongst them; nor the number / [o]f the days, nor the hours, generation after generation, for / [e]ver and ever. The Father will not be hidden from them, from / [this] tim[e] on. Rather, he has accomplished (his) unveiling to them [...] he being revealed ³⁰ [to them] for ever.

These are the three great days, / [which the Fath]er o[f Gre]at-ness has given number to in the reck/[oning].

In contrast, the two deaths that I have pro/[claimed to you a]re [these].

(**104**) The first death is from the time when the light fell to / the

---

*⁴³ ⲡϨⲁ ⲙⲡⲧⲟⲩⲱϨ Smagina 1990:118–9 translates as the 'winnowing of the chaff', treating it as an agricultural image for purification.

darkness, and was mixed in with [the] rulers of darkness; un/til the time when the light will become pure, and be separated from the dark/ness in that great fire. The remainder left be⁵hind there can build and add to that Last / Statue.

Now, the second death is the death in which / the s[ou]ls of sinful men shall die; when / [they will] be stripped of the shining light that illuminates / the world. And also they are separated from the living air, from which they receive ¹⁰ [livin]g bre[ath]; and they are deprived of this living soul, which / [...] in the world; and they are separated and swept / away from this Last Statue [... / ...] and bound on [... / ...] the female will become [...] ¹⁵ their torture and their affliction; for their deeds [...] / those three places; because they have blasphemed and despised the / Holy Spirit since [ev]ery generation of the world.

These are the / two deaths. The first death is temporal; [but] the sec/ond death is eternal. It is the sec²⁰o[nd deat]h!

••• 40 •••

(104,21 – 105,14)

/ *Concerning the Three Things that / were established by the Light.* /

This chapter continues the eschatological theme of the previous. Since the enemy had attacked the light in the beginning, three results became inevitable that would alter the relationship between the two principles in their future eternal separation: the new earth is built over this universe; it will imprison the darkness as in a coffin (?); and the souls of sinners will be condemned and crucified on the enemy.

This doctrine of the final lump, the literal mass of the damned, was an essential part of Mani's system. The tragic loss of some of the light soul, too deeply enmeshed in darkness and sin to be saved, was accepted as an inevitable consequence of the power of evil. In order to ensure that the darkness could never again multiply and rebel against the light, its powers (especially the males and females) are separated so as to sterilise it, and to prevent it planning an attack.

O nce again he speaks to his disciples, these who are not associates in the my[stery*⁴⁴] ²⁵ of his knowledge: Three things

---

*44   Technical term, see note ch. 52.

would be fashioned / by the light through necessity! For there can be no other way / nor other result, to allow them to stay without coming about. For / the darkness, the enemy, mu[st] be bound by them; he who stood up again[st] / the light from the beginning. Due to this, these things have no (other) res[ult], [30] to allow them to stay without coming about. /

Now, the first thing is the new luminous earth, w[h]/ich was set and built on top of this earth [...] / it, namely that alien body [...] built upo[n it]. /

The second thing is this: They will [...] and they [...] [35] the new earth, the coffin [...] (105) of the dark fire, the companion of the enemy.

The thi/rd thing is the souls of all the sinners who have been con/demned by their deeds. They were [...] over them woe; they have been / condemned according to the wicked deeds they had committed, and due to this they will be crucif[5]ied on the enemy, he who had raised himself up against the greatness.

They will / seal up*[45] this final lump when / all the likenesses and images of every shape will be nailed in it. Also, those will be bo[und] / by this last fetter for eternity, and be [plac]ed / as a footstool and a mat*[46] and a rag for this coffin [...] [10] which is the prison of the enemy. It will be placed, being a [bound]ary-/marker and a great void between the two, between the [dark-ne]ss / and the enemy, so that they can not reach one another, nor can they [h]ea/r their voices; rather they will become sterile as they are separated from each other / for [eve]r and [e]ver.

---

*[45] ceλϭe Cf cωλϭ (Crum 333b), citing Ep. 253 and 549, vessels sealed with clay sealings. Smagina 1990:116–7 suggests that the souls 'will make the cover of ...'

*[46] Cf H. 5.4 and 76.23 where it has the meaning 'trample'. Smagina 1990:117–8 translates 'they will be laid as a foundation, and a base, and a cover of this Ark'.

••• **41** •••

(105,15 – 106,21)

*/ Concerning the Three Blows that / befell the Enemy because of the
Light. /*

The eschatological focus continues with further details on the final binding
of the darkness, and the separation of male and female respectively in a
lump (βῶλος) and a tomb (τάφος). Mani uses the description of the fate of
sinners to exhort the faithful to remain firm despite persecution.
    The sequence of content in chapters 39 – 41 provides a good example of
how Mani's lessons have undergone some rudimentary redaction in the
construction of the *Kephalaia*.

[O]nce again he t[u]rned, and says: The darkness itself, the
enemy, / has received three bad blows with three wars; and [20]
worse dangers from the light in those three wars. /

The first: (The enemy) was brought out to the middle and
separated / from his dark earth, whence he had departed. He was
vanquished / in that first war, caught and / [bo]und by the living
soul.

The second blow [25] is the time when he will be dissolved and
melted, and he perishes in / this great fire. He is destroyed and
overthrown, from the images / that are all by which he exists.
And he will be gathered in / [to the] fetter corresponding to his
archetype, and be made like he w/[a]s from the first beginning.

[30] [The t]hird blow that will befall the enemy is the 'rolling back'
/ [at the] end when everything will be separated, and male will
be divided / [from] female. Now, the male will be bound in the
lump, [b]ut the fem/[ale] w[ill be thrown] i[n] to the tomb. For it
will be divided / [... by a great] stone in their midst, for
generat[35][ion upon generation, for ever and] ever.

(**106**) This is the way that the binding of the enemy will come
about, in a fet/ter that is burdensome and strong, one from which
there is never escape; / because [they have achieved] his binding
and bound him for ever. / And they have achieved his being set
apart, and he has been set apart for ever.

[5] Due to this I say to my beloved ones: Hear my words / that I proclaim to you! Gird yourselves for the things o/[f li]fe. Endure the persecutions and trials th/at wi[ll come] to you. Be you strong in these commandments that I have give/n [y]ou, so that you may escape those two deaths [10] and be free from this final bond [i]n which there is no hope of / lif[e]. And you will escape the terrible end of the de/niers and blasphemers who have seen truth with their own eyes, and have turne/d back from it. They will go to the place of punishm[en]t [where]in / there is no day of life. For the enlightening light will bé hidden fr[om t]he[m], [15] and they will be unable to see it from this moment. / Air and wind will be drawn from them, and they will not receive life breath / in them from this moment. Waters and moisture will be taken from them, / and they will not taste them again. /

Blessed is every one who will escape the end of sin[20]ners and deniers, and be free from the ruin that lies hidden for ever!

••• 42 •••

(106,21 – 111,17)

/ Concerning the Three / Vessels. /

This kephalaion begins a sequence of three complex chapters wherein Mani seeks to justify the actions of the Living Spirit in his construction of the universe; and in particular his management of the three vessels of dark elements (water, darkness and fire) by means of the three vessels or garments of light elements (wind, water and fire). Essentially, the Living Spirit discharges down to earth the dark elements from the rulers who are bound in the heavens; and then 'sweeps' them out to the edge of the universe into pits that have been prepared for them. The light elements ascend up through the universe to purity and rest. Since this process must result in some contamination on earth, Mani is at pains to explain that it has been done in the best possible manner.

106.32 – 107.26 The Living Spirit is like a good doctor who discharges sickness and poison (the dark elements) by means of healing drugs (the light elements).

107.26 – 108.16 The light elements cause the dark to be discharged as a child is from its mother.

108.16 – 36 The processes by which the dark elements are poured upon the earth and then swept out to the edge of the universe are carefully managed, so that each occurs at the appropriate time.

109.1 – 111.17 These actions have brought twelve advantages. In the first of these Mani explains that the timing by which each evil vessel is discharged is such as to keep the contamination to a minimum. The other advantages relate to details about the purification of the heavenly realms, and the containment of evil.

Once again the disciples questioned the enlightener, saying t[o h]i[m]: 25 Tell us, our master, and instruct us about these / three vessels that [...] and were discharged fr[om] / above, and how they were discharged and separated from / all [the] rulers who are arranged in the [heaven]s. For it is a ne[ce]/ssity for us to know [the manne]r in which 30 the three vessels have been discharged, while the rulers were [flour]/ishing in their body. /

Then the enlightener speaks to his disciples: [Hap]pen you [kn]/ow, my beloved ones, that when these v[es]/sels [were dis]ch[arged], they were discharged in [...] 35 slaughter, but those [...] these [ves](107)sels from them.

They are like the for[m] / of a man who has fallen into a purulent sickness. Other wounds / and diseases are in his body, and even bile and other po[i]/sons are in his inner limbs. [H]e achieves good 5 health by a wise doctor, who gives him one remedy to drink that causes hi[s] / purulent sickness to break out above, and gives him another medicine to drink / that causes his sickness to discharge below, [and he gives him] / yet another medicine [to drink] that cures his wounds for him [...] / calmly and silently. Through the skill of a 10 wis[e] d[oc]tor, with his effective medicines to consume that t[ake awa]y / all sicknesses [in t]his manner and dissolve all magic, the d[oc]tors shall / [...] they work cures through the aroma of the medicine, other wounds / [...] what is hidden, they at last tear them out from / [...] manifested above and below 15 [... throug]h the aroma of edible medicines that were placed upon them. /

This is also [w]hat these vessels / of water, of darkness an[d o]f fire are like, which are hidden in the body / of all the rulers above; while the Living Spirit is li/ke the wise doctor. These three healing d20rugs are the three garments that the Living Spirit assumes / upon his body: of wind, of water, and of fire. / Through them he has set in order the things below. For by those th/ree garments he has been displayed to the rulers who are / [ab]ove,

with hard-heartedness, with shaking and fear, with [25] derangement; from them he discharged the three ve/ssels, those of water, of darkness and of fire.

The case / of these vessels is just [lik]e a / [ch]ild who is in his mother's [wo]mb and is swathed by sev/[e]n garments. The first [is] the marrow, the second is the bones, [30] [the] third is the [tendons], the fourth is the flesh, the fi/[fth] the veins, the [sixt]h the blood, the seventh / [the sk]i[n of] the bo[dy th]at covers him. The other garment also [... / ... in the wo]mb of his mother. His mother also / [is] ju[st like] this child. The marrow [35] [and the bones, the sinews and fl]esh, the veins and blood and [sk](**108**)in, together with the garment that she wears and the linen that swa/thes her, total nine. Together wi[th] the nine of the child, these and the / others, they shall complete and make eighteen garments. Now, you shall find the / soul of this child is entwined within all these. [5] And look see: When the smell of / the action of the demon, which brings about the stench of birth, wi[ll rev]eal the child; immediately [...] shall / [...] all [these things] and it emerges from a crack that has becom/e visible, while no tear nor wound occurs in the body of [10] the [chi]ld. In the same way as this child [opens up] / the w[om]b of his mother, so is it also with / these vessels of water, of dar[kness] and [of] / fire. The actions that open up his [mother]*47 / to the child, and she shakes him out and reveals [him; these] [15] are the three living garments that the [Living] Spirit [assumed on / his]*48 body.

For by the aspect of the garment of water [... / ...] from the rulers; he moved / [...] they are the poison and / [d]eath with which their veins and entrails are filled.

[20] By the aspect of the garment of wind, in [which] he was revealed / [...] he has swept away and erased the entire destructive shadow / and dirt, discharged it down to the earth. Afterwards / he swept it out and confined it in the vessel of darkness that / surrounds the universe.

Also, by the garment of living fire, [25] through its splendour and

---

*47 Restoring ⲁⲧϥ[ⲙⲉⲩ]
*48 Restoring [ⲣ̄ϣⲟⲣⲉ / ⲁⲍ̄ⲛ ⲡ]ⲥⲱⲙⲁ

vigour, he discharged the fire of the dark[ness f]/rom all the rulers and t[hrew] it down upon this earth. He swept [it] / another time from the earth and confined it in the vessel that surrou/nds all the worlds, and they call [i]t the wall of grea[t] / fire. Now, those three garm[ents], through which he [estab]³⁰lished these three things, he did not peel t/hem off all at once; but h[e strip]ped them off one by one / at the appropriate time [...] down [to the] e/arth [...] /

In this way the universe of the [... ³⁵ ...] his vessels [...] / these vessels like [...]

(109) Furthermore, he continued. He says to his disciples: The us/e of the matter, and the management of these vessels that were swept o/ut and discharged from above to [eart]h, have brought an advantage and benefit of / twelve great deeds. Afterwards, they were swept from the ear[th] ⁵ and pushed outside to the edges of the worlds and to the {extremity}*⁴⁹ / of the zone.

The first deed is this: So that evil-doin/g does not increase in the universe, neither in the creations nor in the tree/[s ... it has set i]tself up in three things.

The [first is / ...]

The second is error [... ¹⁰ ...] Indeed, about this I have spoken to [you] as I / [...] For, if it were so, if [the ves/sel of water] had not been [swept] down from above, but rather the wat[ers / existing up t]ill now in the rulers above [... / ... the] torrents that would flow [...] and the droplets that would ¹⁵ [...] down, so lust would have sprouted / [... i]n the trees and in the fruits as well as all flesh / [...] down [... / t]oday [...] / you could [not] find a single person [...] in the [... ²⁰ ...] a saint does [...] is master of [...] / Not only this, but if the vess/el of darkness had not been swept out and thrown down to the earth, nor swept from / the earth and cast outside the region of the worlds / into this pit; again the drops of darkness, which will drip down from it, and the torrents ²⁵ that will continue to flow down from above to the earth and assume / [the] trees and [a]l[l] flesh, would have multiplied, and the

*⁴⁹ ⲧⲕⲁⲓⲟ

forget/fulness that is in a thousand people today you would have found in / [just] one person. There is not one among mankind [...] him / [...] the thought and the knowledge of the [...] /

[30] [Further]more, if the fire were in the rulers of the worlds of the heavens until / today, and had not been swept out and cast d/[o]w[n] to the earth, and swept from the earth and shut up i/[nside] the vess[el] of fire that surrounds the worlds; / [...] this fire [... [35] ...] abo[ve] through the torrent / [... the tor]ren[t ...] below; (110) and the dark fire wo[ul]d have multiplied in the tree and in fruit / and in all flesh. The power of the fire that is now in a thousand / people, you would have found it occurring in a single person / today. You would not have found a single person embracing [5] the fast in the universe.

Behold, I have taught you about / this single evil that w[as] purified by three archetypes [... / ...] /

The second deed: Al[l] the heavens [... / ...] of the sed[im]ent and the pollution [... [10] ...] so that [... / ...] surpasses in [th]em [...] /

[The third]: The heavens and the firma[ments ... / ... b]urden [...] relieved from the weight-ca[rriers*50 ... / ...] and it ceased being heavy. This rich one [... [15] ...] above.

The fourth: Th[at they might pur]/ify and cleans[e] their dwelling places [... / ...] /

The fifth: Because the great[ness and the rich]ness that dwells in / thes[e shi]ps, as it [...] you might find them [20] [living i]n these ships, purified and holy. /

The sixth: That you might find the mixed, incomple[te], / and unconfined temples above at res[t a]nd purified; since / rest will reach [them] and pass through them and purify th[em]. /

The seventh: [...] nature alone of the vessels, which will [25] advance and extend to their places and sites [... / ...] in [...] /

The eighth: That great enclosures and walls would be made, and / confine everything. /

---

*50 Read ⲉⲥⲉⲓⲧⲉ ⲁ̅ⲛ̅ⲃⲁ̅ⲓ̅ⲉ [ⲧⲡⲱ See 115.5–10

The ninth: When the apostles [...] them, they [30] shall return to the universe and give a sign of [...] / the dissolution of the universe. /

The tenth deed: That they would become releasers and purifier[s of / every]thing at the end of the universe like the fir[e ... / ...] burns [...]

[35] [The] elevent[h d]eed: [...] will make a crossin[g ...] / and the entire rul[ing]-power [...] (111) to the outer land, for they were not envious of this [...] / a man who is richer than them; because the aeons of lig/ht are outside [...] the place [...] of / peace, the place of honour and grace, the place where the j[5]oy of the householders who dwell in it shall never pass away nor / recede.

The twelfth: That you might find all the deeds / of loss hidden from the aeons of light, / because of the wall of fire that surrounds the entire building; and / these [un]clean things are displayed (only)*[51] in its [...] /

[10] There was [a] need for these twelve great deeds b[ecau]se the / vessels that were discharged and swept out from [the firmaments] / to the earth, and were also swept from the earth to the {extr[emity}*[52] ... / ...] the three words of life watch over them that [... / ... ar]e set over them in great power [15] [...] that they might watch over t[hem] at the last time; because / of this, they are firmly se[t t]hus i[n t]hese fetters, in the way that I have told / you.

●●● **43** ●●●

(111,18 – 113,25)

/ *Concerning the Vessels.*

Following the previous chapter this kephalaion provides further details about the vessels, and the creative activity of the Living Spirit in the construction of the universe. The demiurge is termed the Father of Life, an epithet that may provide evidence of a particular stage in the development of Mani's thought. The term is often used in the *Kephalaia* when this god is paired with the Mother of Life; see chapter 9.

---

*[51] ⲍⲱⲧ Probably a scribal error.
*[52] ⲧⲕⲁⲓⲟ Also 109.5

111.26 – 112.18 The Living Spirit poured out the vessels of water, darkness and fire (dark elements) upon this earth; and then scooped them up by means of his three garments of wind, water and fire (light elements). The dark were finally poured into three pits that he had constructed. However, a remnant of each remains upon earth, dark qualities that mar the light.

112.24 – 113.19 The Living Spirit had a particular reason for this process, even though it has some negative results. The dark elements that he poured down from above drew towards them those on the earths below; and thus all this waste could be swept out together into the pits that had been prepared.

113.19 – 25 Now that the levels of the universe have been purified, the light elements are able to ascend through them.

²⁰ [On]ce again the disciples questioned him, saying to him: Wh[en] / the Father of Life discharged these three vessels from / above, they of water and of darkness and of fire, did he perhaps / discharge them to their pits at the edge of the firmament? Or did h/e discharge them first to this earth, and then he swept them from the earth ²⁵ [a]nd threw them to their p[lace]s? /

[Th]en the apostle says to them: As for what you have asked me a/[bo]ut the vessel[s], you must understand this, that when the Father / [of] Life was about to di[sc]harge these three vessels he / [p]oured the three upon this earth, one by one at its (appointed) hour and ³⁰ season. He discharged them and cast them down to the earth. /

[Th]en he bailed and scooped them from this earth in these thr/[ee] garments, they of wind and of water and of fire, which swathed / his body. He poured and made them flow into the three pits / [... w]hich he had [es]tablished during the construc[tio]n of the worlds ³⁵ [...] they [...] something remained (**112**) behind on the face of the earth from these three [v]ess[e]/ls, so that you can find their mark and type display/ed in the universe.

The e[le]m[e]nt that is left in water is / the pungency and the salinity of this salty inner sea that surrounds ⁵ the worlds.

And the remnant that is left from the darkness / is this black mountain that exists in the s[urroundings] of the sunrise. / For when the sun would shine over the world no / sunlight is visible there, because the darkness that gushes / fr[om i]t manifests above it.

And [the re]mnant ¹⁰ that remains behind from the fire, upon the earth, are all the mountains / and islands from where fumes*⁵³ of fire gush up / [an]d are visible. For these things are the remnant of the great ve/ssel, the vestige that was conjoined with this fire that comes up / from the earth; together with the mountains and hills [...] ¹⁵ place[s] where no fruit sprouts on the tr[e]es [...] / greater than that place from the limb and [... / ...] the trees shall not bear / fruit in that place. /

Once again his disciples speak to him: We ask you, our master, ²⁰ to [make clear] and instruct us about the vessels that / surround the universe, and why they were not discharged from above into the / ditches prepared for them (straightaway); but were firstly poured / upon the earth, and afterwards were swept from the earth and cast dow/n into their pits?

Then the enlightener speaks to his discip²⁵les: Happen you know this! When the Father o/f Life discharged these vessels from above upon the earth, he poured them out / for this reason: so that also the water and the darkness and the fire that / exist in these three earths would be drawn a[nd] ascend towards they / that had come down from above, and the earths [would be] purified and c[l]³⁰eansed. Due to this he poured these vessels down to the eart[h], / of water and of darkness and of fire, so that also / the water and darkness and fire that exist in the earths would be drawn up [tow]/ards they that had descended from above.

Now, first o[f] / all, [h]e discharged the water, the waste, [the p]oison of the rule[rs] ³⁵ who are above. He c[leans]ed the firmaments of the [water ...] / he poured do[wn] the [da]rk waters. [Just as the] (113) waters fell from heaven to earth, so also the wat/ers below in the earths were drawn and came u/p from below towards the waters that had come from above to the earths. / The waters [were] purified of the dark poison that exists in them. ⁵ Then he swept them outside and made them a great ve/ssel and a wall of sea that surrounds the universe, / and on w[hi]ch the ships sail.

After the water, he / discharged the darkness. He purified the

---

*⁵³ ⲥⲁⲗⲙⲉ Perhaps from ⲥⲱⲗⲙ Cf Crum 330b.

firmaments and dried from t/hem the darkness with which they are weighed down. He discharged it down to the earth. [10] Just as he had purified the firmaments, so also he puri[f]ied th/e earths. The darkness that is in the earths was drawn up towards the darkness [t]hat had been / [discharged] from above. He swept them both out and s[hut them] i/[n] that [...] of darkness [... / ...] the water.

And he discharged the fire from heaven to earth, [15] [... at] that time again the fire that was shut / [in] the earth below was drawn and came up towards its kind. / Fire was added to fire. After-wards, he swept it out and cast it / into the outer underworld, which [he had constructed fo]r them outside the uni/verse.

In the same way that he purified the firmaments above as a place [20] for the light-givers to journey [... / ...] so also he purified the earths below and sw/ept from them the fire and the darkness and the water [...] / He has purified them for the ascent of these three powers, they of the wind and the water / and the fire, which ascend before the Porter and [25] traverse the earths.

••• 44 •••

(113,26 – 115,31)

/ Concerning the Sea / Giant. /

113.29 – 114.3 The Living Spirit causes his son the King of Glory to turn the three wheels of wind, water and fire. Thus these good elements are set free. However, the waste of the evil elements (water, darkness and fire) that have been poured onto the earth from the three vessels; this he deposits in the sea. Therefore, its water is salty and bitter.

114.3 – 115.4 Also in the sea is the monstrous giant that takes form from the fire and lust, the active evil 'thought', in the waste matter that the Living Spirit has swept down from the sphere (also 136.23 – 26). Consequently, the sea giant has sealed upon him the aspects of the stars and the signs of the zodiac.

115.5 – 31 The divine plan has three purposes: to purify the sphere of the evil elements; to use the sea giant as a fetter to prevent the evil astral powers ascending or descending; to gather in the sea all the good and evil elements that are washed into it. All the good life that comes into the sea will be purified.

[On]ce again the e[nlightene]r speaks to his disciples: After the
[30] Livin[g S]pirit constructed things and the worlds, he came up
and / [s]et himself upon this earth. He gave a sign to the King of
Glory, who / [t]urned the three wheels and caused the wheels
that are found [...] / up above all the mountains; he spread forth
the wind to / [the]m, he breathed on them, he stirred them up, he
washed the earth with the water[35]s. And the waste and the
accretion of the three vessels, they of / [water and of] darkness
[and] of fire, which had been discharged upon (the earth), he
gathered them / [and deposited them in the][*54] sea that is within
the walls (114) and the vessels; because of this sea waters are salty.
/ For they have received salt and bitterness from the washing out
and cle/ansing of the three vessels.

When the Father / of Life came, rising in his ascent to the
heights, he dischar[5]ged the wheel of the stars; he washed it out
and loosened / all the [sedi]ment that was in it. He cast it down to
this great / inner sea like [...] of the mountain. And t[ha]t waste, /
the sediment of the washing out of the wheel, he cast it do/wn
and mixed it in with the sea waters. Its own th[10]ought collected it
together; and (the thought) gathered (the waste) together in / this
w[a]y. It made it fa[s]t and fixed it [...] / The sea giant had
stamped upon him the seal of the seconds a[nd the hours], / the
seal of the days [and months and] / years, the impression of the
stars and the signs of the zodiac[*55] [...] [15] He came into existence
from them and was discharged from their power / and cast into
the sea. The images and the seals and aspects and / doctrines and
counsels of [...] were sealed upon the body / of that giant, because
he is the residue of them all. Consequently, / each star that will
shine, and each sign of the zodiac that will tu[20]rn: of one he shall
be its inducement, and of another its confirmation. H/e was
discharged into the sea like this, the way a cloud / might discharge rainwater into the midst of the sea. They compelled / him
totally through the action of the power and the helms[man]/ship
of the angels. He was swept down to the mill, the pla[ce w][25]here
he was constructed in the [sett]ing up of the universe; and the /
sea also conceived him [...] for its part [...] / it being his chief

---

[*54]   Restoring e.g. ⲁϥⲥⲁⲩ̄ⲅⲟⲩ / [ⲁϥⲕⲁⲁⲧ ⲙ̄ⲙⲁⲩ ϩⲓ̈ⲥⲛ̄ ⲧ]ⲑⲁⲗⲁⲥⲥⲁ
[*55]   See 157. 24 – 25

sculptor and chief cra[ftsma]n. It sculp[ted h]/im in a likeness, he being changed more than the other residue of the sea / bodies.

This matter is comparable with [a] [30] craftsman who might take the stamped impressions of many co[i]/ns and cast them on the fire, and mould them [to a sin]gle image. / These thousands of impressions and thousands [of sha]pes [are perfected] / and make a single body [...] /

(115) This is also the case with the sea giant, who too was moulded / and sculpted by the power of the lust inside him / from many doctrines and counsels th/at belong to the residue of the wheel of the sphere.

[5] The archety[pe] of the giant was constructed for three things.

The first: / That the sphere would be [re]lieved and purified of the burden pres/e[nt in] it. In the same way that the ten firmaments were purified and [re]li/eved [of] the burden of the three vessels; so / was it also done to the sphere, that it too might be relieved [and] puri[10]fi[ed] of the burden and the waste inside it. /

The second: That he might add a {fetter}[*56] and a prison to the wheel / and the signs of the zodiac that are bound to it, so that when / they wish to go up above, you can find the s[e]a / giant dragging them back as by an [i]ron {fetter}, [15] and they are unable to go up; and when the powers / of the wheel would take a decision on a guileful thing, and it enters their / mind to come down to the earth, they are not able to descend because / of this stake that is nailed to the wheel upon the {}[*57] / of the firmaments. This is one. However, this other one, because of its [20] sleepless watchers that are set over it, it is turned all the time. /

[The t]hird thing: That the [wind] and the water and the fire that gush from / [the] c[ircui]t of the sea, [and the r]ivers that flow upon the face of / [the ear]th discharging into the se[a], and the rainwaters that come to gr/[ound], and the wast[e] and rebirth that come [25] [dow]n to it; that sea will be a hostel / [and g]athering place for all of these.

---

*56 ⲟⲩⲱϣⲛϥⲧⲟ Also 115.14
*57 ⲕⲁⲣ.ⲍ

As for all the power and the li/[fe] that comes down to the sea, and in the breath that the / sea gi[ant] will breathe and draw it into him that he might disturb the sea / [... a] fullness and a [...] becomes between his movement [30] [...] purify; but the sea / [...] (116)

••• 45 •••

(116,1 – 117,9)

/ Concerning the Vessels. /

The point of this chapter is the foreknowledge of the powers of light that has enabled them to prepare places to hold and contain various evil forces that arise during cosmic history, until their final imprisonment with the dissolution of the universe. Thus: three ditches for the evil vessels; the sea for the sea-giant; a place for another monster that arises from the sea, and which the Adamant vanquishes (also 136.27 – 137.4); gehennas for the waste of the darkness; 'hostels' for various evil powers who rebel; places (?) for the abortions; a prison for the watchers; cities for the giants of old.

Understand also this other (matter): Before these / vessels were discharged and swept down from heaven, fi[5]rst three ditches were fashioned and constructed for them, / in which they would be bound and fettered. /

Before the sea giant was discharged from the s/phere, the Father of Life constructed a place for [him i]n / this great sea that is within the walls, whereon the [10] ships sail, and where the fullness shall [... / ...]

Also, before the [...] / was displayed to the worlds [...] the earth [... / ... f]ell to the sea and its thought shaped / it, the Father of Life constructed a place for it in [the ... [15] ...] below the four mountains, above / the mountains of the heavens above [...] / that [...] a great plain it di/gs in Matter in the midst of the worlds. When / the Adamant of Light was sent to it, he hastened after it to [20] that place, smote it and threw it between mountains in / the place made ready for it [...] is set fast / upon it till the end of the universe.

Before / the waste and dirt of the darkness were swept out from / creation, [ge]hennas were constructed [i][25]n which the waste might be cov[er]ed till the dissol[ution] of the universe. /

Before the rebels r[ose u]p, they whose co[rps] rebelled / in the ruling-power abov/e and below, they [...] / outside, and also the tyrants in [wh]ose heart it lay [to ty]³⁰rannise amongst the murk and [the clo]uds and win[ds and] / spirits and storms; for them were constructed in the great outer [s]/ea seven host[e]ls, places whence / they are thrown into the depths and the da[rkness ...] /

Also, before the abortions [fell ... ³⁵ ...] to the earth, there was set apart [...] (117) they are gathered in and dwell therein.

Again, before the / watchers rebelled and came down from heaven, / a prison was fashioned and constructed for them in the depths / of the earth, below the mountains.

⁵Before the children of the giants were born, they who had [no] knowledge / of righteousness in them nor divinity, / thirty-six cities were assigned and co[nstructed] for them wherein the children / of [the giants would] live; they who would come to beget from each / othe[r, they w]ho shall spend ten hundred years alive.

••• **46** •••

(117,₁₀ – 118,₁₂)

/ *Concerning the Ambassador.* /

The point of this chapter, which connects it to the last, is again the foreknowledge of the light. Although entitled *Concerning the Ambassador,* his advent is actually only one of a number of discrete moments in the overall plan of the light chosen to illustrate the idea of determinism.

(1) The Third Ambassador is evoked before the beginning of time, and thus prior to the start of the process of salvation, which is his principal purpose in the drama.

(2) The sun and the moon are prepared for their tasks in the salvific process.

(3) The Judge is emanated.

(4) Christ is ordained in advance of the sects coming into existence, to render them harmless.

(5) The stars and the signs of the Zodiac determine the fates of mankind.

(6) The gods of destruction are made ready to dissolve the universe.

(7) The first architect, the Great Builder, and his angels are summoned to construct the new aeon.

Once again, hear this other lesson that I would teach you! /

Know that before night and day / were differentiated in the universe, the Third [15] [Am]bassador was summoned. And, afterwards, he was sent to this void / and outer waste that he might purify the light, / and separate night and day from each other. /

[B]efore the light was released and freed and ascended / through this zone, the Father of Life made beautiful for it the ships [20] of light. He constructed them so that it might be purified in them, / and be sculpted and fashioned in good order. /

[Bef]ore sin had multiplied and had made a kingdom in the flesh, before / the acquitted and the condemn[ed] were set apart from each other, / the Judge [w]as sent forth and revealed. [25] His throne was created and placed [i]n the living atmosphere, so that he would be / [a] just Judge, so that / there the righteous and the sinners would be set apart and tested / [a]nd separated from each other.

Also, befo/[r]e the error and offence of the sects were disp[30][l]ayed in the universe, the blessed Chr/ist was ordained and brought forth against them, that he might render their error harmless. /

Again, [befo]re mankind had been engendered, some were named / ['rich' and] others 'poor' on earth / [...] upon them. Before they die, (118) they who will die are marked out by the stars and the signs of the zo[di]/ac in the sphere. They are appointed for them; in the[m] are their births. / And their root[*58] is bound up with their zodiacal signs; and they are compe/lled by them and brought to an equal judgement [5] in accordance with their deeds and their sins. /

Again, before the universe is dissolved, [and the] entire earth, / the destroyers were appointed and instructed for its di/ssolution.

And before the ne[w] aeon was [built and] / made be[auti]ful and marked out [10] [the] Great Builder [w]as summoned, the first architect and the / angels who are with him, who would build and make beautiful the / new aeon.

---

*58   I.e. people's fate.

••• 47 •••

(118,13 – 120,20)

/ *Concerning the Four* 15 *great Things.* /

The entire 'ruling-power', the collectivity of evil cosmic forces, is apportioned into the four parts of the universe. Three of these are: the ten firmaments; the eight earths; and the surrounding walls and vessels. The fourth is the wheel of the stars, and here are bound the leaders of all these evil rulers, the seven planets (although Mani's system demands the introduction of two ascendants instead of the divine sun and the moon, see 168.7 – 16) and the twelve signs of the zodiac.

Mani explains that this had to be very carefully arranged by the Father and Mother of Life, when they constructed the universe, so as to balance the leaders against their powers. He develops an extended analogy to show that a king is only equal to his retinue, who in turn are equal to the kingdom. Thus, the gods are able to keep control of the evil forces in the universe, although the stars determine the entire created order.

O nce again the enlightener speaks: The wheel of the stars, whi/ch· is displayed to you, is a great mighty thing! Also, it is one / among the four great things; since the whole ruli[n]/g-power is assigned to four parts.

20 The first part is the powers who occur in the ten firmame/nts that exist above the wheel, and the rulin/g-power that is bound in them, as it is imprisoned within them in the heaven/s that are above.

The second part is / the eight earths that are below; the four that are composite, 25 and the four places of darkness. The second part / extends from this earth, upon which mankind walks, towards / the underside.

The third part is the [wa]/lls and the vessels that surround the worlds. / They are the four mountains and the three vessels; 30 with what is in them, and the ruling-power that is trapped within them, / and the powers who are masters over them.

The fourt[h] / part is the sphere of the stars that [is appointed] with [gr]ea[t] / diligence, as it is ordered in a [... m]any [...]; / that of the Father of [L]ife, [and that of the Mother of] (119) the living. Its [...] very [...] with diligence, / because of the great and cruel powers, and the titanic figures, [who are] / in it; they being suspended from it. So, all the first-born and the / leaders of all the rulers, they who were existing in the th⁵ree parts, these were garnered. They were collected together, seized, / bound and assigned on this wheel. Each was apportioned / by these three parts. They were distributed, en[twin]ed, / and weighted against their companions of the same size.

Still, for its part, the w[he]el / is equal to them in its strength; the po[wers] of ¹⁰ the enmity who are bound on it. [Ind]eed, they were suspended on [the] circling [w]he/el because of their cruelty; so that, d[u]e to / the wind and the motion in which they go round, they comp/rehend not the place wherein they are set. For if / they had been bound in the heavens, the heavens would not have had the strength ¹⁵ to support them. Again, if they had been assigned on the earths, on the / fixtures that are below, they also would not have had the strength to support them. / Rather, they were suspended from the wheel of the circling stars; so that / the power and the light that should come up from b/elow can be received, and given to the heavenly ones ab²⁰ove them. Conversely, whatever will fall from above, / whether cold or hot, the wheel / of the sphere will also take it and cast it out / [u]pon the entire earth, upon all the wood.

Behold, the ordinance / of the wheel is in this form. For the powers who are entwined on the ²⁵ wheel are like this: a king mastering his / kingdom by this mighty legionary force of all the lea/ders of the kingdom; and with all the armour / [o]f the soldiery that is collected together for him; and also with / [the] mass of the pro[perty] of the kingdom; and the beautiful lustful aspect ³⁰ of the [wo]men who are collected together for him; together with / [...] property [...] and those cattle / [...] that have been distributed about among his r(120)etinue. Yet, if you ask about that king, he is matched / with all his retinue. His retinue, for its part, / is matched against his entire kingdom. Judgement shall come forth fr/om him, vindication and condemnation, to his entire kingdom; ⁵ by his wisdom, skill and strength. /

Now, just as for this king, who is matched against the measure of his entire ki/ngdom by his wisdom, skill and st/rength; so also is it for the / powers [w]ho are bound on the sphere as compared to the ruling-power, and the [10] powers who exist in the entire zone. Like the king towards his r/etinue; so too is it that this totality is gathered / to the sphere, to seven leaders, to twelve sig/ns of the zodiac. As all the cities are gathered to the king, again they gather / to the leaders of the universe. All that is done [15] in the universe above and below: the battles / and the disorders and the captivity and the hunger and the l/ust and the property; so shall they increase and diminish through / these leaders. They are the motivaters of the whol[e] creatéd order; / the totality being gathered in to them the way that I have to[20]ld you. I have opened your eyes!

••• 48 •••

(120,21 – 124,32)

/ *Concerning the Conduits.* /

This long and detailed chapter is amongst the most difficult in the *Kephalaia;* not least because the decisive term ⲗⲓϩⲙⲉ (lihme)[*59] used in the title and throughout is unknown. Here I translate the term as 'conduit'. The import of the term ⲛⲟⲩⲛⲉ ('root'), which seems to be closely related to it, is also unclear. However, the essential idea is that heavenly bodies are inextricably attached to the earthly; and that the three lihme are conduits through which the divine life can be drawn to ascend and be purified, while the demonic waste is poured down through them. In the next chapter, 49, Mani explains that these conduits are spiritual; and thus can never be entangled nor cut by the astral bodies as they turn though the heavens. The significance of the roots is deterministic; and they must also be spiritual. In chapter 46 Mani explains that mankind's 'root' is bound up with their zodiacal signs (118.3); so this could be translated as 'fate'.

120.25 – 121.12 The first conduit is the root of the powers in the heavens; and stretches from them to their bodies and carcasses that were stripped off by the Living Spirit and cast down to the earths. Therefore, the upper worlds are psychic and pneumatic (soul and spirit); while the worlds below are somatic and ptomatic (body and carcass). Life is drawn up through the conduit to be purified in the heavens; but any waste is poured back down through descending conduits.

121.13 – 17 The second conduit stretches from the heavenly cities to the five kinds of trees. For Mani vegetation was particularly rich in divine life.

*59 See the discussion in Smagina 1990:121–2; and Vycichl 1983:102.

121.17 – 32 The third conduit stretches from the evil heavenly powers to the five kinds of flesh.

121.33 – 122.4 The roots of the wheel of the stars stretch not to earth, but to the heavenly worlds. From these it receives its life.

122.5 – 15 The disciples question Mani. If the stars are not connected to earth, how do they control the fates of mankind and other life on earth?

122.16 – 123.15 Mani explains that when the Living Spirit constructed the universe, he correctly did not bind the stars to earth; although they are bound to the sea giant (see chapter 44). However, when the Ambassador displayed his image to the demons in the heavens and they ejaculated, the sperm fell down on the wheel, the earth and the sea. Subsequently all life on earth developed; and thus the stars control its destiny.

123.15 – 28 The disciples understand, and ask why one conduit is greater than another.

123.29 – 124.22 The first conduit is greatest, because it is bound in all the earths. Then the second, because much life is drawn from vegetation, the Cross of Light, which covers the whole earth. The least is that connected to mankind and other fleshly creatures, because these only cover a small part of the world in the south.

124.22 – 32 Mani's concluding comments.

Once again the enlightener speaks: There are three conduits that e[x]/ist through the entire zone, from the abyss to its heights.

25 The first conduit is the root of all the powers a[b]/ove, they that exist in all the heavens. They are cast off / and fettered on the earths below; because the earth [be]/low is the 'stripping off', the garment and the body of the powers [th]/at are above the heavens.

For when the Father of Li[fe] 30 constructed the heavenly worlds, he di[vested th]em of their bodies, [he] / threw them to the earths below.

So, the up[per] worlds / are of the soul and the spirit; b[ut the worlds] / below are of the body and the carca[ss ...] (121) Now as for this, he [...] the powers of heaven; he se/aled it on their bodies and their carcasses that are on the earths, so that / when life comes up from the fullness of these earths, / it can be entirely drawn up to the heights in the roots of what is heavenly, th5at are fastened in their bodies. And also, all life can be purified in that place. / However, the waste that will be swept from the puri/fied one who ascends to the heights will be let fall to the ground / through the conduits of these conduits, and will be poured down [...] a/nd thrown to the underside. This is the first conduit, wh10ich comes from the powers of the heavens to their bodies and their / carcasses that are upon the earth; also, from their bodies and [their] c/arcasses that are on the earths to the powers of the heavens. /

The second conduit is the one that comes from the temples and dw/ellings and cities that exist in the heavens down to the ground, to [15] the five shapes of tree that grow upon the earth. The life comes / up from the trees to the temples and cities. Life*[60] to/o, and the residue of the heavenly ones, comes down to the trees in a / conduit.

And the third conduit is all the / powers and householders who dwell in all the firmaments, [20] whose roots come down from them to the five wo/rlds of flesh that creep upon the earth, being fixed to one another. / Now, the power and the life that shall be gathered in from the worlds / of flesh are dispersed among them in various shapes. The / powers above shall draw them to the upper side through conduits. [25] [The was]te too, and the l[u]st and the evil-doing and the anger th/[at] will be greater in the powers of [heave]n, shall be poured to the ground thr[ough] / their various conduits. They shall be discharged upon mankind / [and] the other remaining animals. When what is heavenly will wash / the waste and the stench and the poison down on the creations [30] of the flesh below, in their turn the creations shall be greate/r [i]n lust and anger and evil-doing against each other / [throug]h the action of their fathers who are on high. /

The apostle [say]s: [St]ill, look at the wheel of the stars! It has no / [root in this earth], but its roots are bound in the to[35] [tality. The wheel of stars], then, receives life through the power (**122**) and the life that asce[nd fr]om the earths through conduits / and the firmaments above. It (also) takes life from those conduits / that receive up to the firmaments and the heavenly worlds / above it, it takes life out from that place.

[5] Then the disciples questioned the enlightener. They say to him: Look, / in that the wheel has no root in this earth, from where did the stars / and signs of the zodiac find this authority? They became masters over these five / fleshes and five trees. Even though

---

*[60] Probably a scribal error from 121.15

you have told us that / the wheel has no root there! For you said to us that every 10 thing, if it can be reduced from the earth, the heavenly powers above / draw it through a conduit. Also, we see / that every thing that a person will attain, whether it be weal/th that comes into his possession or poverty that will / accrue to him, or his sickness and health; he attains it thro15ugh the signs of the zodiac and the star under which he shall be born*61. /

Then he says to his disciples: Nevertheless, what I proclaimed to / you, namely that the wheel has no root therein, I have recounted to / you properly. It is set aright in its position. For when / the Living Spirit, the Father of Life, constructed the heavens and 20 the firmaments above, he bound their roots in / to the earths below; in their carcasses that he had stripped / from them. Yet, when he constructed the wheel, [he] did not / bind its root in to the e[arths], but he bound the ro/ot of the wheel by the s[e]a gian[t].

And when [the] 25 Ambassador came, he displa[yed] his image / and purified and brought the light o[ut from] all [the] heavens. M[a]/tter, however, which is present in all the rulers, spurted o[ut] / against the image of the Ambassador. It went u[p] / in order to reach it, but reached it not. It dropped back and fell to the [under]30side. Now, when it had fallen from above, it / separated out into three parts.

The first part / fell to the wheel; anoth[er part fell to the earth; an(123)o]ther part fell to the se[a. By means] of the part that fell to / the sphere, [the r]oot was bound in the trees and flesh. / Therefore, because of this, they received au[thor]ity and became masters in the five / worlds of the flesh and the five worlds of the tree. Through 5 the nat[ure] that came dow[n upo]n the wheel / the root was bound in the trees. Also, by means of the abortions / that came to the ground, another root was bound in the fleshes. Therefore, because / of this, the st[a]rs and signs of the zodiac received authority over the trees / and the fleshes: through the root of sin that fell do10wn; and [the ro]ot of the abortions that were aborted there, they fell / to the ground. However, the[se] other conduits that [the] Living Spirit has bo/und in the e[a]rths, they that the soul of the elements c[o]mes u/[p thro]ugh to the

*61 Cf 117. 32 ff. for more on Manichaean concepts of astral determinism.

heavens; tho[se] (conduits) are not bound to the whe/el. Rather, they are [pl]undered from them by the [p]owers on the wheel, [15] that hang from it.

The disciples of the enlightener say: / We beseech you, our master, that just as you have in/structed us and put together this lesson on [...] / you have told us about the prototype of the conduits. / The first is the one that comes from the firmaments to the earths, and [20] the one that comes from the wheel to the sea giant. / That is only one. So, the other root is the one that comes / [fr]om [the temples] to the trees. The third is bound / by means of the abortions in the f[leshes]; also in the fleshes the fathers of the abort/[ions] who are in the heavens [...] are bound and twined, and the[y] that [25] [...]

We entreat you, our master, that you might in/[str]uct us [... about] the conduits, the one that is greater than its / [partn]er [...] as more life and soul is drawn / [...] than its partner. /

The enlightener [says] to his disciples: You have inquired about a [30] [...] and y[o]u have asked about this lesson in superiority*62, great / [... the ea]rth from which much life ascends / [...] the Father of Life has drawn them. (124) He has fastened them from the powers [...] he has bound them in / the earths. (These conduits) are the ro/ots of the ent[ire] ruling-power that the life of the living so/ul is drawn up t[hrou]gh, it coming up f[5]rom the whole earth, from all the mountains, fiel/ds and islands. After that first great root / is the root of the trees, which is bound to the temples / and the buildings above. For there also is much great life / coming up from the tree and the entire Cross, [10] being drawn up from them to the uppe[r si]de like / a gr[eat] ho[s]t. What, however, is lesser [...] of / their conduit [...] he takes up [...] / the roots [...] the earths, they [...] the whole ea/rth in all the worlds. Again, these of the trees are present in [15] the whole earth, whether small or great; but the root of / mankind [...] is not present / in the whole earth, other than only this world of the / south. Therefore, even now these fleshes do not make [...] in the entire wo/rld of the south [...] there is a small [20] part of them in

---

*62 I.e. the lesson is about the superiority of one conduit over the other.

[...] of the upper side / of the world of the south in [...] / in number than the [...]

I have ins[tr]/ucted you about the roots [...] them, [I] / have taught you that they are bound by their [roots ...] i^{25}n with one another. They stir one [anoth]er, they draw / life from one another through the action of the [powers] a[b]/ove, which stirs the nature that dwells in th[em] all. / Now, when the Matter that is in t[hem] will be crushed and [de]/spoiled, then t[h]at Matter too shall [...] ^{30} its members and overturn them and [...] / each other [...] stir [... / ...] (125)

••• 49 •••

(125,1 – 125,24)

/ *Concerning the Wh[eel and the Conduits].* /

The conduits are spiritual (pneumatic). Therefore, they can neither be cut by, nor entangled in, the wheel of the stars as it circles in the heavens.

His disciples say to him: Convince us, our master, ab/out this other thing. How does the wheel circle over the conduits, ^{5} which extend from the heavens to the earths, and it not cut them? Or why / shall the conduits not get entangled in with the wheel / as it circles and drives [... through the u]niverse? /

The enlightener says to them: The reason that the conduits shall not be cut, / for they are not cut, is because they are spiritual. Thus ^{10} the conduits are like the waters through which ships / sail. You shall find the prow that is in position in the / front part of the ship divides the waters, casting t[h]em back / and forth. So, when it parts the wat[ers] / and that ship opens up the water with its c[leaving] pro[w], ^{15} immediately and without delay the wat/ers [min]gle with each other again behind the ship; and the pa/th of the ship shall not be discernible in the midst of the waters. /

Just as when a bird flies up in the air, for its / path is not visible in the air,*^{63} ++ and in the way of mankind, ^{20} in the sun within the

---

*^{63} The text seems to be corrupt here: perhaps a line has dropped out

conduits. They also shall not be tangled up / in them, and neither shall you find their path through the air known. /

This is also the case with the wheel. It turns through the conduits and / the air. The wheel shall not cut the conduits, nor / are the conduits them[selves] entangled in the wheel.

••• 50 •••

(125,25 – 126,29)

/ *Concerning these Na[mes]: God, Rich One, / and Ange[l]; who they are. /*

The many divine emanations in the Manichaean system exist at various levels, depending upon their function in the overall history, and on the directness of their evocation from the supreme Father. In this kephalaion Mani distinguishes the three categories of 'god', 'rich one' and 'angel'.

He then applies these to three distinct moments: the archetypes in the eternal land of light; the emanations who have entered into time and the cosmos; and those who belong to the households of the Great Spirit, the Beloved of the Lights, and the Ambassador. This last sequence is probably intended eschatologically, these being principal figures in the three series of emanations: descent, creation and redemption.

[Onc]e again the enlightener speaks: This one, a name is given to him in / the world. For people pronounce it with their mouths: 'go^{30}[d', 'ri]ch one', and 'angel'. Who are they? Who are the gods? Or / [who] are the rich ones? Or who are the angels? Who are these / [three] archetypes?

His disciples asked him. They say: T/[ell] us, our master, who they are! /

[The a]postle [speaks] to them: There are these three archetypes ^{35} [in the land of light, and there is no measure to] them!

[So], the ones who are call[ed] (**126**) 'god', are the gods whom the Father has summoned / from himself. He has establ[ished them] after the likeness / of his greatness.

---

which finished the analogy of the bird's flight and introduced another analogy about mankind.

Conversely, these who are named / 'rich [...]', are the evocations of the first ri[ch] go⁵ds [of] the Father; because, when the Father had summoned (the first), / they themselves summoned evocations. They called them / 'rich'.

They too, the rich ones, have summoned their / evocations. They call them 'angel'.

These are the three / [archety]pes who occur in the land of light. There is no measure to apply to ¹⁰ them!

Once again, listen! Other persons / who are named 'god' are the emanations who have / come f[r]om the Father; the evocations of the Father whom he summoned forth. / They came out to the contest and humiliated the enmity. /

Conversely, the 'rich ones' are [the ev]ocations of these first living words. ¹⁵ They too, the rich ones, have come and performed and fulfilled the plea/sure of the greatness; [in the] worlds that are above and / below.

On the other hand, the ones who are named the 'ange/ls' are the evocations of the rich ones; who had come from the three / living words. They have been sent in an embassy and ²⁰ an apostolate to this building. They have come to the entire divinity, / which is established in silence and in hiddenness. [An]/d, also, they have come to all the souls who have been entangled in the en[emy]. / They have brought them hope and confidence.

On[ce again] / the enlightener speaks: Again, they are called 'go[d]', ²⁵ all the gods who belong to the household of the Great Spirit. /

Conversely, the ones who are called 'angel', are al[l] the angels / who belong to the household of the Beloved of the Lights.

The ones who are called / 'rich', are all the rich ones who belong to the house[hold of the] glorious [Amb]/assador.

••• 51 •••

(126,30 – 127,23)

/ Concerning the First Man. /

The First Man descends for battle with his armour of the five light elements. These are his garments or sons, the living soul that becomes mixed with the darkness, and which ensures the final victory.

O nce again our light father speaks: When the [First] / Man came forth [agai]nst the ene[my ... (**127**) ...] garment [...] the darkness with the garment / [of] living fire. With that garment he withered / the tumescence (?) of the enemy; he brought down i[t]s foolery / and its vanity. Now, this one alone was sufficient [5] for them. [Y]et, si[n]ce the living fire was weakened, because of this / he added [to it another fou]r garments: that of the wind, that of the water, that of the li/ght, and that of the a[i]r. And this, (why) has he given the four? / He gave them s[o] th[a]t they would be helpe[r]s to t[h]at god, / wh[ich i]s the living fire; so that [...] not [10] with[in] the living f[ire], and penetrate it; and [the po]ison / and the [enmi]ty cut it off.

While the fire received / a bl[ow and] a wound in its body; yet still, / [...] all the powers of da[rk]ness because of it [...] It / [...] necessity [...] brothers, to cause them [15] to receive a blow and a woun[d to]o. The power of the en/emy mixed in with them. Rath[er, ex]cept [the air]. The darkness did not / mix in with it, nor was the burning of the enemy able to penet/rate it. Nevertheless, even the one that remained behind without / the wound, which is the air, it stripped off garment and [20] power. It gave it to its [fo]ur brothers in its place; so that by / that [ga]rment of the living air they would become strong, and / [...] profit, and endure, namely its other four brothers. And it / [be]came for them [...] life.

••• 52 •••

(127,24 – 129,4)

25 *Conce[rning] the [...]*[64] *of the Light.* /

The harmony and common purpose of the divine has enabled the light to overcome, and ultimately to condemn to eternal imprisonment, the evil forces of darkness who rebelled against it. They were disunited in their attack, and thus failed; just as happens between kingdoms in this world. Mani uses this lesson to exhort harmony in truth amongst his followers.

[Onc]e again the en[li]ght[ener] speaks to his disciples: [Now as to what affects the] / light, behold, at the beginning the darkness was strong against it / [...] no disunity [...] exists in the light. /

[...] how far [... the lig]ht that came forth from [... 30 ...] in that place in a / [...] alone / [...] (128) the greatness of the light with one another for ever, / and nor did one of them transgress the command and or/der that his brother had entrusted to him forever.

However, the da/rkness, the enemy, was doomed and overcome; because 5 of the arising of disharmony it was divided within itself. Even the kin/gdom .was divided within itself; [and] ev[en] the [powers, who had] left / their abyss behind and come up fo[llow-ing] it, were do/omed because of the disunity that was present in all of them. / The darkness was destroyed, and its other powers were humiliated, because 10 the p[ower] of that first light functions in the same way / as the kingdom of this world. As long as its [associates in the m]yste/ry*[65] are in agreement with it, th[at] kingdom [...] and / they marvel at it and it receives glory, the one that [...] and it sur/passes and is even more exalted than this other kingdom, which is about [to burst out] against [it].

---

*[64] It would be tempting to restore †[ⲙⲉ]ⲧⲉ 'harmony', since the theme of the chapter is the concord of the light as opposed to the disunity among the powers of darkness: see K 128.19. The four-letter lacuna, however (if correctly transcribed) would seem to be too long for †[ⲙⲉ]ⲧⲉ, and it would also be surprising to find no definite article following ⲉⲧⲃⲉ

*[65] Cf PsBk1. 164.29? (Psalm 121) ⲛϣⲃⲣ̄ⲙⲩ̄ⲥⲧⲏ[ⲣⲓⲟ]ⲛ̣ ⲙ̄ⲡⲣⲟⲟⲩⲉ and 51.14 104.24 128.11.15

¹⁵ Still, the kingdom, [the one that] its associates in the mystery [are in agreement]*⁶⁶ / upon, is compelled to condemn that (other) kingdom; and the[y] / are humiliated and come under the hand of this kingdom that is set up against it. /

In exactly the same way, you yourselves, when you are decid/ed and all agreed with one another, and at a single mom[ent] ²⁰ when you are of one mind about this living truth that is / unveiled to you, then it is possible for you all from y[o]/ur least to your greatest to conquer the sin that is set u[p ag]/ainst you. Should you be divided i[n] / this truth that is unveiled to you – may it not happen! – the [conse]²⁵quence of its happening is that you will be condemned by it a[nd] / also humiliated under [the ha]nd of [s]in, and you / [...] under all its other powers that are set up / [... / ... ³⁰ ... / ... **(129)** ...]

Neither be di[v]ide[d ... a]t your beginning nor / [a]t your end, and you will conquer those above and / those below; and bring under your feet every thing / [t]hat is and that will be!

••• 53 •••

(129,₅ – 131,₉)

/ *Concerning the First Man.* /

This chapter discusses the way that the kingdom of darkness and its powers were doomed from the time of the descent of the First Man. He snared the evil forces by his garment of living fire (see further chapter 51); and thus drew them out of their storehouses. The Living Spirit then constructed the universe out of them; and the storehouses were left barren, like a marsh when all the birds and fish have been netted.

Mani develops further analogies: this is like the human body, where the limbs depend upon the head (see also 84.21 – 25). If a limb is cut off the person remains alive; but he dies without the head. Thus, once deprived of Matter and the evil powers, the storehouses were devastated like headless limbs. Similarly, this is like a dead body, once the soul leaves it.

Once again the enlightener speaks: At the time when the First Man was sent / to the war in the first garment of / [living fire],

---

*⁶⁶ Restoring [ϯⲙⲉⲧⲉ] instead of [ⲡⲁⲣⲝ] of the ed. pr. For ϯⲙⲉⲧⲉ ⲉⲝⲉⲛ see Crum, 189b.

which he gave to the first nature that ex[10] [ists ...] in t[h]at single garment. / [...] he hunted Matter, the tho[ug]ht / [of death, ...] and all its other powers.

[W]hen / [the First M]an came up from the [abys]s, / [... the] Living [S]pirit brought the rulers whom he had [hun]ted [15] [...] element, that [...] of [the land of] dark/ne[ss, that] he might construct from them this universe and fashion / everything appropriate for the greatness. From that time on, / the place of the storehouses of the elements [...] / he destroyed and laid waste the [...] [20] all that were in it.

Just like a marsh, / of which the fish and birds are snared in a net, a/nd only the waters are left behind and the reeds and / the plants that grow in it, this is also the case with the store/[houses of] death. The [First] Man snared their counsels and [25] [their k]in that were [in them], and the storehouses were left b/ehind in their [dwelli]ng place.

So then, the case / [of] the land of darkness is like this, as is that of the storehouses / [t]hat were in it.

[J]ust as the body of man / has [ma]ny lim[bs] in it, [30] [the land of darkness] has [storehouses from] its beginning / [...] all [the limbs] that (130) hang from the great head of the [body]. A si[ngle] root / is the root of them all, because they all hang from / the great head that is on top of the body. Should a limb be cut / from the tip of [the]se small [h]eads, [5] the great head that is on top of them [al]l stays in / its place the way that it is [...]*[67]/ you find this person alive. Al[l] these sm[all h]eads / are firmly set in it [...] / Wh[en] they will cut from them [... [10] ...] all of them, these little [heads] shall [... / ...] the corpses, because they might see [... / ...] be firmly set [...] / in the body, which they joined wi[th it ...] /

In exactly this way, it is also the case [that] [15] the storehouses of darkness are the same, the things from which the [darkness gushed] / forth.

------

*[67] For the notion that the head is the root of the limbs, and its relationship to the extremities, see also 84.21 – 24 and 280.26 – 29

Also, while that Matter / and all its other powers are present in the depths of the / store[ho]uses, they too are alive. Firmly set / were their kin in them, to do whatever they wished ²⁰ in their store-houses. However, from the time when they took the [po]/ison of this nature, they were deprived of (Matter) and it was separated from them, / and all its powers. Those [store]houses and e[le]/-ments became inactive and were devastated, [no en]ergy wa[s in th]/em to do anything.

Just like a bod[y: When] ²⁵ the soul shall come forth f[rom it no] energy shall be found i[n] it, / nor anything ste[ady] at all, because [the] / soul that was in it leaves and has come forth. For [i]t, the ene[r/g]y*⁶⁸, does everything [...] /

This is also the case [with ... ³⁰ ... (131) ...] / when [...] in them [...] / every thing that pleases them in those storehouses [... / ...] the elements that are in them; but when they [took] ⁵ from [th]eir midst death, which is Matter, a division*⁶⁹ [... / ...] storehouses and elements [... / ... a] body that is dead [... / ...] land without life as it has no [... / ... i]n it.

••• 54 •••

(131,10 – 133,3)

/ [Concern]ing the Quality of the Garments. /

The Living Spirit constructs the universe out of the mixture of darkness and light resulting from the deliberate sacrifice of the five garments or sons of the First Man. This is then held in place by his own five sons. Mani compares the Living Spirit to an architect who builds a palace for a king. This metaphor is then extended: the Father of Life (i.e. the Living Spirit) as a perfect carpenter, and the Ambassador as king in this universe.

[Once again] the enlightener [speaks]: At the time when the F[ir]st / [Man ...] he gave the leadership to his five [sons / ... the] Living [S]pirit and the Mother of Life [...] ¹⁵ as the entire ruling-power is entwined and crucified [... / ...] they were poured out

---

*⁶⁸ Reading ⲧⲉⲛⲉ[ⲣⲅ]ⲓⲁ for ⲛⲉⲧⲣⲉ[...].ⲓⲁ of the ed. pr.

*⁶⁹ ⲡⲁⲣⲝ Only here in the chapter as a noun; the root is the same as ⲡⲣⲁⲝ in the previous chapter.

and mixed with each othe[r], / the light with the darkness and the darkness with the li[ght]. /

At that time the Living Spirit called one of [h]is / sons, one rich with power. He gave to him the le[adership] [20] of the garments. Now, he himself [...] of [... / he] hung them and set [them up ... / o]f the Father of [Life ...] he set up / all things [... / ...] he opened [...] ten firmaments [... [25] ...] the wheel of the stars [... / ...] them and the [... / ...]

The Living Spirit is l[ike] / this: Just as [...] and an archite[c/t] who might bu[ild a dwell]ing for the king, and divide it up into [30] separate houses and [separate ... / ...] everything that is requ[ir]ed (132) for beauty [... / ...] and he cleans them. And also the stones [... / ...] them for beauty and {loveliness}[*70], and he a[r]/ranges them and makes them so that should the king come and i[n]habit [5] that [palace], he might glorify him. /

[F]urther[mo]re, the Father of Lif[e resembles a] / wise and skilled ca[rpent]er [... / ...] before [it] was worked [... befo]/re it w[a]s established and made beautiful and [... c]arpenter [10] [...] works in it, but [... / ...] in him in his [...] / in his understanding, and he brings the sa[w ... and] / the a[d]ze, and cuts it into separate piec[es ... / ...] it and he pulls the [...] [15] it with the {plane}[*71] and he smooths it. He shall make many [... / ...] wooden implements, arranging them shape by shap[e]; / he cuts and produces wooden implements from it, / wooden [imple-ments] of different kinds, (such as) dishes, bowls. This wood, that [... / ...] since previously it had not been worked before it was sealed [20] by [the ski]ll and wisdom of this dextrous carpenter. / He [cut] it up into different sorts of implements usefu[l / to hi]s master.

So [is it] also with the Father of Lif[e. / In his] wisdom he has [...] in limbs [... / ...] palace [... [25] ...] in it or in a [... us]eful [... / ... th]e ships of light [... / ...] all [the] other works [...] in the [... / ...] so that when the great king comes, h[e] who / is the Third Am[bassador], who [...] [30] he mig[ht] dwell in this universe [...]

[*70]   ⲘⲚⲦⲢⲞⲞⲨⲦⲈⲚ Cf 162.3 and 206.14 for the same phrase.
[*71]   ϬⲀⲛ

live. The li[ght], / however, that is in it [... (**133**) ...] wise, and he takes it up / [to the] land; but the waste and the darkness / [will be] gathered and thrown down to the abyss.

••• 55 •••

(133,4 – 137,11)

5 *Concerning the Fashion/ing of Adam.* /

133.7 – 135.26 Since Adam and Eve were fashioned by the evil rulers, after the image of the Ambassador displayed in the heavens, some of the disciples believe that the human figure must have divine approval. Mani explains that this is not the case. The Ambassador displayed his image so as to free the living soul from Matter in which it was entangled. The human image is merely a copy of the divine, fashioned in lust, and very imperfect. Mani develops a parable about a beautiful and noble woman who is forced to come out from her honourable seclusion, and display herself to the lust of every man, in order to help her beloved brother.

135.27 – 136.20 In a similar way not only mankind, but also many other powers in the universe, have received the stamp of the divine image. This image could not have originated from the worlds of darkness.

136.20 – 137.11 Not all forms of life have been generated from sexual intercourse. Mani gives three examples: the sea giant; a second monster that rises from the sea and is overpowered by the Adamant; vegetation. Like mankind, these also were not brought by the King of Darkness into the universe. Instead, they are composite forms of life that come into being during the history, and thus are not solely the products of either good or evil.

[Once more his] disciples questioned the glorious one. They say to [him: / There are some amo]ng us telling us that / we [know (?) ...] that the (Ambassador) consents about 10 [tha]t f[igure] of flesh; he who shall be fashi[oned / ...] at another time. And next, he says: / [The Ambassa]dor displayed his image in / the un[iverse. The] rulers and the powers of the universe saw / h[is image], and they formed their shapes after his 15 likeness, who are Adam and Eve. Behold, you (pl.) see that / g[o]d con[sen]ts to its happening; because of this, he has dis/played his image to the rulers; and they constructed [... / ...] If he was not consenting to humankind, he would not have / uncovered his image, nor they fashioned 20 mankind after his likeness! /

[The]n speaks the glorious one to his disciples: Regarding the
Amb/assador, the occasion when he came displaying his image,
/ he [d]id not come so th[a]t he might reveal his image to the
ru/[l]ers in the universe. Rather, he came and displayed [25] to the
universe be[cause of h]is soul and his son, who is / [...] every [...],
that he might enable him to live [... / an]d make for him a
release; and to free (the soul) from / every bond and all the fetters,
in which it is entangled and bound. /

Still, you, look and see! The ru[30]lers and the authorities, in that
they had no form in / [...] him, they lusted for his (134) image.
They reflected upon themselves, that [they] had no [one] / like
him in their creation. They sealed hi[s im]a[g]e / in their heart,
within their soul. Afterward[s, they] / built it according to his
likeness; they formed Adam and [Ev]e. [5] They sealed the image
of the exalted one in their [soul]. So, they / [co]pied with an
imitation; but they have not [copied i]n / truth! Rather, just as [...
/ ...] it is made as these, for [i]t came [...] / but it is not l[ik]e him
in truth. [Again, so too] [10] is this figure of ma[nkind. They
copi]/ed it against the image of the exalted one [...] /

Similarly the [t]ree, for while it is like the [... it is] not [copi]/ed
in truth.

This matt[er is comparable to] / this: As a great, fre[e] woman [...
[15] ...] within her [... / ...] rich in wealth [...] po[ss]essions; / she is
also beautiful in her beauty, and is virtuous in her / modesty. She
walks in a free and reputable position. / The fame of her beauty
has spread in every c[i][20]ty. She sur[passes ...] Behold h[er] /
chamber [...] one who is mad, because [of] / the nobles and the
great ones. Al[so], they lust / for her beautiful face. They did not
[...] her, because / she is hidden in her palace [... [25] ...] within in a
[...] / meet that woman [...] his so[n]; / or rather the head [... t]hat
garment. / This free woman shall [...] leave the cha[mber] /
behind her and come to the street [...] her head [...] [30] and she
reveals her [face and her beauty ... (135) ...] because of her beloved
broth[er]. This wom/an, on whom no man ever looked, nor did
they ever see / her fa[ce], as she neither desires nor rejoices [... /
...] leave her chamber behind her, and come in the midst of [5]
mankind [...] and everyone view her. The / hones[t] men and
the nobles, even the servants too, and the / [... l]ook at her.

In accord with this simile: Again, [this] too [is] how / [...] the Ambassador becomes [... / ...] as this free woman [10] [... not] according to wantonness, in pride, nor / [... she co]nsented to the outer world, she [... / ...], she revealed her face and her [beau]ty / [...] but only due to the constraint of grief / [about] her [bel]ov[ed one].

Now, this too is the way [15] of the Third Ambassador, when he came / and display[ed his] image with a show towards all the powers. / [He did] not [co]me so that all the rulers and the author/[it]ies would sculpt a form [after h]is likeness. R[ather], / he came because of his son being crucified in the totality; [20] [fo]r he would release him, free him, and rescue him from / oppression. Yet, when the rulers looked o[n] him, / [th]ey lusted for his image. They fashioned after his / [like]ness Adam and Eve, without the consent of the gre/[at]ness.

Now, behold, I have e[nl]ightened you [about the a[25]nswe]r to this question, for which you asked; that y/[ou may] happen to commit it to memory. /

[Understa]nd also this other (matter) that I will teach you. For, [a]s / with Adam and Eve, whom the rulers fashioned and / [se]aled after the image of the exalted one, so too [30] this [i]s how a manifold divinity and many powers / [and] angels [... received] the stamp of that image, (**136**) which was displayed to them. For, in the majesty of the l[ig]/ht and (the image's) love, they glowed with their desire and they were undone. / Th[ey] were eager for their lust; like a m[an who looks] / to the majesty of a lusted after face, and [...] [5] and he is eager for the {}*[72] of the desire.

This is [als]o the case / with those powers, when they looked on that majestic / and beautiful [imag]e, they {} [...] / a first image. They received the stamp of th[at image], / which was displayed to them. They copied [... wh][10]ich th[ey co]pied out in a likeness, it being made [... / ...] the ones that they had put forth, which had received a [stamp of this im]/age; but inward even to the rocks [... / ...] which occur from place to place. The {} of that image, /

---

*[72] ϣⲓⲅ Also 136.7.13 Smagina 1990:120 relates the word to ϣⲱⲕ 'dig deep'.

which was displayed in the universe [...] [15] they received a stamp, it being revealed there, and an impress. / Now, this new birth that they begot in a new [...] in / the world, is Adam and Eve. [There is not a] form / in their world since the beginning like it; because that / [im]age [occ]urs not in the worlds b[20]elow.

Not all the figures that have been fashioned / were fashioned by birth from displayed intercourse. / Rather, there are other figures fashioned / [...]

One of them is the sea / [gi]ant, the 'sweeping' from the sphere, which the [Father] [25] of Life discharged into the sea. Its own fire / and thought fashioned it [in] / a figure.

The second figure is the one / [that] fell to the earth. It made the sea its womb. Its own l/ust became its sculptor. It alone fashio[30]ned it to a nature, which is the root of / death. Yet, when it came up from the sea, it [...] / that it might destroy the works [...] (137) of Life. They immediately sent against it the Adamant / of Light, the great 'instruction of vigour'. He humbled it / in the districts of the north. He has trampled underfoot and set h/imself upon it, until the end of the world.

[5] [The] third figure is the nature that fell on wh/[at] is dr[y]. It fash]ioned the tree and set itself there. / [... the] new figure that was fashioned / [... d]isplays.

So, in accord with the essence they / [... the dark]ness; but yet th[ey] did not come with the King of [10] Dark[ness to the wo]rld. Rather, their fashioning [came] about / [...] they are composite and have been displayed in the world.

••• 56 •••

(137,12 – 144,12)

/ [Concern]ing Saklas and his Powers. /

137.15 – 138.19 Consequent to the previous chapter this kephalaion begins with the question as to how Adam and Eve received the seal of the image of the Ambassador, even though they who fashioned them (led by Saklas and his consort as in other accounts) had not themselves directly seen this image. Mani explains that sinful Matter, which had originally seen the image during the seduction episode, led directly through its subsequent generation to those who shaped Adam and Eve. Thus the seal of the image was retained.

138.20 – 141.14 The next section is essentially a separate kephalaion, loosely linked to the previous passage. In repetitive style Mani explains how the various human senses take in, retain, and can then produce from memory ('storage facilities') earlier perceptions. In an excursus (140.22 – 141.1) he comments that the heart governs the senses, and develops two brief similes.

141.14 – 142.11 Spiritual entities guard the gates of the senses (the orifices of the body) like watchmen at a camp. This understanding of the body as the micro-cosmos full of powers is characteristic of Manichaeism.

142.12 – 143.32 When the Light Mind enters the body, transforming the old man into the new (see ch. 38) it takes over the control of the senses, oppressing the old guard that were directed by sin. Now the senses close to the perceptions of lust, and are open to righteousness. In the final part of this section (143.24 – 32) the rule of the Light Mind is referred to as that of the Holy Spirit, an unusual and interesting shift in terminology.

144.1 – 12 Mani concludes by exhorting his hearers always to guard their senses, secure in righteousness, so as to attain the rest or peace that is eternal salvation.

[O]nc[e again the di]sciples questioned the e[n]lightener. They say to him: 15 All [these a]bortions, am[o]ngst them are Saklas and his / consort and the ones whom they have served [...], they are the ones that shap/ed Adam and Eve. How did they find this beautiful image / laid over their shape, even though when it was / displayed to their fathers they were not in existence? They never saw 20 the image of the Ambassador! And how did they take / the seal of the image of the Ambassador? They added it to / [the] shape of Adam and Eve. /

The enlightener [speak]s to them thus: The sin that spur/ted out from the rulers, which is Matter, shot up 25 [tow]ards the image of the Ambassador. It was cut off from [tha]t place / and came down to the earth, for they did not accept / [it wi]thin the firmaments. When it came do/[wn to] the earth, it formed the tree. It was established / within the wood and formed the fruits. And when 30 [the] abortions fell [to] the ground, to the earth, at the [second] time / [... / ...] (138) fruits, it assumed the[m] and spoke in the ruler, / their leader. He says to his companions: Come! Give me yo/ur light, and I will construct for you an image aft[er] / the

likeness of the exalted one. What he said, they did: they gave ⁵ it
to him, and he constructed [...] /

Again the enlightener says: The sin that s[purted out ... / ...]
which is the Matter that saw the im[age of the Ambassa]/dor and
that formed the tre[e and was established i]/n [i]t; afterwards it
came up in the [fruits ...] ¹⁰ It went in to the rulers [...] they /
formed Adam and Eve after the [likeness of the] exalt[ed one]. /
Through the energy of the sin that had s[een the image of the] /
Ambassador, it went into the (rulers) [through the fruits. It] /
assumed them and they [t]oo sculp[ted ... they] ¹⁵ begat each of
them according to his destiny [...]; / one he resembles, one he
does not resemble.

Behold, I have taught y/ou this lesson, how the rulers shaped
Adam and / Eve by the action of the sin that went into the[m] /
through the fruits, and he was ordained after the image of the
exalted one.

²⁰ Once again the enlightener speaks: The moulder placed in the
/ form of Adam and Eve limbs, outside and wi/thin, for percep-
tion and activity. He*⁷³ was apportioned / house by house*⁷⁴. For
everything that his perceptions and / elements will receive exter-
nally there are internal storehouses ²⁵ and repositories and cavi-
ti[es; and] / what is received in to them is stored in them.
[When]/ever they will be questioned about what is deposited in
their internal store/houses, they bring out what they have received within a/nd give it to the questioner who requested it of
them.

³⁰ In this way his faculty*⁷⁵ [...] / outer [limbs] to look at [...] /
every type with[in ...] also [the fa](**139**)culty of the eyes [has]
houses and caviti/es and repositories and stores within, so that
every image / it might see, whether good or evil, whether /
loveable or detestable or lu⁵stful, it can receive into its storehouses
and / repositories. Also, when the faculty of the / eyes is pleased
to send out the image that it saw / and took in, it can go in to its
storehouses [at the] / time and think.and seek [...] ¹⁰ and it brings

---

*73   I.e. Adam or the human form.
*74   I.e. the physical and mental senses are distributed in the appropriate
places throughout the body.
*75   Lit. 'thought'.

it out [and] gives it to the questioner who requested it / and the one who wan[t]ed it. Whether it be something from / lu[st*76 ... or a]n image of love [or ... / ... something] hateful. And thus shall that faculty (of the eyes) / produce and do what it does in each category.

15 The faculty of the ears has its own storehouses / also. Every sound it might receive, whether good or evil, / shall be taken in and placed in its houses and inner repositor/ies, and it is guarded in its [...] for a / thousand days. After a thousand days, if someone comes and 20 asks that faculty about the sound that it heard / [at] this time and took into its storehouses, immediately / it [sh]all g[o] into its repositories and seek and review / and search after this word, and send it out from where it / was first put, the place in which it was kept.

25 [In] like order, the faculty of scent / [s]hall function just as that of the eyes and that of the auditory organs. / Every [o]dour it shall smell it shall take in [to it] and / [d]eposit in its inner storehouses. Every time it will be / [a]sked by a questioner, it shall go in 30 [...] and [...] storehouse and remember / [...] (140) only these things.

However, even the mouth and the tongue within it, / and the taste organ, have a faculty dwelling in them. / Again, that faculty too, o/f taste, has thus cavities and repositories 5 set apart for it. It too receives these tastes and gathers them / in. A[nd] at any moment when someone will ask of a taste, if / [...] it shall send it out and remember tha[t] taste. / It shall snare and give even the mar[k of] th[a]t taste; / give its memory to the qu[est]ioner who asks for it.

10 Again, the fac[ul]ty of touch by the hands is also s[o]: / When it might touch, touch shall [receive i]ts memory. / And it [takes] it in to its inner repository [until] / som[eo]ne will ask this faculty for the memory. [Immediately], / it shall go in again and bring out the memory of this tou15ch that it made, and give it to whoever asks for it. /

And the faculty of the heart that rules over them all is much / the most like this. Every thing that these five fac/ulties will receive

---

*76 Reading ⲉⲛ[ⲓⲟⲩⲙⲓⲁ

and put in store for / the faculty of the heart it shall receive and guard. 20 Any time that they will ask for their deposit it shall send out / and give every thing that they gave to it. /

For the counsel of the heart is like the king. / All the ad[v]isers*77 of his city and the leaders of his a[r]/my are placed with him. Any time if his genera[ls] 25 will entreat him for whatever they wish, he shall give them the ad[v]/ice and opinion by which they move. /

Furthermore, it is like a cellarman: [Eve]ry thing that / will be entrusted to it by them, and given to it, it shall receive / and put in separate vessels and places. Any time 30 [... / ... / ...] (141) in the place that it put it.

This also is the way of / the faculty of the body. The vision that the eyes will se/e and give to it, and it receives it in, it shall bring out again / from the storehouses wherein it had placed it; and give it to whoever asks for it.

5 Again, [the] sound that the ears will hear and give to it, / and it receives it from them. At any time when someone will ask it for that so/und, it shall bring out and give the sound of the ear[s] / to whoever has asked it for that sound. It shall bring out and / give the sound of the ears to whoever has asked.

10 Again, [the] faculty of smell in this same pattern; and that of taste / i[s] of the same [ty]pe. The touch by the han[ds ... / ...] they shall bring it out in to [... / ...] And whenever they will as[k it] for it, it shall bring it out / and gi[ve it].

Once again the enlightener speaks: 15 Indeed, watchmen are a[t] these doors guarding them, / and bolts are fastened on the doors at the hands of the gu/ards that guard them!

Just like watchmen guarding a c/amp with towers and watch-posts. As the holding rooms come*78 / out from there and the bolts are upon the gates, the guar20ds control the bolts of the gates while they sit at the entrance / [of] the watchposts. So, someone who

---

*77 Lit. advices.
*78 Reading ⲉⲡⲉ ⲛ̄ⲣⲓ ⲉⲓ ⲁⲃⲁⲗ for ⲉⲡⲉ ⲛ̄ⲣⲓ.ϥ ⲁⲃⲁⲗ of the ed. princ.

belongs to their city as a fellow / [cit]izen of them, belonging to their country, for him they shall open / [the ga]te and receive him in by their will. However, the foreigner / who comes they shall prevent, and leave him stand²⁵[i]ng at the gate. They shall not yield to let him enter. / Again, another one whom they will receive in, with great trouble before / [they] take him in, you shall find many holding rooms [... / ...] that [...] there are a mass [... / ...] them. The number of d[oor] bolts ³⁰ [...] are [...] Whenever someone will wish / [...] the bolts at his hand, opens (**142**) the gate and brings out whoever is hidden within. /

The enlightener says: This body too is like the mighty c/amp. And the gates of the camp with / their guards are like the orifices and organs ⁵ of the body. Now, the orifices of the body are of sight, / hearing and smell; and they that send o/ut words. There are many sentinels and a ma/ss of guards placed over the limbs of the body, guarding / their orifices. And the faculty in it is the di¹⁰rective of the body, the queen of the entire camp; so that / whenever it wishes it can open, or when it wishes it can shut. /

However, if and wh[en] the Light Mind comes, it shall tu[rn i]n / to the orifices of the body. The rulers, who [a]re the door gua[rds], / shall h[in]der and restrain it from en[ter]ing. ¹⁵ They shall bind the circu[it] of the body so that the foreign[er] can not / enter it.

Nevertheless, the Light Mind / by its wisdom and awe and diligence shall hum/ble the guards who are set at the body's orifices. / When it finishes humbling them it shall take fr[o]m them bolts ²⁰ to all the orifices of the body. Now, the orifices that had been ope/ned before to the parades of lust, to receive i/n the sights of pleasure, to transfer the [wor]/ds of the practice of li[f]e's concerns, to receive in the t[astes] / of the different foods and unclean meals together ²⁵ with the sin therein; whoever stops receiving th[is] in, / his heart and mind shall follow after.

So, now, bec[ause] / the b[olt]s to the body of the righteous person are in the hands of / the Light M[in]d within, he is open [to receive] / i[n] all that is pleasing to God. He is op[en to take] i[n] ³⁰ by his eyes the visions of lov[e ...] and / righteousness. Indeed, due to this, the si[ghts and] the [ad]ornme[nt of the gar] (**143**) ments of kings, which are woven with gold; and the garments of silken wom/en, which are woven with gold and pearls, / made beautiful for the shape of lust; first they were lovable / before the eyes of the chosen person. Yet, now, by the [5] power of the Light Mind that has suffused him and / lived in the body he has humbled lust, the goddess of the bo/dy. The parades of lust have become loathsome in the presence of the righteous pers/on. However, the aspects of divinity a[nd] / righteousness and humility and scorned clothes are pleasing to him.

[10] Again, [these] ears were first opening to empty sounds an/d to the melodies of lust, to the secrecies of [wic]kedn/ess. All these were pleasing at first, at the time when he / he[a]rd them. Yet, now, by the power of the Light Mind, / the sounds of lust and the words o[15]f magic and evil mysteries have become loathsome in his presence; / as he is not pleased to hear them from this time on. Rather, he likes all the time / to listen to the sounds of the lessons of righteousness, the / words of the psalms and of the prayers, the praise of the hy/mns and the lessons of truth, and the knowledge of charity. [20] [S]imply, all orifices in similar fashion were opening / at one time to wickedness, but now have opened / to the good. Sin was ruling in the body / this time, doing anything it liked, having none in command. /

Yet, [n]ow, authority has been taken from the sin in the org[25]ans of the body. The Living Spirit*[79] has become lord over all its / limbs. It has bound them with a chain of peace, and se/aled them with the seal of truth. It has opened the orifices of the / body to the good, and because of this the good enter/s them through the ears and the eyes. It dwells in the heart. The H[o]ly Spirit [30] reigns. It does all that it pleases. It annuls / [the] will of [s]in, the beginning and the end. [In contrast], the will / of the [Hol]y Spir[it] comes about, and the purpose of the Light Mind.

(144) The enlightener speaks: About this I tell you my / brothers, my loved ones and my limbs. With wisdom / and skill make yourselves secure at the circuit of the body's orifices, so that the sin that dwells in the body has no power [5] over you. Nor does it take from you your light, nor / scatter it from place to place, nor

---

*79   Perhaps a scribal error for 'Holy Spirit'.

{drive}*80 it from / site to site in various forms. Now, / let this not happen to you, but be watchful people, / secure in your truth. Be you prepared from 10 totality till totality, so that as your rest will come / about and your end subject to this, you guard its mark and / its hope!

••• 57 •••

(144,13 – 147,20)

/ *Concerning the Generation of Adam.*

The structure of this chapter evidences yet again how Mani, as a good teacher and preacher, is able to turn an explanation of the details of his intricate system into a more immediate lesson for his audience.

144.15 – 146.8 Mani explains to a Babylonian catechumen that Adam and the people of the first human generations were greater in size, and longer-lived, because of the stars under which they were born.

146.8 – 147.17 Mani introduces a second and more compelling theme. In these last days the quality and span of people's lives has come down to almost nothing. This is because the divine life and light in the world has grown less and less.

15 Once again, a Babylonian catechumen questioned the en-l/ightener, saying to him: Speak with me my master, and in-s/truct me about Adam, the first man. When / he was fashioned, how did they sculpt him? / Or, how did they beget him? [Rath]er, is his beget20ting like the begetting that is brought forth today, amongst hum/ankind; or not? Does a distinction exist between his bir/th and the one that they bring forth today?

Now, no[te] that A/dam is mighty in his stature, and great is his / size. Even his years are many! He spent many years 25 living in the world. And he is not the only one / we have found to be mighty; but all the others who were / begotten in his generation, many are their years too. Still, these / people who are born today, their st[a]tu/re has been diminished in po[w]er; even their years are lessened. Also, [wh]30y is the birth today, of [the]y who are born, / altered compared with that of these first [...] (145) place to place? See, even the stars and signs of the zodiac continue / in

---

*80 ⲡⲁⲧ/

their positions. Why now have the age and / the years of these last ones diminished, and he has also become smaller, / compared to these ancient ones who belong to these first generations?

5 And for his part our enlightener, in his deep wisdom / and his great understanding, speaks to this catechu/men who had questioned him: They increased, have turned, and diminished; / because there are five types of authorities and / leaders appointed in the sphere of zodiacal signs, and the hea10vens above it. They have names they are ca[lled] / by: the first name is the year; the sec/[on]d is the month; the third is the day; the fou/[rth] is the hour; the fifth is the moment. Now, these five / positions, and these five houses, exist in the sphere and 15 the heavens. These places have five powers, and they are made masters o/ver them. The master of the year exists; the master of the month exists; / the master of the day exists; the master of the hour exists; / the master of the moment exists. In turn one is above his / companion; and in turn the one above is made the master over the one below 20 him.

So, mankind is begotten, and [the ani]/mals. They are born in these powers. And, thus, these powers / have received authority since the beginning of creation till the end of the wo/rld. Now, in the beginning of the generations the powers who were masters / over the years reigned. Therefore, because of this, the offspring 25 [b]orn in their generations and their lifetime: their ye/ars were found to be greater. They attain a long life span in the generation of Adam, and / [tha]t of Sethel his son, and that of the ones who came after him.

Af/ter they ceased to reign, namely the powers who are masters over the ye/ars; the powers who are masters over the months themselves reigned. Like 30 the months, for they are less than the years; again this [is] also the case / with the offspring w[ho were] born in them. Their life span is less / [than the life span of the ones born] in the generation of the powers who master (146) the years!

When the authority of the powers who / master the months was completed; the powers of the days received authority af/ter them. Therefore, like the days, for they are less than the months, / this also is the case with the offspring who were born in them. Their life span [5] is less than the life span of the ones born in the powers who are masters / over the months. Again, even so the offspring who were born in the ho/urs, and of the moments. Their {conduit}*81 is less than that of the m/onths and the days.

Our enlightener speaks to that Babylonian cate/chumen: Do you see, how near the en[10]d [of] the world approaches? The life span of the pe[o]/ple has drawn in to nothing. Their days have diminished. Their ye[ars] have / become less; because the life and the ligh[t that] / was in the world in these first generations was more than that of to/day. Indeed, because of this have they diminished in their stature. Their lif[15]e span has become less for them.

Once again speaks this Baby[l]onian cate/chumen to our enlightener: I entreat / you, my master! How you have instructed and persuaded / me in respect of the years! Why the ye/ars of these ancients increased; or again why [20] these last ones have lessened. You also told me that they have diminished even in their / stature. You say that all these diminished becau/se of the life and the light that was taken from the world.

Now, can y/ou recount to me this other (matter): By what sort of birth was / the entire offspring of mankind made from one man and one [25] woman, Adam and Eve?

The enlightener speaks to that ca/techumen: While well do you ask for this les/son, so yet know and understand it! For the manner of these / first generations is that they are richer in their light and pu/rer in stature. Even their years are greater. Thus, again, [30] even their offspring is much more than the offspring of this tim[e]. / They were spending a longer time [...] in [the w]/omb of their mother. Afterwards, they [...] (147) a number in a single womb. There are times five were brought forth / from a single womb, and times six were brought forth from [a] single w/omb! There are some lesser than this; again, some / greater than this. Indeed, because of this the offspring of Eve multipl[5]ied, and of her children. The earth was filled by reason of them alone; b/ecause

---

*81 ⲁⲓⲟ̄ⲕⲉ See ch.48. It is difficult to maintain the translation as 'conduit' here.

the offspring from the generation of the people of old, who they /
bore into the world, differ greatly from those of today. / Their
conception and their birth is not like latter births, / brought forth
nowadays from the wo[ma]n's uterus.

10 For, they whom they beget today, in these la[st] generations,
they / stand diminished and maimed. And, indeed, one by one
do they bri[ng t]/hem [forth] from a single womb. Hardly two,
or [l]es/s or more. They are even made ugly in their aspect,
being diminished in / their size, and feeble in their limbs. Their
teachings and [their] 15 considerations are full of wickedness,
they are evil. They are drowning, / and they end their life span
suffering. Even death catches them / in haste.

When that catechumen had [lis]/tened to these lessons, he paid
homage and gave glory. He says to the enlightener: / I thank
you, my master, for you have satisfied my heart, and [pers]20ua-
ded me by an exhortation, about these things for which I
questioned you.

<h2 style="text-align:center">••• 58 •••</h2>

(147,21 – 148,20)

/ The Four Powers that grieve. /

Characteristic of Manichaeism is its emphasis upon the real suffering of the
divine, occasioned by the assault of evil. In this it differs markedly from the
docetic tendencies of many gnostic systems. Indeed, Manichaeism universa-
lised the degradation and crucifixion throughout Matter of the 'son of God'
(the living soul) to an extent that seemed shocking to its Christian
commentators.
    In this chapter Mani relates the grief of the Mother of Life, the First
Man, and himself as apostle, for their children according to their respective
levels of concern. He also comments that he grieves not only for the
sufferings of his church; but even for those souls who have not received the
truth, and who will be damned for ever.
    Contrary to the title the text seems only to deal with three powers,
although there are four sources of grief.

[O]nce again the enlightener speaks to his disciples: I am one /
of they that grieve, amongst these three powers that are heart-
broken, 25 who have come from the Father.

The first who grieves is the first M/other of Life. She is sad because of her children who are s/et in affliction, for they were conjoined with the darkness and the / [poi]son. They have been bound with the entire ruling-power. For what was she grieving, / [wa]tching over them taking these afflictions? Whenever she might ^{30} [s]ee them and how suffering is brought upon them, she shall grieve and be unhap[py] on account of them. /

[The s]econd one who is troubled [of] heart is the First Man, whose / [great]ness and kingdom is established in the li[ght] ship / [...] And he too is troubled of heart because of (148) his five sons who are set in the midst of dan/ger. For any time he may see that they are given trouble / {}*82 always he might hear the sound of their / weeping as they cry out because of the blows and wo^{5}unds of the enemy who assaults them daily; and as he sees them / like this constantly, he shall g[ri]eve and mourn on account of his / [s]o[n]s.

The third one who grieves am I. / For since the time when I came into the world there has been no joy / for me therein, on account of the holy church that I ^{10} chose in the name of my Father. I have freed it from the / slavery of the authoritarians, and placed in it / the Light Mind. Always, as I see i[t i]n / tribulation and persecution and being afflicted by its enem[ies], / I will be sad on its behalf. I have also another grief ^{15} apart from this: for the souls who have refused hope / and have not made themselves strong in this certainty and firmness of / [tru]th. They will come forth and be lost and go to ge/henna for ever. Indeed, due to this I grieve for them in that they have / not accepted repentance, nor have they been reconciled with the right hand o^{20}f peace and mercy that I brought from the Father.

---

*82 ⲁⲛⲉⲧⲟⲩ ⲙ̄ⲙⲁϥ

(148,21 – 151,4)

/ *The Chapter of the Ele/ments that wept.* /

This chapter continues from the last the theme of the suffering of the divine. The five garments or sons of the First Man, that is the light elements, must weep and feel the pain of loss four times during the course of their necessary task. That is, to mix with Matter, and to overcome its assault on the light.

148.29 – 149.3 When they first caught sight of the darkness, and understood the task that they would have to undertake.

149.4 – 13 When the First Man their father ascended from the abyss, and left them behind in mixture.

149.14 – 28 When the Living Spirit stripped off the three garments of activity (wind, water and fire, see chapter 30) in the depths of the cosmos, and they realised that they would have to rise up through all the levels of the universe before purification and salvation could be achieved.

148.29 – 151.1 When the Last Statue will ascend, and they weep for those souls who are eternally lost and bound in the darkness. This moment is much the worst, because it is final. Some of the divine itself can never be redeemed. It is for this reason, to preach the truth and thus to minimise everlasting loss, that all the apostles and divine powers surrender themselves to every affliction in the world.

Mani concludes with a final admonition about the utmost gravity of this matter.

Once again he speaks to his disciples: The garments, ²⁵ the sons of the First Man, wept bitterly three times. / Then they were silent. There is a fourth time of weeping, / for they will weep at the end. And then their crying can stop, / and they will never again weep from this time on. /

Now, the first time of their weeping*83 is ³⁰ when they had seen the darkness, the enemy being about to burst out against them. / They understood everything that would happen to them. They were aware of / the one that would rise and come upon them, [b]/ut by necessity they hastened to h[i]m and [fought] (**149**) with him. They mastered him, they detained him. [They / bou]nd him with their body and their limbs, they o[ver/ca]me his death and his fire and his dark[ness]. /

---

*83 Lit: the first weeping in which they wept.

[The] second time that they wept is [w⁵hen the]ir father, the First Man, [ascend]ed from the [abyss] / of darkness and left them behind; that is the time when he stripped [them off] / and left them below. Indeed, when th[ey] / s[aw] how the First Man had risen out of the abyss / and [l]eft them behind, and that they were abandoned in the enmit[y, th]ey ¹⁰ wept and were sore of heart. Still, what could they do, wishing [... / ...] their heart to every affliction. They [remained b]e/hind and grew [s]ick under the pressure of the weighty burden of all the / works, until the end time. /

[The] third time that they wept is when the Living Spirit ¹⁵ stripped off the three garments of activity, / placing them beneath all things. He gave / them a sign to lift their heads and rise to the / heights from that place; and to pass and journey / through all the earths until they should reach the land of tranquilli[t]y ²⁰ and peace, the place of rest prepared for them. So, when / they had seen him, that he had separated himself from them, while they themselves / remained behind after him and had not ascended; at that mom/ent when they stayed behind these three garments wept. / After their crying, they turned their ²⁵ [hear]t to all the heights that were concealed from them, and were of one mind. For / [they would] soar up and come to the heights; and pass over / all [th]ings until the time that was ordained for them all / [...] at the end of the worlds. /

[The f]ourth time when they will weep is when the ³⁰ [S]tatue will be taken up on the last day, and they will weep / [for] the souls of the liars and blasphemers; for they may give / [...] because their limbs have been severed / [...] of the darkness. And also [th]ose souls, (150) when the Statue will go [up / and th]ey are left alo[n]e, they will weep in that they will rema[in] b/[eh]ind in affliction for ever. For they wi[ll be cut / off] and separated from the Last Statue. An[d it is] ⁵ a necessity to take these souls who are ready for loss / [a]s retribution for the deeds that they have done. They go i[n to] this / [darkne]ss and are bound with the darkness; just as they desired it / an[d] loved it, and placed [t]heir treasure with it. At that very moment, / when the Last Statue rises u[p], ¹⁰ the[y wi]ll weep. And then they will scream out loud because they will / be severed from the company

of this great Statue. And they / remain behind for ever. This great
weeping [...] / is terrible, it occurs in front of the souls and [...] /
who are ready for loss in accordance with their deeds. And they
[will] weep [15] with that crying, they will never be silent; /
because they will not attain rest from this time on. /

So, they too are the garments of these elements. This fou/rth time
of weeping is heart-rending for them. It is much w/orse for them
than these other three times of weeping before. This f[ou[20]rt]h
time the weeping is not for themselves. Rather they weep and are
heartsore for these soul[s] / who will be cut off from peace,
because rest will / not come about for them, to allow them to rest
from torment for / ever.

Therefore, due to the result of the erring of so/uls, all the apostles
and the fathers, the reve[25]alers of the good and the true prophets,
surrender [themselves] / to every labour and every aweful necessity. So that the (souls) might be / saved from the second death.
Not a single one of all the a/postles wished to receive his reward
on eart[h]; / but spent all their time in affliction, [30] suffering and
being crucified in their body, so that they might r[e]/deem their
souls from that loss [and] / ascend to this eternal rest [... in the]
new [ae](151)on.

It is not prop[er ...] the wi/se person must constantly be attentive to
this lesson, becau/se (this matter) is heartrending and grief for
the gods and / the apostles.

••• 60 •••

(151,5 – 152,20)

/ [Concernin]g the Four Fathers; / what they are like. /

Mani uses the analogy of the corporeal body to show that some of the divine
teachings are visible in the universe, but others are hidden; like organs and
faculties that can or can not be seen. Thus, the Father is like the directive
faculty (cᴃω) of the body, hidden in his own kingdom. However, the two
light ships of the sun and the moon are the eyes of the body, seen and
seeing. The living soul, despite its apparent silence, is like the body; for it
can be grasped and struck and wounded. Jesus the Splendour is the tongue,

because he can speak about and explain everything, whether it is visible like the ships, or hidden like the eternal kingdom. Therefore, it is Jesus who makes visible the suffering and the healing of the soul.

Once again the apostle [s]peaks to his disciples: / J[u]st as [the] corporeal body has limbs [10] that are hidden, so it also has others that are visi[b]le. [They] / ca[n be seen] upon it, they can be grasped and receive blows and woun/[d]s, whilst [ot]hers can neithe[r] be grasped no[r / receive] blows. So it is also with this entire greatness, as we resemble it. / Some of it is hidden, [15] whilst some of it is visible; [so]me of it is fa/r away from the blows and suffering, whilst some of it / receives blows and wounds.

Now, thus the directive of the bo/dy that lives within, hidden in the storehouses inside / the body and unseen. So it i[20]s also how the Father, the God o/f truth, exists; as he too is hidden in his kingdom, not display/ed before this outer desolation.

Thus, too, / the body has two eyes that are visible and see/n, and are even the body's source of illumination; so there are also [25] these two light ships that shine and are see/n in the entire universe and the whole of creation. / The light has never been hidden, just like the two eyes of the bo/dy.

The living soul too is like this, / it is established in apparent silence. In [30] its apparent [s]ilence it is grasped and receives b/lows from these five fleshes, which destroy (the soul) and str/[ike it. It can] be likened to the mystery of the [corporeal] body, / as it can be grasped and mastered, (152) can receive blows and wounds.

Also, thus / this tongue that speaks, proclaims, reprimands and reveals / about everything happening in this body, in<side and outside, also the considerations [a]nd bod[ily] knowledges>. / The tongue, which is outside, makes it manifest. It also proclaims about [5] the honour and shame of the body. And it speaks, / unveiling the pain of the body [th]at is [s]ick [from] / its sores.

This is also what [Jesus] the Splend[our] / is l[i]ke, who shall be sent fr[o]m the greatness. / He manifests and reveals about everything, both the external and [10] the internal, both what is above and

what is [bel]o[w]. / Be it about the outer aeons that are hidden and
[not disp]l[ayed], / or about the ships of light that are se[e]n. H[e
is the on]/e who unveils about them. He is also the one who
reveals [about the]ir glo/ry, and the greatness that dwells in
them. And regarding this beating [15] and wounding of the living
so[ul], Jesus is the one who reveals it. / He also preaches ab[o]ut
(the soul) and its peace. He revea/ls about its cleansing and
healing.

Behold, I have shown / to you the power of revelation of these four
fathers, and how / each one of them has his appointed work,
whether in [20] secret or visible.

••• 61 •••

(152,21 – 155,5)

/ Concerning the Garment of the Waters: / how great is its Measure. /

The value of this chapter lies in its historical reference; and in the way it
enables the reader to penetrate the rather dense cosmological language used
in the *Kephalaia* about the elemental garments.
    Mani and three of his disciples were stood upon the bank of the Tigris
while in flood. One disciple asks the apostle about the source of these vast
and powerful waters. Mani then explains that the First Man assumed the
elemental garments, including that of water, and used them to combat the
immeasurable demonic army that had assembled to assault the light. The
evil powers were overcome and bound within the universe; which itself will
be destroyed at the end time. As a portion of that flood of water poured into
the demons the Tigris is next to nothing. Therefore, the disciples should
marvel and be secure in the power and greatness of God.

Once again, at one of the times when the apostle entered [in] [25]
to the presence of King Shapur. He gave him a greet[ing], /
turned, and went away from before King Shapur.

He st[o]/od on a quayside that was built upon the bank of the
mighty river / Tigris. At that time it was the month of Ph[ar]/-
mouthi. The river Tigris was engorged with many waters; [30] it
had {surged up}*84 and swelled and {burst forth}*85 beneath the

---

*84 ⲃⲱϩⲧ=
*85 ⲥⲱⲣⲉ ⲁⲃⲁⲗ

great / force of the flood, so that the waters flowed do[wn ... and] / poured into the gates of the city, they [...] (153) only, but the waters flowed into the {}*86 of / the city until they submerged the market place of the city. [...] / are few and the city goes [under ... comes to] / be fear of its wind. Even his kingdom was in 5 great terror because of the enormous size of the flood of these waters. /

So, the apostle was standing there on the quay, w/ith also three disciples standing by him, [le]/aders of his church. They were watching the river engorged / with these many waters. They saw that the waters rose u10p against the city walls, and the flood was even inside / the walls.

One of his disciples then spoke. He says to the apos/tle: H[o]w great is the power of the garment of the wat/er[s]? How far shall [it extend]? That it should enter with the roar of its flood and / fill th[is] river Tigris in its vastness like the mighty 15 [s]ea! It has carried waves from river bank to bank, and run from / wall to wall. The source from which a[l]l these waters burst forth, / how great will it be? For they come and come each year at their [ap]poin/ted season!

Then the apostle says to him: / Why are you astonished at the vastness of the Tigris waters, 20 and why are you amazed by its flood? Still, listen t/o what I am about to tell you, and be truly astonished about th[e r]iv[er] / that came into being during the first time. /

[At] the time when the First Man assumed the elements, and stood / [fi]rm against the first enmity that had come about in the darkness, 25 he defied these great and powerful rulers. They / are immeasurable, greater than the extent or size / of thousands and ten thousands of {parasangs}*87. At the start, when he spread the fight a/[ga]inst them, he gave them fire and wind; and after-wards he gave / [the] garment of the waters to the rulers of death. So they, 30 the rulers, drank in and consumed those waters; / [the way that I told] you in the *Great Gospel.* / Many [waters] poured forth from the garment of waters / [...] the rivers flow. The mouth

*86 ⲩⲧⲏ
*87 ⲩⲃⲱⲱⲥ Measure of length: see Crum 611a (ⲩϥⲱ); and K (Dub). 274.2.5

of the rulers / [...] those [...], the warriors of destruction [35] [... l]a-
boured and brought them forth. There were seven (rivers), (**154**)
like the great river Tigris [that you] see, / flowing in to the mouth
of each one of them, as they shall not / [...] to a single stomach, to
their fill; because / in turn the descent to its stomach shall burn
them with its [5] fire and heat. Those rulers were like / the {}[*88] of
[...] they were not emptied; rain and / [...] their existent days. /

The apostle s[peaks] to t[hat] elect one: The measure / [of th]at
river was expanded seven times, as they flow [10] [...] of the body of
the [... / ...] waters [...] now. Marvel at / [...] as you say: Grea[t is]
its [... / ...] indeed prolonged, for a bearer [... b]ut [...] / you
marvel at this. Marvel first [...] [15] that [...] is the first [...] which
came into being i[n] this / [...] is how great a struggle, since it
has / [...] these creatures of destruction, the mighty giants.
Beho/ld, they are entwined, bound, {}[*89] and {}[*90] in every place. /
They are hidden, not revealed before the eyes of every flesh that
[20] exists on the land of death [...] these rulers / [...] revealed. The
entire universe of flesh will be destroyed / and dissolved [...] all
pass away [... / ...] they will be destroyed with their angry voice,
/ which is mightier than the thunder. Now, as this small stream
is reckoned [...] [25] before the vastness of these waters of which I
have recounted to you. / For only one river from thousands of
rivers of water, from the secrets / that are not revealed, is the river
Tigris upon the eart[h]. /

See [...] and be amazed at the measure of the elements of the
wa/ters. Marvel at the stature of the Man who bore t[30]hem. And
understand how great is t[hat] god, / active in power, the one
whom these waters [... t]/han the stature of the First Man who
[assumed] (**155**) this garment of such size; and how much was
made.

Then his / disciples say to him: We revere you, our master, and
w[e] give / thanks that moreover you have opened our eyes to all
[the g]re/atnesses that are hidden from every person. Yet, to us
you have [5] manifested them!

[*88] ⲋⲁⲓⲱⲉ
[*89] ⲕⲙⲕⲁⲙⲧ
[*90] ⲧⲁⲙⲥˋ Smagina 1990:116 suggests 'hidden' from ⲧⲱⲙⲥ ('bury').

••• 62 •••

(155,6 – 29)

/ Concerning the Three Rocks. /

Mani uses the term 'rock' to describe three modes of absolute stability established by the divine in the universe.

Once again he speaks to his disciples: Three great / rocks, which exist, were appointed by the greatness. They were set in [10] these outer w[or]lds.

So, the first rock is the / [Pillar] of Glory, the Perfect Man, which was summoned / [by the] glorious Ambassador. He set it in this zone / [... he] brought forth its base (?) from the earth to heaven. It bore up under the [en]tire uni/[verse], and became first of all the weight-carriers in [15] [it]s powers. In its firmness it has been set upright, and has made fast / every [t]hing above and below. /

[The] second great and glorious rock is the new earth of / light, which was set upon the earth of darkness. It has squashed / the fastenings of the five storehouses of death. It has established [20] firmness, with great firmness, over and beyond the earth of darkness. / It has flattened, crushed and fixed the root of death. /

[The] third rock is the great thought, which was summoned / from Jesus, the glorious one. He set it in the holy church. / The church gathered in upon it, and has lived in [25] [it]. It has stood firm, with a true fixity, for ever. /

[These] are the three great rocks, they that have come forth in great / confidence, in three great and honoured places. They were appointed / and distributed in three great places of these [self]same worlds. / They were made fast according to the will of the greatness.

••• **63** •••

(155,30 – 156,34)

/ *Concerning Love.* /

Mani reveals the divine nature of love, which is manifested in the world in
the church. In contrast, hate is the nature of the darkness; but it too is
present in this time of mixture.

[Once] again he speaks [to] his disciples: What is love? / [...]
each [...], calling it 'love'.

(**156**) [Lo]ve is the Father of Greatness, who dwells in his /
glorious land. The entirety of the divine has been revealed /
[there]in! These two are a single living body, the Father / [a]nd
his love; because he has given himself for every thing, 5 as he
exists in his aeons. Indeed, due to this, they called the Fa/ther, the
Lord of the totality, 'love'. For he gave the victory to / his aeons
and his limbs.

Again, the beginning of / all the righteousness and the divine
that dwells in / the holy church; they have also called it 'love'. 10
As indeed the church is made strong therein! [These] two, / the
Mind and the church, a single body is also their likeness; /
because, again, the apostle too shall gi[ve] his [own] / self for his
church. [And, again], due to th[is], / the church too calls him
'love'. [So] 15 is it written: There is no love greater than this, for
someone [to give himself] / to death for his friend*91. Likewise,
too, the beginning of ri[ght]/eousness is made of love for the
church, according both to body and to / spirit. While in the body,
in the church here; so in the / spirit, in the heights above.

20 Once again he speaks: What, conversely, is hate? Hate / is the
first death that welled up. It revealed the land / of darkness. This
one called 'hate', because / it has ruined all its perdition's offspring; it sinned even against / a power foreign to it, and ruined
it. Due to this they shall call 25 it 'hated'; for it has caused
destruction, both wounding in / flesh, and what is not its own.

---

*91   Jn. 15:13

Today again it causes wo[unding] / and destruction in all flesh. It
kills them all with / diverse deaths; these that are displayed today
in every/thing, in every type. Even the Cross of Light, the [30]
living [so]ul, likewise too it ruins and kills them; / as it did at the
start. Indeed, due to this have they called i[t] / 'hated', this one
from the hated; the envy from / the envy; the devil from the
devil; the b[a]/d that came about from the bad. (**157**)

••• **64** •••

(157,1 – 158,23)

/ [Concerning] Adam. /

Mani explains that since Adam was fashioned by the evil powers after the
image of the divine Ambassador, he was preeminent over all other mixed
creations in three ways: his image was more beautiful; his soul fitted the
correct distribution of the elements, and thus he had superior intelligence;
the powers of the entire universe were sealed in him, and thus mankind
became the key to the direction of future history.

This final point leads Mani to explain that the creation of Adam was a
deliberate act by the rulers, the focus of their plan to control everything, and
to capture the kingdom of light. He summarises their evil purpose in seven
further points.

Once again he speaks to his disciples, who listen to his / words:
Three great things that are distinct were reveal/ed in Ad[am] the
first human. Indeed, due to this, he was found [5] to be better and
more outstanding than the conjoined powers that are in heaven /
and on earth.

The first: / The image of the exalted one was placed upon him.
The creators / and moulders of his body sealed him after the
shining form / of the image that had been displayed to them
above. [10] Indeed, due to this, the image of Adam was found to be
surpassingly beautiful / beyond any conjoined power above and
below. /

The second thing: Adam was shaped in his structure / throug[h
the li]ght of the first-born of heaven and / [earth ...] the five sons.
Indeed, due to this, his [15] struct[ure] was found to differ from the
structure of even the other creations; / [sin]ce the form of all

creations is different. As for Adam, / the formation of his soul fits over the / correct distribution of the elements. Therefore, he has / intelligence surpassing that of the other creations and ²⁰ beasts.

The third are the teaching/s and counsels and the seal of all the powers above and / below. The creators, who set him in order, gathered them and se/aled them in him. (Adam) and his consort Eve became a dwelling and home / for the signs of the zodiac and the stars; and the months, the days and the ye²⁵ars. For the seal of the entire universe is stamped upon / Adam. Indeed, due to this, heaven and earth moved because of him; / trouble and disorder arose on his account between they that are g/ood and they that are evil. So, the good induce him to life / because of their image and shape placed upon him; while the ³⁰ [wi]cked were drawing him to death, so that they would have po/[w]er through him and they would conceive the kingdom, and through him humiliate / the entire universe.

Furthermore, understand that / [the ru]lers determined and formed Adam so that they would be masters t/[hrough him a]nd c[onceiv]e the kingdom because of seven things.

(158) The first: He became the enlightener in their creati[o]n; instead of the li/ght of the image of the Ambassador wh[o] had displayed himself to them / above. For they all desi[re]d / the likeness of the image of the Ambassador. Their heart ⁵ was drawn after it.

The second: So that they would scoop up / the light through him and restrain and obstruct it / from its ascent to the heights. /

The third: So that because of the image of the Ambassa/dor that is placed upon him the entirety of the divine ¹⁰ that is above and below would be humiliated; on account of the likeness of the splendour, of / the beauty of his superiority. For he is superior in his appearance t/o all creatures.

The fourth: [He] is a / seal-ring and a new impression, so [that] / all births who will be begotten might be brought forth after his s[eal].

¹⁵ The fifth: That might be displayed through him all the skil[ls]

/ of the powers, they above and below, secret and / manifest; and that they might determine through him the totality, and / every thing be revealed in him. /

The sixth: That there would come to be a great protection for them [20] through the image of the exalted one that was placed upon him; for as the heavenly would / [...] even rulers; and no evil thing would be done to them on account of Adam. /

The seventh: That he might become chief and king and master over all creatures; / and they might conceive the kingdom through him.

••• 65 •••

(158,24 – 164,8)

[25] *Concerning the Sun.* /

This chapter presents a series of teachings about the divine nature of the sun, and the life-giving qualities of its light, compared with the evils of darkness and the night. It may have been redacted from separate sources. D. McBride (1988) has argued that it evidences heliolatry native to Egyptian Manichaeism; but that would be difficult to prove without a parallel non-Coptic text.

158.26 – 161.30 Mani reveals the greatness of the sun, which so many people and the false sects have not understood. The Old Testament God, here termed Satan, has attempted to obstruct the worship of the light in his law. Mani outlines seven benefits of the sun, contrasted with seven evils of the night.

161.31 – 162.20 Five archetypes or qualities presented by the sun.

162.21 – 163.8 Three further qualities that correspond to the mystery of the Father.

163.9 – 164.8 Mani's concluding comments and admonitions to his disciples. He quotes a saying of Jesus from the *Gospel of Thomas.*

Once again, the apostle is sitting down among the congreg/ation of his disciples, one time, and the sun shone forth. He beg/an to recount to his disciples about the greatness of the su[n] / and its divinity. How was it fashioned after the [li]ke[30]ness of the first greatness? He was revealing to them.

He [say]/s, it is the gate of life and the vessel of [p]/eace, to this

great aeon of l[ight ...] (159) However, since Satan knows that it is
the gate of the / souls' departure, he placed an exclusionary
judgement / in his law that no one worship it, saying: / Whoever
will worship it can die*92. He has otherwise called it: 5 The light
that will be nullified. He has hindered the souls from /
themselves turning their faces towards the light. He has caused
them to deny / the light of their being.

Now, people are blind abou/t everything! They have not understood the greatness of this great light-giver. / They have denied
the grace of this great light that shines upon them. 10 They have
not perceived its greatness and its divinity. / No[r], also, have
they understood the good things that it does for them, / even
today, as they are entrenched in their body; when it / comes to
th[is] world and shines. Behold: How many are the ch/arit[ies]
that it does for mankind! Yet they, for their part, de15ny its graces,
which they know not. Every day, wo/uld this great light-giver
shine its light, it shall do seven / good things for them. Shall they
not see them? /

[The] first good thing that it does for them is its light, which it /
shines upon them. It opens the eyes of all mankind. 20 They see
underfoot as they walk by it. It takes away / the blindness of the
night, which made them blind with its darkness. /

[The] second: When (the sun) is come to the world, with its
coming / it shall bring calm and peace to the entire world. With
its / coming it shall also take away from them all the fear and
t25rembling, which their heart is filled with the whole night; for it
shall / ta[ke] away the darkness present by its light, and sweep it
out. / Also, this is how it extinguishes fear by its calm. /

The third is its vigil; because when (the sun) comes to the wo/rld
all sleeping mankind shall arise 30 and awake. And the watchmen too shall cease from / watching. The guards who sit at the
gates of camps, they / [bre]ak vigil at the watchposts, because of its
light that has shone / [upon them in the w]orld.

(160) The fourth: It shall nourish, and give strength, taste and

---

*92   Deut. 17:2–5

scent; / to the trees and fruits and vegetables, and all the herbs, / and the flowers and grasses, which are upon the entire earth. /

The fifth: When (the sun) shines in all the world, [5] the evil reptile and the sharp-toothed beasts that are filled of / wickedness, they shall flee to hiding in their dens. /

The sixth: When it shines its light, the wou/nd of any person is eased from pain. Its light shall me/lt away the evil arts of every doer of wickedness.

[10] The seventh: (The sun) shall display and manifest to the wo/rld the sign of the splendour of the aeons of ligh[t], from which it has / come out; it here in this world being their sign. It / brings light to the whole of creation.

Behold: How gre[at i]s the fo/olishness that has befallen the sects of error! [15] Not only that they have not perceived the mystery of [the div]/inity of this great light-giver; but also, even all the benefits / that it does for them. They forget them. They do not perceive t/hem.

Now, just as I have shown you the sun, / which does seven good things in the world, hear al[20]so what I teach you about the night, for it has all wickednes/ses therein. Every occasion, would the night fall, it sha/ll do seven evils in the world. /

The first wickedness that the night shall do in the world / is the darkness, with which it shall fill the entire world; beca[25]use when the sun sinks from the world and dra/ws to it its rays, at that instant the shadow / of the night shall spread out over the whole world. The eye[s] / of the people fill with blackness. They neither see nor wonder / with their eyes, because of the darkness of the night which shall fill the whole wor[30]ld.

The second evil thing that / the night shall do is its fear; because when its / shadow looms forth, its fear and its trembling shall possess all of mankind. The entire world shall fil[l] / of the night.

The third: W[hen the night] (161) falls, all creatures take up re-volt. / They rebel in their heart, to do wickedness and perdition. /

The fourth: The heaviness of sleep shall lay upon them, and they

/ fall asleep; they slumber and doze, and they are like ⁵ these corpses in the night.

The fifth is its / ugliness; again, when the night would fall, the form / of the people shall be hidden in the darkness and the ugliness of the night. / The beauty and the form of men and women shall not be displ/ayed before one another, because of its darkness and its ugliness; ¹⁰ which it shall spread out over all their forms. /

[The] sixth occasion is when the night would fall on / the world. At that instant evil people shall come / out to do wickedness; the adulterers, and the robbers and pois/one[r]s. The evil beasts shall come out, and all the reptiles ¹⁵ that are filled with wickedness, from their dens. And they sta/lk in the night. Also, the demons and fiends find power / to do wickedness in the night. Again, the blows and buffets and / wounds and discharges shall torment people in / the night; because in it the whole of evil shall find strength.

²⁰ The seventh: The night shall display the sign / of the darkness, its father. It has arisen out of its essence; / because this night that came out of this first darkness has / been displayed in the world. Note this night, the shadow / of this first darkness, the one that is entwined and bound in all things ²⁵ above and below.

Behold, I have tau/ght you about these seven wickednesses of the black night; / the ones that it shall do daily in the world, in the ni/ght. The sects have not seen this black night: / what it is; nor from whence is its essence. That all these evils ³⁰ find strength in it! /

[On]ce again he ramified. He says to his disciples: / [There are] five archetypes occur in the sun, it making them / [...] as it finds the world.

(162) The first is its light; for it illumines by its light / the world, and all the creatures who exist in it. /

The second is its beauty; because when it shines, it shall / flood beauty and loveliness upon all creatures ⁵ and everything. /

The third is its peace; for, again, when the sun would / shine on the world, all people shall receive affect/ion through it, and give peace to one another. /

The fourth is the life of the living soul, which it shall release 10 from all the bonds and fetters of heaven and earth. /

The fifth: It gives a strength to the elements; and also it gives a / scent and a taste to the entire Cross of the Light.

So, / you yourselves see that its light illumines / more than all lights that occur in the world. 15 Also, its beauty [i]s more beautiful than all the beauties of mankind. Again, its pea/ce is more surpassing than all the powers and guards who ex/ist in the world. Its releasing action, by which it releases / the living soul, is a full day ahead of / all releasing actions! The strength that it gives to its li20mbs is a great strength, being mightier than all strengths! /

Once again, there are another three archetypes made apparent by the sun, in res/pect of the mystery of the first greatness. /

The first is the filling up of the disk of its ship; because / its ship has filled up every season, and shall not wane at 25 all, the way that the ship of the moon wanes. This continuous filli[ng], / by which it is filled, displays the my/stery of the Father, the great greatness; from whom all the powers / and the gods have come forth. He shall never wane, / nor shall lack ever exist in him!

30 The second: (The sun's) light surpasses the light of / all the stars, and all the lights that occur in the [universe]; / corresponding to the mystery of the light of the Father; for his l[ight sur]/passes and is greater than the light of his a[eons].

(163) The third: This sun is very high above / all else. It surpasses the height of all the mountains and / hills that exist upon the entire earth, corresponding to the mystery of / the Father of Greatness; for he is high above all the household 5 of his light-earth. Also, because the Father himself / is high above all the heights and the mountains of his / light-earth. He is 'filled up' in his image [all] the time / and every hour from eternity to eternity! /

[Beho]ld the two mysteries I have taught you, O my b[e]lov¹⁰ed ones! The mystery of the night and that of the day, which daily come / forth in the world. Now, the mystery of the li/[g]ht and the mystery of the darkness are displayed dai/[ly] in the created order. The sects have not seen them in their / [error]! The mystery of the first great light is ¹⁵ [the] sun, which is this second light-giver, the one that comes dai/ly to the world. It displays all [the] marks o/f its graces, displaying and signifying on its own behalf / that it is good, out of the essence of the good. / It came from the good Father and appeared in ²⁰ this world.

In contrast, this night that is made of fe/ar exists after the mystery of the darkness. Behold too the myster/y of its essence! It displays it in the wo/rld in all these wickednesses. It displays this my/stery daily in the world, but the sects kno²⁵[w] it not in their error. They do not distinguish the my/[st]ery of the light from that of the darkness. Indeed, concerning this myste/[r]y that is hidden from the sects, the saviour cast an allusion / [to] his disciples: Understand what is before / [y]our face, and then what is hidden from you will be unveiled to you*93.

³⁰ [Once] again the apostle speaks: You are the children of the d/[ay and] the children of the light. However, you <[...] the character of the darkness> are the children / [of the night a]nd the children of the darkness.

(164) Yet, blessed are you, my beloved ones! Blessed are your / souls, for you have known the mystery of the day and / that of the night. You have understood, that the day exists after the myste/ry of the light, but the night after the mystery of the dark⁵ness. They have not arisen from one another. Blessed is he / who can know this mystery and distinguish these two esse/nces, that of the light and that of the darkness, the ones that have not arisen / from one another; so that he can inherit life eternal!

---

*93 Ev. Thom. log. 5

••• 66 •••

(164,9 – 165,24)

/ Concerning the Ambassador. /

The solar theme is continued from the previous chapter to this one, entitled after the Ambassador as the principal god who dwells in the sun. Mani compares sunrise and sunset to the first and last moments of the history: when the First Man came and shone over the darkness; and when the Last Statue will ascend, leaving behind him eternal death. The entire 'second time' of the cosmos and of mixture is thus the daytime for the creatures of flesh and darkness, between eternal nights both before and afterwards. Mani uses this lesson to exhort his disciples to preach the truth, whilst there is still time for repentance.

10 Once again he speaks to his disciples: Pay attention, look / [and] understand in the way that I show you. / Two great mysteries are apparent in this shining sun, / at its rising and setting. Now, at the moment / when it rises and is visible in the universe, 15 all creatures of flesh shall lift up their heads fr[om their sleep] / towards the splendour of the sun, <and open their doors*94>. While at evening / time, when the sun sinks from the universe, / all people from every place and even all beasts / shall go in to their dark hiding places. The popula20tion of the entire universe shuts their doors*95 and dark night / overcomes them. They go inside and stay within the dark nig/ht in their hiding places. /

Very great is this mystery revealed by the sun! / For when the sun rises and [be]come[s] visible at the beg25inning of the day all people open their doors, and / all of humanity and every creature emerges onto the ear[th] / to destroy this Light Cross that is established i[n] / silence.

This pertains to the mystery of the First / Man, because when he came out from the grea[t]30ness he shone forth over all the children of darkness. At that mome[nt] / all the children of darkness came forth from their stor[e]/houses, its powers and its armies, abandoni[ng] their cav[es] / and their black abyss. They

---

*94 Or 'mouths'.
*95 Or 'is silent'.

destroyed the [outer] body / of his five sons, who were swathed over hi[s b]o[dy, in (**165**) t]hat first struggle.

Again, when / the sun sinks from the universe and sets, / and all people go in to their hiding places and / houses and conceal themselves; this also pertains to the mystery [5] of the end, as it presages the consummation of the universe. For, / when all the light will be purified and redeemed i[n] / the universe at the last, the collector of all things, / the Last Statue, will gather in and sculpt it/self. It is the last hour of the day, the time [10] when the Last Statue will go up to the aeo[n of] / light. The enemy too, death, will go in to / bondage; to the prison of the souls of the de[ni]iers / and blasphemers who loved the darkness. They will go in / with it to bondage and the dark night overcomes th[em]; [15] and thenceforth this name 'light' will not shine upon them.

Behold / the two mysteries made visible daily in the sun, / which is this splendrous light-giver. /

Now, [b]ecause of this I say to you, my brothers and loved ones: / Take trouble and train yourselves, and preach to the so[20]uls that they might seize the moment, while alive, for their / repentance. As long as there is time to do the good, / before the door is shut and the souls are kept back, stopped / at the gate of life; and they become part of the treasure of the enemy. /

[Wh]en his disciples heard this, they were frightened and alarmed and disturbed <[saying: We ...] in great agitation [...] for we would be saved from death [to dwell in the] imperishable [aeon] for ever>.

••• 67 •••

(165,25 – 166,16)

/ *Concerning the Light-Giver.* /

This chapter is again based upon an analogy about the sun. This time Mani plays on the title 'enlightener', used both of the sun and of himself. The believers are compared to the sun's rays extending across the entire earth; and Mani promises to draw them all after him to the eternal kingdom of light.

Once again he speaks to his disciples, while he sits / in the midst of the congregation: Note how the sun, the great / light-giver, comes with its splendour when it ^{30} shines over the universe, and its rays shall extend over / the entire earth. Again, when it is about to set, its ra/ys shall [disappea]r and sink. It does not leave [behind] a single ray / [on the earth].

Again, this is also what I am like! (**166**) In the image of flesh, wherein I have been set, I have been displ/ayed in the universe. Also, all my children, / the righteous elect who are mine in every / country, are like the sun's rays. At the moment, when I will ^{5} come forth from the universe and go to the household of my people, / I will gather toge[ther] all the elect who have believed in me / to that place. I will draw them to me, each one of them at / the time of his coming forth; I will not leave any one of them / in the darkness.

Now, because of this I say to you: ^{10} Every one of you who loves me, let him love all my children, the / blessed elect, for I am with them. I / alone. How so? For my wisdom anoints th[em] / all. The great glorious one lives in all of them, and every / one who will love them and mix with them in his charity ^{15} may live and be victorious with them; and be saved from the black / universe.

••• **68** •••

(166,17 – 30)

/ *Concerning Fire.* /

Fire is one of the five light elements. Nevertheless, this brief chapter also evidences Mani's delight in classifying all aspects of the world, to establish a totally integrated system.

Once more he speaks: This fire, which burns and is apparent to^{20}day in the world, it does five works. /

The first work that it does is this: It incinerates / and burns wood, and everything that shall be placed upon it. /

The second: It separates four aspects of the wood, which / are these: fire and light, ash and sm^{25}oke.

The third: It gives a taste and an {aroma}*96 to / whatever will be cooked on it. It also gives heat and ch/eer to whoever will be close to it.

The fourth work that [it] / does: All craftsmen shall work the / utensils that they will fabricate in it.

The fifth: ^{30} It sh[all] display light, and the people see by [it].

••• 69 •••

(166,31 – 169,22)

/ Concerning the Twelve Signs of the Zodi/ac and the Five Stars. /

Mani is asked to explain the distribution of the twelve signs of the zodiac and the planetary stars. Since he subscribes to the astral fatalism found throughout gnostic and esoteric systems in late antiquity, he identifies them as evil rulers from the worlds of darkness. However, it is noticeable that this causes a variety of structural problems for his system, all of which are apparent in this chapter.

In Manichaeism the demiurge is one of the light gods, the Living Spirit, unlike the case with many of the other dualistic traditions. Thus, it is constantly necessary to explain why evil powers are given a place and a role in the universe.

The characteristic pentads of Mani's system, here the five worlds of darkness from which the evil powers originate, can not be made to fit the distribution of the twelve zodiacal signs.

Perhaps of most interest, Mani is clearly aware that the ruling powers are commonly understood to be the seven and the twelve (as in Mandaeism). However, since for him the sun and moon are divine vessels, he must develop his teaching about the two ascendants (the two lunar nodes when the moon crosses the ecliptic of the sun). In this chapter there are two obvious attempts to reconcile this matter.

O̲nce more, during one of the times, the apostle [is sitting down] (**167**) among the congregation. A disciple stood before him and question/ed him. He says to him: We entreat you, our master, that you may recount / to us and explain about the twelve signs of the zodiac / that are set in the sphere. How are they determined?

---

*96 ⲚⲂⲞ

Or to what place do they belong, 5 according to their essence? Or else again, these five stars that circle / in them, from whence are they? Or why has the demiurge appointed them / as the authorities and leaders? He is the great construc/tor who has appointed the entire creation; and he has bound and fix/ed them on the sphere. Now, we entreat you, our 10 master, that you may satisfy us about these things that are hidden from all mankind. /

[Th]en he speaks to that disciple who had questioned him: Whether / these twelve signs of the zodiac that are fixed on the sphere, or these fi/ve stars that circle upon them; those and these are rulers, all of them, / according to their essence. They are all enemies and rivals to 15 each other <one oppresses another, they threaten each other>. They plunder one another by the action of the great / craftsman who has formed all the worlds. He has gathered / [them] and bound them on the sphere above, which circles const/antly. Now, while it circles and tumbles them, so they shall do every/thing that they desire, above and below, according to their plea20sure. Nevertheless, a guardian is over them, a debt-collector a/bove them; compelling, extorting, and taking what is theirs / away from them!

Now, this is how it can rightly be understood. They were / [s]eized from the five worlds of darkness, and bound on the s/[ph]ere. Two zodiacal signs were taken per world. Gemini 25 [an]d Sagittarius belong to the world of smoke, which / is the mind. In contrast, Aries and Leo belong to the wo/rld of fire. Taurus, Aquarius and Libra be/[long] to the world of wind. Cancer and Virgo / [an]d [P]isces belong to the world of water. Capricorn 30 [an]d Scorpio belong to the world of darkness. These are / [the] twelve rulers of depravity, the ones that wicked/[ness] shall not [...] For they cause all the evil and / [... in the wo]rld, whether in tree or in flesh.

(168) And understand also about these five stars, the leaders: from where were they / formed? The star of Zeus (Jupiter) was generated from / the world of smoke, which is the mind. In contrast, Aphro/dite (Venus) came about from the world of fire. 5 And then Ares (Mars) belongs to the world of wind. Hermes (Mercury) / belongs to the world of water. Cronos (Saturn) belongs to the world / [of] darkness.

And also, the two ascendants are counted to / fire and desire, the dry and the / moist. They are the father and the mother of all these.

10 An[d al]so, the sun and the moon, which are counted in with them as a / rule <[counte]d to their kind, but why did they count them in with them?> so that they would reign over them. You will discover they subjugate them at / every moment.

These seven we have named, the five stars and the / two ascendants: They are the doers of wickedness that do every wi/cked and bad act in every land, the whole of it, abo15ve and below, in every creature, in the dry / and the moist, in tree and flesh.

Once more I reveal to you about these signs of the zodiac: [They] are / distributed, appointed on four sides, three per angle in / these four places. And they are fixed to this revolving sphere. Ari[es], 20 Leo and Sagittarius, they three belong to a single side*97. / In contrast, Taurus, Capricorn and Virg[o], / these other three belong to another side. And then, Gemini, / Libra and Aquarius belong to another side. Scorp[i]/o, Pisces and Cancer belong to another corner. Now, th[ey] 25 are placed like this, appointed to these four parts, and distribute[d] / on the sphere.

So, when the side of A[ri]/es, Leo and Sagittarius will be plundered by the guard/ian who is over it, who extorts from it and the leaders [w]/ho move upon it; at that instant shall affliction st[r]30ike all the four-footed creatures below. / However, when [the side] of Tau[rus], / Virgo and Capricorn will be plundered; [affliction] sh[all] (169) at once befall the herbs, together with the vegetables and / all the fruits of the trees. Yet again, when / the side of Scorpio, Pisces and Cancer will be plundered; / scarcity shall befall the waters upon the earth, 5 and drought be from place to place. / Conversely, should the side of Gemini, Libra and Aq/uarius be plundered; deformity and stuntedness shall befall / the form of mankind from place to place. /

Behold now, I have explained to you about these tw[el]ve 10 signs

---

*97   The circle of the zodiac is quartered, with each set of three houses grouped as by an equilateral triangle. Thus Aries, Leo and Sagittarius are not consecutive signs; but rather the first, fifth, and ninth houses.

of the zodiac: They were fashioned from the five / worlds of darkness, and bound on the sphere.

Also, I have taught / you about the other five, the stars: They too came about / from the five worlds of the land of darkness.

I have recounted / to you also about the [t]wo ascendants: They are se[15]t to the mystery of fire and desire. They / are the dry and the moist, the father and the mother. /

Again, I have revealed to you about the sun and the moon: They / are strangers to them. Still, because of the constraint of the arrangeme/nt, in that the thing receives light, and as they belong and plunder them; [20] because of this they were counted in with them in relation to the calculation of / the number. For, the sun and the moon are from out of the greatness, / not belonging to the stars and the signs of the zodiac.

••• 70 •••

(169,23 – 175,24)

/ Concerning the Body: It was [25] constructed after the Pattern of the Uni/verse. /

Astrology connects this chapter to the last. However, the basic theme here is the correspondence between the micro- and macro-cosmos. The chapter appears to be redacted from a number of separate sources or Manichaean lessons.

170.1 – 20 The structure of the human body and its organs accords to that of the universe.

170.21 – 172.29 The events that occur in the watch-districts of the five sons of the Living Spirit, the conflicts between evil powers and the gods, correlate to those within the individual as the new man struggles with the old. Compare 92.9 – 94.16.

172.29 – 173.20 Demonic rulers exist in the organs of the four worlds of the human body.

173.21 – 174.10 The zodiacal signs correspond to parts of the body vertically from the head to the feet.

174.10 – 175.4 In a second schema the signs are arranged in a circle from the right temple of the head round to the genitals, and returning up the left side of the body.

175.5 – 24 Thousands of evil rulers exist in the human body. They cause illness within, or suppurations on the surface.

[Aga]in, on one of the occasions, the apostle is sitting do/[w]n among the church in the midst of the congregation. He says to his / disciples: This whole universe, above and [30] below, [re]flects the pattern of the hum[an] body; / [as the f]ormation of this body of flesh ac(170)cords to the pattern of the universe.

Its head is like / the first-fruits of the five garments. And, from its neck / down to the site of its heart, it resembles the pattern / of the ten firmaments. And again, the heart accords to [5] the wheel of the rotating sphere. And, from its heart / down to its intestines (?), is like this atmosphere / that extends from the sphere down to the earth. The [male] part / of the body corresponds to this great earth. And also, from its / intestines (?) down to its loins is [10] like the three earths. And also, its shinbones to the pa/ttern of the space in which the Porter stands. / Its footsoles to the great earth upon which the Po/rter is stood; and the four fastenings that are under his / feet. Its liver to the vessel of fire. [15] Its flesh to the vessel of darkness. Its b/lood to the vessel of water.

Now, this is how / the small body corresponds to the macro- / cosmos in its firmaments, in its orderings, in its / mountains, its walls and its vessels. As I have [20] made clear to you!

Once more, I reveal to you: / There exist five great camps in this / great outer zone, of which the five sons of the Living / Spirit are masters.

So, in the first watch-station / above, of which the Keeper of Splendour is master, [25] on the battlement of all the works, is found his authority / over the three heavens. Then the ones below him [... / ...] the great King of Honour. /

The second watch, of which the great King of Honour / is master, his own authority (extends) over the seven [30] firmaments beneath him.

The thi[rd] / watch, of which the Adamant [is master, his authority] (171) rei[g]ns from the firmament down below to the [earth]. / [And he] invigorates, according to his authority, the sphere and the [wo]/rlds of the atmosphere; and the other four worlds that are appointed on / this earth.

The fourth watch, over which the King of [5] Glory has power, is the three wheels. And his / [auth]ority lies over the three earths upon the hea[d] / of the Porter.

The fifth watch is the wat/ch over which the Porter is authoritative. Again, he is / master, according to his authority, over this great earth [10] he stands upon, and the four fastenings under / his feet.

Affliction has come about in these five watches from ti/me to time.

So, in the watch of the Keeper of Splendour, / s[in] desired to spurt up towards the image / of the Ambassador. Yet, they barred it from that place, [15] and it fell back down in shame. /

Again, an earthquake and treachery occured in the watch of the great / King of Honour, which the watchers who had arisen / at the time and had [...] they who were sent came down, / until they were humbled.

Also, in the watch [20] of the Adamant, the abortions came to the earth and fashioned [the] / figure of flesh.

Again, in the watch of the King of Glory, / a commotion happened in these three earths abo/ve the Porter. The pathway was obstructed for / [the] ascent of these three wheels; that of wind, that of [25] water, and that of fire.

Also, in the watch of the Po/[r]ter, the fastenings beneath were laid bare and strained their / [ch]ains. A great [ear]thquake befell that place. /

[Like] these five watch-[stations], which exist in this great / [... these fi]ve camps, which I have recounted (**172**) [to] you. This is also the case with this body that the e[l/e]ct wear. There are another five camp[s] / there, and the Light Mind is watching over them, and the new / man who is with him.

The elect person who will con[5]trol and subdue the configuration of his face, which is above his bo/dy, and guide it towards the good; he resembles / the mystery of the Keeper of Splendour, who rules o/ver the watch above the zone.

Whoever will become master / [over] his heart and subdue it; he is the sign of the great [10] King of Honour, who subdues the seven heavens.

Wh/oever will become master to his genitals and subdue his lust; he is / the mystery of the Adamant of Light, the one who / subdues Matter.

Whoever will subdue the stomach and / become master to the fire that is in him, and also purify [15] the nourishment that comes in to him; he resembles the likeness / of the King of Glory, the one who turns the wheels, sending / the life above.

Whoever will become master over the ruling-po/wer that is beneath in his feet, and bind it with the / chain of peace; he is like the Porter, the one who subdu[20]es with his footsoles the abysses below.

Also, the teaching / of wisdom, which circulates in that body: to / the likeness of the Virgin of Light, who goes up and / comes down in this zone, above and be/low.

Also, love and joy, faith [25] and truth, in which the person should l[iv]e: they are / to the likeness of these two light ships. For, the living s[o]/ul should go up in them and become free through them; / and it ascends from the abysses below and arrives at [the] / heights above.

Once more, understand this other (truth): [30] There exist four worlds i[n th]is body of the f[lesh], / and there exist countless times seven rulers [in the b]ody [of the four] / worlds!

So, the first w[orld is from its] (173) neck up; and also the seven rulers who are / in this upper world are these: the two organs of sigh[t], / and the two of hearing, and the two of smell. / The other one is the mouth, which is the organ of taste.

[5] [The] second world is from its neck down to / its entire upper torso. And also, the seven rulers w[ho] / are in this second world are: its [two] arms / that accord to the pattern of its two ears, which [oc]/cur in its first world above; and i[t]s [10] two breasts that are to the pattern of its organs of smell; / and the two eyes of its heart;

and the gullet of the stoma/ch between the two breasts, which in the che/st is the pattern of the mouth.

Once more, there exist seven / rulers in the third world of the body, [15] which are these: the fat, the lung, the sple[en], the liv[e]r, the gall, / and its two kidneys.

Also, the fourt[h wo]rld b/elow. There are another seven there of this same kind: its / two buttocks (?), and its two testicles, and its two loins; / and the member out of which the seed comes, that begets [20] all the forms. /

[O]nce more the enlightener speaks to his hearers: Ari/es and Taurus, Gemini, Cancer, Leo, / Virgo, Libra, Scorpio, Sagittarius, Ca/pricorn, Aquarius and Pisces; these are the twe[25]lve signs of the zodiac that occur in the worlds above, on / the sphere. They are interlocked and bound on this turning wheel, the one in whi/ch they are [...], fixed, and planted. And, regarding [a]ll these twelve / signs of the zodiac, this is how they were appointed and made leaders / [...] on the sphere beneath the heaven that is the wheel of the [30] [stars]. Now, they are appointed like this, they are thus, so that you can find the head of / [...] and you find the tail too [... / ...]

Again, they occur like this, (174) these that we have recited, one after another in this body. They are counted / by order and number from the head to the / feet. Its head is Aries. Its neck and its shoul/ders are Taurus. Its two arms Gemini. [5] Its upper torso is Cancer. Its stomach is / Leo. Its belly is Virgo. The v[er]tical spine / and its intestines (?) are Libra. Its genitals / [S]corpio. Its loins are Sagittarius. Its knees ar[e / Capri]corn. Its shinbones are Aquarius. [10] The soles of its feet are Pisces.

Behold, these / are also distributed one after another. They exist in this body, / as if turned to the side and bent to the pattern of the twelve signs of the zodiac. / They too are thus, arranged one against another, head / to tail, a[s] they occur on the wheel [15] [...] up.

Also, they are counted by / order and number of the body and all its members. / So, we have proclaimed that these are turned to the side, bent, and spread / out; because from its head down to its / hip shall count six to its left, and another six to its right. [20] The six that are down its right are these that I / will recount: the right temple is Aries; its right shoul/der is Taurus; its right arm is / Gemini; its right rib-cage is Cancer; / its stomach is Leo; the right side of its reproductive organs [25] are Virgo. Conversely, the other s[ix] about which we have spoken, / which are to its left, in contrast they come / from its hip to its head: its left [...] / is Libra; its left rib-cage is Scorpi[o]; / its left breast and left kidney [is Sag][30]ittarius; its [left] elbow [is Capric](175)orn; its left shoulder is Aquariu[s]; / its left temple is Pisces. This is how / the creator of the body himself has appointed them. He has [set] / them in order and arranged them, one against its companion, head to [tail].

[5] Once more he speaks: Listen to this other lesson that I will pr[ocla]/im to you. Understand that there exist many powers / in this body. They are the house-dwellers who are made the leade[rs] / in it. There are eight hundred and forty times ten thousand [ru]/lers made chiefs in the human b[o]dy! They are distributed and [10] set firm, quartered according to house. The count and / number of their houses is two hundred and ten times ten thousand. /

When all these rulers come creeping and [m]ov/[ing with]in the body, they will meet one another; and they shall / beset and destroy one another, and [...] [15] in them there. When [... t/il]l they shall erupt from the body of the person who [will] / die; and make putrid boils and sores and [bur]ning wounds / in the body. Either they might have made hi[m] sick with[in]; / or else they might come forth upon his outer side. Those woun[20]ds shall first be squeezed and discharge their liquid, / and empty out their pus, until they are squeezed [... / ...] and the suppuration forced out from the wound. Afterwards, / their scars [shal]l close over; and they are healed and obtain relief f/rom the places that came out upon them.

••• 71 •••

(175,25 – 176,8)

/ Concerning the Gathering in / of the [E]lements. /

This chapter discusses the sequence by which the light elements will be gathered in and ascend up to the eternal kingdom at the end of time, the destruction of the universe. This corresponds to the eschatological path taken by each soul: to answer the summons of salvation, to become one with the Light Mind, to ascend up the Pillar to the moon (the First Man), then to the sun (the Ambassador), and thus to the aeons.

[Onc]e more the enlightener speaks: In what way shall / [the] elements be gathered in, from one to another?

The l^{30}[igh]t shall be gathered in [to] the fire, and the fire itself gathered / [in to the water, and the wa]ter gathered in to the wind, and the (**176**) [win]d gathered to the air, and the air gathered to the answer, / [an]d the answer gathered to the summons. Also, the summons / [to the] purified Mind, which is the intellectual. The intellectual to / [the P]illar of Glory, [the P]illar of Glory to the First ^{5} [M]an, the Man to the Ambassador, the Ambassador / [to] the aeons of greatness.

They are gathered in like this; / but, [they] will be gathered on one occasion only, and go up a/[b]ove to the place of rest for ever and ever.

••• 72 •••

(176,9 – 178,23)

^{10} *Concerning the worn / and torn apart Garments, or the tattered Clothes, / or the Elements, the C/ross, and the rest too. /*

The divine light soul (or elements) that descended at the beginning of the history with the First Man was devoured by the evil demonic forces of matter. During the course of the history it has experienced different forms of degradation, and of salvation, depending upon its position and role in the conflict. Since it was the armour (or the five sons) that the First Man had assumed at his descent, it frequently receives various names that are variants on the concept of a garment. In this chapter Mani explains the different terms and roles during the history; but emphasises that they will all return to a single form and a single name at the final victory.

Once more the apostle is sitting in the congregation of his [15] disciples. He says to [hi]s disciples: What is this lesson / [that] is written in [the scriptures]? It proclaims the name the 'great garm/ents', but what then are these 'great garments'? Or again, this / you sometimes call the 'rags', what are those / 'rags'? Or the 'worn and torn apart'? Or what are [20] the 'images and the tattered clothes'? Or what is this name: / 'light element'? Or conversely, what is the 'Cro/ss of Light'? Or why named otherwise: the 'couns/el of life'? Or what is the 'soul that is slain'; being killed, / oppressed, and murdered in the enemy? What are all these names? [25] Look, they are written and sealed, according to memory, / by a multitude of scriptures. Now then I ask you, / so that you may tell me: What are they? Or how have they changed / with all these names and become set in altered forms, / namely all these?

His disciples say to him: [30] You, our father, are the source [of] all wisdoms. [Th]/erefore, we entreat you that you may open o[ur e]/yes about all these things. Te[ach us these wisdoms], / since you are the fount of [all wisdoms]!

(177) Then speaks the apostle to them: It is proper for [yo/u] to understand this. The garments that are named / 'great garment' are the five intellectuals that [make per]/fect the body of the Pillar of Glory, the Perfect Man. [5] They were purified by the coming of the Ambassador. /

In contrast, the ones named 'rag': the rags are the devoured enlightening power. / It is compounded and entangled in [the bo]/dy of the universe in the rulers who are above, who / exist in all the firmaments. Also, its shine is t[10]hat which lights up and is displayed in the stars of the chain and the powers / [of the] course. And likewise, these rags that are entangled in / these [thre]e [ear]ths below, above the head of the Port/[er ...] on the earth that is under the Porter. These are / [named] the 'rags', because [...] set [... 15 ...]

However, the 'great worn and torn apart garments', / which we have proclaimed, is this entangled living power. / It is reaped, cut, and devoured. / It is overpowered by the five worlds of the flesh, wh/ich creep as they move from place to place.

20 On the other hand, [these] we have termed the 'images and the great / tattered clothes' [...] are the three great garments / of the wind, the fire, and the water. These the Living Spirit / cloaked upon his body. With them he set in order thing/s in the universe. With them also he emptied the vess25els. He swept them out and laid them bare in front of the Por/[t]er at the foundation of all things. /

Conversely, '[the ele]ments', we have called them this name, are this / [pow]er that remains in all things below. It rises up / [in] the wombs of all the earths, gathering together, and pouring 30 f[ort]h upon [a]ll thin[gs].

And then, the '[Light] Cross' / [we have termed] this bound 'light power'. It / [...] all [...] upon the earth, in (**178**) the dry and the moist.

Also, the one name[d] / the 'counsel of life' is the summons and the / [obed]ience. It moves in all these powers that we have named. / It awakens them, gives them ease, and drives them 5 to their movement.

The one named 'the soul [that is s/l]ain', which is killed, oppressed and murdered; it is / this power of fruit, vegetables and seeds. They shall be th/[r]eshed, plucked and cut down; and they / give nourishment to the worlds of the flesh. Further: the wood should it be dr10y, and the garment should it become ragged, will perish. Again, it is [a pa/]rt of this entire soul that is slain and killed; s/ince also even this whole part of it they kill / [...]

For all these names [... / ...] are a single [...] since the beginning, it [...] 15 as it enlightens; but they separated into all these parts / in this first contest. They became set in all these altered / forms, and these many names. Of course, / if now all these var[iet]ies are laid bare, and stripped / of all these appearances, [and] parted from all 20 these names; they will gather together [and] make a single form, / and a single name, unaltered and unchangeable

for ever in the / land of their first essence, from which they were
sent forth / against the enemy.

••• **73** •••

(178,24 – 180,26)

25 *Concerning the Envy of Matter.* /

178.26 – 179.16 Mani begins by outlining four crucial moments in the history
when Matter (hyle), the driving force of the darkness, has displayed the
envy that is the essence of its nature. It envied: the First Man; the image of
the Ambassador; Adam; Christ and the apostles.
   179.16 – 28 Furthermore, it has caused envy for Mani himself, and his
church. The apostle turns the discussion into a warning to his listeners that
sin will never be content to leave them secure in their faith.
   179.28 – 180.19 Mani illustrates the point by recounting the typical actions
of an envious person against the faithful, in every church since the beginning.
   180.19 – 26 Final admonitions to be steadfast in the faith.

Once again the apostle speaks to his disciples: [The] / entirety of
envy is this first nature that occu[red] / in the worlds of darkness.

In this envy that [...] / in it, the First Man [...] its poiso[n ...] 30 its
evil-doing. His garment[s] were [...] / it cut them and drew them;
[...]

(**179**) It envied the first image of the Ambassad[or], / which he
displayed to it in the heights abov[e], / i[n] his form that it saw. It
established the seal and the i[m]/age of flesh, and put the
impression of t[h]at image 5 on flesh, its very own birth. /

[The th]ird time it envied Adam, the fir[st / hum]an. It seized a
power from him, and bore it forth from a / [rib of] of Adam's
[flesh].

The fourth time / [it en]vi[ed] all the firs[t-bo]rn and the first
f[a10thers; an]d the blessed Christ who is the father of / all the
[apostles]. Again, he too, it envied his / [endurance upon] the
wood of the cross. It envied [the] fa/[thers of r]ighteousness. It
was jealous of the [... / ...] all congregations of [... th]eir love over

him, [15] [which] is among them, by the desire of its wickedness. It
has [...] t/hem.

Furthermore, I myself was sent now, in this / last generation. It
has envied me. For it wishes now, at the end, to be / god in its old
land. After it had caused envy for me and / fulfilled its jealousy
there, it also envied all my righteous[20]ness and my entire church
and the whole assembly / [of] my catechumens. It could not bear
to see a / single wise and true person, upright and stead/[fa]st in
his deeds. Rather, it shall envy you with / [i]ts jealousy and
wickedness; every one, whether [25] [a] great person or a disciple, a
man o/r a woman, a male catechumen or a / female catechumen. They who are in truth, being perfect in / [the] faith. These
of this kind sin shall not be content to [... /

...] cho[o]sing a single day. He was strong [30] [...] they are of it,
but he has separ/[ated himself. He] spoke with them so that he
might do (**180**) [a]mong them his will, whether outside or
within. / While [in]side, he wounds them by his envy, with /
[s]icknesses and pains and physical afflictions; and outside /
with false reports and lying accusations [5] that he spreads as
rumours after them. He makes [t/he]m hated and stinking
among mankind, more and / [m]ore. He shall return to burst
against the teacher and the righteous e[lec/t] person. He who
preaches, manifestin[g / the] mystery in the revel[at]ion of [... [10]
sa]ve by him his lamb[s ... / ...] in his hands. More and more it
shall envy [... / ...] speaking after him with [...] words [...] / Now,
these who are lesser in power, they [... / ...] negligent and
confused i[n their] contorte[d] faith [...] [15] they fall from the faith.
This is the desire [of Mat]/ter, the thought of death. This is the
envy of its wi[cke]/dness, that it casts upon the entire kindred of
life / from the very beginning until my time, from m/e too to
my church.

Therefore, it is appropriate [20] for the wise person that he be steadfast and strong, / and stay with his truth and hope. And he not be
/ defeated nor cowed, nor give himself to the en[vy] / and hatred
of dark Matter. Rather, he will stand firm [... / ...] in God and be
strong and stay [with] [25] his hope and his [faith]; and he
overcomes [...] / Whatever would cover me comes before him.

••• 74 •••

(180,27 – 181,31)

/ Concerning the living Fire: / It is present in Eight Places.

The living fire is one of the five light elements, and its origin is the eternal kingdom. However, the First Man also swathed it upon his body at his descent; and so it is present in this universe, from whence it is purified. It equates to the consideration amongst the five intellectual qualities.

30 Once again the apostle speaks: The [holy] living f[ire] / is present i[n] eight places. /

The first place wherein it is, is this [light] land [where it is present and] / exists. It is established beneath [it ... (181) ut]terly beyond the totality. It is the foundatio[n and / ba]sis of that great earth, and the consideratio[n / th]at is beneath them all.

The second pla[ce / whe]rein it is, is the Father, the God of truth; because 5 [the Fathe]r is established in his great, mighty consideration. / So, [firs]t in the Father. The other powers that came from him / were revealed through him, and (the fire) too came w[i]/th them [and was revea]led by them.

The third / [place wherein it is], is the First Man, h[e] wh[o ... 10 ...] armour. Again, it is this fire [... / ...] on the body of the Perfect Man. /

[The fourth is this fir]e that was purified from all the [light] powers, / [which is i]n the outer wall, in the ship of the day. /

[The fifth i]s this fire that is in the light-giver of the night 15 [...] within the water. /

[The] sixth is this f[i]re that is purified from the totality. The Living [Spirit] / swathed it upon his body, over the summons and / the obedience. He has established many things by it. He / went down and stripped himself of it before the Por20ter.

The seventh is this living fire that is of / the new earth, and is the consideration. For it is the first / foundation in the new earth, it they built anew [... / ...] the first course, that is a crown for the entire earth. T[hey] / are below the totality, over the entire earth of da[rkne]ss ²⁵ [...] in it, in the [...] whole [...] /

[The] eigh[th] is the fire that shall be revealed in this [... / ...] person, and it signifies fear and war. Furthermore it / [...] it displays and manifests its sign in / [its ter]ror. It shall be r[ev]ealed in these two light ships.

³⁰ This i[s the way] that the holy living fire exists in these / [eight places].

••• 75 •••

(181,31 – 183,9)

/ *[Concerning the Letter (?)]* /

In this kephalaion the summons and the obedience are considered to be letters, a motif also found in the Hymn of the Pearl in the *Acta Thomae*. These two are the essence of redemption, the call to knowledge and the answer of knowledge, otherwise jointly termed the counsel of life. In Manichaeism the prototypical moment is the salvation of the First Man by the Living Spirit; and the call and answer are themselves divinised as, respectively, the sixth sons of each of these two great gods (92.1 – 4).

However, the point of this chapter is that the letters contain all know-ledge of what has happened and what will happen; and thus it emphasises the divine foreknowledge and consequent control of events. As usual Mani connects the primordial event to the present, and makes it relevant to his audience. The Light Mind, which is the call to salvation within the church, is also an all-knowing letter. Similarly, the response of the people in their good works is also a letter; and so Mani can assure his listeners that everything they have done and need is known to Christ.

[O nce again he speaks to h]is disciples, preaching the wo(182)[r]d of life. And thus he speaks to them about the su[mm/o]ns and the obedience: Consider the summons, which was sen[t f]/rom the Living Spirit in the beginning. He sent it [to the First] / Man. It is a peace letter and greet[ing] ⁵ that he wrote and sent to his brother, in which all the [tid]/ings are written down, together with everything it will / [bring ab]out and establish by [th]at summons. That / [summ]ons, the First Ma[n ... / is o]rdained to happen.

The an[swer that was sent from [10] the] First Man came to the heigh[ts, to the Living Spirit]. / That is also [a] letter, [which was sent from] / the First Man to the Living Spirit, [in which] all [the tidings] / are written down; and [every] w[ar] / and the struggles that he had waged. It did [...] [15] in the answer that the First Man [... / ...] everything that had happened and everything [that would happen], / all [t]hat had been done and whatever is made ready to be done by him. / The Living Spirit knew a[ll] the wars and the dang/ers and the contests that the rulers had waged against the First Ma[20]n.

The Light Mind also, which came from the beloved Chris/t and was sent to the holy church, is a / letter of peace too; in which all the reve[la]/tions and wisdom are written down [...] / all [...] in the light and everything that had happened [... [25] ...] it was prior to all mankind, and all that [...] / to happen at the last in it, as the holy church / shall understand all things.

This creation also [...] / this light product, that shall be generated from the holy church / and go to [...] is [a letter] [30] too; since all the [g]ood works tha[t the] holy ch/urch performs are written down in i[t. Every / thing] that it may entreat its father for, so that [... e]/ase in the world. And at the last [... r]/est before him. They are present in [... fa(183)s]ting and prayers and good works that [... / ...] them. It shall go up and be rev[eal]ed b/efore the blessed Christ. He shall answer it [... / ...] he [gives] power and makes it at ease [... [5] ...]

Indeed, [d]ue to this, I say to you: / [...] each [...] and entreaty, since a [... / ...] prayer. Everything that you will ask [for / ...] will be given you*98, if [... / ...] perfect.

---

*98 Mt. 21:22 Jn 15:7 16:24

••• **76** •••

(183,10 – 188,29)

/ [Conce]rning Lord Manichaios: / how he journeyed. /

This important chapter has clear historical context and content. Mani is so
busy answering the calls of King Shapur, (who does seem to have given him
and his teaching some real protection), that a disciple wishes that there
could be two Manis! The apostle replies that the world has scarcely been able
to accept him alone. With authentic frankness he recounts the trials of his
missionary journeys and the opposition of the authorities in various lands.

[Further, it] ha[pp]ened one time while our master Manichaios,
/ [our] light [enl]ightener, was staying in the [ci¹⁵ty] of Ktesiphon. Shapur, the king, enquired / after and summoned him.
Our master stood / up and went to Shapur the king. Afterwards /
[he] returned and came back to his congregation. When he had
been a / [sh]ort while sitting down, before delay elapsed, King
Sha²⁰[p]ur enquired af[te]r him another time. He sent, he called
f/[o]r him. Again (Mani) returned, he retraced and went to King
Shapur. / He spoke with him and proclaimed to him the word of
Go/[d]. Again he retu[r]ned and came to the congregation. Also,
a third / occasion, King Sh[ap]ur enquired after and called for
him; ²⁵ and [he] returned to him once more. /

[T]hen one of his disci[pl]es made a retort, Aurades by name, /
[the] son of [Kap]elos. He says to our enlightener: Please, / our
master [Manich]aios, give to us two Manis resembling you; /
[pass]ing for you! Good, peaceful, and ³⁰ compassionate [...]
disciples in righteousness [like] you / [...] one Mani will remain
with us as you; / [and the other go to] King [Sha]pur, his [mind]
at ease, / [and proclaiming it] to him.

(**184**) W[h]en our enlightener heard these words from that
[dis]/ciple, he shook his head. He says to him: Now be[ho/ld], I,
a single Mani, came to the worl[d to / p]roclaim in it the word of
[God]; and [do] ⁵ therein the good will that had been ent[rusted to
me]. /

Then look, I, one Mani alone, have not been permitted [to] / speak freely in the world; I [...] / that I find room to fulfill [the good will] / that has been entrusted to me. Ye[t], I have done [the will of the mys¹⁰ter]y, which I preach in the [living] tru[th]. /

[Fo]r the world loves the darkness; [but] it h[ates / the lig]ht, because its works are evil*⁹⁹. [Still, I, I have travelled] / so that I would do the will of the l[ight, and spr]/ead the truth far and wide, in accord with what the[y entrusted to ¹⁵ me]. And, behold, the world bears down on me with [... / ...] upon me with its sects. They give me no place [to prea/ch] therein, and besides I am a single Mani. / I came to the world, and they have not given me time to pre/ach according to my will. They have not accepted me. ²⁰ On the other hand, if we do as [...] as you have spoken / [to us], what might we do then? How were [... / ...]? Rather, this [... / ...] to you, and recount it to [you].

At the time when I sail[ed] / the sea in the ship, I went [...] ²⁵ I found it necessary [...] / the life that is with me in the world [... / ...] I stirred the whole land of India [... / ...] all the people who dwell in it [... / ...] all of them to me, so that they might bear ³⁰ two to three times [...] / in their land according to their heart [... / ...] and the wise man [...] / they {}*¹⁰⁰ [... (185) se]t them against me. At that moment I ceased finding l[i]/ght, I ceased speaking freely with the voice that is / of truth, which is entrusted to me.

Now behold, [... / ...] in India. It may act against me in its [... ⁵ ... and] accept the greater ones and the counsellor[s / and the] satraps and the governors who are found there [... / ... I was] difficult [for] it, it stirred not [... / ...] because they belong to it [... / ...] from all the sinners [... ¹⁰ ...] to me. I was more difficult for it than [all] these / [... did not acce]pt me, and it persisted to [... / ...] it. For the world loves [the] dark/ness; [bu]t [it hates] the light, because its wo[rk]s / [are evil.

I crossed] the seas another time. I took [... ¹⁵ ...] India. I went up to the land of Pe[rsia. / I le]apt from the sea and went [... / ...] the land of Persia and its ci[ties ...] / in this living truth that is wi[th me ...] to the [li]ght of [... / ...] proclaim [... the] powers and the

---

*99 Jn. 3:19 Also 185.12 – 13
*100 ⲍⲱⲱⲛⲉ

[au]thorities [... [20] ... / ...] and the holders of authority [... / en]lightener [...] in the land of Persia [... / b]ody [...] because of this truth that I proclaimed, si/[tt]ing in their midst [...] to one another. S[ee [25] n]ow, [... / ...] in their land [...] to me the power. The Father [... / ...] livi[ng ...] all occasions. The one who [... / to] it [... / ... [30] ... / ...] in the land [... / ...] (**186**) how strong is it? (The land) tolerates the kings and accepts [the / s]atraps and the governors who are ther[e. It] / stirred [amon]g them, it was not defeated in their midst [... / ...] it was not able to accept [the truth that I pro[5]claimed] there. It did not [...

I] / came [out] from the land of Pers[ia]. I went up / [to Me]sene, the city that [... / ...] in this truth that is in me, in [... I / proc]laimed this knowledge; I separated [the light from the darkness and] [10] d[iscriminat]ed life from death, what is go[od from] / what is evil, the righteous person from the sin[ner. I proc]/la[imed] the path of life and the command[ments ... / ...] Yet, when they had heard the voice [of truth and life], / the [rulin]g-power and the swarm of demons [... [15] ...] and the race of mankind [... / ...] under wickedness and hatred, they [... / ... they did not] allow me, [nor] did they / [permit me] to preach [the tr]uth in [tranquill]ity, the way that it / i[s]. See: In [...] [20] for they tolerate the kings, they acce[pt ...] and the / caesars and the satraps a[nd the governors who] are f[ound] / among them. Yet, the truth that I proc[laimed] among [them], / they did not accept it; and [... they did not listen] / to the voice of life that I cried out [among them].

[25] Again, [fr]om that place I came to the land of Babylon, the [ci]/ty of the Assyrians, and walked in [it]. I went in [to] / the [other] cities, and spoke in this truth [of the life that is with] me. I / proclaimed there the word of [truth and li]fe. / With [the voi]ce of the proclamation I se[parated the light from the dark][30]ness there, what is good from [what is evil ... / ...] the powers who are master [over ...] (**187**) their envy to the heart of the kings and the leaders / there. They and the sects of that place, they / [were s]et against me. Even as you yourselves see, they have w[aged] / some great wars [wit]h me. The lawle[ss] judges [5] [took] me, they watched. They and their rulers and the[ir / lea]ders took me in the midst of their land. If as / [...] to me the protection of the

Father, who does [not] hel[p / the lawless]. Yet I, he helps me at [all] times / against his [enemy]. Still, they would not permit me in B[a¹⁰bylon] a single day to journey in their land. /

S[ee no]w: How great is the land of the Assyrians? / [It is abl]e to tolerate the kings and accept the eparchs / [and the gen]erals and the caesars and the governors / [... i]n it. It did not stir, nor was it [defe]ated before [them ¹⁵ ...] but, on the other hand, to me, it stirred and was disquieted [... / ...] It waged against me a multitude of struggles. [Therefore, I] le[ft be/hind me] the Assyrians.

I went to the land of the Medes and Par/thians. At that place I played the harp of wisdom; [I] / spoke in this living truth [th]at is with me. The [whole] land ²⁰ [of] the Medes and the Parthians stirred, it shook [... / ...], to accept the hope of the life that I [proclaimed]. Yet see: How great / is the land of the Medes and the Parthians? Many / [ci]ties are found there. It was able to accept the kings / [an]d the leaders who were there; but, on the other hand, it was not able to acc²⁵[e]pt the power of my truth. It stirred, it all shook just as / [...]

Then the apostle speaks to that disciple: / Indeed I, a single Mani, came to the world. / All the cities [of the] world stirred, they shook. (The world) did not wi/[sh to] acce[pt m]e; unless I humbled its rebelliousness ³⁰ [...] I have subdued its powers and brought / [...] all that were there. I have planted in it / [...] I have sown this [s]eed of life. I chose (188) a few from among the multitude [... / I], one Mani alone, came to the world; and [... / ...] all the powers of the world stirred. A turmoil ar[ose] / before me. And thus, if tw[o] Manis had [come] ⁵ to the world, what place would be able to tolerate them, or [what land] would / [be able] to accept them?

I, a singl[e] Mani, [d/id] come, and walking on tip-toes [... / ... no] pl[ace] was found for me wherein I could stand [fast ... / ...] on the fullness of my feet, [and walk on ¹⁰ the] earth like everyone, and do there [... / ... / ...] all of you, pray to God that he might [... / ... fe]et henceforth, this single Mani, who is [among you / on that d]ay, that [...] will happen [... ¹⁵ ...] he might do the will of the living ones [in the] / holy [ch]u[rch]. However, you, blessed are you i[f] / you make yourselves strong in this truth that I have given to you; so that you may be / [confirmed] in it, in the life which continues for ever and ever. /

Then, [whe]n that disciple had heard these things, he says to [20] the apostle: Blessed am I my master! [I], and all my other brothers / who hear these great things from you, we know that w[e] / all are among the living. And we are alive by your advent t[o] / us! We have found the truth more than all people who are in the wo/rld. Who of us will be able fully to repay you for the good[25]ness that you have done us, our father? Only the Father who se/nt you is sufficient fully to repay you for this / toil. For the recompense that you desire of him, the God who has / sent you, is this: every prayer you entreat of the Father, / may he grant you your prayer and your co[nsolation].

••• 77 •••

(188,30 – 190,10)

/ *The Chapter of the Four K[ingdoms].* /

In this lesson Mani takes as his text a saying of Jesus, and develops his own teaching from an analysis of the terminology used by the saviour. To share not only with the righteous elect, but even with catechumens, is a deed beyond any achieved by the greatest kingdoms of this world. It will bring an eternal reward.

It is notable that this kephalaion speaks of the indwelling Holy Spirit, rather than the to be expected Light Mind (and see 143.24 – 32).

Once again the apostle speaks: There are f[our great kingdoms] / in the world.

[The first is the kingdom (**189**) of] the land of Ba[by]lon and of Persia.

The s[ec/o]nd is the kingdom of the Romans.

The thir[d / is the k]ingdom of the Axumites.

The fourth is the kin/[g]dom of Silis.

These four great kingdoms e[x^{5}i]st in the world; there is none that surpasses them. /

Yet, I, I say to you in truth that whoever [will give] / bread and a cup of water*101 to one of my disciples on [account of / the name of G]od, on account of this truth that I have m[an]if[est]/ed; [t]hat one is great before God. [He s]ur10passes these four great kingdoms, which are so g[reat]! / He does more than their armies, because t/hey did not listen to God's truth, nor did they h[el]p / r[ighte]ousness.

Not only this, but whoever will [give] bread / and a cup of water to a catechumen of the [truth, on acc]ount of the 15 name of God and on account of the truth [that is manifest]; / that one is brought near to the [truth. Hi]s end will t[u]/rn to rest for ever.

[Just as the saying] that the [g]ood savi[our] / uttered: W[hoever will give bread and a cup of water] / to one of these least [of the faithfu]l who believe me, on account of the name 20 of a disciple [...] /

Now, [the] savi[our] is callin[g] these saints 'least of the faithful'. / So, I, behold I have proclaimed of the catechumens / [th]at whoever will fellowship with catechumens who are / with the knowledge, and helps them, he surpasses these [ki25n]gdoms that I have counted for you; because all these kingdoms / know not the truth of God. For they {}*102 / the lust of the world and care about livelihood. /

Indeed, due to this, I tell you that these two persons / whom I have named, [the] faithful catechumen and the faithful ri30[ghteous one, are the] ones in wh[om] the Holy Spirit dwells. / [...] he sees [...] Indeed, because of this (190) [he] will give them alms and fellowship with them. / [He] gives it for the Holy Spirit that dwells in them. / The Holy Spirit too will give his thanks be[fore] / his true father. And the true father will repa[y] 5 his reward at the last day because of / the Holy Spirit that dwells in these saints./

How great is this truth that I have unveiled for you, / {}*103. Due to this I have told y[ou]: Bless/[ed] are these who will hear and believe [it, and] set their 10 [h]eart upon it with a single mind [...]

---

*101 See Mt. 10:42 Also 189.13 – 14.18 – 19
*102 ⲃⲉⲗⲏ
*103 ⲁϯ ⲁⲡⲁⲥ

••• **78** •••

(190,11 – 191,8)

/ Concerning the Four Things over which Peo/ple kill each other. /

The four obsessions of mankind are food, sex, riches, and strife for glory. Unlike faith and truth, all these are mortal.

On[ce aga]in he speaks to his disciples: Th[ere are] f[ou]r major ¹⁵ [things] in the world over which a[ll people / on earth kill] each other. /

T[he firs]t thing is [the obsession] of people; in that they would eat / [for the swell]ing of their body [...] /

The [sec]ond is [sexual inter]course; [...] fornication ²⁰ [...] fornication [... men] and wo/men {}*¹⁰⁴ in it with each other.

The third / thing is w[ealth; and ...] the useless riches in [which] / they shall pride themselves without [...] from it. /

The fourth is war; and the d[ispu]tes, the {}*¹⁰⁵ ²⁵ and the trials that they instigate against each other. / Someone is victor [o]ver another, [wi]th each o[ther] / in tyranny, so that they have received a name in the world. /

All people, they who side with these four major things that [a]/re on every tongue [in the] world [...] ³⁰ they struggle so that they might generate them [... a]/mong them.

However, I say to yo[u ... **(191)** whoever wi]ll accept faith and invite it in together with this ph[ysi]/cian whom I have brought, and he separates the light from the darkness, / the good from the wicked; he remains in [... / ...] in only-begottenness, in godliness and o[b]⁵edience. That one surpasses a[ll] people / who run after these four worldly things [...] / For they will not remain with them for ete[rni]/ty; rather they shall leave them behind and die.

---

*104 ⲃⲉⲗ︦ⲏ
*105 ⲗⲉⲅ.ⲉ

••• 79 •••

(191,9 – 192,3)

10 *Concerning the Fasting of the Saints.* /

Once more the enlightener speaks to his disciples: The fa/sting that the saints fast by is profit[able] / for [four] great works.

The first work: S[hall] / the holy man punish his body by fast-ing, [he sub]15dues the entire ruling-power that exists in him. /

The second: This soul that comes in [to] him in the ad-m[ini]/stration of his food, day by day; it shall be made holy, [cl]/eansed, purified, and w[ash]ed from the adulteration [of] / the darkness that is mixed in with it.

The third: 20 Th[at] person shall make every deed a holy one; / the mystery of [the children] of light [i]n whom there is neither corruption / nor [...] the food, nor wound it. / [Rat]her, they are holy, [there is nothing] in them that defiles, as they li/[ve] in peace.

The fourth: They make a [... 25 ...] the Cross, they restrain their hands from the hand / [... not] destroy the living soul. /

[The] fasting is profitable to the saints for these four great / [wo]rks should they persist; that is if they are constant in th/[em] daily, and cause the body to make all its 30 [memb]ers to fast [with a] holy [fa]st. /

[...] faith. They who have not strength / [to fast d]aily should make their fast (**192**) [on] the lord's day. They too make a contribution [to the wor/ks] and the fasting of the saints by their faith and their / alms.

••• **80** •••

(192,3 – 193,22)

/ The Chapter of the Command ⁵ments of Righteousness. /

Summary of essential precepts held by the elect and the catechumens; arranged in two sets of two (by three).

The first righteousness of the elect has three parts: to refrain from all sexual activity; to take great care not to harm the light soul trapped everywhere in matter and especially vegetation (the Cross of Light), for instance by plucking fruit; and not to consume meat or alcohol (192.8 – 13). These correspond to the three seals of mouth, hands and breast discussed by Augustine (signacula oris, manuum et sinus, *mor. Manich.* VII, 10; IX, 18); and also referred to in eastern Manichaean texts.

The second: to multiply wisdom, faith and grace.

The first righteousness of the catechumenate: fasting, prayer and almsgiving. The catechumens had to support the elect who could do no labour, farming or cooking.

The second: to give someone to the church; to share in their good works; to construct something. The catechumens were allowed to marry and procreate, but were expected to compensate in this way.

[Once more] the enlightener speaks to his disciples: Know [and] / understand that the first righteousness a per[son] / will do to make truly righteous is this: he can embra/[ce] continence and purity. And he can also acquire 'the rest ¹⁰ [of the] hands', so that he will keep his hand still before the Cross of Li[gh/t]. The third is purity of the mouth, so that he will / keep his mouth pure of all flesh and blood; and not take any taste / at all of the 'wine' name, nor fermented drink. This is the fir/[st] righteousness. If a person will do it in his bo¹⁵[dy], he is pronounced righteous by all mankind. /

Then, the second righteousness that he should do is this: / He can add to it [...] wisdom and faith so that / [...] from his wisdom he can give wisdom, to every person who will he/ar it from him. And also from his faith he can give faith, ²⁰ [to th]ese who belong to the faith. From hi[s grace] he can give freely / of love, shower it upon them, that he might join them to him. / For, when that one acquires a great riches [...] / in righteousness. By this second godliness / he may cause others to be sent, resembling him in [righteous]²⁵ness.

Just as this righteous one should fulfill the se/cond and become a perfect elect; so too, / if the catechumen shall be a catechu/men of the faith, he is perfected in two stages. /

The first work of the catechumenate that he [30] does is fasting, prayer, and almsgiving. Now, the fa[stin]/g b[y] which he can fast is [th]is: / he can fast on the [lord]'s day [and rest from the] / deeds of the world. [And] the pra[yer is this]: (193) he can pray to the sun and the moon, the great li[ght-givers. The alms]/giving also is this: he can place it [...] / in the holy one, and give it to them in righteous[ness ...] /

[The] second work of the catechumena[te that he] [5] does is this: A person will give a child to the [ch]/urch for the (sake of) right-eousness, or his relative [or member] / of the household; or he can rescue someone beset by troub[le; or] / buy a slave, and give him for righteousness. Accordingly, every [go]/od he might do, namely this one whom he gave as a gift [for righ][10]teousness; that catechumen [...] / will share in with them. Thirdly: / A person will build a dwelling or construct some pl[ace]; / so they can become for him a portion of alms in the holy ch[urch]. /

If the catechumen shall ful[fill] [15] these three great works, these three great alm[s that he] / gives as a gift for the h[oly] church [...] / which these alms will achieve. Also, that cate[chu]men / himself, who gave them, he can [... / ...] as he shares in them. The catechumens who will give [...] [20] have great lo[ve ther]ein, and a share of eve[ry] grace / and good in the holy church. They will find many / graces.

<h2 style="text-align:center">••• 81 •••</h2>

(193,23 - 196,31)

/ The Chapter of Fasting, for [25] it engenders a Host of Angels. /

For the Manichaeans the human body and its digestive processes worked in a very literal way so as to purify the divine light, and thus to discard the evil waste matter. Consequently, as Augustine comments, they believed that they 'breathed forth angels (*Conf.* III.18, IV.1)'.

In this kephalaion one of Mani's disciples, an archegos (leader), re-counts how he had joyfully counted the number of angels engendered by the fasting of the elect in his church. However, for some reason (the relevant passage is fragmentary) he had had a change of heart; and now he asks Mani to release him from this responsibility. He seems to be fearful that he might inadvertently sin. However, Mani encourages him, and points out that this kind of responsible position in the church is very necessary. It brings much more good than the actions of people who are only concerned with their own spiritual edification. Mani charges him to use his abilities for the growth of the church.

[Onc]e again, it happened one time while the apostle is sitting do[wn] / among the congregation. One of his disciples stood up in front of [him]. / He says to him: I have heard you, my master, saying: / 'Seven angels shall be engendered by the fasting of eac[h 30 on]e of the elect; and not only the elect bu[t / the] catechumens engender them on the lord's d[ay'.

The / work] of fasting is this in summary. Now, I, I have [... / ... have p]assed since I became leader. Fif[ty / elect were with m]e in the church over which I became the head. (194) [They stood befo]re me while they fasted every day. / Now, I [took account of the fast]ing that a person performs at these thr/[ee lord's da]ys singly, and I found that each one of these [el/ect] had engen-dered seven angels by their fasting. So, I 5 [counted the] fasting of the[se] fifty people at the three lo/[rd's da]ys: they totalled three hundred and fifty angels, as seven / [an]gels are reckoned to each one of the elect, who engender / [th]em daily through total fasting. I counted these thr[ee] / lord's days when these fifty people fasted, and [I 10 multi]plied by three. I found: the number of angels en/gendered by them totalled one thousand and fifty, and I / [was grateful] on account of the great profit and go[od] that I had achieved / [on these three] lord's days.

However, I was made to change and beca[me tr]oubled of / [heart]; I had supported [...] this person had committed a sin because of the words [... 15 ...] because of a church, to build [it / ...] to construct it, or because of another necessity / [...] he has sin therein, in these / [...] do I myself sin, I pray, because I command [... / ...] to construct them [...] I shall question myself in my heart 20 [...], saying [...] t[h]u[s / ...] he alone, and he [...] and he [... / ...] and he takes [...] and he [... / ...] them [... / ...] in the presence of God, who will [...] him alone and he supports [.... 25 ...] it is more than [...] my words [...] / the ordinance of their church.

Now I entreat you, my m[aster], / in th[at ...] the worthy thing
[...] {obligates}*106 to restrict me to my own [s/e]lf. Consent and
[acquie]sce with me, that I may withdraw to pray[er. / ...] that I
may walk in the midst of my brothers lik[e] ³⁰ the elders.
Perform this grace for me and re[le]ase me from this power / [of]
protection of the gods and an[gels]. /

Then, when the apostle had heard [this word of] that [dis]-
(195)ciple, recounting a[bout ..., he] / performed him this grace.

The apos[tle says to the disciple]: / The saying that you uttered, in
th[at ... / ...] by your own mouth! 'I k[n]ow that t[his] is a [go]od
thing that is ⁵ achieved by virtue of these fasts, in which these
[h]oly peo[ple] / have fasted on the lord's day'; as i[f] / knowing
that this thing is entirely beneficial. Then why do they [ask
ex/empt]ion from it? For in these words that you have uttered in
my presence / you make [...] as if you had not known anything
true; ¹⁰ because if you had understood the truth and known [the /
be]nefit, your heart would not have come after you to ask
exemption from [the go/o]d. If you are [e]ager.

You were not ill to make us say it, nor do you [...] / many times.
Truly, if you did know the [tru]e benefit / and found your body
ailing, sic[k and] ¹⁵ troubled, and you having pain many times,
then [... And you] / do not cease from doing the work with which
you have been entrusted / the whole time you spend [set] firm in
the [body / ...]; as you will go to this great l[and] of rest wi[th the]
/ children of the living. [And you ent]er with glory and [victory
to] ²⁰ what you had set your heart upon. You confirm yourself
upon them. Indeed, it [will be / to]ld to you: 'A divine work has
come about, [your bo]/dy has been found safe for you [...] there
being no blemish nor de[str/uction] nor pain for you'. And after
all these things, I wi[ll / ...] you, so that you wish [...] to complete
the good, together with ²⁵ that which I have assigned to you.

Now, if you can ask exemption from this matt[er] / and this
divine work, are there also others like you / to decline it? Then
indeed, all this sort of benefit and / every divine [wo]rk: whoever
will do it? For wise people [... / ...] who know the truth, who are

---

*106 ⲧⲙ̄ⲧⲁϩ

like you, shall not att[30][ain the benef]it [...] that you have given
them. They will commit this sin [... / ... so]ul. However, I, this is
how I have (196) [...] elders / [...] you in it, and you do the work
that I have proclaimed / [to y]ou [and assig]ned to you, and a
benefit co[mes about / i]n your life. Even if others should
{strive}[*107] 5 [to] ask exemption [...] do not {strive} / [to a]sk exemption from it. And also, [si]nce thus I am telling / you in truth [...]
that greater is the [gl/ory a]nd the victory and the goo[d] of the
one who preaches, building / [the] church; than that of the
brother who turns [h]is heart in[10]w[ard] and keeps himself to
himself, and edifies only himself. /

Ne[vertheless, o]n the matter of the word that [you have] uttered:
'Suppose I have si/[n] at the time when I shall proclaim some
word by my [mou/th] concerning building a church or alms' [...
/ ...] your heart is pained [...] or you are afraid because the person
15 [...] concerning the church's work and the helping of they who
/ [... as] he commands he edifies by his word, and has no sin /
[ther]ein.

However, the person who speaks, commanding / [...] some thing
[...] his own need, just as / [...] his [f]lesh [... fo]urteen; or he
hastens 20 [...] works that are defil[ed ... / ...] themselves to take his
o[wn] care. Therefore, the one who speaks / [...] of this matter, is
set utterly in sin. / [...] he is silent and does not proclaim [... /
an]y word.

In contrast, you, I assign to you this a[25][lo]ne: Have you power to
preach and to build the chu/r[c]h of God, for your toil will be
reckoned to your benefit. /

W[he]n that disciple heard these things from the apos[t]/le, he
paid homage to him. He says to him: My mast[er], I have received
/ the word that you have proclaimed to me. I will preach and
bu[ild] 30 the church. Only, may your power and glory / aid me!
(197)

[*107] ϧⲃⲁⲩⲃⲉⲩ Also 196.5

••• 82 •••

(197,1 – 200, 8)

/ The Chapter of / Righteous [Judgement]. /

A disciple, one of the teachers, asks Mani as to whether righteous anger is a
sin or can be justified. The apostle asserts that anger in the service of
righteous judgement can be constructive; and he distinguishes it from other
kinds of anger that are unacceptable. A strong reprimand can lead to
repentance.

Mani uses the analogy of a wise doctor who will on occasion use a cool
remedy, and at other times a hot one. These correspond to the two aspects of
love and fear; and Mani points out that both of these are revealed in the
heavenly sun and the moon. Thus they are able to purify the divine soul that
passes through the totality. Therefore, the disciple too is right to use both
aspects, in his dealings with the brothers and sisters.

[Onc]e again one among the disciples who [...] [5] apostle. He says
to him: I beseech you [that / y]ou may convince me about this
lesson, if I may ask you. For [you have to/ld] us that [...] and you
give [...] is / [...] their brothers [...] the judgement [... / ...] in
accordance with right[eousness ... [10] ...] is [...] a brother or a
s[ister]; / and you find, while I speak with them in humility and
quietne[ss, t/h]ey themselves [are o]bdurate and do not listen as
they r[ush / i]n [...] headlong and reach the end and are lost. /
[T]hrough anger, then, I will [...] before [him]. That pe[rson] [15]
shall wither and be subdued instantly and come to the place [...] /
with righteous judgement.

So, now I b[eseech] / you, my master, that you may instruct me
about whether there is [si/n] for me in this anger with which I
shall be ang[ry]? W[hy] / do I have sin therein [...] for his
benefi[t and I [20] am] in no way ashamed nor am I [...] muzzled
[... and / n]ot at all sure about the judgement [...] And because I
do not / know if this anger [... with] which I shall be angry, /
whether it [...] why what will happen [... / i]t.

Then the apostle speaks [to] [25] that teacher with [words] of sweetness [... / ...] this anger [with] which you shall be angry, you are
making in it [a / j]udgement of righteousness [...] difficul[t]
people / [...] repentance. Their anger and wickedness and evil-

doing [... / ...] is only a scare and a rebuke; because [... ³⁰ ...] For the anger alone <is> the scare, and when [... / ...] you would censure and upbraid that brother with words [th]at / [sc]are, you are shaming him to good use, so that you might strip him of / [the] obdura[cy ...] in this [... / ... ³⁵ ...] h[i]s heart [... (**198**) ...]

However, you have heard [... / ...] the anger. For this is the anger that lets you find o[cca/sion to] lust after an evil thing with sin [in it. / ...] liste[n] to him [...] and he is ang[ry with ⁵ a]n anger [...] look at him [... / ...] and he is violent [...] he does not utter constructive [wo/rd]s [...] compose[d] anger; [he is] / angry in his pride and boastful/[n]ess. <They> speak ill in that they would [...] him*¹⁰⁸. And they do not honour him [as ¹⁰ he] is angry and abuses and curses, and wishes to humilia[te / the m]eek, in retaliation and violence against / [h]is ill-treated brothers. He engenders the things that [...] / or else if someone will falter and commit sin [...] / and does not accept judgement. He is angry or he walks in his own [... ¹⁵ ...] not of the opinion of his brothers. / [Th]ey reprimand him about it, and he assumes anger and commits an / evil de[e]d in h[i]s anger. This is the evil anger [... / ...] and zeal.

[... c]all it anger. / [...] Whenever you may produce evil or [... ²⁰ ...] two or one [...] becomes obdurate and [not] / listen to you. You see him [...] he humiliates himself, ass[u/m]ing up to now a [...] You understand that they [... / ...] harshness to you [...] them with ha[r]d words, / in cruelty and harshness. And they will not be able to name [i]²⁵t anger; rather its name is the strong reprimand / that leads to repentance.

For you are lik[e] / a wise doctor, whose hand is sensitive in [... / ...] the wounds that he shall heal are severe [... / ...] sometimes he shall place [on the] wound [a] remedy that is [hot], ³⁰ sometimes a r[emedy that is cool ... (**199**) ...] after the blow. Corresponding to the simi[le ... / ...] this too is how it happens [... / ...] There are some, if he shall take the reb[uke*¹⁰⁹ ... / ...]

---

*108 Perhaps read ⲧⲉϥⲙ̄ⲛ̄ⲧϣⲟⲩϣ(ⲟⲩ) [ⲟ]ⲩⲱϣ ⲣ̄ⲫⲗⲁⲩⲣⲟⲥ ⲝⲉ ⲉⲩⲛⲁ[ ] ⲁⲣⲁϥ, with the last two letters of ϣⲟⲩϣⲟⲩ being assimilated into the beginning of ⲟⲩⲱϣ by homoiteleuton. Cf 202.6 where the scribe wrote ⲛ̄ⲧⲁⲣⲟⲩⲱ for ⲛ̄ⲧⲁⲣⲟⲩⲟⲩⲱϩ.
*109 Reading ⲉϣⲁϥⲝⲓ ⲧⲉⲡⲓ[ⲧⲏⲙⲓⲁ] Cf line 6 below, ⲉⲡⲓⲧⲏⲙⲓ[which

Through the hard word [... 5 ... the] blow that shall be cured by the remedy [... / ... of] people if he shall [take the] rebu[ke*110 ... / ...] with the humbling word, just as this [... / ... he]aled by the cool remedy [... / ... the wi]se person is like this underst[anding] doctor [... 10 ... s]peaks to hi[m] as he is subdued corresponding to error [... / ...] in humility. Also, this one who will speak to him [... / ...] he spoke [...] so that [... / ...] they of g[o]dly opinion. And [... / ...] so that he might [... 15 ...] the brother in two aspects [... / ...] love, but the other one with fea[r ... / ...] obduracy in one of his bro[thers / ...] foolishness. He may speak with [tho]se ones with [great] / fear [...] of evil-doing and hate. Fe[ar], however, 20 leads to repenta[nce ...] Yet, this one [... / ...] as even he is [...] he reckons words and what is [...] / in the aspect [...] and he upbraids th[at] brother / until he brings him to re[pentan]ce.

For the light-give[rs that are] / in the heavens shall be revealed with these [two] aspects, 25 in the aspect of love and the aspe[ct of / f]ear. They display these t[wo] aspects / of the powers above that are in the heavens, because of their soul that p[asses] / through the totality. For in these two appearances, the aspect / of love that is beauty and sublimity, together with the other asp30[ect of] confrontation that is in them, they shall purify / [in th]em the powers above.

Also, you too, wheneve[r / you st]and fir[m] in these two aspects, so long as / [...] the truth and the watchful teaching, you [... **(200)** ...] through yourself. They will question you stealthily [about these / an]d other matters, nor will their anger [... / ...] but wherever your heart and your [...] / your treasure will also be for you in th[at] place*111.

[Wh5e]n that teacher heard that lesson, h[e sa]id: / This is truly told, my master [... / ...] told me. I know that he who will reprimand [... / ... tr]uly he has a victory therein.

---

should also conceal the same.
*110   See note above.
*111   Mt. 6:21

••• 83 •••

(200,9 – 204,23)

¹⁰ *Concerning the Man who is ug[l]y / in his Body, [but] beautiful / [in his Soul]. /*

This chapter begins with a touching story about how Mani publicly embraces one of the elect, despite his deformity, in front of the assembled congregation who are laughing at his ugliness. It is the inner new man, formed by the Light Mind and religious practice, that is of lasting value.

This then leads Mani to develop an extended parable about pearls in their shells (the living soul in the physical body), pearl divers (the apostles), and traders (the sun and the moon). Mani like Jesus frequently used parables for effective teaching, and this motif of the pearl without price has an obvious heritage stemming from the Gospels through early Syriac Christian literature.

However, one distinctive feature of Mani's teaching was his desire to combine religious truths with total scientific knowledge, in order to establish a complete and integrated understanding of the world. Thus this parable begins with a lengthy discourse on the formation of pearls and their shells. While such features are of great historical interest for modern scholars, they did make Manichaeism a rather static religion, its teachings too easily undercut by advances in science.

[Once] again it happened one time, while the apost[l]e is [sitting among / a] great gathering, as some [... be]fore ¹⁵ [the] teachers and elders [... / ...] by the leaders and first citi[zens]. Now, he / [is s]itting down in their midst. All of a su[dden] one / of the elect came in to his presence, but no[t ... / ... he] is an elect [... ²⁰ ...] his commandments. He is an ugly [man] in his / [bod]y, having {}*¹¹² [... / ...]*¹¹³ in his midriff; but he is perfec[t in] his [h]oly righteousnes[s]. / He is a man who is upright in his truthfulnes[s. /

W]hen he came in, he spread himself on the ground and paid hom[age ²⁵ b]efore the apostle in love. The mass[es o/f] well-born men and free women cast their [ey/e]s about and saw that elect crying o/ut in his joy, exulting loudly and giving praise. When [they] / looked and saw him, ugly of body, havin[g] ³⁰ {}, they

---

*112   ⲕⲁⲕⲣⲁⲗⲉ ⲛ̄ⲉⲗⲟⲩⳓⲉ Also 200.30
*113   Smagina 1990:122 restores κυρτός 'bent'.

[a]ll mocked him and [sc/of]fed at him. They were speaking to one another a[bout him] / with laughter and scorn [... but the laugh]/ter did not trouble [that] ele[ct. (**201**) He was paying hom]age all the time, giving praise [... / ...] the glorious one stood u[p / from the ju]dgement seat; where he is s[itt]ing. He drew and gathered him [in / to him], and hugged him to his body, kiss[ing] ⁵ that elect. He sat do[wn / ...]

And [when] he had sat upon his judgement seat [... / ...] with the entire congregation of well-born men a[nd] / free women sitting before him. He says to them: W[h]/y do you laugh at this man, in whom the [Lig]ht Mind ¹⁰ and belief dwell? For what reason a[re you / g]aping at a person who is ugly of body [... / ...] in front of you because of the flesh [... / ...] outwardly; yet within great is [... / ...] is like a great [... ¹⁵ ...] if he has no worth by his deeds, by [his / p]rayer and fasting and humility. He is like [a] / sharp [k]nife that might devour its [... / ...] its humiliations [...] that you see [... / ...] he destroys [...] and [... ²⁰ ...] while the [o]ld man [... / ...] you [...] he sculpts [... / ...] he is perfect in his limbs [... / ...] a young royal child, who is beautif[ul ... / ...] shape, as the beauty and loveliness is despoiled [... ²⁵ ...] the image that is fixed outwardly [... / ...] and is displayed and unveiled to you. / Its heart would not bear you to laugh at this old man [... / ...] because whoever will laugh at him possess a g[reat / sin] be[f]ore God. For the [saviour] says: ³⁰ [He who sha]res something with these least of the faithful, who [... / ...] their angel sees the face of the Father daily*¹¹⁴.

(**202**) [...] all heard these words [that the apost/le] uttered about this elect [... / ...] they gazed at him, he [... / ...] and he was in their presence like the [... ⁵ ...] truth, when its worth is per-fected*¹¹⁵ [... / ...] upon him. When they were settled, they sat [... / w]hile his disciples stand.

They [paid homage, saying] / to him: Tell us, our master, [... / ...] how (pearls) came about and were formed in [the s]e[a ¹⁰ ...]

---

*114 Mt. 18:10
*115 This phrase recurs at 203.16 (see also 201.15), and links the two halves of the kephalaion. Presumably, the ugly elect is compared to a perfect pearl, which then leads the disciples to their question about how such are formed.

+The enlightener says to them:*116+ Pearls shall ar/[ise not] in every place in the sea, nor be formed / [in the s]ea as a whole. Rather, in various places that are in this s/[ea], pearls are formed in them [... / ...] that [sea, in whic]h the [pearls] shall be formed 15 [...] this [... / ...] what the sea shall [... / ...] its fire {blazes}*117 above and comes [down ... / ...] and it makes foam like the drop of water that flows / [...] down in rainwater [... 20 ...] is the water [... / ... d]own first [... / ...] foam and comes down [... / ...] the sweet waters [... / ...] the waters. This drop of water shall [... 25 d]own to the sweet waters and [...] / and they absorbed them and were combined with the [... They did not / d]escend to the depths of the sea, but they [... / ...] it floated on the surface of the waters [... / ...] to it. The foam and the pearl-shell shall be formed [... 30 ...] this wholesome drop [... / ...] it, and it becomes a pe[arl ...] / that makes a drop of rainwater [...] / waters [...] (203) it not being whole. It breaks and separates out into [m]any droplets, / and it has time to become a drop of sweet water [...] / and comes up in the sea of [...] rain / [a]nd sweet water; and it is accomodated in the shell, which 5 at first is foam. They shall be joined with each other at [this] / time, and are shaped and become a great pea[rl], / a great and valued kind. When, however, a / drop of rainwater falls, and that drop / breaks into many droplets and various {particles of water}*118, 10 they shall be formed into and be confined in [n]umerous pearls; / in the shell and the pearl-shell. One might [for]/m two pearls, another may form three, / others may form five; some mould more than t/hese, so[me] fewer.

Now, when you might [find a] 15 whole drop, and the shell receives it, it shall become a great and valued [pe]/arl as its worth is perfected. [However], if / these two droplets will have time (to adhere) to one another / before any {water particle} escapes, and they mix with e[ach / o]ther, and the shell [...] before they break into [... 20 ...] within [...] in a great kind [... / ...] the drop of rain, which [... / ...] another one, that [... / ...] the [w]aters form them in [... and] / in a great, valued commodity.

---

*116 Corrupt text reads ⲡⲁ]ϫⲉⲩ ⲙ̄ⲫⲱⲥⲧⲏⲣ ⲁⲩ ϫⲉ
*117 ⲃⲱϩⲧ
*118 ϫⲗⲁϣϫⲗⲁϣ unknown word, presumably a reduplicated synonym for ⲧⲁϯⲗⲉ 'droplets'. Also occurs as ϫⲗⲁϣ in line 18 below.

. Behold, [I, 25 I have] taught you how / sea-pearls shall be formed. I have told you that as a pe/[a]rl shall come into existence by means of rainwater that has [ti]/me to become foam, the pearl-shell shall come into existence by means of the foam, a/nd the foam itself comes into being by means of the transformation*119 and the [...] 30 of the sea.

Then immediately at the time when [... / ...] the pearl divers know it, they shall [...] and they / [... d]own to those places [and t]hey bring pea(204)rls up from the depths of the sea, and / each pearl diver finds according to the fortune that is / [ordai]ned for him. The pearl divers shall [gi]ve them to the traders, and the t/[ra]ders give them to the kings and the nobles.

5 This is also what the holy church is like. / It shall be gathered in from the living soul, / gathered up and brought to the heights, raised from the s/ea and placed in the flesh of mankind; while the flesh / of mankind itself is like the shell and the pearl-shell.

10 [The] booty that shall be seized is like the dr[op of / r]ainwater, while the apostles are like the divers. / The traders are the light-givers of the heavens; the kings and no/b[le]s are the aeons of greatness.

[F]o[r a]ll the souls / that ascend in the flesh of [ma]nk[ind] and 15 are freed shall be brought back to the great aeons of light. / A place of rest comes about for them, at that place in the ae/ons of greatness.

You to[o, my] / b[elo]ved ones, struggle in every way so that you will become good pea/rls and be accounted to heaven by the light diver. 20 He will come to you and bring [you] back to [... the] great / chief merchant, and you will rest in the life for e/[ve]r. You have [... / ...] and the light.

---

*119   ⲭⲱⲃⲉ

••• 84 •••

(204,24 – 208,10)

[25] *Concerning Wisdom; it is far superior when on the Tongue / than in the Heart of the Person. /*

Mani uses the analogies of a child who is born, and of fire that blazes from wood, to explain why wisdom is superior when it is proclaimed to when it lies silent in the heart.

However, wisdom is not always listened to, nor well-received. In a second speech Mani extends the same two analogies, showing that strangers may reject a child, and the blind can not see the fire.

O nce again, on one occasion, one of the disciples sto/od up before the apostle. He questioned him, saying: / I entreat you, my master, that you might instruct me. [30] Behold, when a person will be taught wise wisdom / in his heart, and he seals it in his doctrine, so sh[al]l you find / him rejoicing greatly about it. .However, [sh]all his [... / ...] to him, more th[an] when he may proc[laim ...] **(205)** and utter it. He shall be enlightened by it, and [t]hat [wisdom] / shall shine forth the more in him. It is unveil[ed be]/fore him, and through it he assumes power and truth. /

That disciple speaks further before the a[po][5]stle: I understand [...] / that this word I have uttered is correct. I know that the w[i]s/dom I have been taught is spread through my heart and perfected in [m]y / soul. (However), it is not found like the splendour in me, so that I regard it / [ad]vanced, except when I shall proclaim it [10] by my mouth and utter it to others. Indeed, when / I proclaim it, I am giving it to the ears [of] / others to hear. Would I do these same things, even if I had never heard it / in [my] days of being? Would I desire greatly and [m]y / [h]eart be drawn to the wisdom I now proclaim? [I entreat [15] y]ou, my master, that you might instruct me as to [w/hy] this wisdom becomes more advanced when I / [p]roclaim it, than when it is sealed in my heart.

Then / the apostle [s]peaks to that disciple: Well / [do] you ask! And great is this lesson for which you have sought, [that is] w[20]hence comes my great joy, on account of this wis/dom that I utter? [...] it is superior in my mouth when / [I] proclaim it than when it is set in m[y heart]. / [Y]ou yourself rejoice in it; and the other one who / [h]ears it from you, he shall rejoice in it, and be enlightened 25 [by] it and receive thereby permanent strength. /

For like this matter, just so a small b/[o]y who is conceived in the belly of his mother. He / [... he] turns in his mother's womb, filling her womb. / [The m]other knows and understands that this child she conceives 30 is alive within her. She rejoices over him until / [the tim]e when she gives birth. And he comes from her alive with his / [limbs whole] and perfect in beauty, without defect, (206) [in] the living open air that is more sp/[ac]ious than the first air he was in. / [He] fills his eyes with the light and speaks with his livi[ng] voice / in the way of they who are born.

Now, the time w5[h]en this woman conceives the child in her belly, / her joy at conceiving him in her womb is not so [ve]ry great as / when she gives birth and sees him; and is full of his / [be]auty and stature in the space of a single moment. / [T]he love and joy over him shall be a hundred 10 [t]imes greater than it was, now that she has given birth and seen him.

For / the first time when she conceived him in her belly, / [h]is beauty and the sight of his eyes was hidden from his m[o/th]er; but when she gave birth to him she saw his beauty. His / s[t]ature and his loveliness came before the e[ye]s of his f15athe[r a]nd his mother and all his relatives. They shall rejoic[e] / over him more and more when they look upon him / face to face and see his beauty and delightfulness. /

Just as in this simile, the wisdom that is present [in] / the heart of the person is like the living child who is co[nceived] 20 in the belly of his mother. And when he / is taught and seals it in his heart, it becomes like / the child who shall be born, and they see his beauty. /

So, in this way, the wisdom that the person proclaims, speak[ng] / it from his heart, shall be advanced more and mor[e]. 25 Its enhancement and glory shall double from the time when the bea/-uty and splendour of the saying will be displayed before the eyes [of / t]hey who hear it, and it shall also advance for you [... / ...] your hearing, and you are astonished at what you proclai[m]. /

Once again, the wisdom is like [superscript 30] this, while it is hidden in the heart of the person. [Bef]/ore he has uttered it, it is just like [the blaze] / of fire that is hidden in wood. An[d] that wood is [set aflame] / by the blaze of the fire, but the garment of fir[e that exists in] / the wood is not apparent. Indeed, you can see [...] **(207)** wood and they put them in a single house. It is impossible to [put li]/ght to that house as long as the light within [...] / until the time when they are added to the fire, and the light [comes f]/orth from them. It is possible for that entire house [to be] [superscript 5] lit by the light of a single piece of wood. /

This is also the case with the wisdom that is in the heart of the person. [It] / is like the fire that is hidden in the wood, as its light is / not [d]isplayed. For its part, the wisdom is like this: its li/ght is hidden and its glory is hidden in the heart; but when [superscript 10] the person will proclaim it, its glory shall be displayed be/fore the eyes and the ears of a multitude.

Once / again, for a second time this disciple speaks to the apostle: / So, if the wisdom is like the paradigms / you have taught me, why are there some people who shall h[superscript 15]ear the word of wisdom and rejoice in it and give glory / to it; when others shall listen to it and neither rejoice / [i]n it nor receive glory amongst them? /

[Beh]old, the apostle speaks to him: I will persuade you and / satisfy you about this belief, so that I teach you with cl[superscript 20]arity of vision.

For in this respect the wisdom is / like this child about whom I have told you, the one who / [was] born from the woman. Now, when he will be born, / his father and mother and family circle shall / [r]ejoice over him. However, you find others grieving by reason of him, [superscript 25] [s]ince they are strangers to him. These are not reckoned among his family. / [They do n]ot rejoice over him, because he is not of their race. /

This is also [the case] with the wisdom. When / it is proclaimed by the mouth of the teacher, these who / are [a]kin to it shall receive it to them and rejoice in it; [superscript 30] but [those] who are strangers to it neither rejoice in it / [...] nor receive it to them. /

Just like the light of / [the fire, which I] proclaim[ed] to you, that shall come from the wood / [and be apparent o]utside before the eyes of every one. (**208**) So, [wh]oever looks shall see the light that has [come / fro]m the wood; but whoever is blind does not see the / [fir]e.

This is also the case with the wisdom, / when it will be pro-claimed. The person, in whom is the ⁵ [Mi]nd, of him is the wisdom. Whenever he may hear it, / he shall receive it in to him; but the one who has no Mind in him is a / stranger to it. He neither receives it in to him, nor shall he listen to [it]. /

When that disciple heard these things, he rejoiced gre/atly. He was persuaded in his heart about what had been proclaimed to him. He made obeisanc[e] ¹⁰ and sat down.

••• 85 •••

(208,₁₁ – 213,₂₀)

/ *Concerning the Cross of Light: / [...] trample / upon it.*

The divine light that is crucified in matter throughout the cosmos, (a uni-versalisation of the christological themes of incarnation and atonement), is symbolised and even personified in a number of figures. The Cross refers principally to that most rich source of light: vegetation and all plant life, where the divine hangs on every tree or bush or herb.

In consequence the elect, who hoped to be saved in this one life rather than suffer reincarnation, were at great pains never to harm the Cross; excepting the necessary pain involved in its liberation through the digestive system of the elect themselves.

In this chapter a disciple is concerned about the inadvertent harm he might do in such situations as when sent on a mission journey, or when himself requested to ask for alms. The elect had to take great care wherever they trod, and it was the catechumens who prepared their diet, offering it as alms to them. Mani is anxious to assert that any tasks undertaken for the building up of the church, and thus for the ultimate salvation of the light, even where short-term pain is inflicted on the living soul, can cause no sin. He was very practical in his role as an apostle, and clearly aware that the divine teaching must not lead to self-defeating passivity in the face of the world. Here he uses the analogy of a good doctor who must first cause pain before healing can be achieved.

¹⁵ Onc[e] again another disciple questioned the apostle, saying / to him: I have heard you, my master, say in the congregation / of

the church, that it is proper for the person to watch / his step while he walks on a path; lest he trample the Cro/ss of Light with his foot, and destroy vegetation. Also, it counts firs[t] 20 for any creep-ing creature, lest he trample upon it and kill it with his foot. /

However, on occasion the superior, [who commands me], may send me to some foreign coun/t[ry] about a godly matter [...] of the church. / Sometimes, also, a teacher [of the] church where I am, or / some of the foreign brethren, may [ask me] about a portion of al[m]25s, concerning some food that they need. I know / that what I do is good, as I am obeying the one who commands [me], / who sends me on the road to a foreign country. Again, if I [take] / up the alms and it is brought to the church, the br[others] / and the sisters can take their sufficiency of it. I know and perce30ive that I have therein a great success, by this matter. [Never]/theless, I am also afraid lest in any way I commit a sin when [I wa]/lk on the path, as I trample upon the earth, [tre]ading on [the Cro]/ss of Light, and make [...] **(209)** without force in my sole on the path, as I walk o[n it].

[W]/hen the apostle heard these words from that [dis]/ciple, he says to him: You have recounted the lesson [like] / this, and it is well composed. Still, listen, and I may well per[suade] 5 you about it! Now, when you walk on [your] / way about some godly matter, as your command[ing] superior / sends you, you do no sin therein. For y[ou are] not [wa]/lking there about some lustful matter, nor concerning [... / ...] of advantage, wherein is sin; but you make y[our] 10 walkway due to the work of God, as you hasten [... not] / because of your own desire. /

[I]ndeed, I, I tell you (pl.) with a great voice: / Every elect and righteous person who walks on a path / due to the work of God, and though w[al]king upon the ear[th] and though 15 treading with the soles of his feet on the Cross of Light, / he does no sin therein. Rather, a crown and palm-branch is his entire path; / because he walks not by his own desire, / nor hastens about an acquisition a[nd] worthless things, / as he tramples upon the earth and the Cross of Light.

20 [H]owever, the other person who hastens on the path because of his own lu/st and [...] of his body, as he [...] / his own about an

acquisition and [...] things [...] / a total sin is the walkway of that person, / walking on the path of sin and error.

25 [...] behold, I have told you (pl.): Any one who, if his teacher will send him, / goes on a path about some godly matter, a total victory / is his path. Still, you (sg.) also recounted this: 'I trample u/[p]on the earth and the Cross of Light, I oppress with my / [sole]'. As you say: 'Perhaps I have therein sin because of 30 [the de]ed'.

Again, do not be afraid even with this; because the / liv[ing soul] is like this. As a person, (210) if a disease will take hold of his limbs, and his heart / [is sl]ow, his soul distressed, and he has pain in his di[se/a]se. He seeks after a doctor to cure him, to make him strong of heart. / And he cures, attends to, and gives him health 5 [from] the disease that has risen up against him. So he thinks about this. /

[And] a wise person comes, knowing the formulas proper to a skilled / doctor. If he shall achieve a healing of the one whom he [... / ...] it, he recites over him the formulas that he knows, / and he even tramples with his foot upon all his limbs! 10 That [pe]r-son, who is ill, knows that this person / is trampling upon him so that he might achieve a healing; rather, not do/ing this to him out of some enmity he had / against him beforehand. Instead, all that he does, / he does to hi[m that] he might make a healing of his body. 15 And he expels [the] disease and the pain, trampling upon him / to occasion this benefit. That person, who is ill, he can / bear no anger nor hatred against this doctor, who tramp[les] / upon him. He can not hate him out of enmity, because he kn/ows that he does this to him to his benefit.

20 However, should someone come and trample upon him in en-mity; he may / hate, prevent and not permit him! For he kno/ws that he tramples upon him in enmity; and as he strikes / out of a wanton whim, he piles another illness upon his di[se]/ase.

Again, this too is the case with the living soul; whether in the earth, 25 or in the Cross of Light. Should you walk a[long] / upon it on the path, should you trample the Cross, it may take no reckon[ing] / against you in anger nor wrath. For it knows that

[you] / walk upon it for relief and healing, to proclaim on its behalf. [You] / walk because of it, to reveal its mysteries. Also, the di[str]³⁰ess of the bones, which you have oppressed, befits not si[n], / but is set towards the victory. As the savi[our] has said: [Where] / your heart is, your treasure also will come to [be there]*¹²⁰. (211) Again, because of this nothing will be lost for you du[e to] / the distress of the bones and your toil; rather, it all accumul[ates] / to the relief (of the soul).

Also, as to this other (case) that you have [rec]/ounted: 'The occasion when a teacher would come up to me, or some foreign brethren, ⁵ and I speak about the alms; perhaps that word / will lead to a wound, and hurt the [Li]ght Cross?' / Again, do not be afraid even in this; because there is a dist/inction between words! For this is not any saying. Rather, the wo/rd that wounds is this: should a person utter a sayi[ng] ¹⁰ for the sake of the murder of a person, or the murder of animals, or for [the sake of] / the murder of trees and the Cross of Light, the ly/ing word and the wrathful and the bitter, or a word of en/vy and [...] only, or a word of accusation, which some/one will spread against his brother; this is the [wor]d that wounds [...] ¹⁵ Should the person utter it, it befits [si]n; because [he has br]ought forth / from it the demons [...] concerning this / [...] the righteous person, or [...] / all of them, which I have proclaimed, in order that [...] his word to the fet/ter; because anyone who would [...] his word to the [fet]ter. ²⁰ And again, he [...] his coming forth, they will bind him in / the place wherein he has bound his [...]

Nevertheless, so far as [... / ...] word for the [...] not go [...] / nor will they write it [...] wound [...] / word for the release of the soul [...] for the mystery ²⁵ [of its] healing; because the righteous person, who speaks to the nee/[d of the] alms, speaks to its healing and its gathering in. /

[He is li]ke this, a wise doctor who might turn back [... / ...] his disease. As a wound is in his body, he cuts / [...] this person who is ill, in his wisdom, [... ³⁰ ...] he [...] this wound, and he cuts it. After these things / [...] and he places the soluble drugs upon it, so that / [they will be able to diss]olve. He might incise it with the

---

*¹²⁰ Mt. 6:21

iron, and he casts it out (212) [f]rom him, with the soluble drugs.
And the wound is purified / [fr]om the fever. After these events,
he shall place the soothing drugs / [...] and it heals up. That
person, who is ill, he shall give / [...] but he shall not [... ⁵ ...] he
[shall not] generate anger in his heart against him; beca/use he
knows that he is making the aspect of his benefit and his /
heal[ing]. After the cut that he may make, and the cauterizing
that he may / do there, he shall even give rewards to the doctor!
He gives / his thanks and is a friend to him his whole life
through.

¹⁰ Again, this is [how] he is like the doctor, namely the elect /
person who encourages the alms-giving and gathers it / in,
bringing it to the church. Also, the alms / is like the person who
is [ill], because the power of the ene/my is mixed in with it [...] it
is gathered ¹⁵ [...] to the c[h]urch. It will be purified in the image
/ of the saints. That [alms-giv]ing will not be able to be saved /
without toil and pain, because they [... / ...] which they che[w], /
as they eat it [...] and other pain. ²⁰ However, there is no other
mode for the alms than this, because he / is its gateway to come
forth [...] from the world / in affliction.

Similarly, the holy church / that the apostle shall establish in the
world. For with/out toil and pain the elect shall not find strength
to become free f²⁵rom the world. Rather, only by the consideration of [...] / and that of prayer, and of self-control, and of [...] /
and of only-begottenness, and of withdrawal, wo[unds] / and
lashings, the discipline of the chains, the [... / ...] At first these
things [... ³⁰ ...] and these pains [...] they inherit [...] / for ever and
ever. Whoever [...] / he has not rest therein, in the land of the
living ones. Again, this / is [also the case] with this living alms-
giving. It shall suff[er] (213) pain for a while, and an eternal rest
[co]/mes to it from the saints.

However, this I command / you, my brothers and my limbs: Let
no pers[on] / unleash his hand and strike this living Cross [...] ⁵
wantonness and gluttony. Rather, be a leader [fo]r (the alms-
giving) / by word to the catechumens. For even the word, see, /
we utter it as you utter it. Thus (the alms) exist / in great distress,
and you should be mindful to eat it. Do / not eat it in wantonness
nor dissipation nor revelry ¹⁰ nor gluttony. Rather, eat it in great

hunger, and / drink it in great thirst, and take care of your b[o]/dy with it.

Then speaks the apostle to that di/sciple: Behold, you have heard what I have proclaimed to you / about your own longing. You have no s[i]n therein.

[15] [W]hen this disciple heard these things, he was persuaded and rejoiced greatly. / He says to him: I give thanks to you my mas-ter, for you persuade / us, as to occasion, about everything. You give ease to our heart with / loving-kindness from now [...] by the ears [...] / living will live [...] by your lessons of life [20] [th]at we have heard from you.

••• 86 •••

(213,21 – 216,30)

/ The Chapter of the Man / who asks: Why [am] I / sometimes at peace, and trou[25]bled at other times? /

Mani explains to a disciple that the Light Mind cleanses the soul and makes it a new man, at peace and untroubled. Nevertheless, even such a person still remains prey to disturbances and emotions caused by his star signs. Also, food and drink, being a mixture of light and darkness, can lead either to peace or disturbance depending upon the level of its purity. The positive and living balance of the nourishment becomes greater on account of justified souls who have come into it through transmigration; and thus these ally easily with the light within the person, and he is at peace.

Mani remarks (216.4 - 6) that such justified souls are those who have perfected their deeds, and 'their dues have ceased (ⲁ ⲛⲟⲩⲱⲃⲓⲁⲟⲩⲉ ⲱⲁⲛⲉ)'. This sounds very like the Buddhist doctrine of karmic consequences, and may provide important evidence that Mani was substantially rather than just superficially influenced by Indian teachings.

On the problematic question of the 'roots' and 'conduits (ⲗⲓ?ⲙⲉ)' see chapter 48.

[On]ce again a disciple speaks to our enlightener: I beseech you, / [m]y master, that you might explain to me this lesson I would ask you. /

Sometimes [I] am peaceful in my heart, as my consideration / [is constructive], and all my doctrines are ordered and in place. I conduct [30] [...] my wor[k]s, as I utter my words to all people /

[with swe]etness. I am peaceful of heart in the gladness of the Mind. (214) Even my body is carefree, and my soul / [rejo]ices in wisdom and true knowledge.

There are also times / when I shall be troubled. My doctrines are confused. Gloom increa/ses with them, and grief and anger and envy and lu⁵st. I am troubled, struggling with all my might that I would sub/due them; not finding the strength of mind to subdue them at that hour nor / day when they surged up in me. And all these evil teachings / and wicked considerations come forth. They have tormented / me. I do not comprehend, because there is no single shape in all these cou[ns]¹⁰els that have entered me. Are they revealed to me, or / ind[eed did] they enter me from outside and have been shaken in to me? I / do not know if they have wakened within me alone, have / re[belled] inside me and set themselves up against me. I do not know / about [th]at. Howe[ver, th]is only I understand: that ¹⁵ I shall be ver[y] badly confused in all my doctrines. I shall / do [...] in my [work]s, and you find my word is worthless in / my mouth. I shall not find how [...], and I become a source of trouble and confus[ion] / for my brothers. Even my body rises up against me, and sick[ens] / for that entire day.

Again, there are other times [y]²⁰ou shall find my heart carefree, as I rejoice and am glad. My wisd[om] / is sweet for me, and the preaching. My heart is drawn to the fas/ting with which I fast. I shall not wish to stop p[raying]. / You find all my doctrines tranquil, while my other thoughts are j[oyful], / my body being carefree. I shall not slacken as I recite psalm[s, and ²⁵ not] stop saying prayers. I am right indulgent [to] / my brothers, because I am governed by the / constructive state.

So now I beseech you, my master, / that you might persuade me about these two matters. I have tested them [in] / my own body, but not comprehending the ma[nner] ³⁰ by which [they] come in to me. /

Then the apostle speaks [thus] to t[he di]sci[ple]: / Well do you ask about this lesson. B[ehold], I [will explain] it [to you]! (215) Understand this: The soul that assumes the body, / [w]hen the Light Mind will come to it, shall be purified by the power o[f] /

wisdom and obedience, and it is cleansed and ma[de] / a new man. There is no trouble in (the soul), nor confusion nor [dist]⁵urbance.

However, when a disturbance will arise for [him] / and he will be troubled, this disturbance shall go in to him in [...], / first through his birth-signs and his difficult stars that [...] / they turn over him and stir him and trouble him with / lust and anger and depression and grief, as he wi¹⁰lls. Also, as he wills, the powers of heaven shall trouble him through the[ir] / roots, to which he is attached.

Again, there are times you shall find the [powers / of] heaven are peaceful and tranquil for him, and it comes to [... / a] difficult part comes into him by the nourishment that he has eaten, / or else indeed in some [...] or in the water that they have drunk. ¹⁵ Again, trouble and confusion and anger [will] increase in him, a[nd / l]ust multiplies upon him together with depression and grief; becau/se of the nourishment of the bread he has eaten and the water he has drunk, / which are full of bothersome parts, a vengeful counsel. They shall / enter his body, [mixed in] with these foods, and they ²⁰ even become joined in with the wicked parts of the body and / the sin that is in him; transferring the anger and the lust and / the depression and the grief, these wicked thoughts of the body. /

Now, [beh]old, I have explained to you that should you be troubled [... / ...] them through the c[ondui]ts and the r[oot]s of they above [... ²⁵ ... the f]ood that comes in to you.

There are times, however, / [if] you shall find that the nourishment that comes into you is pure [... / ...], so it is greater in light and life w[hile the / wast]e is less in it, and the evil-doing is diminished [f/rom it]. Even the atmosphere above is still, being purified through the [... ³⁰ ...] also the image is calmed from [... / ...] increases in you through (**216**) [th]ose good parts of the food that come i/[n] to you. And they find you at ease and tranquil, as you are / well gover[n]ed in your abodes because of / [the] living [p]art, which is greater on account of the light of these [ju]stified souls ⁵ that are in it. The ones that have perfected their deed/[s]. Their dues have ceased, while their soul is carefree / [...] they have been allied with these living souls that / [are p]resent in

you. Due to this you shall find them in you, / [c]alm in tranquillity, and they come from you without tro[10][uble; a]nd you are
found flourishing of body. Even your de/[eds] are determined,
being well constructed after their manner, and your doct/[rines
are in] order, as your words [...] your soul is ca[re]/free within
you, ascending like a bird. /

Behol[d, I have] explained to you the determination of this lesson
for which you [15] asked: Whe[nce] come [th]ese bad counsels and
considerations / in to you, these vengeful thoughts that trou[bl]/e;
and also whence come in to you these good counsels / and sweet
doctrines, when your Mind is cal/med for you. I have told you
that when [your bo]dy*[121] is troubled, you [20] shall be troubled by
the conduits of they below, the difficult parts / that come in to you
by fo[od and the] act of eating. Aga[in], when / the conduits
above are calmed from you, even your fo/od that has come in to
you is clear and pure. Your heart shall be found / ordered in its
place, your counsels at peace from disturb[ance].

[25] Then, when that disciple had heard these things, he glorified
[... / ...] the apostle. He says to him: You are glorious and
bless[ed]! / The living [...] that came from you have been added
to us. We [... / ... b]elieve you. For everything that we ask of you,
you [per/suade] us about it with sweetness; you [... [30] ... the so]uls.

••• 87 •••

(216,31 – 218,32)

/ *Concerning the Alms, that [...] / life in the Church.* /

Although all the sects of the world may make offerings of alms in the name
of God, it is only the holy church of the elect that can purify the light. Thus
the elect are the only means for its release; and they themselves depend
wholly upon the catechumens, who give the alms.

Mani compares the catechumens to good earth in which the good tree of
the elect can grow. Similarly, the living soul can only ascend to rest
through the sun and the moon, and again these light-givers will only rest
in the land of light. So, too, both the elect and the catechumens will finally
find rest in the land of light.

---

*121 Reading ⲡⲥⲁⲛ [ⲡⲉⲕⲥⲱ]ⲙⲁ

Once [again, it] h[appened one time. The enlightener sat] (217) in the midst of the congregation. He says to his disciples: / All these alms are donated in the world because of the / name of God; that is every sect overall (uses) his name. / Their catechumens give them in the name of [5] God. Everywhere these alms will be received for him they are accompanied / by sorrow and affliction and wickedness. [There is no] / rest nor open door that they can come out by and find an / opportunity to go to the God in whose name they were given; ex/[ce]pt only the holy church wherein the com[m][10]andments of alms are established, thro[ugh which] they fulfil / the will of the exalted one.

Now, the holy church / exists in two forms: in the brothers and / the sisters. Indeed, when these alms reach the holy / c[h]urch, they shall be [redee]med through it and purified and r[15]est therein. They shall come from it and [go] to the / God of truth in whose name they were given. / Thus it is this holy church itself that is the place of re[st] / for all those alms that shall rest therein; / and it becomes a doorway for them and a conveyance to that land [20] of rest. Also, the holy church / has no place of rest in this entire world exce/pt for through the catechumens who listen to it, as [...] / only with the catechumens who give it rest. For / [it]s honour is with the catechumens, through whom it shall be pass[25] [ed on].

What does the assembly of catechu/[me]ns resemble? It is like good earth / [...] in which the gardener shall plant a good tree. [Beho]ld, / [th]at good tree transforms the power and the [... / ...] of all earth, and it produces good fruit. [30] [Th]at [gardener] sets at ease the tree of life, and he r/[ests himself].

This too is the case with the [holy] chu/[rch]. It is like a good tree. (218) The assembly of the catechumens is li/ke this good earth that shall receive the good seed. / See how large is the assembly of the cate/chumens! For it is like good earth, since i[5]t also shall receive to it the holy church. / It shall provide for it, and give it rest from all its deeds / and sufferings. It shall become a place of rest for it, / [s]ince (the church) rests in it everywhere. The place wher[e]/in there are no catechumens does not have the ho[ly] church [10] resting there.

Likewise this [liv]ing sou[l] / that today is set in mixture; for it wishes / to [as]cend and go to the house of its people, but it kn/ow[s a]nd understands that it has no open door in all the powers / of heaven and earth. For they are its oppression that [15] [...] it everywhere. Indeed, it has no open door / except the sun and the moon themselves, the light-givers of the heavens [... / ...] they become the place of rest for it. And they become a door that opens for it / [in] the coming forth, and (the soul) comes out through them to the country of the household of i[ts] / people. Again, further in, also the light-givers of the heavens have no [20] place of rest amongst all the powers of heaven; except for the lan[d] / of light, that has indeed been theirs for ever.

So, thus / the living soul is purified of all afflictions; / and they provide a rest for it, and open a door that opens to the house [of] / its people.

Also, it is the case that the land of lig[25]ht will become the final receiver for the light-givers of [the] / heavens, and they will rest themselves therein and rule in it [for] / ever.

Again, this is how the [ho]ly church / shall become the place of rest for the alms of the cat[e]/chumens; and the catechumens themselves become the [30] place of rest for the holy church. Nevertheless, both the former and the [latter], / the place of rest wherein they will be at peace [is the land] / of light. (**219**)

••• **88** •••

(219,1 – 221,17)

/ *Concerning the Catechumen who found / fault with the Elect: why he is angry.* /

Mani castigates a catechumen for finding fault with the elect, though they are sometimes angry, and do not always behave righteously. He compares the elect to a sweet scented and spice-bearing tree. Certainly, its branches may give off acrid smoke when burnt. Nevertheless, the tree is not cut down; but rather, it is carefully cultivated for the good things it produces. Similarly, the elect are placed in an evil material body; and this may cause them to be angry. The catechumen should know about the mystery of the two essences. Mani points out that the elect do not blame him for his frailty, for living in the world. Rather, they love him, and seek always to help him. So, too, this catechumen should always look to what is constructive.

Once again, it happened one time. A catechumen stood ⁵ before my master, the apostle. He says to him: / If when I see a righteous one being angry and resentful as he quar/rels with his friend, turning his anger on him a[nd utterin]/g ugly words, not giving in to him; [at that] / moment when I see them arguing with each other [... ¹⁰ ...] it is obvious that they are not righteous, / [...] and it is obvious that they are not established in the truth / of [...] condemn them. Directly I shall find fault, s[a]ying: / If these are righteous, why are they / angry? For what reason do they quarrel with each other? ¹⁵ Why would one abuse another, as if they had nothing in the un/iverse on which they stand firm? /

Then our enlightener spea[ks] to tha[t] catechumen: / The [saying] that you have uttered is not a constructive saying. You [do] not re/peat it well. Do not be [in]structed by foolishness [...] ²⁰ that it comes to be in you. Rather, know and understand / what you see [...] is clear to you, that these / [...] it shall produce oil [...]-plants. Its aro/ma, and the spices that [shall come] from it, is made use of / by kings and [...] Just as this tree that produces ²⁵ sc[ente]d oil: If a person plucks a bough / and cuts a branch off it and puts it on the fire, / it shall give off abundant smoke / [...] separate from it; but no person [... / ...] this scented oil that has come from it should give ³⁰ perfume to the smoke and ash, and they take an axe / [...] and destroy the entire tree! Rather, they shall make the other / [...] the cultivator of that tree and they nurture it b/[ecause of the s]c[en]t that shall come from it. /

This [is also the case] with the elect. [They are] gods (**220**) as they stand firm in the image of the gods. The divinity / that is planted in them came to them from the heights and / [dw]elt in them. They have done the will of the greatness. /

F[urther], when they will be troubled and angry and resentful, ⁵ [they] curse each other. However, do not you be troubled in yo/ur heart. You know, once and for all, they are established in a bo/dy that is not their own, hating the flesh of sin that makes the oth[er] / dwell in a foreign land. Due to this they shall be angry, / and say and utter hard words ¹⁰ to each others' faces. Still, when you might see them / angry and wrathful, do not doubly criticise them; do not / speak against them; do not reject them in your heart; / and do not distance yourself from them. Do not ask why th/ey are angry or why quarrelling would aris[e] ¹⁵ be[tw]een them. For you have known the mystery of the t[w]o essences, / you have understood that [wha]t is good and what is evil dwell in / every person. You have also understood that the saints bear a great bur/den on their shoulders. So, inasmuch as you have known / all these things, it [is n]ot constructive [to] utter words like this about ²⁰ the saint. For you [your]self have unde[rstood] that they carry / a great burden, they are establis[hed in] the body that is not the/ir own.

Understand also this other [point]: You st/and in sin constantly! You spend your lifetime in eat/ing and drinking, in lusting after women, gold [and] ²⁵ silver. Your hands are always free to beat the Cro/ss of Light. Behold, you are stuck in all these sins. / The saints watch you as you commit them. Neverthe[less], / they neither mock you nor hate you. Nor are they distant / to you. Nor shall they say, 'Inasmuch as he sins like this, I ³⁰ will not be his teacher'. Rather, they shall accept [you] / in love and sweetness; they shall speak wit[h you] / in the wisdom of God, teaching you as you [... / ...] your dissipations and your deeds [...] (221) that are sins, and they perform for you all these charities. / They say to you: 'You are our brother. You / are one of our congregation, a companion who will journey with us to the land / of light'.

Behold now, you see how great is the love ⁵ that they have for you! They bear with you as a friend. / For your part, this is told to you so that you may love / and honour them. Do not speak against them when / you may see something disgraceful among them, being wrathful / with each other.

Then, when the apostle had utt¹⁰ered these words to that catechumen, he was persuaded / in his heart. He says to him, weeping: Forgive me / my sins, for I have truly understood, my master, about all these things / that you have taught me. For when quarr/elling will arise among the saints [... ¹⁵ ...] because the old man too dwells in their [b]ody; / and due to this they shall take offence [... and] / they {dispute}*¹²² with one another.

---

*¹²² ⲗⲉⲅⲗⲉⲅ

••• 89 •••

(221,18 – 223,16)

/ The Chapter of the Nazo[20] rean who questions the Teacher. /

A member of one of the Jewish-Christian sects seeks to trap Mani by asking him whether his God is good or evil. Presumably he was expected to answer along the lines of Marcionite dualism, with its rather naive division of moral attributes, wherein the good God is wholly loving and merciful without any judgemental qualities. However, in marked contrast, Mani replies that God is a judge. He then explains that while a judge is responsible for the administration of justice, any harm that befalls a sinner he brings upon his own head. Equally the righteous have nothing to fear, for they will receive their reward.

Once again, it happened one time, a Nazorean came before / the apostle. He says to him, I will ask you one wo/rd! You, for your part, persuade me with a single word; / but not many words.

The apostle speaks to him: [25] So, [if] you are able to utter to me a single word, then I / [my]self will also utter to you a single word. However, if / you may ask many, then again I too will proclaim to you / a multitude!

That Nazorean says to the a/postle: Your God, to whom you pray, as you believe in him, [30] is he good or evil?

Then says the apo/[stle] to that Nazorean: So, pay attention, / [see you have] not [asked] a single word; but you have asked a / [mass of words! Then] the apostle says to him: A (222) [ju]dge is my God.

And then also that Nazo/rean says to him: Yet I see that there is no city / judge not wont to do evil! For everywhere that a ju/[d]ge is, there are lashes, should he strike people [5] with them. There are racks, should he punish them o/n them. There are neck chains at his disposal, should he cast them upon them. / Also the sword, that he should put them to death by it. The judge shall / do all these things in the city, but all of them are wickednesses. / Look now, you see that the judge is an evil-doer!

[10] The apostle, in turn, speaks to him: The judge is / not a man of

wickedness, but rather the work counteracts wickednes[s], /
limiting the evil. Nevertheless, what you have recounted is that
the jud/ge shall go and punish, kill and slay. He acts / like this
that he might annul the evil and impede [15] the wickedness in the
pe[rs]on; and lay it upon the head of the sinn/er.

At any rate, pay attention to this: You shall find a great / many
people, free and good, are before the / judge's seat; and he shall
not sin against them, [n]or shall he / ruffle their clothing! Also,
he shall not cause them reason to fear [so] [20] l[o]ng as they have
not sinned. For his part, he shall not err against these / among
them. However, the occasion when, if someone will do some
wicked/ness, and the ones whom he has sinned against catch
him, and they seize and bring [him] / before the judge; he shall
indeed bring his sin and his wi[ck]edn[ess] / upon his own head.
Now look and see: [25] The evil shall not come about from the judge,
nor shall they call / him 'sinner'; rather the one who does the
wickedness, [he] shall / set his wickedness upon his own head.
Al[so], he who has done / what is right and beneficial; again, he
shall be paid recomp[en]/se for the goodness that he has done.

Again, th[is] also [i]s the way [30] of God. And he too is a judge of
souls. [Should they] / obey the devil and do this that is evi[l;
should they not be won] / over to the truth and the knowledge
that are in [...] (223) wickedness [...] and he condemns them by
their works. / He shall not accept them at their last, rather they
shall be made a portion of the d[ev]/il whom they have loved.
Even as the saviour has said: [Whe]/re your (pl.) heart is, your
treasure will co[me to be] [5] there*[123]. Thus these souls too, according to [their heart] / and according to their treasure, which they
have placed before the dev[il, they will] / count to his portion.
Nevertheless, God has not done anything that is ev[il to] them, /
rather they to themselves. It is their own deeds th/at shall condemn them and cast them in the gehenna of burning. [10] On the
other hand, these who are people of good deeds acc/ord to their
goodness. He shall recompense them the goodness, / and give to
them the kingdom of lig/h[t], and make them heirs in life
eter[n]al. /

---

*[123]   Mt. 6:21

Beh[o]ld now, you see God, that [he] too [is a jud]ge. [15] He shall
not do what is evil; but rather as he limits the evil, he takes / it
away.

••• **90** •••

(223,17 – 228,4)

*/ Concerning the Fifteen Paths; and whether the Ca/techumen would have
avoided causing his [20] Wealth to go on the Three Paths to Gehenna. /*

In Manichaean teaching each soul, at death, is faced with three possible
futures (e.g. see chapter 92): eternal salvation for the elect; eternal damnation for hardened sinners; or rebirth for the catechumens. In this chapter
further intricacies become apparent, for there are in fact fifteen possible
pathways: four to life; three to hell; and eight to transmigration.

The kephalaion is concerned with a question posed by one of the elect.
Given that each soul follows the direction or the pathways of a person's
actions in life (their 'wealth'), how can catechumens avoid the damnation
caused by their deeds prior to conversion?

Mani's answer evidences a firmly deterministic view of salvation. Each
apostle elects his entire church before becoming incarnated in the world,
freeing the heavenly forms of each member before they are even born (see
also chapter 1). Thus the catechumens are marked out before conversion, and
angels waylay their deeds that would otherwise have drawn them to hell, so
as to purify them through transmigration. When then the catechumen later
converts, these deeds have been cleansed and are ready to travel to the moon,
and thus along the path to life, together with the first good deeds resulting
from conversion. This is an especial grace (226.10).

In the final section (226.28 – 227.26) Mani uses an extended analogy to
show that a persons deeds may precede, accompany, or even follow after an
individual soul's own ascent to salvation. As in chapter 86 these teachings
appear to be influenced by the Buddhist doctrine of karmic consequences,
although thoroughly integrated into Mani's system.

The following chapters are also concerned with transmigration, again
evidencing a redaction history to the *Kephalaia*.

Once again, an elect stood up before the apost/le. He says to him:
I beseech you, my master, that you might instru/ct me and
persuade my heart about this lesson I would require of you. / For
we have heard thus from you: 'Fifteen pat[25]hs are drawn out in
the zone. Four paths are pure and belong / [to the] light, leading
up to life. Eight other paths are / [mixed], leading above from that
place. The light shall go / [u]p and become free through them; be

purified and go in / [to the] ships. However, the waste is separated and thrown ³⁰ [dow]n to transmigr[a]tion and the other three paths of / [waste ...] discharged to the gehennas'.

You have explained / [that the three] paths that belong to waste, the ones that are drawn to the gehennas, (224) [a]re drawn from the fleshes. O[n]e of them is the appetite for / [lawl]essness, that of people and of all flesh. The second is the / [...] all bodies, which is slaughter, [with] which / all flesh is consumed. The third is the damaging action*¹²⁴, which ⁵ [...] the Cross of Light and every body; together with the / r[est] of the error and the blasphemy that wounds the gods. /

Th[ese th]ree paths have you taught us, that they lead to the gehennas. / And you have also [told] us that every person shall follow after hi[s] / de[e]ds, whether to life or indeed to death.

Now, I beseech ¹⁰ y[ou], my master, that you might speak with me and explain / the lesson of the catechumen. How does his end come o/ut? For from the first, before / he rec[eives] the faith of God, these three paths draw him / on. [The a]ppetite in h[is] bones; the appetite of his fornication; and ¹⁵ the damaging action that comes from the wounding. So then, is his / richness drawn (to gehenna)?

From the first, before he becomes a ca/techumen, do these three paths lead to transmig/ration, they of the gehennas? If indeed they are drawn to gehenna. Then, / does he entirely go following after his limbs to bondage? ²⁰ If indeed this will happen thus, as according to me, it is very difficult / for him to live. For there are a multitude of catechume/ns set in the world, walking in err/or and derangement, before they receive the faith of / God. To where will their end come?

²⁵ Then the apostle speaks to that elect: You have [ask]/ed well for a great lesson! I am the one who will en[li]/ghten you and reveal to you how (it) [is]. /

Now, this is how it is for you to understand (about) the souls of the [ele]/ct and the catechumens that shall receive the hop[e of] ³⁰

---

*124   Lit. 'word'. Also 224.15

God and enter the land of the living. / So that their forms could be chosen in the heights: before / he is born in this human flesh and befo[re the a]/postle is manifested in the flesh, still abid[ing ...] (225) he shall choose the forms of his entire church and make th[em] / free, whether of the elect or of the catechume[ns]. / Now, when he chooses the forms of the elect and [the] / catechumens, and makes them free from abov[e], 5 afterwards he shall come down immediately and choose them. /

Now, when he comes and finds them amongst various sects [and] / heresies, he shall choose them by his light word. / And when he chooses them and makes them free from the error of / the sects, even all their deeds that occur in madness 10 come to him through transmigration. The angels shall / guide them to the places wherein they will be purified; becau/se, each catechumen, none of his de[ed]s shall / go to the gehennas, on account of the seal of the faith and the k/nowledge that is stamped to his soul.

Like a royal horse, 15 stamped with the seal of the king, that some person will stealthily muzzle / and take in to his house on account of the mark that is / upon it!

This is also the case with the catechumen, / stamped with the mark of the faith and its / seal of truth. The deeds that he was doing from the 20 first times, none of them went to the gehennas on account of / his form that was chosen from the start, being established a/bove in the heights. For it too, his form, / shall have pity upon him. It shall not leave his deeds to their error. / Just like his latter works that he shall do, for they shall not go 25 [to] the gehennas, on account of his faith. Just so is it also with these / former works that he did, as his form is / first chosen in the heights. They too shall not be lost. /

[Rat]her, they shall be drawn only to the transmigrations and suffering. / [Afterw]ards they come into the h[an]ds of the angels and are purified. 30 [...] you know this, that when they only shall [... / ... p]erson in to the truth, and he receives the knowledge and (226) [the] faith; and he begins to fast and he prays and he does g/[oo]d. At that moment, these new deeds that he has done, / [the] fasting by which he has fasted and the prayer he has prayed / and the alms he has given to the saints, all

these shall [5] [...] and nullifier of his first deeds in e[very] place /
wherein they will be found. /

Happen you know that from the first day when he left the former
/ error behind, wherein he was, and he received the right hand /
of [p]eace and trusted and became established in the rank of the
true ca[10]techumenate; at that moment he can receive this grace /
and so believe! These first fasts that he has made / sha[ll g]o up
[and] be received in, in the light ship / of the night. An indication sha[ll be given] there. Immediately all his / first deeds, that
he did before he [15] received the knowledge, shall be freed from
every place wherein they are / [bou]nd and snared. They shall
loosen their bond and asce/n[d] from heaven and earth, from the
trees and the fleshes. / They are loosened from every place
wherein they are and go / to the heights with this first fasting
and this first [20] prayer; the principal of all his deeds. For it is / the
holy sign of his liberation, and cause for / the departure of all his
deeds; the former and the latter. /

For his deeds shall not continue outside, awaiting him in e[a]/ch
place, until he comes out from the body and frees them al[l] [25]
and sends them to the heights. That catechume/n has the ability
to free all his deeds / by his own hand, while being in his body. /

Now this matter is like this, the way [som]eone / might dwell at
a city, while his enti[re] following [is present] [30] in the cities and
the dwellings and the villages [of the country]. (227) As long as,
overall, the king is living in t[hat] place, / you shall find his
entire host living in those [dwelli]ngs / that surround it. Also,
whenever he may [give ... / ...] the sign for departure to the
country, when he wishes [...] [5] to it, an indication is given by
him to his entire follow[ing] / so that he might set out on the road
and depart [...] / each [pl]ace wherein it is. And he goes to the
place where it i[s]. /

So, there are some among his expedition who shall travel before /
him and be prior to him. And there are others am[ong t]hem
who [10] shall wait for him and travel with him. They depart [at] /
his departure. Also, there are others among them who / shall
come after him, travelling behind him. They continue / [very]
many days and months travelling until they arrive. /

His entire following shall not depart a[t] a [15] single time; but someone shall go first / and another after him, while others shall d/epart with him.

This is also what the ca/techumen is like, with his deeds. / There are some among his limbs and his deeds shall be puri[20]fied while he is set in the body. They are cleansed in / [the] firmaments of the heavens and go before him. / [Th]ere are some also among his*[125] limbs shall be freed wi/[t]h him, at the time when he comes out from / [h]is body. There are others shall be freed [25] [af]ter him from the bonds of the earth and that of the creatures. / [They] go and reach him in the land of the living. /

[Behold], I have instructed you about the catechumen / [and ab]out his l[im]bs, about his other deeds that [... / ... b]y him. Nor also will one be lost, **(228)** [as] the angels hasten [...] He is healed, so that / he [will be ga]thered in, all of him, and go up to the land of the living. / [He] goes and rests himself upon his hope; upon his / good [deed]s that he has done.

••• 91 •••

(228,5 – 234,23)

/ Also concerning the Catechumen; / shall he be saved in a single Body? /

This chapter is concerned with the religious practices and sins of the catechumens. Normally, catechumens would expect to be reborn, on account of their sins, before they could be saved. As the Manichaean laity they lived within the world, marrying and working; but hoping to accumulate enough merit from their fasts and prayers, and service of the elect through almsgiving, to perhaps become an elect themselves in their next life and thus be saved.

228.8 – 230.30 Mani begins the chapter by explaining that it is possible for catechumens not to need to be reborn; essentially by practising perfection and whole hearted devotion to the church, almost as if they were one of the elect. Such catechumens will receive their final purification during their ascent through the heavens; just as the light in the fruit or vegetables offered to the elect is finally cleansed through their digestive systems.

231.12 – 233.1 Mani then turns to the question of prior sins. Those that believers have committed before entering the church are totally forgiven, so

---

*125   Read ⲛⲉϥ for ⲛⲉⲩ

long as they persist in the faith. However, if they return to error they will
be punished in respect of all their sins, both from before and afterwards.

233.1 – 234.20 As regards the life of a catechumen: Mani explains that if
they carefully observe all their due practices over the religious year, the
merit from these will be equal to the sin committed during the remainder
of a normal catechumen's year. Furthermore, the catechumen will be absolved of four fifths of the sin by the protection of the church, and by their
own faith and gnosis. Nevertheless, they will need to be punished and purified for the remainder. Mani finishes with encouragement for the rewards
of the catechumenate; tempered by warnings against back-sliding.

Once again that elect speaks to this apostle: I / heard you, my
master, saying that there is a catechum[10]e[n who] shall not enter
a body other than this one alone; but wh/e[n] he comes out from
his body, his s[oul] shall [... / ...] in the firmaments above, and he
travels to the place / of r[es]t.

Now I beseech you, my master, that you might / instruct me
about the works of that catechumen [15] who does not enter another
body. What are or is / his archetype? Or what is his sign, so that I
will und/erstand it and can instruct my other brothers. For they
would proclaim i/t to the catechumens, in order that they would
be exalted by / that, and ascend in peace to the good.

[20] Then the apostle says to him: I am the one who will instr[u]/ct
you about the deeds of those catechumens o/f the faith who do not
enter (another) body. The sign of that perfect ca/techumen is this:
You shall find the / woman in the house with him, and beside
him she is like these strange[rs]. [25] His house, in his reckoning,
shall be like these lodg[ing] houses. / He says: I am living in a
house for rent by da/ys and months. His brothers and his relativ[es] / shall be, in his reckoning, necessary as foreign people
who take up with hi[m], / while travelling on the road with him.
He [...] [30] they will separate from him, and each on[e ...] may [...]
/ the gold and the silver and the utensils of the [...] (**229**) house.
To him, they shall be like borrowed vessels; [he] / takes them, is
served by them, and afterwards gives th[em to] / their owner. He
does not set his trust on them, nor his tre[asu]re*[126]. / He has with-
drawn his consideration from the world and set his [5] he[art] on
the holy church. Always his conside[ration] / is placed with God.

---

*126   Mt. 6:21 Also 234.9

Whoever transcends all these things, / in [wh]om there is solicitude and concern and love for the saints, / c[are]s about the church as for h[is] house. / Directly, even more than his house. He has placed all his treasure in the e[l][10]ect men and women. For this is what [the] saviour / put in the mouth of his apostle: From today / on, let these who have wives be like they who do not have them; / these who buy be as if they do not buy; these who rejoice be as if they do not rejoice; / these who weep be as if they do not weep; these who [make] a profit in this world [15] be not in wantonness*[127].

These things that [...] / proclaimed were proclaimed about these perfect catechumens / who shall be released from this one body and go / to the heights. They are like the elect in their constitution. / This is the sign of those catechumens who [20] shall not enter (another) body.

Again, there are others who master / self-control and have even [kept the flesh] of every animal away from / their mouths. They are eager for fasting and prayer each / day; helping the church with what has come into their hands / [i]n alms. The potential for evil-doing is dead within them. [25] [...] that is to say, they set foot in the church more than in / their [ho]use. Their heart is with it at all times. Their sitting down and / [s]ta[nd]ing up is like that of the elect. They have stripped / [a]ll / worldly th[i]n[gs] from their heart. [Now, th]at person, / the Mind that is in the holy church [30] [...] at every [m]oment, and its gifts and / [its ...] and its honours and graces that benefit (230) [h]is life. It steers them to the holy church, / also to these who sh[all] come in to the church, whether / h[i]s children or his wife, or a relative / of his. He shall rejoice over those the more; and love [5] th[em, as] he shall set all his treasure upon them. /

Beho[ld], this is the sign and the archetype of these catechume/ns who shall not enter (another) body. Just like the good pearl, / about which I have written for you in the *Treasure of Life* / and which is beyond price. This is also how [10] these catechumens are, these catechum/ens who shall not enter (another) body. /

When, however, they come f/orth from their body, they travel on

---

*127   1 Cor. 7:29 – 31

their way and pass by / in the place above, and go in to the life. / They shall be [pu]rified in the heavens, and they are plucked just as a fruit [15] that ripens is plucked from the tree. In just the same way, this al/ms-offering that passes over to the elect is given likeness / in many forms. It is purified and goes in / to the land of the living. Similarly, the soul/s of the catechumens who shall not enter (another) body resemble (the alms).

[20] However, as for the rest of all the catechume/ns, I have written down in the *Treasure of Life* / how they shall be released and purified; each one of t/hem in accordance with his deeds and his contribution to the chur/ch. This is also how his ascent contribut[es] [25] to him his healing and cleansing. /

Therefore, because of this, it is right for the catechumen to pray at / all times for repentance and the forgiveness of sins from Go/d and the holy church; due to his sins, the [first] / and the last. For his deeds will be collected tog[ether, the] [30] first and the last, and be added to his account.

(231) [Th]en, when his disciples had heard these lessons fro[m him], / they praised him and gave glory to him with great blessings. They / [sa]y to him: Blessed are you, our father, and you are glorious! Bless[ed] / is the hope that awaits us through you, for great is th[is th][5]ing that you have bestowed the souls. Indeed, you have rev[ealed] / to the e[lect] the works and the commandments of the e[lec]t state, / in which they will live. Further, the catechumens / were not abandoned by you. Rather, you have taught them every / step and stair and rung so that they would climb u[10]p by them to the good. Each one of them in accordance with his [potential], and / they attain the country of the living. /

Now, again, we beseech you, our master, that you might continue a/nd recount to us about this lesson that [...] him; and instru/ct us concerning the person who shall [...] [15] and come into the church [...] are elect [and] / catechumens. The first sins that they have committed [in] the wo/rld, before they became disciples, what happens to them? For / some of them worship idols first, making obeisance / and holding in reverence [...] also others among them were firmly [20] set in the teaching of the sects, blaspheming God. / They even profaned the light-givers that are in the heavens. Again, som[e] / of them have committed other sins [... / ... m]urder or a sin committing adultery or [... / a]nd a sin of magic or a [...] of fal[se] witness. 25 [The] other one [...] these in the evil deeds of the wo[rl]d, / if a perso[n] ha[s walked] in them first. Now, when / [someone he]a[rs the w]ord of God, will he be absolved fr[om] / the former [s]ins, or will he [not] be absolved? / There[fore, I entrea]t [you, o]ur master, that you might instruct us 30 [...] and set our heart at rest.

(**232**) Th[en] the apostle [sa]ys to them: Very great is this less/[o]n [that] you have asked me. I am the one who can reveal it to you / [...] thus. Every person who has received the hope / [and the fa]ith and has separated the light from the darkness, and has perceiv⁵e[d the] mysteries of the living soul, he has received the right hand of pe/a[ce] from the Light Mind who dwells in the holy / church. And he begs forgiveness from the Light Mind. /

Understand this: All his first sins / that he committed from the day that he was born until the 10 [da]y when he received the hope of God, and took his heart a/way from all the sects and idols of error, he / shall be absolved of them all. He shall not be questioned about them from this time, / nor receive retribution on their account. If, this is, he may persist in / his belief and [live. If] he [shall not] sin from this time by these fi¹⁵rst [s]ins that he committed. Afterwards, he has been taken f/rom [...] he was absolved and he will be made / [...] from this time in respect of all his first sins. /

Should, however, he return to repeat his first deed/s, and sin by them once again, then he will be accounted 20 for all his sins, the former and the latter. He shall receive / retribution for them all, because God had given repentanc/[e] to him and forgiveness for his foolishnesses; but / nevertheless he was not steadfast in this repentance that God had / given him. So, if he had been steadfast in the cate[chu]²⁵menate, in his faith, and had left behind all his former deed[s], / then he would have been absolved from [all] his sins. / Whether, indeed, an elect in his el[ect state / or] a catechumen in his [cat]ech[ume]/nate. Now, this one who [i]s a catechumen may [stand f]³⁰irm in the catechumenate. The other si[ns that he] / committed, a multitude [of th]em will be / absolved because of his fasting and h[is prayer and his a](**233**)lms.

So, listen how I make clear to you / the works of the faithful catechumens. The cat[echu]/men who truly believes performs fifty fasts, wherein [he] / fasts on the fifty lord's days of the y[ear]. 5 Also, he masters their purification, controlling himself [from] / lust for his wife, purifying his bedroom through / self-control on all these lord's days. He shall [...] / in his eating. He shall not defile his nourishment with the [...] / of fish and all the pollution of flesh and blood. H[e shall not e]a¹⁰t any unclean thing on these lord's days, and [he] also restrains / his hands from wounding and inflicting pain on the living [so]ul. / He keeps to the hours of prayer; he obse[rv]es t/hem and comes daily to prayer. Hour by ho[ur] and / day by day, all these hours of [pra]yer will [...] ¹⁵ his fasting, and his alm[s that he] gives o[n] every da/y of the year. [The a]lms wi[ll be coun]ted [...] to / his good, and the fasting that he has performed, and the g[ar]ment that he has put / upon the saints. A daily communion! And they fell/owship with them in their fasting and their g[oo]d. ²⁰ These shall be counted with these other ones, and half of his wo[r]k is done / for the good, the other half for sins.

Still, the sins t/hat he shall commit half the year shall be se/parated into five parts. He shall be absolved from four of them by / [the] protection of the holy church, by the faith ²⁵ [and the] love of the elect. On the one hand because of this, [and] on the othe/[r b]ecause he knows the knowledge and has separated the li/[ght f]rom the darkness, and has offered a hymn and a prayer to / [the l]ight-giver of the heights. Even the quiet that he has m/[ade ...] Now, by cause of these good things t³⁰[hat he has done, he shall be absolv]ed of four parts, four / [... si]ns that he has committed (234) from the day that he became a catechumen.

As for the rest, / he shall be questioned about a singl[e p]art; and receive / bl[o]ws for (those sins) and retribution. Afterwards he is puri/[fi]ed, whether indeed above or below. He shall be ⁵ purified according to the worth of h[is] deeds, and clean/sed and washed and adorned. After/[wards], he is sculpted a light image; / and [he glid]es up and reaches the land of rest, so th/at [the pl]ace where his heart is, his treasure also will b¹⁰e [th]ere. This is, if he shall be steadfast in his catechu/m[en]ate he can receive recompense for his good things like this. /

If, however, he sh[al]l speak a lie and turn from the truth, then / will be [cou]nted all his sin[s] again, the former and / the l[a]tter. The judgement [that con]demns his sins will be poured upon hi[m].

15 Still, i[f he] shall be steadfast in his faith and / bo[l]d in it, then there will be a destiny for him. He asc/ends another time and is made righteous and is released. And he saves / his life in the life for ever and ever. At the time / of h[i]s coming forth, he can go and rest in the life 20 for ever.

When these disciples had heard t/hese lessons of wisdom, they gave glory to their teacher and thought a/bout the first light, the one that brings understanding through the Mind and [the] / riches of its knowledge.

••• 92 •••

(234,24 – 236,6)

25 *The Apostle is asked: Why when / you drew every thing in the Picture (-Book), did you not / draw the Purification of the Catechumens / who shall be cleansed by Transmigration? /*

Mani was renowned as a painter, and in his *Picture-Book* he depicted details of his complex system. Unfortunately, no trace of this work survives. In this chapter a catechumen asks Mani why he has painted the fate of sinners who will be thrown into hell, and of the righteous elect who will ascend to the land of light; but he has not painted the middle way of the catechumens who must pass through transmigration before being saved.

Mani explains that it is because this middle way is various, with the soul of the catechumen passing through all sorts of possible bodies before it is purified. However, he assures the catechumen that the final ascent is the same as that for the elect, which is painted in the *Picture-Book*.

Once again, at one of the occasions, a cate[chum]e[n ...] 30 stood up. He says to our enlightene[r ...] / Why have you marked every thing [... that ex(235)ists], and what is provided to happen, in the great *Picture (-Book)*?

You have made / clear in that great *Picture (-Book)*; you have depic[t]ed / the righteous one, how he shall be released and

[brou]ght / before the Judge and attain the land of li[ght. You have] [5] also drawn the sinner, how he shall die. [He] shall be [... / s]et before the Judge and tried [...] / the dispenser of justice. And he is thrown into gehenna, where he shall wander / for eternity. Now, both of these have been depicted by you in the [grea]t / *Picture (-Book)*; but why did you not depict [the ca]te[10]chumen? How he shall be released from his bo[dy], and / how he shall be brought before the Judge and [...] reach / the place ordained for him and [...] that he can rest in the / place of rest f[or ever]. For if we can see [...] the path / of the catechumen, and know [...] [15] so have we recognised him with knowledge. If we can also see him / face to face in this *Picture (-Book)* [...] in the / sighting of him! /

Then speaks the enlightener to t[hat] catechumen. It is not / possible to depict the catechum[e]n in the *Picture (-Book)*, b[20]ecause many [...] world[s] and [...] be/[f]ore him from place to place [...] there are / others existing [...] because [... / to de]pict it, since [... / a]lone in a single place [...] you know [25] [...] that the end of the catechumen [...] / his path comes to be with the elect [...] of the e/[l]ect. Look, he is drawn in the *Picture (-Book)* [...] as the e/[lec]t will [...] the catechumen will go / [...] the path of the elect [... [30] ... will] not [g]o in to the land of life / [... of the] elect and the catechumen **(236)** is a single one. However, it is not possible to depict the middle way of the puri/[ficat]ion of the catechumen, / because he shall not be purified in a single place; nor / [clean]sed and washed there.

When that [5] catechumen had heard these things he was persuaded and / [agreed] and kept silent.

••• **93** •••

(236,7 – 239,2)

/ *A Catechumen asked the Apo/stle: When I would give an Offer[10]ing to the Saints, shall I inflict a Wound on the Alms?* /

This chapter returns to a serious problem for the Manichaeans, the harm and pain caused to the living soul by the very process of saving it. This is the theme of a number of the questions addressed to Mani throughout the

Kephalaia; and the apostle is repeatedly concerned to warn against the consequent tendency to quietism (e.g. see ch. 85)

In this kephalaion the problem concerns the task of providing alms-offerings for the elect, as undertaken by the catechumens. Probably it is the preparation of food that is a principal worry: the plucking of fruit, the baking of bread and so on.

In his answer Mani embarks on a complicated analogy concerning a fight, and then he turns it in to his common theme of the wise doctor who must hurt to heal. While the exact relevance of all players in the analogy is unclear due to the fragmentary text, the basic point is certain. The catechumen must not be afraid of causing sin in the task of preparing and offering alms, for this is an unavoidable process that might cause temporary pain, but will certainly lead to eternal rest and life for the soul trapped in matter. The offering of alms is also a means for the salvation of the catechumen.

Once again, another catechumen questioned the apostle. He tells / him: I know that each time I would provide an alms/-offering for the elect, I know and sense that [...] remainder / [...] of the living soul. A sore and a wound is [15] [...] I awake pain for it in various / form[s ...] / nourishment and their management. Indeed, due to this my heart trembles. / I become very afraid.

I will venture to this place to speak / befo[re] you. Perhaps the good I perform will [20] not repay the sin I am doing to the living soul? /

When the apostl[e] heard these things from / that catechumen, he spoke. He says to him: / Do not be frightened of the sin you will commit that day / to the alms! For al[l] that you do [to] [25] this alms on that day you do to [cause it] / to be healed. You are bringing this alms-offering that you have made to life and r/est.

For this matter is like to two people, if / a personal enemy and an opponent of theirs will hit o/ne first and make a sore and a wound [on] [30] his body. Afterwards he smi[tes him] again and [...] / and he hits over his blows and [...] / blows that have made sores on him and [...] (237) strikes him these two times [...] accuses his [ene]/my who has struck him. And this judge questions him to his face about the [...] / of the sores that he has left as marks on his body. And they [...] / on him as if he had split his head. And he is led to judgement and [sent][5]ence, and is punished before the judge of the worl[d. He] / makes retribution for a sore in the sore place, and adds / to him the wound that he had left on this person who had [not yet s]/inned against him. He shall not omit the retaliation of the opponent, [as] he / is judged [...] according to enmity.

[10] After the end, this enemy is condemned for the retaliation [...] / sin against him. Afterwards, the other one is sick [...] / the one whom this enemy has struck, and a wound comes out [o]n him / [...] and he becomes a sick person by cause of his illness, / and he [...] He calls the doctor and shows him his [15] w[oun]d. However, that doctor has no [...] nor / [...] and he takes the knife to him and cuts this wound. Never[th]eless, / when he cuts i[t] the blood shall pou[r o]ut / of his wound. That person shall be pained, but / he accepts those and these things. This doctor has not retaliated [20] nor was harm imposed on him; because he did this thing / to him for healing his wound. All that he did / to him was done for the good; and not directly for e[v]il. /

After the completion, he cuts this wound and lets blood / [f]rom it and heals it. He shall even make [... [25] ...] gifts and compliments. That illness / [and the] healing become a pride for this doctor, and he is given / [honour].

This is also how this matter of [... / ...] before this living soul. When you make / [an] alms-offering [you] are like this under-standing doctor who has [30] [...] he shall heal this ill/[ness ...] strike this alms. At the time (238) [...] it [...] you have struck / [...] it is well and [...] ea/[se] shall [e]xist for it. It is healed by the elect, by the psalms / [and] prayers and ble[ssings]. A glory comes about for this [5] [...] healing [...] it exists [...] it is painful [... / ...] for they shall [t]hank you [...] you. /

Also, [this] is the other person [who] struck the comrade of the [... / ...] sick with his [...] he struck in / [...] he being cruel according to [... [10] ... / ...] living soul [...] upon it [... / ...] that [...] accusation / of [... /

...] [15] like [...] the catechum[en]s / [...] / bec[ome ... / ...] in to the church [...] its / heal[ing], you are wearied [... [20] ... / ... / ...] strips off [a ma]/ss of sins for you [...] only, what you [... / ...] to this alms, the ones that you shall be absolved of [... [25] ...] rather you shall be absolved of other sins that y[ou] / commit through the cleansing and purification [...] / it sh[all] become an intercessor for you and cause yo[u] to be absolved / of a mass of impediments.

Then, when the / catechumen [...] ³⁰ like [...] to the apostle [...] / al[l the] catechumens [... (**239**) ...] and they perform [...] and make res[t] / and healing for the living soul.

••• **94** •••

(239,3 – 240,12)

/ *Concerning the Purification of these Four Elem⁵ents [that have been place]d in the Flesh.* /

Four of the five light elements that descended with the First Man were mixed with darkness and matter. That is: fire, wind, water and light; but not air (see chapter 51). In this kephalaion Mani explains that it is these elements (the living soul), entering by means of food, which are purified in the bodies of the elect. Thus they will attain the land of light. If they do not enter the elect they must continue through transmigration.

However, Mani warns that the pollutions that have been joined to the elements cause dangers for the body. Here he attempts to classify these in four sets of three, linking each of the elements to parts of the body, emotions and states of mind. Thus fire discharges blood, anger, and the humours. Unfortunately, the text for the fourth set is fragmentary, and probably corrupt. The reference to the tree (239.25 ⲡϣⲏⲛ) is unclear; but the fourth element must be that of wind.

[O]nce again, on one of [the occasions], the apostle is sitting [among the] / congregation. He speaks thus: The four elements [are what is] purified. / From the beginning they are holy ones, living ones, and / enlighteners. However, when they undertood [...] ¹⁰ in that first struggle. The waste was [mixed] i/n with them, and the darkness of the enemy was mixed wit/h them. And when they were come in to the body, stri/pping off these polluted garments, they set them in the flesh. / Their pollutions, which they have stripped off, shall be displa¹⁵yed in a [...] and become a danger to the bo/dy.

The discharge of this pollution, that [the fir]e / shall disgorge and place in the body, is [blo]od. / The discharge of the blood is anger. The discharge of anger is the / humours.

Also, the emissions that the waters discharge 20 from them are
lust. The discharge of l/ust is bitterness. The emission of bitterness is f/[e]ver.

The emission that light shall disgorge / is flesh. The emission of
flesh is gloom. / [The] emission of gloom is obstinacy.

The emissions 25 that the tree shall disgorge, they are the
voices*128 / of the winds of shame. The emission of winds of
shame / [is ...]

The emission of the / [tear] is the [...]*129 of these twelve emissions. /

[...] these four elements shall 30 [...] what are gathered in (240) are
[f]ound by the management of this soul food / [that] enters the
body. When they enter / the body, they are cleansed and purified and established / [i]n their living image, which is the new
man. They shall live 5 [...] and receive the Light Mind and be
purified / in their image; and they come forth, being cleansed
and holy. They / attain their first rest.

So, when they shall reach / the elect, this is how they shall be
cleansed and go / u[p to] the land of the living ones; but these that
come to 10 [...] the sinners and pass through them and [... / ...] in
sins. Their end will occur in trans/migration and spirit*130.

••• **95** •••

(240,13 – 244,20)

/ The Apostle asks his 15 Disciples: What is Cloud? /

Mani distinguishes five types of cloud, each rising up from and corresponding to one of the five light elements.
   However, in typical fashion he integrates this natural science aspect of

---

*128   Reading ⲉⲣⲱⲟⲩ
*129   The text has ⲡⲥⲉ[....], with the probable meaning of: "the tear is the
[collectivity] of these twelve emissions.'
*130   The reference here to πνεῦμα indicates a tripartite system of
pneumatics, psychics and hylics; where transmigration is the middle way
between salvation and damnation.

his teaching with the fantastical element of divine and demonic beings populating every corner of the universe. Thus each type of cloud is inhabited by evil rulers that take the relevant opportunity of hail storms or whatever in order to damage the created order. Still, angels are commanded by the Virgin of Light to rush after and seize those rulers, and thus stop them. They are then cast into the seven outer ditches prepared by the light as holding places for the evil forces (see also 116.26 – 33), preparatory to the final destruction of the cosmos.

Mani is thus attempting to explain the constant recurrence of evil in the world, while at the same time asserting the ever-present concern of the light powers and their watchfulness.

In this kephalaion the prominence of the Virgin of Light as having authority over the zone (244.12) is noticeable, for this role is elsewhere taken by her masculine doublet the Third Ambassador (e.g. 82.18).

Once again, the apostle is sitting in the congregation of his d[i]/sciples. The heavens were cloudy that day. / He brought his eyes up and saw the cloud that day. / He says to his disciples: This cloud that is app²⁰arent to you, which you see; I will reveal / and teach you about it, how it ascended! /

Happen you know that it shall be released fr[om] / five places and ascend over this great earth and [...] / and it is revealed and seen in the atmosphere between.

²⁵ So, the cloud shall ascend from fire [to] / the heavens towards the likeness of the Virgin of Lig[ht] tha[t] / she shall display to it. Its sign is the flas[hes that] / occur with lightning storms [... i]ts exchan[ge ...] / And they shall be purified by her towards [...] ³⁰ the light that she shall reveal [... (241) ...] the rulers shall be released by the lightning storms and they are f[re]/ed and sent.

However, [these] angels shall immediately be summoned to them. / So that they will seize them, because they kn[ow] / that they shall never do good. Every place they will tou[ch] ⁵ they shall make dead and a loss. Whenever / the angels will make towards them and come beside [...] / they shall flee in their constraint before them. They go i[n to] / whatever they will meet upon and assume it. Like [a] ro/bber being abandoned and fleeing before one stronger than hi[m], as he ¹⁰ runs after him to arrest him.

Now, those rulers / that shall be freed from these clouds and assume wh/atever they will meet upon [...] in to the [... / ...] that

THE KEPHALAIA OF THE TEACHER

they did not [...] will seize / this thing, whether indeed a [tr]ee to [which] they have found the [15] way or animals or people. Si/mply, every place that they will assume they shall burn a/nd destroy by the fire of their body. Namely, the rulers, [the] chil/dren of fire, they that shall be stripped of the fire. /

In contrast, [the] cloud that shall be raised up from [20] water, and comes above towards the Virgin of Li/ght; its sign is the thunder storms and the booms that / shall come in the atmosphere in various forms and are he[ar]d. / [...] Again, there are times if the rulers that belong / [to t]hem, which exist in the cloud, shall on occasion be constrained [25] [in a] water [clou]d. And they flee from it and aband[on] it. /

Now, [they] too are so, in that every place th[ey wi]ll / [reach], they shall make frost and hail and s[no]w. / [They rui]n the seed-corn and the fruits and the plants; and they / [...] every [pl]ace [that] they will reach.

Again, [ang]els shall be summoned to [30] them who seize them. Still, while the angels (242) [ru]sh after them in order to seize them, they shall make this destruction. /

Also, [the cl]oud that will be raised up from wind / ascends to the atmosphere between, towards the likeness of the Vi[r/g]in that she shall display to it. Its sign is [5] [the s]torm wind that shall blow with bitterness. /

So, i[n] those winds and tempests shall the lives / be p[ur]ified. Again, the rulers will be stripped of the clo/ud of wind and they descend from it, safe in / the[ir] image. All the rivers and the seas that they will [10] reach and arrive at, they shall make waves in them a/nd raise [...] and they [...] the ships. They / wreak destruct[ion ...] and they seize / and bring them [...] /

Also the cloud, the one of light, immediately they will [15] be strip[ped] of it [... / ...] the Virgin. She shall / display its sign too [...] And its sign is / this, in that you shall find it sailing in stillness and calm. / The lives in it shall be clea[nsed] in stillness and calm. [20] Again, the rulers that will be stripped of it [...] / that will come forth [...] they shall put [...] and they take [... / ...] there [...] the [a]nge[ls] / seize them.

Again, the cloud that shall be raised [up] / fro[m] the mingled air comes above towards [the image] 25 of the Virgin. Its sign is this, in that [...] / are pur[if]ied in it in stillness and [rest ... these rulers] / that will be stripped of that cloud and [co]me f/rom it; every place that they will find [...] / they shall make it {}*131 [...] 30 one of [...] unt[i]l [... (243) th]ey are seized and taken to their midst.

Their stri[p/p]ings, that they shall leave behind them in various places / they will have reached, whether the produce of the trees or the offspring [of] / the fleshes, they shall be taken midst [...] wither away. 5 They shall inflict great dangers, but agai[n] / those rulers also the angels shall s[e]/nd to their midst. They bring the light from them and / cast the demons down to these seven o[ut]er ditches / of the great sea; which i[s] the vessel of 10 the waters that are outside the wo[rl]d. /

Then his disciples say to him: Instruct us, / our master. To what place do those seven ditches go / down?

[The apostle] says [to t]hem: / Those ditches and the [...] unt15il they reach the earths below [...] fe/et of the Porter.

Hear also [...] / for sometimes these angels shall be sent to them, / to seize the rulers. Whenever the rulers [... / ...] for the angels rush after them. They beseech them [...] 20 they that are given the command. However, [t]hose [rul]ers / shall be freed from them alone and ass[um]e / [...] and [the fle]sh. They are consumed by this offspring [... / ...] tree and that of flesh. The angels shall set a / [... ov]er them, that they might guard them until the hour when 25 [those r]ulers will be stripped of tree and / [flesh; a]nd they go [u]p above. They shall be gathered / [...] above, and they are poured out / [...] in their first for/[ms ... im]ages in which they first were. (244) They take the light from them, which had remained behind in [t/h]em. And they too are cast down to these seve[n] / outer [path]s that are in the great sea; the place to where these former ones [were c/as]t. They shall reach their mids[t 5 ...] and the light that is in them is taken. /

---

*131 ⲟⲩⲁⲧⲟⲩ(ⲟⲩ)

Beh[old] n[o]w, I have instructed you about this cloud: How / it shall ascend above, and the lives that are in it / are purified. I have also taught you of the rulers that are in it: how / they shall make these {rebellions}*132 and how they shall be {caught}*133. 10 And they are cast to the outer prison by the angels, / when the command is given to them through the power of the Virgin / of Light. She has authority over the entire zone, [and cl]ean/ses [the] life that is in it.

Then, when his disciples / hea[rd these lessons] they glorified him. They say to him: 15 [Y]ou have [instructed us] in all the secrets, the giv/er of [...] of all revelations! We give tha/n[k]s to you, our father, with great confessions. For you have / inst[r]ucted us about every thing. You have given to us great / [...] of the knowledge; so that through them we may give judgem20ent about these things to which we listen.

••• 96 •••

(244,21 – 246,6)

/ *The Three Earths that ex/ist, they bear Fruit.* /

Mani uses the example of human farmers upon the earth to describe the work of the sun and moon in cultivating the field of the living soul, and the Light Mind toiling over the holy church, to bring them to harvest. He then calls upon his audience to be active in the faith, to do the farming of righteousness, and thus to bring forth fruit.

On[ce] again he speaks to his disciples: Thr[ee earths] 25 exist in the universe, and are being toiled over. At first they [... / ...] the farmer in them. Afterwards they bear [good] fruit / to they who toil over them.

One of them is this great ea[rt]h [th]at / people are living upon. They are ploughing in it [...] / it with iron hoes, th[ey cu]ltivate, [making] 30 the furrows, turning it over [... After]/wards they harvest fruit from [it ...

---

*132   ＧλλＮΒλλ
*133   ϩⲱⲣⲧ

(**245**) The] second field is the living soul, the ho[ly] one. / It is mixed in the entire zone, above and be[l]/ow. The farmers who toil over it are these two great [ligh]/t-givers, which journey through the heavens. They are toiling and cultivating [5] it, so that they will draw it towards their aspect. And i[t lea]/ps up and comes to the heights. It goes upwards, ou[t] / from every place wherein it is, and it adds to them. /

[The] third earth is this holy church with i[t]s / elect and its catechumens. The farmer who toi[10]ls over i[t] is this Light Mind. He has freed it, / rescued it, and gathered it in from every place. He has made it for [him] / a throne, a dwelling-place to the glory of his gr[ea]tness. / He made it a good field that it might bear good fruit[s]. / In them it can make its appearance beautiful, be victorious, and ascend to [15] the heights. And it goes u[p] on the ladder of the [Li]ght Mind, / [the] good farmer who cultivates it at all times. /

Now, [ju]st as these farmers toil over these three earths, after/wards [they] receive from them the fruits that are valuable [to] them. / You yourelves be good farmers! Do the fa[20][rm]ing of righteousness. Preach and enlighten every soul! / Open the eyes of the people and reveal to them / [li]fe and death; so that you [like]wise may [become / r]ich by your preaching. Whoever will [... / ...] will make rich and enter into the citizenship o[f [25] ...] If you are silent and you / [do not p]reach to the people, you have no strength to bear fruit. / [...] this one, to find a per/[son ...] enlighten [... / ...] but bear him and he awakens not, and he [... [30] ...] in to repentance. These s[o/uls ...] they go to the perdit[ion] (**246**) that is prepared for them there. Since he is able / [to] do the good [...] you now; this has no power to / strike you and make you weak in the spirit. Rat/he[r, to]il! As you cultivate the good earth, [5] reap f[rom it] the good fruits, that you may / l[i]ve o[f them for] ever and ever.

••• **97** •••

(246,7 – 248,10)

/ Concerning the Three Creations of the Flesh: the ones / that were brought forth [...]; and the ones [10] *that were begotten by the Abortions; and the ones / that were formed of themselves. /*

This chapter shows again how Mani presented his teaching as an integrated science for understanding the entire world. Life arises from the mixed light and dross that fell to earth at the time when the Ambassador displayed his image in the heavens, and the demonic powers ejaculated or aborted in their lust. This matter or sin contained the 'thought' (ἐνθύμησις) or driving force that causes reproduction. Here Mani attempts to classify the different forms of plant life according to various means of propagation.

On[ce again] our enlightener speaks to his disciples: All these / animals that you see, and also the rest of the [crea]/tur[es ...] of the earth, confirm them in three [15] likeness[es ...] them from [... / ...] abortions. Others, / [however, for]m their own selves in their shape [... / ...] Also, their nourishment is thre[e / ... li]ght in them, if they shall wish [... [20] ... / ...] they eat see[ds and] fr[uit / ...] they eat seeds and fruit. / The [...] it entirely, and they [... / ...] the three archetyp[es] from their nature and the [... [25] ...] the time when they are on the ea[rth ... / ... th]ey are seized [...] / in their [... / ...] the Ambassador [... / ...] all powers [... [30] ... / ...] / i[n] it [... / ...] first [...] **(247)** plant them [g]enerally to this name: shoots and grass. It formed / the bad, bitter tre[es], the reeds and the thorns and the [...] / and these others that are like them.

For that th[oug]/ht belongs to the flesh-eating rulers. [St]ill, these [that were] [5] planted (belong to) grass and gourds, since they are in their essence. Nevertheless, [this t]/ho[ugh]t that came down from the rulers, [a]/s they are i[n] fruit and grass first and shall not be planted / in flesh and blood, it formed the trees that shall give nourishing [fru]/it as their gourds are sweet.

Again, this thou[ght] [10] that came down from the powers that eat m[ea]t / and also eat grass and gourds, it has formed the trees / that shall not produce any nourishment. Their / fruits belong neither to good nor evil. /

Behold, I have taught you the growth of the tree. For it was [15] planted from the sin that came down from the [powe]rs of / [...] according to the counsel and teaching of the [...] / them due to them. It grew the tree on the earth and gave fr/u[its] there of different kinds and shapes. /

Furthermore, I also reveal to you another thing about these trees [20] that shall be cut and grow again upon their roo/t; and they produce fruit. There are also others that if they are cut / shall neither grow nor produce fruit. And there are others / if their branches shall be [cu]t they are planted. There are some / [...] and they make fruit and come up and make a tre[e]. And it [25] [produces a bra]nch.

Now these (trees) that shall be cut from / [their] root and flourish and blossom an[ew and / produce] fruit, [t]heir thought is in [their / reproductive pa]rt*134 and the[ir ro]ot. Again, due to this they shall [... / ...] a firmness exists [... [30] ...]

Howev[er], the other trees [that (248) shall be] cut and not grow by their root and repro[ductive / part], their thought that sculpts them / [i]s (in their) twigs. And these others too, from which / branches shall be taken and planted and they sprout, their th[5]ought that sculpts them is in their body / [and subs]tance, as their thought exists in buds [th]at a/[re] in their branches. Also, these others, which shall grow from / the [fr]uits and the seed, their counsel is in their / [fr]uit. Due to this they shall be formed and grow from their [10] [fr]uit.

••• 98 •••

(248,10 – 249,30)

/ *What is Virginal; or, / otherwise, what is Continent?* /

Mani applies these two terms at five successive levels of the light's descent into matter. The archetypal distinction is between the light that remains in the eternal kingdom, which is virginal; compared to that which has entered into time and mixture. Then, at descending levels, the other pairs are as follows: the gods in time who do not enter mixture compared with

---

*134 [ⲕⲟⲩⲟⲩ]ⲛϥ̄

the light that does; the light first purified through the episode when the Ambassador displayed his image, and the light that had to continue through transmigration; the Light Mind and the new man; a human virgin and a person who renounces sex.

Once more, the apostle is sitting down one time among / the congregation of his church. He says to his disciples: 15 W[h]at is the virgin that is named 'virginal'? / Or the [one that] is called 'continent', what is it? Or by what category is / the [vi]rgin called 'virginal'? Or [the co]/ntinent, which is given this name, by what category is it / named '[c]ontinent'?

20 His disciples say to him: Proclaim to us, my master, of these / [t]wo lessons; since all good gifts are given to us through you. /

Then speaks our enlightener to them: / What is called 'virginal' is assigned to the myster/y of the aeons of greatness. And they called it 'virgi25n[a]l' by the category of all the light that did not [taste] / of death, nor come to the enemy's war. / However, what is called 'continent' oc[curs to / the m]ystery of the light that came and was mixe[d with the / dark]ness. It was defiled in bodies [... 30 ...] and went up to the light. [They] called [it 'co/ntine]nt'.

Furthermore, the holy vir[gin]als [... / ...] should they come out against the en[emy ... / ... not] taste death, nor [...] (249) On the other hand, what is called 'continent' [is this li]/ght that mixed with the darkness, was purif[ie]d, came [up f]/rom all the creatures, and was confirmed in the great[ness]. / They called it 'continent' since it tasted [of the l]5ust; but afterwards was cleansed from it and [become an] / holy one.

Furthermore, what is called / ['vi]rginal' is this light that was purified by the ima[ge] of / the [A]mbassador. It wen[t up and] attained [the] he[ights. It was] / confirmed in the image of the gods. Again, what is [called] 10 'continent' is the remainder of this light th[at] / remained behind, from what was cleansed. It goes up [and comes] / down in transmigration. Al[so], there is a part [of] i/t that shall come and attain the form of [hum]an [fl]esh. / Again, that one too shall be chosen in the flesh, [accept] the ho15pe, and become an holy one. And they name it 'continent'. /

Furthermore, what is named 'virginal' is the Light Mind, / should he come and assume the images [of] the ele/ct. However, on the other hand, what is called 'contin[ent]' is / the new man, should it be purified from this old man. And it [20] is cleansed and strips off the sin that is compounded with it, and it becomes / a continent one.

And also, what is called 'virgi/nal' in the flesh, is a man if he has [ne]ver joined himself to woman, / has not been defiled by intercourse. However, [i]n contrast, what is called / 'continent', is the man who has a wom[25]an in the world. Afterwards, he cleanses himself from her / [and] renounces her. And because of this he [...] and he becomes an holy / contin[en]t one.

Behold, I have taught you the categories / [of] the v[ir]ginal and the continent in a great many / [as]pects. For what is virginal, or otherwise what is [30] [con]tinent, is in many forms.

••• 99 •••

(249,31 – 251,25)

/ Concerning Transmigration. /

Mani explains that although both sinners and catechumens must pass into transmigration, the fate of these two categories differs. He compares this to the educative punishment that must on occasion be meted out to erring children, contrasted with that imposed on wicked servants. Thus the catechumens will in the end attain to the light and the life, while sinners will be imprisoned and suffer eternal death.

[Once again o]ne of the catechumens questioned the apost/[le. He says] to him: We have heard a lesson from you, my master. (250) You [have] recount[ed it] fo[r] us and written it down in the books, as you [... / ...] people who come out from their body / [are d]riven into transmigration and wandering, and / [ea]ch one is weighed [according to] his actions. Whether the sinners, you [5] [proclaimed] to us that they are driven into transmigration / [... or] they who have received the faith and have / [...] in the [... dr]iven also into tr/[ansmigrat]ion [... / ...] the catechumens surpass the sinn[10] [er]s [...] and again he too is driven into transmig/ration and t[ak]es hope. /

Then the lord [spea]ks. He told them about these two lessons. [... /
...] one concerning the transmigration of the sin/n[er]; he speaks
to them about the transmigration of the cate[15]chumen.

Now, listen to this lesson that I will recount to / y[o]u, how this
education I will proclaim to you shall be / given to the catechumens during transmigration. /

The [...] education occurs in the world, / by which people shall
educate their children, when [20] [...] foolishness. So, they shall hit
/ [them], but their education is not equivalent with the education
/ that they give to their servants when they shall sin. / For the
striking of children differs from the striking of servants; /
b[eca]use when the child transgresses, he should be rebu[25]ked by
word and harsh lessons are proclaimed t[o sca/re] him. And if
he [...] he is struck [... /

...] educate him. And if [he is in / a p]rison then he is bound by a
chain. Similarly, [bl] / ows and fetters [...] and kill him. He will
neither [be] [30] killed nor be h[i]t [... / ... / ...] For [...] (251) his
[thro]ne in the light, which [... w]/hich he had also uttered [...] /
When that one will be muzzled, they shall [... / ... [5] ...] cut limb
[...] / there is [s]till a [... / ...] / just as you have [...] according to
the edu/cat[io]n of the catechumens [... [10] ...] the education of [...]
/ cat[e]chumen [... / the]ir souls [...] / they are troubled of heart
[... / ...] they are mixed [... [15]...] until they attain [... / ...] the
sinners [... / ...] they shall be still [... / ...] they are cruel; they
shall bind him [... / ... [20] ...] from them [... / ...] to the great fire
from the [...] /

This is the end of [... / y]ou: Blessed are you catechumens [... /
y]ou are chosen and ordained [...] [25] their end is loss [...]

••• **100** •••

(251,26 – 253,24)

/ Concerning the Dragon with Fourte[en] He[ads]; / what it is and [...] /

Many Manichaean texts describe the human body as a microcosmos full of warring demons. Interestingly, here Mani asserts that this is a spiritual but not a physical truth. He proceeds to relate the fourteen headed dragon in the body, with its five refuges, to different parts of the anatomy. The dragon is really the driving force or 'thought' of the body that the righteous person must overcome, so as to receive the victory.

[Once again], one of h[is] disciples asked the [apostle ... [30] ...] is distributed [... / ... / ... **(252)** the] laws of the Magi. They say that there is / [a d]ragon with fourteen heads, and it is gathered / [i]n and [...] den with five refuges. Now, I beseech / [y]ou, my master, that you may instruct me about this lesson. [5] [Wh]at really is a corporeal dragon wi[th] / fourteen heads? Or is it another spiritual lesson? /

Then the apostle says t[o] him: / [The]re is [n]ever a dragon [i]n the f[l]esh with fourtee[n] hea[ds], / as the Magi say! Rather, this is a [spiri[10]tual les]son. It was uttered in virgini[ty / ...] the Magi did not understand [... / ...] all their words that are written [... / ... spiri]tual (?).

Again, this is how this earth / [...] to it, as it is accounted a co[rp]ore[al] drag[on [15] ...] I will instruct you / [...] the dragon is this doctrine [... / ...] of the flesh [... / ...] also the f[ou]rtee[n] heads that are distributed ove[r] / the d[ragon] are these.

The seven sense organs [o][20]n [the h]ead of the body are the two of sight by whi[ch one] / se[es; the] two of sound b[y] which one hears; / [the] two of scent by which one smells; also the to[ng/ue ...] by [which] one selects, receiving / [th]ere the different tastes that occur in every form.

[25] [These ar]e the seven heads of the dragon, the seven sen/[se] organs that are on the upper part of the person; [... / ...] below. The seven of the [tor/so] are these: two [...]; the two [... / ...] ruler [... [30]

... / ... the se]ven [heads that are (**253**) a]bove; so with the ones below they total and make fou[rteen] / heads of the dragon.

Conversely, the five dens about which they have [spo/k]en, where the dragon is congregated and protrudes, / are these: the first is the tong[ue]; ⁵ the second is the lungs; the third is the h[eart]; / the fourth is the spleen; the fifth is the b[lood that] / dwells in them. Again, if it shall look out from them [and / r]eveal its likeness and its observation a[bo/v]e and below, it wages war [by ¹⁰ i]ts fourteen heads.

Whoever will recognise them [wi]th / the dragon, which is the thought of [the b]o/dy, and struggles with it and is victorious and ki[lls] i/[t] in them [... he is called] / the holy righteous one, elect, good person. ¹⁵ He receives the victory without suffering on the day [of h]is com/[in]g forth.

So, behold, I have taught you of the dragon that / [exi]sts with its fourteen heads and five dens, / [wh]erein it is concealed and hidden. It does through them [... / its des]ire all the time.

Then th[a]t disciple says ²⁰ to him: My heart has been persuaded, my master, by what [you have r]e/[count]ed to me. You have taught me of the dragon with the fourteen / [he]ads. Blessed is every one who will slay and kill it; / [and it suffers] loss! He will live for ever and be a person victori[ous / i]n all his deeds.

••• **101** •••

(253,₂₅ – 255,₂₁)

/ [Concer]ning why, if the Person shall look down / into Water, [...] /

This chapter illustrates again Mani's fascination with all aspects of the natural world; and his attempt to create a totally integrated science.

254.1 – 24 Reflection in water is explained as a spiritual mystery signifying the descent of the divine call to the First Man in the abyss, and the corresponding ascent of the answer to the Living Spirit.

254.24 – 255.7 Reflection in water is explained as a physical mystery indicating how humans and other life on earth are inextricably tied to the stars and zodiacal signs (their 'fathers').

255.7 – 11 Reflection also indicates that a child is born head first.

255.12 – 21 Shadows show how the body is fastened to the earth.

This series of loosely grouped teachings may evidence textual development. Also the distinction between spiritual and physical truths, occuring also in the previous kephalaion, may be the link used by the redactor in attempting to order the chapters.

[Once again, one of his d]isciples asked the apostle / [... ³⁰ ... in(254)stru]ct me about this lesson: When / the person is above water and looking down [into / the wat]ers, if he shall see his face reflected why sh/all you find his head turned upside down and a[l]so his fee[t] ⁵ upwards? Yet, when he stares down into the wa[te/rs], his face shall not be visible, nor can he see i[t / th]ere? Then the apostle says to him: Ha[p/pen] you know this, that this universe is established / [of m]ystery, and is entirely full of mystery. [And] this: ¹⁰ The face of people and the shape of trees shall app[ear] / turned upside down in the water as this is signifi[ed] / in [the] mystery of the summons, when it was sent do[wn] / to the [wo]rlds of darkness towards the First Man. Sin[ce / ...] in this way it cast itself down [...] ¹⁵ like a person [who] plunges headlo[ng] into water; / so it is also with the summons. It cast itse[lf] / headlong to the worlds below, with streng[th] / and diligence.

And this too: Shall the pe[rs]/on lift his head up from the water, his face shall not be visibl[e] ²⁰ to him, being bent below. This characterises the m[yste]/ry of the obedience that ascended from below, / from with the First Man his father to the [Liv]ing Spirit. / This is a spiritual mystery that I have [revea]/led to you so that you would understand it.

I[f] ²⁵ you [w]ish to understand another cor[pore]al mystery / on this subject, listen and I may teach you to under[stand it]. / The face of people and of animals [and / of] trees is visible in the water, hangi[ng upside down]. / This occurs to the mystery of the [stars] ³⁰ and the zodiac, which hang upside down and are vis[ible in] / the great sea. For [the face of people a](255)nd beasts and all trees hang on the ro[ot] / of the stars and the zodiac, being begotten from them. / Just as their fathers, who are spread out above, [hang] / upside down; so it is also that the m[yste]⁵ry of their fathers is being revealed to them whenever th[ey sta]re down into the water. This is, that you shall find their [shapes] / inverted.

Not only this, but [the] child / who is born; as the ho[ur] approaches for him to be born*135, he hangs upside down and is born [he]ad first. 10 Indeed, due to this, his mystery shall be revealed / in these waters people [s]tare down [int]o. /

Furthermore, I reveal something else to you: Behold, you will find the shadow of the person who walks along is joined to the earth / all the time. If the person is troubled [...] 15 his shadow up upon the earth [...] / above. It is impossible for him to do [... / ...] on the earth. See, this mystery is [a] great / sign, signifying that the entire body came / from the earth and had ascended from the abyss. Again, d[u]e to this, 20 its shadow is joined on the earth, turned downwar[ds], / and hanging from above.

••• 102 •••

(255,22 – 257,7)

/ *Concerning the Light Mind, why / it does not exercise Forekno*25 *wledge for the Saint as for the Apostle?* /

Mani is asked why the Light Mind does not cause the elect to have perfect and prior knowledge, such as the apostles have, when it indwells them all. He gives five practical reasons why such knowledge could lead to abuse and dissension; but promises that it will be given to them when they ascend from their bodies in perfection.

[Onc]e again one of the elect questioned the apostle, saying / to him: The Light Mind that shall come and be reve/[aled] of the holy church, and assumes the faithful / [and the ele]ct; why shall it not entrust forekno[w30ledge] to them [as for] the apostle? In my opinion, it ought to be unve/[iled] to them in a revelation. Just as / [all things are revea]led for the apostle, so also / [ought they] to be unveiled for the elect and they become 'fore/-[knowers]'; so that they will attain them, be they easy or (256) difficult. You ought to find them, knowing each other's heart; / because the child of the apostle is the Mind. For whoever / [und]erstands i[t] is able to unveil all things from it, / [just a]s with the apostle!

---

*135 Lit: he is about to be born and his hour comes.

Then the apostle says to [5] [him]: You have recounted this well. I am the one who will te/[ach y]ou about it. Happen you know that the Light M[ind], / who dwells in the elect, has the power to perform all these / w[onders] among the faithful, all these signs that you have re/co[unted] to me; but the elect are not able to persist in [10] the great[ness] that may be unveiled to them.

Not only this, but / [firs]t of all: If it unveiled something to / the [ele]ct and they exercised foreknowledge, they would have become an apostle / and none be humble to his comrade.

Second: / [If t]hey were knowing each other's heart, they would have despised [15] one another. If their counsel and consideration / is unveiled from one [to] another, and the shames of th[eir] / body are revealed to each other, not one among them / [...] the other.

Third: They would have made enemies of / one another because of the counsels and evil considerations t[20]hat they shall ponder over together; due to the flesh that / they assume and the sin that dwells in them. An[d] when / each one of them will understand the evi[l] counsel / that his comrade ponders over, he may become an enemy / to him immediately; and they are set firm against one another [25] in disputation.

Fourth: When / he may exercise foreknowledge, they will understand the lifespan [... / ... of] a body and will not await a gr[eat many] / years in righteousness, but [...] / down to the world. And when they will [...] [30] attain the one found be enlightened [...] / up to righteousness.

Fifth: [If] / everything is unveiled to them, th[ey would have] unveiled it [to the ma](257)gicians in the world and these fortune-tellers, and go arou[nd fr]/om place to place taking money to create for them wealth and worldly [ri]/ches.

Now this is why (the Light Mind) shall not give a reve[la]/tion to the elect. It does not add it to them due to these five [thin]gs; [5] but the matter is hidden from them only until the time when [they will come] / forth from their body.

Then every thing that has oc[curred] / and that will occur is unveiled to them!

••• 103 •••

(257,8 – 258,3)

/ *Concerning the Five Wonders* [10] *that the Light Mind shall / display in the Elect.* /

There are five qualities proclaimed and enacted by the elect person who is indwelt by the Light Mind, and who has thus become a new man.

Once again the apostle speaks: The Light Mind shall / enact five light signs in the elect.

The first si/[gn] is the wisdom that the elect shall preach [15] and proclaim in all its shapes and forms / and manners.

The second is the fai/[th]; since after his preaching of the wisdom, that he / proclaims, the others who hear it be[lieve] it. /

The third is [...] [20] in his preaching [...] peace / of heart for the assembly of his brethren [...] /

[The] fourth is love, for he shall love wisdom [...] the / brothers and sisters who are seated [before] him. /

[The] fifth is the fear of legal excommunication that shall ex[25][clude him amo]ngst these who did not receive the hope of God. Also other iniquit/[ous] people who shall be found in the church; it excludes / them with a legal excommunication, on account of their foolishness. /

[The] Light [Mind] puts these five signs in the new man, / [whom he has] purified, cleansed, supported [and [30] cho]sen [...]

Blessed is every one / [who ...] the [M]ind and is diligent in his wis/[dom ...]

The [other] one: These five sig(258)[n]s will be [es]tablished in him and perfected in him, so that / [he] will become a faultless vessel and a pearl with/out [pr]ice for ever at all!

••• 104 •••

(258,4 – 258,25)

5 *Concerning Food: It shall be allocated to / Five Products of the human Body. /*

Food engenders five productions from the human body. These five may all be understood as physical, if the text is read as euphemistic. For instance: spiritual heat; spittle; sweat; semen and sexual juices; children.

[Onc]e again he speaks to his disciples: This sustenance / of various kinds that people gather in / and eat, and enters the body; it shall be distributed [10] to five productions.

The first product is this that shall / issue from the person in rapture and rises up in / the Mind, and it comes out from all his limbs, and is immeasurable. /

The second is this that shall issue from the per/son in voice and word.

The third is this th[15]at shall spring from them in strength and activity. /

The fourth is what is engendered by the pleasure of lu[s]/t in men and women.

The fifth is this / that shall be formed and sculpted in the flesh, a/nd be engendered and come from them. It is this cor[20]poreal creature; only its parents / can recognise this creature that they beget. They are attentive to its desire and its / th[oug]ht and its [lo]ve every day, / all the time. However, these other four forms they neither notice / nor are concerned about; because [25] they are not displayed.

••• 105 •••

(258,26 – 259,23)

/ Concerning the Three Things that are great with / Mankind, as they are running all the time, in that they [...] /

Mani recounts how Christians use the name of Christ in invocations, personal names and oaths. He then asserts the success of his own apostolate, evidencing the same use of his name.

Once again he speaks: Chris[tia]n people [...] 30 sow in the universe for t[h]ree [things ...] /

The first: If the person will spe[ak the name of Christ] (259) on every thing he may lay his hand to to construct.

The [sec]/ond: They will call people who love him by hi[s name]; / and bestow his name upon their*136 children and children's [child]/ren.

The third saying: They will swear by hi[s fo]5rtune and his surety; namely all these who are under hi[s a]/uthority.

And I, Manichaios, who sits before you, / I have sown these three graces; by the grace that was [re/war]ded to me from the Father. For, by the wisdom that I [have manif]est/ed, by the truth that I have revealed and by the truth and [sw]10eetness wherein I have taught people, I have received a [se]/ed and a good sowing*137 with they who are counted to me. Also, by my good and useful tea[ch]ings / that I have revealed; s[e]e, / people who love me are c[a]lled of my name! Also, by the aposto/[la]te of my father, who sent me to the world, they w[ho] 15 are mine accept me for themselves.

Behold, they swear by m[y fort]une / [i]n every place and every city! Who is as great as I in / the universe? Or who was active in this creation / the way I myself have been active, other than my brothers the apo/stles who were before me? For indeed those t20oo

---

*136 Reading ΝΕⲨ for ΝΕϤ
*137 Or read ⲤϮⲚⲞⲨϤⲈ 'perfume'.

were active and laid foundations in the world. / Indeed, due to
this, every one who will believe in me and also be persuaded / to
my word can become with me inheritors in the new / aeon.

••• 106 •••

(259,24 – 260,27)

25 *There is no Joy that shall remain / in the World till the End. /*

Although they are not themselves oppressed, the sun and the moon (here
personified) can never be completely joyful during the time of mixture. This
is firstly because they see the rule of the enemy in the universe; and
secondly they see the oppression of the living soul everywhere before it
reaches them and is finally cleansed.

[O nce agai]n he speaks to his disciples: There is not [o]ne
person / [existing in] the world, standing firm [i]n mixture, for
whom / [j]oy remains to the end.

Not only peo30 [ple], even the sun and the moon, the light-givers of
the heavens / [...] nor are they oppressed, they know not / [... s]et
firm in a summons and an **(260)** [obe]dience. Nevertheless, they
too, they do not rejoice comple/[tel]y.

So, one: Their eyes stare at their enemy, they / [perceiv]e him
and also look at his ugly shapes. / [They s]ee him, that he is alive
and established and is king ab5[ov]e and below, in secret and
manif[e]/st. He does every thing that he wants according to his
wil[l]. /

[The s]econd: They perceive the living soul, they see [i]/t and
that it is ensnared and set in a great [fetter] a/bove and below, in
the tree and in the flesh*138, 10 [...] with every oppression. It is
being pressed, drawn near t/o [and] sliced and eaten as it comes
up / and down; from above below and from below ab/ove. It [is]
despoiled and moved from / body to body.

Now, because of their living soul that is 15 love[d] by them and
honoured of them, when they see it in op[pr]/ession th[ey can]
not [re]joice completely.

---

*138   Reading ϭⲁⲡϩ for ϭⲁⲡⲧ 'wool'.

So, one about the soul; / and one about their enemy whom they see ruling [in] / what is not his own. He is proud and satisfied with / a wealth that is not his own. Indeed, due to this, they do not rejoice in [20] total; but bear up and swallow their heart unt/il they cleanse the living soul and take it from the enemy's hands. / Then they obliterate the death that is their enemy and they g/ather it in [and fetter it in the lump] for ever and / ever.

When they will chain their enemy in the bond at the [las][25]t, then they will rejoice and no longer grieve from this t[ime]. / Also, they become the very same as they were from the [start] / for ever!

••• 107 •••

(260,28 – 261,13)

/ Concerning the Form of the Word, that [... [30] ...] /

The process of forming a word is compared to the production of a coin.

Once again he speaks about the production of the word t[hat comes] / from the mouth and is heard by the [ears]. / He says [... (**261**) ...] and the throat draws it up and the tongue / spreads it out and the teeth cut it and the lips g[at]/her it! The word shall come forth through the power of th[ese five] / members and be heard outside.

Simila[rly] [5] the coin: One shall pour it out and an[othe]/r beat it and another trim it as it is turned, and a[nother] / put the stamp on it and another wipe it in the sieve (?). [Behold], / these five craftsmen shall shape and beautify [their] / coin, and it comes amongst mankind. It becomes a posse[ssion] [10] to be received and given.

This is also the case with the [wor]d, / as it is formed and embellished by five [member]s. / It comes forth and is heard by the ears [of] / others.

••• 108 •••

(261,14 – 262,9)

15 *Concerning the Seed Grain that shall be / formed by the Elements,
[a]/nd also be destroyed by them. /*

The meaning of this chapter is not entirely clear. Perhaps the theme is that
there is a cycle of growth and blight, and that one must inevitably lead to
the other in this world of mixture. As the light elements are saved, so what
is left must be increasingly stricken.

Once again [the] apostle, the builder of the church, spea[ks] to
his disciples: / This seed grain and this barley grain 20 that you
see shall be formed and [...] a/nd beautified by the five elements.
[N]ow, the w[ar]mth / and the cold nourish the seed grain and
the / entire [t]ree. So, just as these things nourish it [... / ...] it is
destroyed [...] throu[g]h 25 [... / ...] hunger.

In this way also righteousness / [gathe]rs the five to it. So, it shall
be chosen by the teachers / [and the ele]ct; and they gather it in
and ornament i/[t ... and] it is well established 30 [...] Now, [ju]st
as they that shall enlight/[en ...] In this way too, a (262) lack and
a shortfall shall occur from place to place through / [t]hem; and
they who have chosen it have gathered it in and beaut/[ified] and
attained it, while an affliction shall arise for it th/[ro]ugh those.

People also shall be caused [to 5 st]umble on their account, through
the energy of Matter / [that d]wells in them. It has poured / [its]
shadow over them, just as it shall also pour its / [shado]w over the
elements and destroy the fruits / [of] all the trees.

••• 109 •••

(262,10 – 264,19)

/ Concerning the Fifty Lord's Days; / to what Mysteries do they correspond? Or the / Second (Fifty)[139]; *to whose Sign (are they)? /*

Mani is asked to explain the significance of the fifty fasts undertaken by the catechumens, that is once weekly on each lord's day; and also of a further fifty held by the elect. He engages in some rather convoluted calculations to reach these totals.

The first fifty correspond to the mystery of the First Man: five powers for each of his five sons or garments equals twenty-five limbs of the living soul. This divine son/s of the Man (note the deliberate Christological reference) has abstained from the food of life in a world of mixture. The doubling of the twenty-five seems (263.4 – 9?) to be calculated with reference to the ascent of the First Man; and then the ascent of the call and answer, which are the counsel of life or means of salvation for the soul.

The second fifty correspond to the mystery of Jesus as the second man: forty days fasting in the desert, seven days in the house of Simon the leper, and three in the tomb.

O**nce** [again] a disciple stood up. He questions the apo[15]stl[e], saying to him: I beseech you, my m[a]/ster, t[o] recount to us about the fifty lord's days during wh/ich the catechumens fast. For what do they fast, or / for whose mystery do they fa[s]t? Or these seco[20]nd (fifty) that is set between the elect, / to whose mystery were they set [a]mongst them? Proclaim t[hi]s also to / [us] and persuade us about it, because [... / ...] you [...]

Then [he] say[s to] / his questioner and they with him: [25] Happen you know that [in eac]h one of these five garments that the [First] / Man summonsed there are five powers. / They shall be counted to the [... each] / other, these five, and five times [...] / their number. However, at the time [...] **(263)** the summons went down. The answer wis[h]/ed to ascend with it. And the summons with the obedien[ce constitute] twenty-five characteristics in their twenty-five limbs, [which] / are the sons of the Man. The summons and [the obed][5]ience were raised to the heights through them.

---

[139]   Smagina 1990:122 suggests that the term δευτέρα stands for Monday, i.e. the second day of the week upon which the elect fasted.

Just as their fa[ther] / the living Man raised himself up through them, by th[ese] / these other ones have set up all things a[bov]e / and below. Indeed, these are what are called p[ente]/cost, the fifty great days that are the [archetypes of [10] the] holy [d]ays. They fasted from their [foo]d, / [w]hich is their own. So, from that time until [the time] of / [the adv]ent of Jesus the Splendour, the glorious one who came [... / ... t]heir food which is the [...] of sou[l, w]hich is / the summons and the obedience [...] [15] that spiritual food. They rele[ased ...] / all these fifty days, which [...] this living food / suffices for all of them. It filled them all with power and rich/ness and life. Light [...] / this living food that [... [20] ...] became rich.

They ceased being fifty days. [They] have gone. / They became the one hundred holy days that are the fifty [d]ay/[s ...] fast [... / ...] that they have joined them wit[h them / ... [25] ... / ... / ...] these mysteries of these first fif[ty / ... these s]econd (fifty) also [in] which the elect / [fast] correspond to the sign of the fifty [... [30] ... the] sum[m]ons and the obedience set them in their (**264**) splendrous [places] at the coming of Jesus. Now, behold, these are the / [great] days of the fifty lord's days that I have revealed / [for the] catechumens.

Behold, these are the fifty da/[ys of] the second (group) that I have revealed for the elec[5][t ...] You enquire about these mysteries. They also occur in / [the teachin]gs of the sects. They have fifty days in which they / f[as]t. They call them penteco/[st, b]ecause the apostles themselves fasted for / t[hese fif]ty days, they revealed them to their disciples.

[10] Also, [Chr]ist himself revealed these fifty days to [them] / on [the d]ay, fasting on the mountain, at the time when the [de]/vi[l] tempted him[*140]. He spent another seven days g[oing i]/n [to] the house [of Simon] the leper[*141], together with the three other [days t]/hat he [spent] in the sepulchre among the dead[*142].

[15] Yet, [... in these f]ifty days. And I, I have b[estowed them] / on the entire church with these fifty days in which / the ca[te]chu-

---

[*140] See Mt. 4:2
[*141] See Mt. 26:6
[*142] See Lk. 24:46

m[e]ns fast, after the myster/y of the First Man. And the other fifty, after the sign of / the s[ec]ond man who was revealed in the church.

••• 110 •••

(264,20 – 265,8)

/ Concerning the Nourishment of the Person, / for there are Powers in it [... / ...] /

The human body images the macrocosmos as a machine for purifying the light from the darkness. As food is absorbed and passes through the digestive system the light is cleansed and exhaled, while the material dregs and their powers are expelled.

[Once again] sp[ea]ks [... ^{25} ...] exis[t ...] / d[a]ily to the body of the person [...] / there are two hundred and fifty thousand seals in it [...] / there are ano[ther] two hundred and fifty thousand rule[rs ...] / they are cleansed and purified and enter [...] (265) by the voice, by the word, and by the [... / ...] quiet with the silence at the time when his heart [... / ...] of God the Father. Also, the twelve [... / ...] rulers that belong to the darkness shall be swept o[ut ^{5} ...] outside in wandering and in tran[s/mi]gration [... / ...] some of them [... through] this tr[ansmigra]/tion, and others among them shall be brought bac[k].

••• 111 •••

(265,9 – 266,2)

^{10} *Concerning the Four Archetypes that occur / in the Eye, and the Fifth that is hidden / in them; to whom do they belong? /*

Too fragmentary to derive the overall sense.

[On]ce again he speaks: There are four a[s]pects among / mankind that perceive, as they perceive [... ^{15} with]out*143 these four that are hidden in them [...] they belong [... / ...] So, [the ...]

---

*143 Reading [ⲭⲱ]ⲡⲓⲥ

that is in the [... / ...] belongs to the fire. The darkness belongs to the ab[yss]; / but the light that perceives what is hidden in a[ll] these things, / being clear, is the living air.

²⁰ [Once] again he speaks: How shall the pupil of the eye [per]ce/[ive]? While [it percei]ves by day, yet come the nigh[t] it [shall not / perceive]. What myster[y] does this matter signify? / [Look], I am the one who will [explain to you what y]ou do not know [... / ...] the pupil of the eye shall not [... ²⁵ ...] the mystery of the [... / ...] is the door [... / ...] below [... / ...] the other four cardinal points. F[o]r in the [... / ...] above. He has [... ³⁰ ...] great [... / ...] they came do[wn ... / ...] living [... **(266)** the F]irst M[a]n came forth from it and kne[w] / all things.

••• 112 •••

(266,3 – 268,27)

/ The Human is less than all the Things ⁵ of the Universe, and he is rebellious beyond them all. /

This kephalaion seems to begin with a clear historical reminiscence. In the latter part there are two typical catechetical lists that appear to have been added to the text.

266.6 – 267.18 Mani stands in a dry river-bed and points to a great mountain, in order to illustrate his theme. The sense of his comments seems to be that if all of mankind (or perhaps all life forms?) were gathered together they would not equal in size this one mountain, and similarly they would be engulfed (?) in a single sea. And the earth has many mountains and seas existing in silence and peace. Nevertheless, it is humanity that blasphemes against God in all his power, saying that God is the one who created the demonic beings.

267.18 – 268.2 A disciple interprets this attack upon monotheism (correctly) as an assertion that humanity does not belong to God. He therefore asks why Jesus the son of God came into the world, and had to suffer torment and persecution. Mani replies that Jesus did not come to save mankind alone. He had various tasks in the divine plan, including a cosmological role (e.g. 94.1 – 11) and his revelation to Adam and Eve.

268.3 – 18 Jesus sent the apostles and revealed five great things.

268.19 – 27 The faithful shall live by three mighty things.

[F]urthermor]e, it happened one time as the apostle is travelling / [on the] road. He came across a great river marked deep in it[s / be]d. That river was dry. When he had le[apt o]/ut, he stood in its

midst and filled [his] eyes [10] [with its brea]dth and length and
deep bed [... / ...] he lifted his eyes up and saw a great mo[untain]
/ beyond that river.

After he had stood / [in] that place in the midst of the river, he
shook his [head]. / He [sa]ys: If one of all these five wo[rlds [15] of
the f]lesh [...] today on the surfaces of the earth [... / ...] out from
[...] which is deep. They will make it like / [...] and they set
them in order [... / with o]ne another, one [wi]th one upon the
earth. They all [... / ...] up to the heights against the elevation of
this mountain [... [20] ... corresponding to] its height; they will
neither come to breadth corresponding to / [its] breadth, nor to
width corresponding to its width, [nor / to] depth corresponding
to its depth.

Not only this, b[ut e/ach] one, all of them from their smallest to
their g[reatest / ...] a single sea [... [25] ...] single [...] but [...] / that
[s]ea and they are swallowed an[d ... / ...] is in it [... / ...] they are
in [...] earth [... / ...] many [m]ountains [... [30] ...] sea in it, they [...
/ ...] are very [gre]at in their fa[shion ... / ... t]hey did not guard
against him [... / ...] the silence and they [... **(267)** ...] blasphemed
hi[m] not, neither against his l[i/gh]t that is displayed, no[r] do
they utter {}*[144] blasphemies / [a]gainst his power that supports the
totality, nor against the / [e]ssence that is displayed indicating
the totality, [5] [nor] against the good works of righteousness. [They
/ re]count no cause of evil after Go/[d].

However, [the i]dol of ill-fated human[it]y [... / ...] the one that
will be unlike anything, that is equal [... / ...] great works; and it
was found evil [by] [10] God, the Lord of all. It even blasphemed
again[st the] / power that supports the totality, against its hol[y]
light; [and / it] profaned its glorious wisdom, bringing forth / the
cause of every sin. They say that / every disgraceful wickedness
and defilement, the rulers and the [15] demons and the fiends and
the satans, they say that they have co/me from God, that he is the
one who [es]tablished them [... / ...] they came not from him,
and they give false testimony / about him.

Then, when he had recounted this, / at that instant one of his

---

*[144] ϩⲁⲣⲡⲥ`

disciples speaks [20] to him from amongst these who are standing before him: T[e]ll / [u]s, our master, and instruct us about this lesso[n]. /

Now, [i]f this idol of humanity does not belong [t]o / God, according to what you have said about it, why did Jesus come to / [the] world, the son of the Living God? He has been reve[al[25]e]d therein! He suffered tribulation and persecution. They hung h/[im] on the cross, and his enemies perpetrated against him the tor/[ment] and shame of their evil-doing. /

[The ap]ostle [says] to him: Jesus did not come and s[a/ve the] world because of mankind alone, but [30] [... he] came and revealed on earth / [...] was strong outside in / [...] And [whe]n he had finished doing his (268) [t]ask outside [i]n the great u[ni]verse, he came [... / he wen]t further with Adam and Eve and revealed [to them]. / Even so, he sent the apostles to the good, / [g]enera-tion by generation, and revealed to them five great thin[gs].

[5] [Firs]t: He told them that they belong to the race of ligh[t. /

Se]cond: He unveiled to them about the aeons [of the gre/atness], how they occur; and he taught them about [the / manner of] the darkness, how it t[o]o exists. /

[The th]ird time: He proclaimed to them about the [l]ight great-[ness], [10] how it has been active against the pow[er / of] darkness and conquered it. /

Fourth: He taught them that he came to the province of death [... / ...] that is flesh, until he should find profit and bring / them from the gate of the underworld below, for [they had] been swa[ll][15]owed into it.

Fifth: He explained to us / that the rebels shall be bound in a great fetter, they who / shall [r]ebel against the g[o]od and against the righteousness t/hat is proclaimed by the apostle. /

Once [again] the apostle speaks: All the faithful who believe [20] this tr[u]th shall live by three great mighty things. /

The first: They have been counted to the race of faith and truth, this / living one that enlightens.

The second: They have received the right hand and / the peace that came to them from above. They have believed the [a]/postle who has been manifested.

The third: They a[ct] [25] with restraint and charity to the Cross of Light, which g[rie]/ves in the totality, being present in what is visible and what is / not vis[ib]le.

••• 113 •••

(268,27 – 269,13)

/ The Chapter on whether any [Lig]/ht comes from the Three Vessels.

Mani taught that the universe was layered, with eight earths and ten heavens, and carefully constructed for the purification of the light. The term 'vessel (ⲙⲁⲛⲍⲓⲟⲣⲉ)' is variously used in this complex cosmology. However, the reference to such surrounding the universe would seem to indicate the three vessels of water and darkness and fire that the Living Spirit first poured down from the heavens, and that he then swept out to ditches prepared for them at the edge of the universe. See chapters 42 – 45, especially 112.20 – 24. In any case, this kephalaion explains the mechanism by which light may be further refined, even from these vessels.

[30] Once again the disciples questioned our enlightener. They say: [Preac]/h about this bit of life and light that comes from [these three] / vessels that surround the universe [...] / life comes up [...] /

The apostle s[a]ys to them: [... **(269)** ...] b[u]t should the [...] ascend [... / ...] light of the rays that [...] which are received, which shine a[n/d] go in through these great open gates, through these doo[rs] / firmament by firmament. For four [gates [5] o]pen in each world, distributed at the four points of the comp[ass, / op]ening downwards to the vessels. So, due to this, the [light / of the] rays shall go in through these openings and it shines on [that] pla[ce], / and pulls through them the light and the little pi[llar (?) / that ex]ists there. From that place [it] shall be poured [out [10] to the] firmaments. It shall also be clarified in these firmaments [... / ...] a part there is cleansed and it is [all] taken u[p wi/t]h the living ones. However, its other part [...] shall all [be cast] d/[o]wn.

••• 114 •••

(269,14 – 270,24)

15 *Concerning the Three Images that / are in the righteous Person. /*

The elect have three 'images (εἰκών)' in them: the corporeal; the psychic; and the spiritual, which is the new man formed by the Light Mind. The living soul that enters the elect through food is cleansed as it rises up through these three, being stripped of all the corporeal and then the psychic accretions brought by mixture. In the spiritual image the light virgin perfects it.

This latter term is used variously in Manichaean texts. Here she is described as a guide, just as is the eschatological Light Form who comes to greet the departing soul with her three angels carrying the victory prizes. However, in this context she represents the perfection of the elect soul. Essentially the virgin is the manifestation of the soul in all her chastity and power.

Once again our enlightener speaks to his disciples: Thr/[ee] images occur in the elect person. /

[The fi]rst is the [s]piritual image, which is the new man, wh 20 ich the Light Mind shall form in him; and it goes [i]n / to him and dwells in him.

The second image is [the] rem/nant and remainder of the new man, which is the py[ch]ic image / that is bound in the flesh, as the old man [... si]nce the / times of this psychic image.

The other one is the [corp]oreal image 25 [that is] added to them all.

These three images / [...] entirely. When it will [... / ...] through the nourishment of food. If it shall sink [... / ...] down to the corporeal image. [And] the corporeal, / [that] is in it, shall divest itself of it and place it in the [...] image. 30 [...] again it rises up and falls to the [...] image; / it [sh]all divest itself of the psychical of the enemies, which [... / ...] anger. The lust [... / ... / ...] with it.

Then sh[all] a [light] vir 35 [gin come and] reveal [the] spiritual image (270) that is [there], which [is] the n[ew m]an. / T[h]at virgin acts as a guide. [She g]/oes on before and it is extended to the heights abo[ve, / and] received in to this spiritual image. And she scu[lpt⁵s] it and adorns it with the new man [wi]t/[hi]n. It is sealed with all the limbs of this light vir/[gin] who is present and dwells in the new man. /

So, this is [h]ow this living limb shall be [puri/fied] and live, the one that comes in to the body of ^{10} [the ri]ghteous one from without through the administration of food of various ki/[nds], like this. The living soul shall be clea/n[sed] entirely every [d]ay and traverse these three [im]/a[ges]*145.

So, it shall divest itself of the body, which is not its own, / in the corporeal. It shall also divest itself of the souls ^{15} that are not its own, these that are mixed with it in the psychical [... / ...] anger and desire and [...]-ness / and foolishness and envy and strife; and these other / wicked teachings that are not its own.

However, in [the] / spiritual image itsel[f] it shall live and be joined with [lo]^{20}ng-sufferingness, the perfection of faith and love / that reigns over them all. It is the virgin of / light who robes the new man and who shall be cal[l]/ed 'the hour of life'. S[he] is the f[irst], / but s[h]e is also the last.

••• 115 •••

(270,₂₅ – 280,₁₉)

/ The Catechumen asks / the Apostle: will Rest / come about for Someone who has come out of the Body, i/f the Saints pray [over] ^{30} and make an Alms-offering [for him]? /

In this extensive chapter the question concerns the effectiveness of prayer for the dead; and how to reconcile such intercession with the doctrine of retribution for one's sins (the familiar theme of grace versus deeds). Whilst this second problem is not clearly answered in the readable portions of the text, the chapter is of particular interest for evidencing (albeit only implicitly) Manichaean practices as regarding the dead; and the role of the elect or the saints within believing communities.

270.31 – 271.12 Framing sequence and statement of the catechumen's question.

---

*145   Reading Ⲙ[ⲉⲓ]/ⲕ[ⲱⲛ]

271.13 – 26 Mani replies that supplications made by the elect in faith will be granted; for such petitions have been made by the gods since the beginning, and the right has been passed on to the church.

271.26 – 273.9 Mani explains the archetypal supplication whereby the Mother of Life besought the Father for a helper, on behalf of the First Man; and was granted the Living Spirit that saved him from the abyss.

273.9 – 14 Reiteration: the saints will similarly be granted their prayers.

273.15 – 20 Mani begins to recount a second archetypal episode with a brief description of the constituent parts of the universe.

273.20 – 274.21 The great gods of the first and second emanations beseech the Father for a leader to undertake the process of salvation, the mechanisms for which they have put in place. They are granted the Third Ambassador.

274.22 – 29 Reiteration: the faithful elect and catechumens will similarly be granted their requests.

274.30 – 277.3 (and see 274.16 – 19) Highly fragmented account of a third supplication regarding the liberation of the living soul; and perhaps further episodes concerning Jesus Splendour et al.

277.4 – 278.23 List of four victories achieved by prayer for the dead; with reiteration. Here perhaps might also be found Mani's answer concerning the problem of retribution for past sins.

278.23 – 280.1 Analogy of the process of intercession, and explanation.

280.1 – 19 Mani charges the catechumens with their mission, and receives the thanks of his original questioner (framing sequence).

O nce again, it happened one time wh[ile our enlightener is sitting] / in the midst of the co[ngreg]ation. A cate[chu]me[n ...] / stood u[p] in front of him and sp[oke, questioni(**271**)ng] him. He says to hi[m: I be]seech you, my master, [that you / may] recount to me of this lesson; if I ask you it! [About / the] entreaty that the person makes in his pr[ayer, / if he] beseeches charity for someone who has been released from h[is ^{5} bo]dy.

Tell me: The entreaty and the prayer by which / [the] saints pray, beseeching for [someone; do they / h]elp him any? How is it benef[icial] for him; or el[se does it / he]lp him not? For we have heard from you [just so, th]at / each one shall receive retribution according to his deeds.

^{10} So [n]ow, I beseech you my master, that you may instr[uc]t me / about this lesson for which I have asked you; whether [it is] tru[e]? / [F]or it is very great and honoured amongst pe[opl]e. /

[Then] the apostle speaks to him: As to the qu[esti]on / for [which] you ask me, the entreaty occurs and the true pra[yer] ^{15}

occurs! For every elect [Manich]aean*[146] person, / [if he] beseeches charity in total faith, he is [claimi]ng a / [re]quest from our compassionate Father. So, if he is beseec[hing] over him/[sel]f alone, he shall be favoured his entreaty; [bu]t i[f] again he is / [be]seeching on behalf of someone else, he shall be granted [hi]s r[20] [eq]uest.

For this entreaty has been since the beginning [... / ...] the gods first made entreaty of their Father. They were granted / their entreaty and their request. For its part, the [h]oly church / that assumes the flesh is established in [pray/er, and] entreaty above [a]ll, and the pure request [...] [25] him and the son, the Christ. They shall give him it, na/[mely] these first ones that are prior to him.

I will inst/[ruct y]ou how it is that they shall / [beseech] their entreaty from the first ones; or in what form / [they shall en]treat [their req]uest, they who have asked for it [30] [...] every thing. The Great Spirit, the Mother / [of Life, she claimed and pra]yed and besought and glorified and praised (272) the first established on[e; who] is the Father. She [beso/ught] him an entreaty. She claimed of him a request. [She / received] a great gift; she and the many powers / [wi]th her.

She besought an entreaty on behalf of the First Man, [bec[5]ause of h]ow he had come forth and thrown himself dow[n. / He became] distant from the Mother of Life. He separated from her and g[ave / him]self; in great affliction. He joined war on [earth / with] the destruction and the grief and the weakness; in the worlds [of / dark]ness; in the abysses made of fear; in the midst [10] of the demons' d[i]t[ch]; amongst the powers of the dev[il]! /

Indeed, h[e is l]ike a king standing in the mids[t of] / h[is] enemies. And when the Mother of Life petitioned and prayed and [gl]/or[ified] and praised the Father, the [f]/irst established one, she did petition him that he might send [15] a po[wer]; a protector and redeemer and helper for the s/on of God who is set in affliction.

---

*[146] The reconstruction in the ed. princ. of ⲙ[ⲙⲛ̄ⲭ]ⲁⲓⲟⲥ should be treated with caution. This form of self-designation does not occur elsewhere in the text.

No[w], just as / [she] had [beso]ught and interceded, so likewise was her pray[er] / fulfilled and received in to the presence of the Father of Gre[at]/n[ess]. He turned and gave to her her entreaty: the great [power], 20 the Living Spirit, the giver of ease. The Mother of Life and the Living Spirit came with / gr[ea]t power to the [bo]/rders of the territory. They brought the First Man up fro[m] / that war and struggle, wherein he is se[t]. /

He gave himself as a grace for the Mo[th]er of Life. [He] 25 became estranged and far from her, the one whom his enemi[es] (place) / in great affliction, the one who is in the land of [dark-ness] / since he [became] weak.

The Living Spirit gr[asp]ed and t[ook him i]/n. He freed him. He set him r[ight and gave] / him [e]ase in the land of res[t ...] 30 the Living Spirit, the first giver of e[ase ...] / the will of these three. The w[el]comer [...] / find with the welcomer that [...

(273) ...] a great power [...] of the loved one [...] / the First Man who had been f[a]r away. He had become dista[nt]. / She [had] besought on his behalf. He was set fast in affliction. (The Living Spirit) [went] / to the place of destruction and weakness, the one that freed 5 and redeemed him and gave him ease from the affliction. He se[t him] / right with rest and joy. He has himself become rested, [wi]/th him for ever.

See [no]w, I have taught you [the fi]/rst entreaty that the Mother of Life besought by [her] / prayer. They granted her her entreaty.

Thi[s] also is the case [with the prayer] 10 that the faithful saints [... o]/ver the one who has been released from his body. They shall be granted their / entreaty just as the Mother of Life was given the entreaty th[at sh]e / besought on behalf of the First Man. She was given the First Man / by the entreaty for which she besought the Father.

15 [...] a/nd they built the universe and completed it with its firmaments, / with its wheels, with the ships of light that are in the heights, / with its fastenings, with its earths and its walls, with its / vessels. They completed the universe and set it right 20 by the fathers of light.

Then, the Great / Spirit stood with the Beloved of the Lights, the Great / Builder with the Living Spirit and the First Man. These / five stood to prayer; they glorified and praised the Father, / the first established one. They besought of him an entreaty. They [25] [clai]med of him a request, that he might give them the power / [...] the leader, a guide to all the things / [of] activity that they had constructed. That he might come and purify / [the] living [so]ul that is set in affliction. /

[They prayed and be]sought their Father, and he received from them their pr[30][ayer ...] he gave them their entreaty and their re/[quest ...] he summoned from him / [...] which is the Third / [Ambassador. H]e, he came from the power of his (274) [g]reatness. He saw the entire [soul], how it is entangled [in / a] chain and set fast. [It] sees the things of ac[t]/ivity that his brothers have constructed, that have come from [the hei/ghts]. Again, he saw the living soul, that it is entangled and set [fa5st] in a great torture. It is oppressed in the stink of the abys/[s that] is joined with it.

And therefore, he, the Ambassa[dor / ...] in his charity. [S]o, he revealed his way, / before this underworld that is dug deep down, / [to f]ree the living soul. He redeemed it from all the fleshes [10] of death wherein it is pained. He gave it ease. / H[e] set it right in the place of rest and joy.

And / again, he too, the Ambassador, he fulfilled the will / of these three; the will of his brothers who had besought / the Father for him. They claimed of him a request, together with [15] the [...] of the Father, the one that [...] he gave the entrea[ty / that they had besought] of him.

The third is the transferral / of the living [soul] that he had fre[ed]. He released it and / gave it ease from the affliction. He became king and first to / the entire b[o]dy.

Behold, I have instructed you as to [20] the second entreaty by which they [first] besought the Father. / They were given the Third Ambassador. /

Now, happen you know this lesson: Each perfect elect / and every catechumen who believes, being / in the truth and set firm to prayer in faith, if he bese[25]eches and [inter]cedes with faith, [wheth]er indeed for himself [or] / else for another who has been freed from his [bo]/dy; his entr[eaty] and his request [that he ask]/ed for shall [be] granted for him. Just as the entreaty of his fathers was granted [...] / they who besought the Father for the Ambassador.

[30] Again, let us come to the third entreaty wh[en they besought h]/im the third time [...] / display[ed] his image [...] / he hid his image from the [... (275) ...] he stood firm [... / ...] they revea[led ... / ... / ...] the light [... [5] ... the F]irst Man [... / ...] mock [...] to him in [... / ...] which is exalted [... / ...] garment [...] they were fr[e/e]d [... [10] ... / ... / ...] to him [... / ...] their voice [...] the bod[y ... / ... p]rayer [... [15] ...] it [...] beseech [...] the bo[dy ... / ... / ... / ...] beseech [... / ...] she besought [...] in [... [20] ...] be free [... / ... / ... / ...] Ambass[ador ... [27] ...] and also [...] (276) with the living ones and [... fo]r ever [... / ...] the firs[t ...] from the [... / ...] he gave him the hope [...] /

Also, [Jes]us the Splendour perfec[ted] the will [... [5] ...] the will [... / ...] they found the li[gh]t [...] the wil[l] of the [... / ...] that he had [...] he gave them the power [th]at / is Jesus the Splendour. H[e granted] the will of the elements. / [... [10] ... / ...] for ever. This first [... / ...] he was humbled, he was made free [...] / the [...]-ness is displayed [to] his enemies. He received the hope [... / re]veal [...] Jesus the Splendour, the light power [... [15] ...] and [the] entreaty of the [...] of lig[ht ... / ...]

Now, just as this entreaty [... / ... / ...] the fig[ure ... / ...] that they have [... this] is also how [... [20] ...] the figure of [...] you are set fir[m ... / ...] Happen you know this: Every one [... / ... k]nows, he has perceived [... / ...] all the things [... / ... [25] ...] out from [... / ...] within him [... [29] ...] upon him [... (277) ...] will fre[e] him, [an]d they give him ease [... / ...] in it, and they [give h]im rest and [... / ...] and the petition of the hol[y] church. /

[Happen] you k[no]w: That per[son] who enacted the [5] [alm]s and the remembrance for the person who had come ou[t from the b]o/[dy]; he made this peace. He besought an entreaty [...] / his four great victories th[erein].

The first: [... / ...] of the living soul that is entangled and bound i[n the] entire [uni]/verse. For it shall be freed and clea[nsed] [10] and purifi[ed] and redeemed by cause of him.

The seco[nd]: / He shall make rest for the holy church, b[y the al]/ms that he enacts for the person who has been fr[eed] / from his body. The [...] children of the [chu]r/ch rest upon it. The [...] that living [so]ul, [15] the one that was [...] in the [ho]pe / [...] it shall surpass and be purified [...]

The th/[i]rd victory is [... / ...] the Father [... / ...

The fourth (?) ... [20] ...] who had come out from his body, they [...] him, as he had [...] / alms on his behalf and a remembrance for his br[other; / whether] his father or his mother or his s[o]n / [o]r else [his] daughter or his relative [who / sha]ll come out from his body. He has made alms for [his [25] ... f]rom him. He did not lack his ho[pe / ...] but he enacted for him a remembrance [... / ...] of the church.

The catechumen [... / ...] this alms for a person if he has come out [fr]om / [his body]; as his limb [...] these four [... [30] ... / ...] the sins from the one who has [... / ... / ... (278) ... / ...] a brother [...] a relativ[e ... / ...] sick [...] his [... / ...] sin [... [5] ...] from the affliction [... / ...] the way [...] catechumen [... / ...] in his [...] /

So, [...] reward for it [...] the other five [... / ...] he did not remember [...] the catechumen [... [10] ...] He redeemed the living [person] who is entangled [... / ...] entirely. He has [...] his father, the first [... / ...] he made redemption for the s[oul / ...] that he had fre[ed / ...] the light has pity [15] [...] the way als[o ...] a request [...] Cross [... / ... a]ffliction. Again, just as he has [... / ...] of the light [... / ...] give ea[s]e for his [... / ...] grant the entreaty and the re[quest [20] of] this catechumen. He besought for the soul / [...] him, that had come forth from the world. They shall make [... / ... e]ase. It shall be freed from affliction and come forth [... / ...] for ever.

D[u]e to this whole matter [... / ...] like a person [...] a relative [25] [...] if he had sinned he was hung and bound [... / ...] he did it. Afterwards, a comrade [... / ...] or his father or his brother rises and goes [... / ...] for he who was bound a promi[se ... / ...] it shall be determined [... [30] the mast]er whom he had bound [... / ...] before [the chi]e[f ... / ... (279) ...] and he petitions [...]

(Mani) says: You have [asked me / about the s]in of his relat[iv]e who is boun[d ... / ...] and the intercession that his [kin/sma]n shall make there before this per[son], ⁵ who had bound him, [for these other] masters.

Now, by cause of the [re/l]ative of this bound person who beseeches / [that] they might free him, and with the help of they whom he pe[titi]oned / to give something so as to aid either h[e o]r / these others; this person shall fill these other master[s] ¹⁰ with charity. And he frees his kinsma[n a]nd achi/eves for him rest.

Again, this too is what / the matter of this person is like, the one who was f[r]ee[d] / from his body. Afterwards a male / and or female catechumen, or a household member of his, [expresses] his ¹⁵ love towards him. And he performs a remembrance in the church / on his behalf; and the saints beseech for him a [s]in-entreaty / through the entreaty and the remembrance that they shall perform [on] his behalf / in the holy church. They shall release that soul / and it comes forth from this affliction to ease.

Indeed, this living soul ²⁰ that was freed by cause of this other soul; it / [t]oo, that living soul, it shall be redeemed in the name / [of] that person. It is redeemed*¹⁴⁷ and purified and at[tains] / its first essence. Also, it shall become h[is co-]/helper and beseeches for the soul of the one who has been freed ²⁵ [from h]is body. He shall petition charity for it and forgiveness / [of sins] from the powers of light.

Just as eas/[e has come about] for the living soul by cause of this soul, / [this is how] this soul [sha]ll find ease and escape / [tha]t [body]. It goes in to the land of ³⁰ [light ...] soul that was redeemed because of it / [...] comes about for it; and it (280) [goes] to the land of [li]fe and rest [...] /

[Then] speaks the apostl[e to t]hat catechu[men]: / I, I have entrusted you al[l; these cat]e/[chu]mens of the faith. For, so long ⁵ [...] make alms-offerings and remembrances and [... / for these] souls that have come out from their body [... / ...] So long as they are set fast in distress becaus[e / ...] of the alms that you give him, and the cup of wat[er / ...] the saints by it. [What] you are doing

*¹⁴⁷ Perhaps read ⲥⲱⲧϥ 'cleansed'.

[is] a great good ¹⁰ for this living soul that is set / [...] in transmigration [... / ...] you will perform for it a remembrance as you redeem / i[t] from thousands of afflictions and ten thousands of transmigr/ati[on]s; and you bring it to this brother.

Then, when ¹⁵ that catechumen heard these things he prai/sed [and] made obeisance and glorified. He says to him: I am grate/-ful to you my master, with great confessions. For / you, [you have] {opened}*¹⁴⁸ for us every thing. You have instructed us / entirely; with your [wisdom].

<h2 style="text-align:center">••• 116 •••</h2>

(280,20 – 282,6)

/ Concerning why if a [Nail] is cut / the Person shall not be sick; but if a Limb is c/ut he shall immediately be pained. /

Mani compares the different responses of parts of the body to the growth patterns of tree varieties.

O nce again one of the disciples questioned the apostle. He s[a]²⁵ys to him: Tell me, my master, why / when limbs are cut from the body / of the person he shall be pained? While if the hair / on the head of the person's body should be shaved, and [the nai/ls o]f his hands and feet be cut, he does not notice it [...] ³⁰ Some of these even now shall grow an[d ...] / again. Just as the na[ils*¹⁴⁹ ...] / so the hair shall grow and [...] / cut a finger, he in [...] / on the limbs of the [bod]y that you [... (281) ...] him [...] since this time to the [... / ...] the body ag[a]in.

So, [I besee/ch you], my maste[r], that you might instruct me of the m[atter] / for [which I have ask]ed you.

Then the a[po⁵stle] speaks to him: I am the one who will instruct you [about the / less]on for which you have asked me! Happen you know th[at / the] body is like the earth, wh[ile these] limbs als[o ... / ...] of it are like the trees. There are varieties [...] / of tree

---

*148 ⲡⲱⲣⲡ
*149 Reading ⲚⲒⲉ[ⲉⲃⲉ]

you shall find growing on the earth. They ar[is]e ^{10} and grow
again and stand firm. They have not [... / ...] Again, there are
others that if they are cut shall not [grow / ... / ...] and they grow,
as they are li[ke / ...] which shall be cut and grow [...] and ^{15} [...]
they too that occur [...] / they shall be cut and not grow, resembling [... / ... neither] grow nor shall they [... ^{23} ...] it [sh]all please
him on [...] and grows [... / ...] in impurity [... ^{25} ... / ... / ...] from
him. This flesh that is corrupt / [... **(282)** ... / ...] in the liv[in]g
flesh and they [... / ...] are somewhat sick.

Behold, [I have tau/ght you] about this lesson for which you have
asked me [... the] ^{5} disciple heard this homily [... / ...] he sat down.

••• 117 •••

(282, 7 – ?)

/ *Concerning why Some shall delay to come / forth from the Body, and
Oth*^{10}*ers die in an instant.* /

The fragmentary kephalaion may have continued on to the next leaf, 283, of
which virtually nothing survives. Since it is impossible to tell where chapter
117 finished, the few legible words from that leaf are transcribed under the
next chapter heading.

Onc[e] again the disciples questioned the apostle, say[ing] / to
[him]: We beseech you, our master, th[at you might] / instruct
us about these people who shall [... / ...] and their soul is released
from [their body ... ^{15} ...] if he shall fall upon [...] /

The [sec]ond*^{150} [...] if he shall fall [... / ...] one [... / ...] one hour
[... / ...] ^{20} others who shall [... / ...] and they remain. They shall
delay until they [... / ...] he is freed, and they delay to come
toward [... / ...]

So, now, we bes[eech / you, our mast]er, that you might [...] and
say [... ^{25} ...] which names shall be freed, as they [... / ...] release
them.

Then he says to the [... / ... the] matter that [...]

---

*150   Reading ⲡⲙⲁϩ [ⲥⲛⲧⲉ]

••• 118 •••

(283 – 284)

[...]

The mostly destroyed leaves 283-284 perhaps contained the end of chapter 117, certainly the whole of chapter 118, and the beginning of chapter 119. Only a few words may be read, and no overall sense of the contents is achievable.

(**283**) [... [10] ...] upon [... / ... / ...] from [... / ...] thus [... (**284**) ... [5] ... a]ll of them [... [11] ...] that they shall [... [14] ...] seven people [... [15] ...] Again, he too, this per[son ...] the time when [... / ...] of the light [... [19] ...] the universe [... [20] ...] is revealed [... / ...] take to the light [... / ... utt]erly, the way that he exists [... [25] ...] from [... / ...] these other three [...]

••• 119 •••

(284,? – 286,23)

[...]

Mani describes the First Man in distinctly Christological terms as the only begotten and first righteous one, who was approved and sent forth against the enemy. The point of the lesson or sermon is that the disciples should model themselves after the steadfastness of the son of God, to whom they belong.

(**285**) [...] and the [righte]o[usness ...] is more than [the / ...] the voice through them.

The a[postle] speaks / [to] them about these four [... / ...] people; because they had recounted to him from [the hour] [5] and time.

This one, whom they called 'approved' [... / ...] they approved him in the midst of the ae[ons of] / light. These numerous multitudes set him a[part], / and he came forth against the enemy. They gave this name [... / ...] this matter [... [10] ...] who are numerous, that are in the aeons of light and who [are without]*151 / measure or number.

This one, [whom they called] / 'righteous', because he is the first righteous one who / had no sin amongst all of the aeons that belong to the light / and the thought [... 15 ...] they knew him, so that [... becau]/se he is the first catechumen [wh]o obe/yed his Father, who had sent him with five sons [...] / perdition.

This one also [whom they called] / 'only begotten', because he was established [...] 20 pour [...] enemy.

So now, I / tell you, my brothers and my limbs, that these / [whom] they have called 'approved', they [... / ...] after the likeness of the First Man; they called [... / ...] to yo[u ... 25 ...] two in ten thousand after the likeness of the First Man [... / ...] 'righteous' after the likeness of the First / [M]an. For, just as he was without sin among the [... / ...] Man. He gave victo[ry] to them [... / ...] you and they who are unyield[ing 30 ...] are without sin among the souls of the / [...] to them the word of life, that / [...] hope of life. They are establishe[d / ...] in love and friendship [... (286) ... cate]chumen [...] the cate[chume/ns ... / ...] the rebel[s]. / Again, just as the only begotten ones from your [onl5y] begotten race and you [...] according to flesh [... / ... o]nly begotten also from gold and silver and / all the [...] of the universe.

Just as your father, [the / F]irst Man, himself stood firm in the / [midst] of all the worlds of darkness. He did not love [the] 10 worlds of darkness, nor did he lust for them! Rather, / h[is] thought and love for the household of his people is / in h[i]m. Anything else that the enemy [...] with his / violent de[e]ds. Behold, (the First Man) toils and struggles; so that (the enemy) would be separat/e [from] them and be cast out from them. And he purifies them and ma[ke]s them 15 f[r]ee, and makes them as they were from the beginning. /

You too, so long as you stand firm in this / bo[dy ...] and all its lusts after the likeness of yo/ur [liv]ing father [...] the worlds of darkness. /

---

*151   Reading ⲚⲈ[ⲦⲞ ⲚⲀⲦ]/ⲰⲒ Cf 153.26

[...] may they discover the remembrance of the household of his
²⁰ peo[ple], as he remains in this [place ni]ght and day. /

When his disciples heard these lesso[ns], they rejoiced and gave
[g]/lory. They praised their father and made obeisance to their
teacher. H[e] / sat down and they rejoiced and were glad and [...]

••• **120** •••

(286,24 – 288,18)

²⁵ *Concerning the Two Essences. /*

In this chapter Mani makes a forceful attack upon monotheism. The initial
context is unclear, but possibly he is preaching directly to Christians. If
there was nothing apart from God at the beginning, then where did all the
evils in the world come from? He scornfully asks his listeners why they
reject evil deeds, surely they should perform them if everything comes from
God! Indeed, by not doing so they are committing the double crime against
their God of rejecting his deeds, and then forgiving the sins of those who
fall into them.
Alternatively, if evil did not come from God, the Manichaean position,
his listeners have lied against God who will judge them. Mani asserts that
Jesus, like all the true apostles, taught dualism. Here Mani develops the
favourite proof-text about the good and evil trees, in its five-fold version (see
30.20 48.14 – 19 and kephalaion 2). He ends by warning that at the last
judgement his listeners will receive their condemnation.

Once again, when our father looked, he saw a [...] / person [...]
before him. [He] says [... the] / two essences that are present at
the beginning [...] the [lig]/ht and the darkness, that which is
good and that which is evi[l, life and] ³⁰ death.

You, however, the creatures of the [... / i]s a single essence that
exist[s ...] / every thing, [from] which everything came abou[t ...
/ ...] it, the evil and the [... (**287**) ...] God. Now, therefore, if the [...
/ ...] among you that only one essence exist[s ... / ... a]nd they say
that there is nothing else [apart / from] God.

So, tell me that lying, fal[se] ⁵ testimony, slander and accusation,
sorceries [for] / sake of adultery, theft, the worshipping of id[ols],
/ robbery, the consuming fire, [...] {}*¹⁵² that i[s / i]n the body of a

---
*152 ⲧⲥ/ⲧ

person like a moth, the lustful[ness] / and fornication in which people revel, the [... [10] ...] struggling with his breath as he shall not be quiet a si[ngl]e hour, / the insatiability of Mammon that the pers[on] shall [...] / as he shall not be satisfied for his lifetime, all these idola[tries], / the evil spirits that are like the night [... / ...] what they are or who cast them in the heart of peop[l]e so [15] [that] they both would die by them, and be tortured / [on their] account.

If they came about from [the] G/[od o]f truth*[153], then why do you annul [... / ...] them not. If they are his, you do them! [...] / will receive two woes: one, that you did not do them; the other [...] woe [20] [...] received it, because you annul them and [... / ...] them. You forgive their sins upon the [... / ...]

For if God has hi[mself] created them, / the one who does them [h]as [no] sin therein! If they did not come / [about] from him, nor did he command them to be d[on]e, [25] [y]ou are the one who will speak a lie against God, saying / [that] all [these e]vil things come about from him [... / ... f]rom him, and you may bring two woes to the place. / [...] God (brings) a judgement against you, for while it / [...] through his beloved son in the [30] [manner of] all [the apos]tles, he proclaimed l[ik]e ess/[ence ...] do these evil things, he set a [... / ...] saying that these evil things are / [...] which is the wicked (288) [...] for in this way [... / the] bitter trees that give not fruit [... / ...] the hard earth.

Once again he says: [... / ...] the father plants it, they will [... [5] ... / be]loved [...] every fruit that is o/[n these] five tre[es ...] he and his belov[ed] son / [and hi]s holy spirit and the entire kingdom of they that [... / ...] they say th[at] [10] all the [wic]kednesses are his. They come about from / him. He is the one who established them because of this [... / ...] to separate the good from the darkness. / You will [be c]on[de]mned by this in the presence of God with a great [...]*[154] / an[d be]fore his beloved son and his h[oly] spirit [15] at the last [da]y, at his advent.

You shall [come f]/rom your body and see these things that I have recou[nted to] / you; that they occur in truth before the Jud[ge] / of truth, the one who shall not favour anyone.

---

*153 Read [ⲡ]ⲛⲟⲩ [ⲧⲉ ⲛ]ⲧⲉ ⲧⲙⲏⲉ
*154 Perhaps read ϩⲉⲛ 'judgement'.

••• 121 •••

(288,19 – 290,28)

²⁰ *Concerning the Sect of the Basket.* /

The interpretation of this chapter must remain speculative whilst the import of the crucial term ΝΟΒΕ ('basket'?), which is the description of the sect under discussion, remains unclear. From the context it may very tentatively be suggested that these were a sect of fruitarians, and that the basket (if this indeed is the meaning of the word) implies something like 'pickings' or even 'windfall'.

This could explain Mani's analogy about the universe, which leads on to the cosmological details in the latter and very fragmentary part of the kephalaion. Otherwise the relevance to the earlier discussion is uncertain.

Onc[e] again, on one of the occasions, as our enlightener is si[tting / ...] in the midst of the land of Babylon, a m[an came] / before him, a presbyter belonging to the [sect]*155 / of the basket. He is a worshipper of idols. He [... 25 ...] of the apostle. This presbyter [...] / who belongs to the sect of the basket.

Why [do they call / it] the sect of the 'basket'? For I see the [...] / when it hangs from the tree, they shall not [... / ... w]hen it will be picked in the [... 30 ...] they shall call it [...] in these ways [...] grapes [...] / grapes. It shall not be called [...] / will pick from the vine [... (289) ...] the basket [... / ...] their apples in various ways [... / ...] on their tree and they put them in the basket [... / ...] immediately [...]

The ap[ost]⁵le speaks to the presbyter of the sect of the basket: So, [the un/i]verse in which you stand i[s l/i]ke a tree; while you are [li]ke the frui[t that h/a]ngs from the tree. Now, if you [your]-self had been plucked from the univers[e] / with the basket, then well could you call yoursel[f] ¹⁰ the son of the basket! However, if up till n[ow] you are entangled in / the universe; how then do you call yourself the so[n of] the bas/ket, b[e]fore you are plucked from the universe like [a] fr/uit? For as long as it hangs from the tree, it shall not be call[ed] / 'alms'. And you too, as long as you

---

*155   Reading ⲉϥⲏⲡ ⲁⲛ [ⲁⲟⲩⲙⲁ]

are entangled in [the] uni[15][verse] you [shall not be] w[ell] called the son of the [ba]sket. /

He raised his hand to his disciples: B[less]ed / [...] the children of the basket on account of their alms-giving, the ones that [...] / from the universe. He has released them and they [... / po]sses-sions[*156] from the houses, from the gold and silver, from [20] [...] and in [...] they shall be placed in the basket, w[h]ich / [is] the holy c[h]urch!

Then he says to him / [... / ... /...] The[n [25] ... / ... / ...] and the great [... / ...] and the great Mind that is [... / ...] this Youth that is with the [... [30] ...] thirty-six angels [... / ...] twenty-two angels [... / ...] but [...] of the twenty-two [... (**290**) ...] the seven pillars that stan[d ... / ...] the sea that surrounds the universe [... / ... f]our angels that are distributed to the [... the / un]iverse, supporting the mightiness [... [5] ...] below, which is the earth of al[l] the heavens / [...] these other five gods, the sons of the Man, they that [...] / the [un]iverse is stood firm [...] the summons / [and the] obedience [...] the splendour of the [... / ...] holy [ch]urch and the Adamant of Ligh[t [10] ...] they are become en/emie[s ...] they guide it.

The third also, [... / ...] below, there are twelve powers stan[ding f]/ir[m] there. However, the number of the twelve images [...] / the three great pillars of mightiness that [...] [15] pi[ll]ars supporting the disk [...] the other thr[ee / ...] they are the garments that the [Li]ving Spirit / [...] he put them at that time [... / ...] that threw them, together with [... / ...] which is displayed therein [...] this [... [20] ...] perfect before [... / ...] great Porter [... / ...] in his power [... / ... / ...] these are the three great [... [25] ...] against [... a]/re in the midst of people [... / ...] knows [... / ...] entrusts his soul to them [...]

[*156] Reading [ⲚⲬ]ⲣⲏⲙⲁ

••• 122 •••

(290,29 – 295,8)

30 *Concerning the 'Assent' and the 'Amen'.* /

The edited and published text of the *Kephalaia* currently ends in the midst of this chapter at page 291 (Böhlig 1966); although page 292 has been made available in an article that discusses the liturgical context (ibid 1985). However, W. -P. Funk, who is now editing the remainder of the codex, has kindly provided me with his working text of the Coptic for the entire kephalaion. It is from this that the translation of chapter 122 has been completed.

291.4 – 292.8 The assent and the amen are convictions proclaimed by the community at prayer; as in Christian practice. In this chapter Mani asserts their divine archetypes in the summons and the obedience, the two gods that embody the will to redemption. Thus the First Man was redeemed from the abyss; and in the present time they are incarnate in the holy church. Therefore, the assent and the amen uttered by the congregation seal the redemption for which they ask.

292.9 – 25 The assent and the amen also bear forth a beautiful living image sculpted by the faith of the believers; and which ascends daily to the land of rest.

292.26 – 294.22 The assent and the amen are also a great power; for in prayer they bring help both to the sick and at times of temptation.

[O]nce again, one of the disciples [... / ...] to him: Tell me, my master, [... (**291**) ... the] name that we may utter over the blessing [... / ...] we bless, and also the prayer [by] which we pr[ay]. / Tell us: What is the 'assent' and the 'a[men']? /

Our enlightener [s]ays to him: The assent and the a[men] 5 have come about from these great ones of the powers. They were given the na[me] / as the assent belongs to the summons and the amen [belongs to] / the answer.

Just as the summon[s an]d the obedience [ar]e / the ones that opened the portals of mercy and entreaty / for the First Man, so they also became portal[s for the Mo]ther 10 [of Lif]e and the Father of the living. The Firs[t] Ma/n sought and found his redeemer. [An]d [also] the Mother / of Life and the Father of the living sought [...] / this runner, who came forth from them, who is the / First Man; but the summons and the obedience became the 15 portals for them.

Now, in this way they have become portal[s f]or the ae/ons of greatness towards the First Man, and the s[ou]l that was / [c]onjoined with death. They became helpers [...] of the / First Man during his ascent. They gave him [...] / the Father of Life and the Mother of Life [...] [20] They are purifiers of the living soul, be[ing] he/[lp]ers and bestowers of remembrance for it, be it either in [... / ...] in the tree or in the creation of flesh [... / ... the] holy [c]hurch [... / ...] the earth [... summ]ons and the obedience that [25] [...] the portals [...] in the holy church / [... he]lpers, bestowers of power and collectors / [...] teacher [... / ... / ...] purified for thei[r s]ake [... [30] ...] a letter [... / ... (292) that] it might be uttered over the psalm and over [the prayer, / with] the entreaty and the supplication. For, whenever o[ne will / b]less and respond to the assent and the a[men, / the] assent and the amen [shall] seal the blesser. Also, [when] [5] the congregation will beseech an entreaty wi[th / a questi]on, and they all answer and say 'verily an[d / ame]n', they shall seal the entreaty that the congregatio[n] has / as[ked] for and besought. /

Hap[pen] you know that the assent and the amen [are] a great per[so]n [10] [w]ho exists in [... / al]l of you, and you rejoice in him with great jo[y]; / be[caus]e he came to you profitably. He has agreed befo[re] / you to bring forth by him a new birth daily, / [v]ery go[od] and honoured in the presence of the living ones abov[e]. [15] [S]o, when grea[t cro]wds of people utter the assent and the amen, / happen you know that the sound / of all the people who respond shall collec[t] / and come together, and it fixes and sculpts [...] / it is [for]med and makes a good image, ver[y] beautiful [20] and honoured. It goes up to the land of tranquillity and / peac[e]. It receives all their grace, because [... / ...] it gathering what has ascended from [a]ll [these] / who responded. For it was uttered by th[em / a]ll. It separated and attained the land of tr[anquillity] [25] and peace by their joy and their alms. /

Happen you know that the assent and this amen are [a great] / power. Whenever one will be found in [... / ...] in bodily danger [...] / sick [...] they pray for it [... [30] f]or the [ass]ent and the amen; and [... / ...] in his sickness, and he improves [... / ...] with power, and they entreat [... (293) ...] utter over it [...] being sick [... / ...] one is found among you; while the hand of the pursu[ers / ... / ...

⁵ a] great [he]lp comes to him from the assent and [the amen / ...]
over it.

Again, it happens [... / ...] among the elect [...] / awakens in us,
and it is established [... / ...] in evil counsels, and he is set firm
[and ...] ¹⁰ his [compani]ons, and he confesses his sin and [...] /
as he will beseech for himself charity, so that if [G]od / will
{spare}*¹⁵⁷ him this temptation that [... / ...] his [... / ...] and they
call over him the assent and the ame[n ...] ¹⁵ immediately there
is a power come from the assent and [the] amen. / It annuls the
lust and the temptatio[n t]hat he has carried [ar]ound / in him.
And also, whenever a prayer will be be[so]ught / over that person
[... the a]men / that [...] hi[m], as he utters it [...] ²⁰ immediately
there is a great power come to him ou[t] from / the assent and the
amen. It helps him and [... / ...] in [...] / the assent and the amen
go up to the ships, and they [... / ... ²⁵ ...] upon him in the [... / ...]
power [... / ...] in it, a[s] the [... / ...] at a place [... / ... ³⁰ ...] Now,
whenever he may see them [... / ... / ... (294) ... / ...] from him [...
/ ...] but [...] he [... / ...] his voice in [... ⁵ ...] and they who guide
will [... / ...] he is saved [... / ... / ...] the voice of this person [... /
...] his enemies [...] they took his goods [... ¹⁰ ...] because [... / ...]
on account of this judgement / [...] also [... / ... / ...] for [... ¹⁵ ...]
evil [... / ...] they called over him [... / ...] who is master [... / ... /
...] to the heavens and the ships [... ²⁰ ...] helps [... / ...] whenever
[...] / the [assent] and the amen.

Behold, [... / ...] the assent and the [amen ... / ... ²⁵ ...] him, your
own cry / [... / ...] answer [... / ... / ...] ³⁰ and the ame[n ... / ... / ...
(295) ...] the pursuers [... / ...] him [... / ...] it might be uttered from
God [... / ...] for it might be uttered [... ⁵ ...] they named it [...] from
the apos[tles, / the] first fathers [...] fame, bu[t ... / ...] not.

Then, when the father [... / ...] like this, he glorified and he [...]

---

*¹⁵⁷ ⲟⲩⲱϭⲉ ⲁⲃⲁⲗ

THE LIGHT AND THE DARKNESS

APOSTLES

PROPER NAMES

Adiabene ⲁⲇⲓⲃ 16.1
Ardashir ⲁⲣⲧⲁⲝⲟⲟⲥ 14.29.31 15.24. (27)
Artabanus ⲁⲣⲧⲁⲃⲁⲛⲏⲥ 14.28
Assyrians ⲛⲁⲥⲥⲩⲣⲓⲟⲥ 186.26 187.11.17
Aurades son of [Kap]elos ⲁⲩⲣⲁⲇⲏⲥ ⲡϣⲏⲣⲉ ⲛ[ⲕⲁⲡ]ⲏⲗⲟⲥ 183.26-7
Axumites ⲉⲍⲟⲙⲓⲧⲏⲥ 189.3
Babylon ⲧⲃⲁⲃⲩⲗⲱⲛ 15.30 186.25 (187.9) 189.1 288.22
Babylonian ⲃⲁⲃⲩⲗⲱⲛⲓⲟⲥ 144.15 146.9.16
Baptists ⲛⲃⲁⲡⲧⲓⲥⲧⲏⲥ 44.25
Christians ⲛⲣⲱⲙⲉ ⲛⲭⲣⲓⲥⲧⲓⲁⲛⲟⲥ 258.9
Hystaspes ⲅⲩⲥⲧⲁⲥⲡⲏⲥ 7.28 12.18
India ⲡⲅⲛⲧⲟⲩ 184.27 185.4.15
Indians ⲛⲅⲛⲧⲟⲩ 15.25.29
Jews ⲛⲓⲟⲩⲇⲁⲓⲟⲥ 12.27.30.32.34 19.3
Judas Iscariot ⲓⲟⲩⲇⲁⲥ ⲡⲓⲥⲕⲁⲣⲓⲱⲧⲏⲥ 12.31 19.4
Ktesiphon ⲕⲧⲏⲥⲓⲫⲱⲛ 183.15
Magi ⲙⲙⲁⲅⲟⲩⲥⲁⲓⲟⲥ 252.1.9.11
Manichaeans ⲙⲁⲛⲭⲁⲓⲟⲥ (271.15)
Medes ⲙⲙⲏⲇⲟⲥ 187.17.20.22
Mesene ⲧⲙⲁⲓⲥⲍⲁⲛⲟⲥ 15.30 186.7
Nazorean ⲡⲛⲁⲍⲟⲣⲉⲩⲥⲁⲓⲟⲥ   Ch. LXXXIX
Parthia ⲧⲡⲁⲣⲑⲓⲁ 14.29
Parthians ⲛⲡⲁⲣⲑⲟⲥ 5.25 16.1 187.17.20.22
Persia ⲧⲡⲉⲣⲥⲓⲥ 7.28.30 12.18 14.30 15.30 16.1 185.(15).17.22 186.6 189.1
Persians ⲛⲡⲉⲣⲥⲏⲥ 15.29
Purified ones ⲛⲕⲁⲑⲁⲣⲓⲟⲥ 44.27
Romans ⲛⲅⲣⲱⲙⲁⲓⲟⲥ 16.2 189.2
Shapur ⲥⲁⲡⲱⲣⲏⲥ 15.28.31 152.25.26 183.15.17.19.21.24.32
Silis ⲥⲓⲗⲉⲱⲥ 189.4
Simon the leper ⲥⲓⲙⲱⲛ ⲡϣϭⲓⲧ (264.13)
Susiana ⲧⲭⲱⲣⲁ/ⲡⲕⲁⲅ ⲛⲟⲍⲉⲟⲥ 15.31
Tigris ⲧⲓⲕⲣⲓⲥ 152.28.29 153.14.19 154.1.27

MANICHAEAN SCRIPTURES

(Great) Gospel ⲡⲛⲁϭ ⲛⲉⲩⲁⲅⲅⲉⲗⲓⲟⲛ 5.23 153.31
Kephalaia ⲛⲕⲉⲫⲁⲗⲁⲓⲟⲛ passim
Book of Mysteries ⲡⲧⲁ ⲧⲱⲛ ⲙⲩⲥⲧⲏⲣⲓⲱⲛ 5.24
Picture (- *Book*) ⲧⲅⲓⲕⲱⲛ Ch. XCII
Prayer of Sethel Ch. X
Prayers ⲛϣⲗⲏⲗ 5.26
Psalms ⲙⲯⲁⲗⲙⲟⲥ 5.26
Treasury of Life ⲡⲑⲏⲥⲁⲩⲣⲟⲥ ⲙⲡⲱⲛⲅ 5.23 230.8.21
Treatise ⲧⲡⲣⲁⲅⲙⲁⲧⲉⲓⲁ 5.24
Mani's *Epistles* ⲛⲉⲡⲓⲥⲧⲟⲗⲁⲩⲉ 5.25
Mani's *Writing* (for Parthians) ⲧⲅⲣⲁⲫⲏ 5.25

CITATIONS

Deut. 17:2-5 (159.4)
Mt. 3:10 (58.18-19)
Mt. 6:21 (200.3-4 210.31-32 223.3-4 229.3 234.9)
Mt.10:42 (189.6-7.13-14.18-19)
Mt. 18:10 (201.30-31)
Mt. 21:22 (183.7-8)
Mk.12:36 (40.13-14)
Lk. 6:43-44 (17.5-9)
Lk. 22:3 (19.2)
Jn. 3:19 (184.11-12 185.12-13)
Jn. 8:38 (35.32-34)
Jn. 15:7 (183.7-8)
Jn. 15:13 (156.15-16)
Jn. 16:7-9 + ff (14.7-11)
Jn. 16:24 (183.7-8)
I Cor. 7:29-31 (229.10-15)
I Cor. 15:9 (19.7-8)
Phil. 2:7 (12.25 61.21)
Ev. Thom. log. 5 (163.28-29)

NAG HAMMADI AND MANICHAEAN STUDIES

FORMERLY

NAG HAMMADI STUDIES

1. SCHOLER, D.M. *Nag Hammadi bibliography, 1948-1969.* 1971. ISBN 90 04 02603 7
2. MÉNARD, J.-E. *L'évangile de vérité.* Traduction française, introduction et commentaire par J.-É. MÉNARD. 1972.
   ISBN 90 04 03408 0
3. KRAUSE, M. (ed.). *Essays on the Nag Hammadi texts in honour of Alexander Böhlig.* 1972. ISBN 90 04 03535 4
4. BÖHLIG, A. & F. WISSE, (eds.). *Nag Hammadi Codices III, 2 and IV, 2. The Gospel of the Egyptians.* (The Holy Book of the Great Invisible Spirit). Edited with translation and commentary, in cooperation with P. LABIB. 1975.
   ISBN 90 04 04226 1
5. MÉNARD, J.-E. *L'Évangile selon Thomas.* Traduction française, introduction, et commentaire par J.-É. MÉNARD. 1975. ISBN 90 04 04210 5
6. KRAUSE, M. (ed.). *Essays on the Nag Hammadi texts in honour of Pahor Labib.* 1975. ISBN 90 04 04363 2
7. MÉNARD, J.-E. *Les textes de Nag Hammadi.* Colloque du centre d'Histoire des Religions, Strasbourg, 23-25 octobre 1974. 1975. ISBN 90 04 04359 4
8. KRAUSE, M. (ed.). *Gnosis and Gnosticism.* Papers read at the Seventh International Conference on Patristic Studies. Oxford, September 8th-13th, 1975. 1977. ISBN 90 04 05242 9
9. SCHMIDT, C. (ed.). *Pistis Sophia.* Translation and notes by V. MACDERMOT. 1978. ISBN 90 04 05635 1
10. FALLON, F.T. *The enthronement of Sabaoth.* Jewish elements in Gnostic creation myths. 1978. ISBN 90 04 05683 1
11. PARROTT, D.M. *Nag Hammadi Codices V, 2-5 and VI with Papyrus Berolinensis 8502, 1 and 4.* 1979. ISBN 90 04 05798 6
12. KOSCHORKE, K. *Die Polemik der Gnostiker gegen das kirchliche Christentum.* Unter besonderer Berücksichtigung der Nag Hammadi-Traktate 'Apokalypse des Petrus' (NHC VII, 3) und 'Testimonium Veritatis' (NHC IX, 3). 1978.
    ISBN 90 04 05709 9
13. SCHMIDT, C. (ed.). *The Books of Jeu and the untitled text in the Bruce Codex.* Translation and notes by V. MACDERMOT. 1978. ISBN 90 04 05754 4
14. McL. WILSON, R. (ed.). *Nag Hammadi and Gnosis.* Papers read at the First International Congress of Coptology (Cairo, December 1976). 1978.
    ISBN 90 04 05760 9
15. PEARSON, B.A. (ed.). *Nag Hammadi Codices IX and X.* 1981.
    ISBN 90 04 06377 3
16. BARNS, J.W.B., G.M. BROWNE, & J.C. SHELTON, (eds.). *Nag Hammadi Codices.* Greek and Coptic papyri from the cartonnage of the covers. 1981.
    ISBN 90 04 06277 7
17. KRAUSE, M. (ed.). *Gnosis and Gnosticism.* Papers read at the Eighth International Conference on Patristic Studies. Oxford, September 3rd-8th, 1979. 1981.
    ISBN 90 04 06399 4
18. HELDERMAN, J. *Die Anapausis im Evangelium Veritatis.* Eine vergleichende Untersuchung des valentinianisch-gnostischen Heilsgutes der Ruhe im Evangelium

Veritatis und in anderen Schriften der Nag-Hammadi Bibliothek. 1984.
ISBN 90 04 07260 8

19. FRICKEL, J. *Hellenistische Erlösung in christlicher Deutung.* Die gnostische Naassener-schrift. Quellen, kritische Studien, Strukturanalyse, Schichtenscheidung, Rekonstruktion der Anthropos-Lehrschrift. 1984. ISBN 90 04 07227 6

20-21. LAYTON, B. (ed.). *Nag Hammadi Codex II, 2-7, together with XIII, 2* Brit. Lib. Or. 4926(1) and P. Oxy. 1, 654, 655.* I. Gospel according to Thomas, Gospel according to Philip, Hypostasis of the Archons, Indexes. II. On the origin of the world, Expository treatise on the Soul, Book of Thomas the Contender. 1989. 2 volumes. ISBN 90 04 09019 3

22. ATTRIDGE, H.W. (ed.). *Nag Hammadi Codex I* (The Jung Codex). I. Introductions, texts, translations, indices. 1985. ISBN 90 04 07677 8

23. ATTRIDGE, H.W. (ed.). *Nag Hammadi Codex I* (The Jung Codex). II. Notes. 1985. ISBN 90 04 07678 6

24. STROUMSA, G.A.G. *Another seed. Studies in Gnostic mythology.* 1984. ISBN 90 04 07419 8

25. SCOPELLO, M. *L'exégèse de l'âme.* Nag Hammadi Codex II, 6. Introduction, traduction et commentaire. 1985. ISBN 90 04 07469 4

26. EMMEL, S. (ed.). *Nag Hammadi Codex III, 5.* The Dialogue of the Savior. 1984. ISBN 90 04 07558 5

27. PARROTT, D.M. (ed.) *Nag Hammadi Codices III, 3-4 and V, 1 with Papyrus Berolinensis 8502,3 and Oxyrhynchus Papyrus 1081.* Eugnostos and the Sophia of Jesus Christ. 1991. ISBN 90 04 08366 9

28. HEDRICK, C.W. (ed.). *Nag Hammadi Codices XI, XII, XIII.* 1990. ISBN 90 04 07825 8

29. WILLIAMS, M.A. *The immovable race.* A gnostic designation and the theme of stability in Late Antiquity. 1985. ISBN 90 04 07597 6

30. PEARSON, B. (ed.). *Codex VII.* (in preparation)

31. SIEBER, J.H. (ed.). *Nag Hammadi Codex VIII.* 1991. ISBN 90 04 09477 6

32. SCHOLER, D.M. *Nag Hammadi Bibliography, 1970-1994.* (in preparation)

33. WALDSTEIN, M. & F. WISSE, (eds.). *The Apocryphon of John.* A Synopsis of Nag Hammadi Codices II,1; III,1 and IV,1 with B68502,2. 1995.

34. LELYVELD, M. *Les logia de la vie dans l'Evangile selon Thomas.* A la recherche d'une tradition et d'une rédaction. 1988. ISBN 90 04 07610 7

35. WILLIAMS, F. (Tr.). *The Panarion of Epiphanius of Salamis.* Book I (Sects 1-46). 1987. ISBN 90 04 07926 2

36. WILLIAMS, F. (Tr.). *The Panarion of Epiphanius of Salamis.* Books II and III (Sects 47-80, *De Fide*). 1994. ISBN 90 04 09898 4

37. GARDNER, I. *The Kephalaia of the Teacher.* The Edited Coptic Manichaean Texts in Translation with Commentary. 1995. ISBN 90 04 10248 5